LABOUR AND POVERTY
IN KENYA
1900-1980

LABOUR AND POVERTY
IN KENYA
1900–1980

PAUL COLLIER

and

DEEPAK LAL

CLARENDON PRESS · OXFORD
1986

Oxford University Press, Walton Street, Oxford OX2 6DP

Oxford New York Toronto
Delhi Bombay Calcutta Madras Karachi
Kuala Lumpur Singapore Hong Kong Tokyo
Nairobi Dar es Salaam Cape Town
Melbourne Auckland

and associated companies in
Beirut Berlin Ibadan Nicosia

Oxford is a trade mark of Oxford University Press

Published in the United States
by Oxford University Press, New York

British Library Cataloguing in Publication Data
Collier, Paul
Labour and poverty in Kenya, 1900–1980.
1. Poor—Kenya—History—20th century
2. Labor supply—Kenya—History—20th century
I. Title   II. Lal, Deepak
305.5'69'096762   HC865.Z9P6
ISBN 0–19–828505–1

Library of Congress Cataloging-in-Publication Data
Collier, Paul.
Labour and poverty in Kenya, 1900–1980.
Bibliography: p.
Includes index.
1. Labor supply—Kenya.   2. Poor—Kenya.
3. Income distribution—Kenya.
I. Lal, Deepak.   II. Title.
HD5840.5.A6C65   1986   331.12'09676'2   86–1352
ISBN 0–19–828505–1

Set by Hope Services, Abingdon, Oxon
Printed in Great Britain
at the University Printing House, Oxford
by David Stanford
Printer to the University

ACKNOWLEDGEMENTS

The authors wish to thank the World Bank's East Africa Department as well as its Research Committee which financed most of the studies on which this book is based and the ILO for financing the study underlying Chapter 5.II. They would also like to thank Mark Leiserson in particular for his help and support over a number of years in making this study possible. The views expressed are the authors and should not be identified in any way with the World Bank or its affiliates, or the ILO.

CONTENTS

List of Tables   ix

List of Abbreviations   xii

Introduction   1
   I   *The Evolution of Ideas on Three Major Issues*   2
  II   *On Method*   12
 III *Plan of the Book*   15

PART ONE: HISTORY

1 Coercion (1800–1948)   21
   I   *The Pre-colonial Economy and Labour Organization*   21
  II   *The Colonial Impact*   26

2 Compassion (1948–1968)   39
   I   *The Colonial Government's Interventions in the Labour Market:*
      1945–1952   39
  II   *The Emergency, Uhuru, and After: 1952–1968*   42
 III *The Growth of Education*   54
 IV *Labour Force, Employment, and Wages: 1948–1968*   58

3 Competition (1968–1980)   73
   I   *The Policy Environment*   73
  II   *Poverty, Income, and Land Distribution*   77
 III *Wages and Employment*   85

PART TWO: ANALYSIS

4 Some Simple Theory   99
   I   *The Experts and the Kenyan Employment Problem*   99
  II   *Determinants of the Wage Structure*   99
 III *Summary*   113

5 The Functioning of the Labour Market: Agriculture   115
   I   *Introduction*   115
  II   *Smallholder Labour Allocation*   116
 III *The Plantation Labour Market*   139
 IV *Adjustment Processes in the Agricultural Labour Market* 143

6   The Functioning of the Labour Market: Non-Agriculture   154
    I   *Introduction*   154
    II   *Institutional Segmentation?*   154
    III   *Skill Acquisition during Employment*   169
    IV   *Adjustment Processes in Non-Agricultural Labour Markets*   196

7   Consequences for Migration, Unemployment, and   242
    Urban Poverty
    I   *Education and Migration*   242
    II   *Unemployment and the Structure of Employment*   243
    III   *Unemployment and Household Poverty*   248
    IV   *Urban-to-Rural Migration and Remittances*   249

8   Poverty and Growth   252
    I   *Introduction*   252
    II   *Malfunctioning of Rural Factor Markets:*
          Consequences for Poverty and Growth   254
    III   *Rural–Urban Interactions I: Urban Employment*
          as a Substitute for Credit   257
    IV   *Rural–Urban Interactions II: Land Concentration*
          and Absenteeism   267
    V   *A Framework for Analysing Growth and Poverty Redressal*   270

9   Conclusions   274

Bibliography   279
Index   289

LIST OF TABLES

1.1	Wage Employment and the Labour Force 1902–1948	31
1.2	The Occupational Structure of Employment by Race	32
1.3	Population 1911–1962	37

2.1	Annual Number of Strikes, Employees Involved, and Man-Days lost 1962-1974	47
2.2	Education Department Expenditure by Race, 1926	56
2.3	School Enrolments	57
2.4	The African Male Labour Force by Age Group	59
2.5	Enrolment in Schools by Race, 1938–1968	60
2.6	Skill Composition of Nairobi African Wage Labour Force	61
2.7	Africanization of the Private Sector, 1964–1968	61
2.8	Years of Education of African Male Urban Employees, 1968	63
2.9	African Earnings by Skill, 1968	63
2.10	African Real Wages by Sector	64
2.11	Earnings by Age for the Uneducated, 1968	66
2.12	African Wages in Private Industry and Commerce	67
2.13	Wage Differentials in Teaching and the Civil Service	68
2.14	Employment by Sector, 1951–1968	69
2.15	Educational Qualifications of Male Migrants to Nairobi, 1964–1968	70
2.16	Educational Qualifications of the Nairobi African Labour Force, 1957	70

3.1	Estimated Land Use in Kenya	75
3.2	Poverty in Kenya, 1974	79
3.3	Trends in Absolute Poverty, 1963–1974	80
3.4	Distribution of Income in Kenya by Economic Status of Households, 1974	81
3.5	Distribution of Income in Kenya, 1974	82
3.6	Changes in the Distribution of Income and Consumption in Central Province, 1963–1974	83
3.7	Landholdings of Cultivators of Land on Smallholdings	84
3.8	Distribution of Income in Nairobi, 1969 and 1974	85
3.9	The Distribution of Educational Attainment	87
3.10	Employment by Sector, 1968–1978	88
3.11	Employment by Skill	90
3.12	African Real Wages by Sector	92
3.13	Median Salary for Citizens	93

5.1	The Hiring In and Out of Labour by Farm Size	120
5.2	The Allocation of Smallholder Labour	122
5.3	The Contribution of Labour Transactions to Smallholder Factor Proportions	123
5.4	Commodity Specialization	133
5.5	Wage Income by Type of Job, Murageto Sub-Location	136
5.6	Hired Labour per Acre: Central Province 1963	144
5.7	Smallholder Labour Force, 1963–1974	147
5.8	Land Use by Man/Land Ratios, 1963	148
5.9	Distribution of Cropping Area by Major Crops, 1961–1974	148
6.1	Education, Hierarchy, and Firm Size (Unskilled)	159
6.2	Education, Hierarchy, and Firm Size (Skilled)	162
6.3	Union Membership and Wages, 1968	162
6.4	Upper-Quartile Relative to Lower-Quartile Basic Salary among citizens	166
6.5	Collective Agreements, 1973–1978	167
6.6	Average and Median Monthly Gross Cash Remuneration in Selected Occupations, 1972	170
6.7	Estimated Quit Rates among Nairobi African Wage Earners	180
6.8	Hypothesized Training Investment of the Firm in a Non-Quitting Worker	182
6.9	Training Investment of the Firm as a Percentage of the Mean Wage	182
6.10	Quitting and Seniority of Trained Insurance Clerks	184
6.11	Earnings and Job Change by General Skill Level	185
6.12	Education and Training of Non-Manual Workers	189
6.13	Education and Skill Level (Manual Workers)	190
6.14	The Flow on to the Labour Force	198
6.15	Rates of Stock Accumulation	199
6.16	The Change in the Demand for Labour by Education due to Industrial Change	202
6.17	The Change in the Demand for Labour by Education due to Occupational Change	203
6.18	The Educational Profile of the Non-Agricultural Wage Labour Force in the Early 1960s	204
6.19	Changes in Employment by Education, 1961–1977	205
6.20	Quit Rates by Reason for Quitting and Education among Skilled Manual Workers	207
6.21	The Total Incremental Demand for African Labour by Educaton	209
6.22	Demand–Supply Imbalance by Education	209
6.23	Earnings by Occupation in Kenya, 1953–1977	211
6.24	Long-Run Real Wage Adjustments	212

6.25   Increments in Earnings by Education Level   215
6.26   Unemployment of Form IV Leavers   216
6.27   Average Delay between Leaving School and Starting Work   216
6.28   Education of Workers Hired/Promoted in 1971 and of all
         Workers, by Selected Occupations   220
6.29   Educational Selection Criteria used in 141 Jobs for Form IV
         Leavers, 1968–1970   222
6.30   Education and Experience of Persons Hired/Promoted during
         1971 in Selected Occuptions   223
6.31   Earnings Functions for Skilled Manual Workers   230
6.32   Information Identified by Firms and by Conventional
         Earnings Functions   230
6.33   Unemployment Prospects by Examination Performance,
         1968–1974   232
6.34   Flows on to the Labour Market by Education and Job Type,
         had Bumping Operated, 1964–1979   234
6.35   Characteristics of the Nairobi Male Unemployed   238

7.1   Nairobi Population Annual Growth Rates, 1969–1979   243
7.2   Age- and Sex-Specific Net Migration to Nairobi   244
7.3   Educational Qualifications of Male Migrants to Nairobi   245
7.4   The Propensity of Male Non-Nairobi Form IV Leavers to
         Migrate to Nairobi   246
7.5   The Nairobi Male Labour Force by Economic Activity,
         1969–1979   247

8.1   An Estimate of the Loss of Output due to Allocative
         Inefficiency   254
8.2   Regression of Crop Output on Liquid Assets   259
8.3   Smallholder Characteristics by Selected Income Groups and
         Province   261
8.4   Sources of Non-Farm Income   263
8.5   The Distribution of Remittances   264

LIST OF ABBREVIATIONS

ACIE	Association of Commercial and Industrial Employers
ATAC	American Technical Assistance Corporation
CBS	Central Bureau of Statistics
COTU	Central Organisation of Trades Unions
EATUC	East Africa Trades Union Congress
EES	Employment and Earnings Survey
FKE	Federation of Kenya Employers
IBEAC	Imperial British East Africa Company
IDS	Institute of Development Studies (Nairobi)
ILO	International Labour Office
INBUCON	International Business Consultants
KANU	Kenya African National Union
KAU	Kenya African Union
KAWC	Kenya African Workers' Congress
KFL	Kenya Federation of Labour
KISA	Kikuyu Independent Schools Association
NSSF	National Social Security Fund
PWIF	Plantation Workers' International Federation
SPSCP	Smallholder Production, Services and Credit Program
USAID	United States Agency for International Development

INTRODUCTION

There are three general public policy issues for which labour market analysis is crucial and which are the focus of this study. The first concerns the existence and relevance of so-called 'surplus' labour in developing countries. This is of relevance for forming judgements on the viability of 'big push' type developmental policies, as well as in the estimation of shadow wage rates for project analysis. The second concerns the spread effects of what has been termed capitalist growth. Whether the income expansion at certain 'growth poles' trickles down fairly rapidly to other groups in the economy will depend in part upon the functioning of the country's labour markets. The final set of public policy issues concern the changing pattern of income distribution in the course of development. As the labour market mediates the earnings of different groups of workers, its functioning is again of importance in both explaining the past pattern of income distribution as well as its likely evolution both with and without certain policy interventions.

It might be thought that there are clearly formulated alternative theories of the functioning and evolution of labour markets in developing countries which one can 'test' with historical time series data on the relevant variables. This is not the case. One can, though, amongst the existing babel of views distinguish three general explanations of labour market phenomena in developing countries.

The two dominant 'theories' are, first, various versions of the theory of 'surplus labour' and 'dualism' associated with the names of Lewis, Nurske, and Ranis–Fei, and secondly the conventional neo-classical theory of wages and employment. Thirdly, there are various institutionalist explanations which are largely *ad hoc*. Sometimes, explanations claiming to be alternatives to neo-classical views are mainly product differentiated variants of conventional theory!

Much of the seeming discord in the area can be ordered into some coherence if certain conceptual categories and the logical status of statements made under conventional theory are firmly kept in mind. To this end we begin this introduction with a brief excursion through the development of ideas on the role of labour in development found in the next section. Besides providing some conceptual focus for this book, this exercise will also help in setting the stage for our explanation in the following section of the currently unfashionable method of analysis we have adopted in forming judgements on the functioning of labour markets and the three policy issues outlined above, through the study of wage and employment trends and structures in Kenya.

I   The Evolution of Ideas on Three Major Issues

There are three major sets of issues relating to labour in development, which though interrelated can nevertheless be separated for our purposes. These concern, (1) notions of unemployment (both its causes and cures) and its relationship to poverty, (2) the likely trend of average labour incomes in different types of development sequences, and (3) the determinants of the structure of wages in an economy, and its evolution over time in response to alternative types of growth mechanisms. We briefly outline the evolution of thinking on these three sets of issues in turn.

(1) Unemployment and Poverty

(a) 'The State of the Poor'   Unemployment is a relatively recent concern of economics (see Garraty for a historical survey). The mass open cyclical unemployment in currently developed countries, which has been observed by economists since the mid-nineteenth century and whose dynamics they have been keen to explain, was a by-product of the rise and growth of the industrial system and the accompanying urbanization. The contemporary concern with unemployment in LDCs is more like the concern with poverty, destitution, and beggary to be found in the European writings about the 'State of the Poor' since the fifteenth century. In their chronic form these were novel problems for fifteenth-century Europe since in the preceding feudal societies of the Middle Ages unemployment and destitution as 'normal' states were virtually unknown. Feudal societies were designed to provide a place for every member.

In normal times unemployment was quantitatively unimportant and confined to individuals who had broken loose from their environment or had been cast off by it and who in consequence had become beggars, vagrants and highwaymen . . . mass unemployment, definitely unconnected with any personal shortcomings of the un-employed, was unknown to the Middle Ages except as a consequence of social catastrophes such as devastation by wars, feuds and plagues (Schumpeter, p. 220).

The breakdown of medieval society (in the sixteenth century), the sub-sequent agrarian revolution, and later (in the late eighteenth century), the industrial revolution, led to large changes in production relationships. Des-titution and unemployment became a major problem for the newly emerging landless proletariat. Though over the long run the new methods of production would raise the overall demand for labour, in the short run the inevitable bottlenecks in the process of adjustment meant that the spectre of incipient mass unemployment and destitution was ever present. The ensuing paradox of poverty amidst progress was to haunt European societies with increasing frequency from the latter half of the eighteenth century. With the rise in the long-run demand for labour following the spread of the industrial system, the fear of chronic technological unemployment receded in Europe. Then cyclical instability became the major source of open unemployment, for which a 'cure' was not found until the Keynesian revolution of the late 1930s. The current unemployment problem in LDCs is rarely identified as being of this latter Keynesian sort.

It is the notion of 'unemployment' current in the pre- and immediate post-industrial period (sixteenth to early nineteenth centuries), which was synonymous with the problems of poverty and destitution, which is most relevant for developing countries.

Since the end of feudalism pauperism has been recognized as a social evil in most European countries. Altruism apart, it was the danger to civil order from vagrancy which lent urgency to the alleviation of poverty: once the link between poverty, crime, and vice was perceived. Since the early part of the sixteenth century the administrative solution for providing relief to the swelling numbers of beggars and vagrants was usually found in some form of public poor relief, of which the Elizabethan Poor Law of 1601 is the most notable instance.

(b) Wage Fund and Neo-Classical Theories of Unemployment Various explanations were provided for low end poverty and the associated 'unemployment', which need not concern us (but see Garraty and Schumpeter op. cit.) except for the one which even today continues to be persuasive. This was the Malthusian 'principle of population'. As Schumpeter aptly puts it, this is because 'the most primitive of all theories of unemployment is that people cannot find work at living wages because there are too many of them' (Schumpeter, p. 273).

This view formed the basis of the subsistence theory of wages which continues to thrive in development economics in the form of assertions about horizontal (perfectly elastic) supply curves of labour, as in the writings of the dualists or labour surplus theorists. But today the Malthusian *biological* theory of long-run labour supply has been replaced by simple *assertions* of a horizontal supply curve at some 'conventional' minimum level of wages. Moreover, in the nineteenth century, Marx had rejected the Malthusian explanations but substituted his own in terms of a 'reserve army of the unemployed' which exerted downward pressure on wages leading to the same iron law of subsistence wages. This view is still current.

All these notions of disguised unemployment and 'surplus labour' imply a continuing excess supply of labour till a stage is reached in the process of development when the surplus has been exhausted and the real wages of workers begin to rise (the so-called Lewis turning-point). Till then, though there is no overt open unemployment, the poverty of the masses will remain unalleviated and be associated with a 'slack' in the labour market, represented by a perfectly elastic supply of labour at a 'conventional' wage rate.

Clearly, in such a model with a perfectly elastic supply of labour at a fixed wage, (which we can term a *Fixwage Model*) there can be no question of full employment till the 'surplus' labour is worked off and the only relevant question is how, when, and through what processes of growth the economy reaches the Lewis turning-point — which can then be identified with 'Full Employment' (see Lal, 1978). Nor, however, is there any short-run involuntary unemployment of the Keynesian type in such a world. The so-called unemployment problem is in fact the long-term problem of the development of a 'fixwage' economy, which is directly related to the second set of issues discussed below — namely the path of real labour incomes in the course of development.

The subsistence wage theory determined the supply curve of labour. The other important component of the classical theory of wages and employment — the wage fund — determined its demand.

The wage fund doctrine held that the total wage bill was constant, as the demand curve for labour was a rectangular hyperbola. This wage fund was predetermined by the total amount of circulating capital required for production, and consisted of the real wages advanced by capitalists to workers. Dividing this constant real wage fund by the volume of employment yielded the average real wage. The wage fund theory was used to counter the mounting demands (from the mid-nineteenth century onwards in England) of trade unions to raise wages. The classicals argued that this would not solve the problem of poverty as with a given wage fund artificially raising wages would merely lead to lower levels of employment.

With the marginalist revolution at the end of the nineteenth century, the marginal productivity theory replaced the wage fund doctrine as the leading theory of factor pricing and more specifically for the demand for labour. Utility maximization, given workers preferences between income and leisure, determined the supply of different types of labour, while the flexibility of wages guaranteed full employment. These models can then be termed as *Flexwage* Models.

In the perfectly competitive world, posited in Walrasian general equilibrium theory, it is easy to show that because of cost minimization by firms (which is the technological analogue of the behavioural assumption of profit maximization) the wage rate will equal the value marginal product of labour. An excess supply of labour would imply that wage payments in excess of labour's marginal product were being made somewhere in the economy. The appropriate remedy would be a wage cut to get back to full employment. Keynesian economics was to deny the efficacy of money wage cuts in reducing involuntary unemployment. It shifted the focus of policy in developed countries to the management of the aggregate level of demand in the economy.

(c) Economic Structure and Keynesian Unemployment   But is Keynesian involuntary unemployment also likely to occur in LDCs? There is an important reason related to their economic structure which makes it unlikely that Keynesian

unemployment will be a serious problem in most developing countries. As is well known, some stickiness of money wages is necessary for Keynesian unemployment to occur and to persist. If the labour market behaved as a purely casual labour market, where on each 'day' there was a spot market for labour in which a market clearing equilibrium wage was established, there could be no involuntary Keynesian unemployment. To explain the occurrence of Keynesian unemployment, therefore, it is necessary to delineate the characteristics of the economic structure which does not allow spot market trading of labour services.

In identifying these characteristics it is useful to outline the major contrasts between the most common forms of labour in pre- and post-industrial societies. As is well known, a major characteristic of pre-industrial societies (as of most current LDCs) is the predominance of self-employment. This contrasts with the importance of wage and salary employment in post-industrial societies.

A self-employed worker combines in his person and personal enterprise (or in his household) all those characteristics which, due to the division of labour, are separated in industrial firms. These are labour, entrepreneurship, and capital. A variation in the demand for the output produced by these 'factors of production' will be reflected in an instantaneous change in the implicit value marginal products of the various 'factors'. There cannot be any 'involuntary' unemployment, therefore, of the self-employed.

By contrast, in a system of wage labour where individuals have specialized functions to facilitate the division of labour, the variations in a firm's output demand (or price) will alter the derived demand for the various factors. If each of these factors were hired each day in a spot market, then again a market clearing price for their services would be established on each and every day and there would be no Keynesian-type involuntary unemployment.[1] An important feature of post-industrial production processes, however, is that they require labour with firm-specific skills. This means that both employers and employees have an interest to maintain a fairly long-term employment relationship. For if the worker leaves the firm, the employer loses any investment he may have made in his firm-specific human capital. But as the value of the worker (and hence his wage) is higher to the firm in which he has acquired some firm-specific human capital than in another firm, the worker might have to accept a lower wage in a new firm. This means that, in industries dependent upon firm-specific human capital, there will be an inherent 'small numbers' bargaining situation (akin to bilateral monopoly), as the returns from (and costs of) firm-specific human capital will need to be shared between employers and employees. Along with problems of moral hazard, this intrinsically game theoretical problem makes spot contracting infeasible. The alternative labour contracts devised will tend to have the Keynesian feature that in the face of unforseen short-run changes in the demand for a firm's output (or in its price), employment will be variable but money and (assuming price stability) real wages will be sticky.

It is industrialization, therefore, with its accompanying need for specialized wage labour with firm-specific skills, which creates the type of 'fixwage' labour markets in which Keynesian-type unemployment can occur. By contrast, in the labour market form typical of pre-industrial societies — self-employment and most wage employment being of the casual spot contracting kind — the labour market will work in the flexprice manner posited by conventional competitive theories.

Thus in the process of development, as a country's economic structure comes to be dominated by modern industry, its aggregate labour market behaviour is also likely to shift from being 'flexprice' to 'fixprice'. As most LDCs, in this sense, are still at a stage of development where their labour markets (except in the relatively small, so-called 'formal' sector) are flexprice, they are unlikely to suffer from the type of involuntary unemployment emphasized by Keynes.[2]

(d) Search Unemployment   Another line has been taken in more recent writings on LDC labour markets, in explaining high levels of (in particular) open urban unemployment in many LDCs. Recognizing that this unemployment is not due to, and hence cannot be cured by Keynesian methods, theorists have provided explanations in terms of expectational models of job search in an urban labour market with an institutionally fixed wage above the market clearing level. These models do not deny the marginal productivity theory of factor demand, but like the subsistence wage theories (which are also not inconsistent with marginal productivity theory) imply a rigid wage in one sector. Depending upon the recruitment patterns for labour in the high wage sector, in a general equilibrium model — where in all other respects perfect competition rules — 'equilibrium' open unemployment can be shown to occur.

(e) Conclusions   The major conclusion of this discussion of the evolution of views of the causes and cures of unemployment, is the slippery nature of the concept. But all the varying notions, whether they are related to those associated with poverty, as in the eighteenth- and nineteenth-century debates on 'the State of the Poor', to the cyclical problems of the Keynesian variety, or to the more modern variants of voluntary unemployment associated with job search, have two things in common.

First, they all reflect the fear of transitional 'disequilibrium' effects on the levels of living of the 'weaker sections' of the population flowing from economic change, such as those associated with the agrarian and industrial revolutions (both in the past and those currently taking place in many LDCs) and (in modern times) with more mundane changes in economic circumstances during the trade cycle.

Secondly, these perceived unemployment problems (except for those associated with notions of 'surplus labour', on which more below) are all short- or medium-run, in the following sense. They are the result of immobilities, bottlenecks, and other rigidities which prevent an economy from attaining an instantaneous new 'equilibrium' when some major economic or institutional change occurs. For in any actual historical process of change we would not expect infinite speeds of adjustments (particularly in terms of spatial mobility or relative price and wage changes) to emerging imbalances between the demand and supply of labour in different lines. It is the nature of the obstacles in the path of such adjustments, as well as the speed with which they are removed, which determines the quantitative importance of transitional disequilibrium phenomenon, such as unemployment. As such, in understanding and clarifying the 'unemployment' problems of contemporary LDCs, it is particularly important not to confine one's attention to a particular short period of time but to look at the phenomenon in a longer historical perspective. Only then can we determine whether (in some sense) these problems are endemic, because the adjustment processes are inherently sluggish in particular economies, or whether the man-made (and hence removable) obstacles are preventing speedy adjustments.

(2) Labour Incomes and Growth

The combination of the subsistence wage theory of labour supply and the wage fund theory of labour demand results in the classical theory of growth and development of Smith, Ricardo, and Mill (and also a part of Marx) which rightly led to economics being labelled the dismal science. We need not concern ourselves with the precise mechanisms of the classical growth model, as neither the Malthusian elements nor the diminishing returns to land built into it are now found to be persuasive by scholars.[3] Nevertheless, the belief in a horizontal supply curve of labour from a traditional to a modern sector is still prevalent, particularly in the influential dual economy models of Lewis and Ranis-Fei. Moreover, the wage fund doctrine underlies the literature on the optimal development of a dual economy, and its byproducts in the theory of the optimal choice of techniques and the determination of shadow wage rates.

(a) Full Performance versus Full Employment Models From an omniscient planner's viewpoint, once a horizontal supply curve of labour is postulated, the optimal level of current employment will be determined by the share of current output that is available for consumption. Assuming all wages are consumed, and all profits saved and invested, the volume of current employment (given the exogenously fixed wage rate) will be determined entirely by the supply of available consumption goods; whilst the levels of employment in the future will depend upon both the expansion in co-operant reproducible factors of production allowed by current and future level of savings, as well as the

overall consumption savings balance at each date in the future. Given an exogenously determined rate of labour force growth, the assumption of a 'fixed wage', and public distributional preferences about intergenerational equity, the optimal time path of employment, consumption, and accumulation could be determined. This in essence is the model underlying the development of a fixwage economy with surplus labour and the determinants of the time path of the shadow wage rate in the economy.[4] In these models there is a clear trade-off between current and future employment levels which are determined by the share of the wage fund in each period to total output. An increase in employment at any particular date implies that the wage fund at that date must be greater and hence savings and capital formation lower. The latter in turn will determine how much output of wage goods can be generated in the next period, and thereby the amount of employment that can be offered. In these dualistic models a simple planning interpretation can be given to the notion of 'full employment', which will be the date by when the 'modern' sector would have grown sufficiently to 'absorb' the available labour surplus in the sense that the marginal product of labour and hence wages in the traditional sector will start rising (see Lal 1978 for a further elucidation of such a concept of 'full employment').

By contrast to the above model, which following Hicks (1973) maybe termed a *Full Performance* (rather than a Full Employment) model, the neo-classical model of development (as for instance that propounded by Jorgenson (1961, 1967)) does not have a fixed institutional wage (either in the agricultural sector as in the Lewis and Ranis–Fei models, or in the high-wage modern sector as in various job search models of the Harris–Todaro variety). The wage rate is variable, and there is no disguised unemployment. Thus these are *Flexwage* models which have *Full Employment* at all times, even though there may be dualistic features in the labour market — due for instance to the industrial supply price of labour being higher than the alternative marginal product of such labour in agriculture. The most important reason for this dualism is likely to be the loss in the share of family income that might accompany a rural migrant's move to an urban job. But as in peasant family farming, the share in the family income will be determined by the average product of labour (which will be higher than labour's marginal product); the migrant's supply price for urban work is likely to be at least equal to this income he will forgo if he takes up an urban job (see Sen 1975, pp. 54–6, for other sources of dualism in the labour market).

The 'surplus labour' *fixwage* classical models move asymptotically towards the neo-classical *flexwage* model after the Lewis turning-point. Thus the two models have different implications for the trend and structure of wages and employment only during the 'surplus labour' phase. Jorgenson (1967a) has presented a brief outline of the different predictions on these scores that the two approaches would make.

First and most important, the assumption of a constant agricultural real wage rate over time (which includes interseasonal constancy) is the hallmark of the 'classical' as opposed to the neo-classical approach. For the latter the real wage rate variations depend upon the twin influences of the demand and supply of agricultural labour over time. Secondly, 'according to the classical approach, the agricultural labour force must decline absolutely before the end of the disguised employment phase (that is before real agricultural wages start rising); in the neo-classical approach the labour force may rise, fall, or remain constant' (Jorgenson, op. cit, p. 65). Thirdly, if the terms of trade between industry and agriculture are roughly constant,[5] then according to the classical approach labour productivity in the modern sector remains constant during the phase of disguised unemployment, whilst on the neo-classical approach it is always rising.[6]

Thus it can be seen that these two alternative theories have very different implications for the likely trends in average labour incomes during the development process, particularly for the 'poor' in traditional activities, and one of our purposes is to see which is broadly consistent with the evidence on wage and employment trends in our different countries.

(b) The 'Principle of Population'   Before ending this discussion of alternative views on the long-run evolution of labour incomes and the structure of employment in the process of development, it may be useful to partially exorcise a ghost which since Malthus continues to haunt those obsessed with the 'principle of population'.

The underlying fear is of the continuing immiserization of labour through its excessive breeding in countries with limited land and natural resources. The crudest form of this fear is based on the law of diminishing returns to increases in one factor of production, and the pure arithmetic of calculating per capita income as a ratio of GNP to population. Thus, if an infant is born to a cow, per capita income goes up but if born to a human it goes down![7] But men are not merely receptacles for output; they are also producers. So as Kuznets asks,

why, if it is man who was the architect of economic and social growth in the past and responsible for the vast contributions to knowledge and technological and social power, a larger number of human beings need result in a lower rate of increase in per capita product? More population means more creators and producers, both of goods along established production patterns and of new knowledge and inventions. Why shouldn't the larger numbers achieve what the smaller numbers accomplished in the modern past — raise total output to provide not only for the current population increase but also for a rapidly rising supply per capita . . . ? (Kuznets, p. 3.)

The answer is usually provided by assuming diminishing returns to labour so that growth in the labour force will necessarily imply (*ceteris paribus*) a fall in per capita output. But at least since Adam Smith it has been known that, due both to the expansion of production possibilities through foreign trade and the ensuing world-wide division of labour, as well as the possibility of any increasing returns which may be associated with the domestic widening of the market (with more domestic consumers with the same average purchasing power), this outcome is not inevitable, even in principle.

Nor does the relative scarcity of natural resources in many LDCs provide any reason (in an open economy) to expect an increase in population to lead to immiserization. As Kuznets succinctly states, 'The scarcity of natural resources in the underdeveloped countries is primarily a function of underdevelopment, underdevelopment is not a function of scarce natural resources.' (Ibid. p. 9.) Japan, Switzerland, and more recently Hong Kong and Singapore have limited or virtually no natural resources compared with Indonesia, Nigeria, and the Congo, and yet the former set of countries have succeeded in developing; the latter have not.

In fact, if we consider a two-good model of an open economy, trading at constant (or improving) terms of trade, then an expansion of the labour force relative to other factors of production need not, following the arguments of Rybzynscki and Stolper–Samuelson theorems, necessarily lead to any fall in the real wage (income) of labourers.

Moreover, for Keynesians it is investment which leads to savings, and the inducement to invest depends upon the expected profitability of investment, which according to Keynes was high in the nineteenth century because of 'the growth of population and invention, the opening up of new lands, the state of confidence and the frequency of war over the average (say) each decade' (Keynes, p. 307).[8]

As Hicks (1977) notes, there are two assumptions of the steady state growth model which colour thinking on population growth. The first is the implicit assumption that the inducement to invest does not matter, and hence there can be no Keynesian lack of confidence. This may not be too implausible when we examine long-run growth processes. The other assumption, however, is that

a steady-state expansion, in which capital per head was constant and there was no technical progress, would show no gain in productivity. The expanded population would be absorbed, but that would be all. In such a steady state there would be no rise in real incomes and no rise in real wages. But in this steady-state theory is there not an important element which is neglected? Is it not the case that expansion as such, even population-based expansion is favourable to productivity? (Hicks 1977, p. 23.)

There is at least one plausible economic model of induced technical change in agriculture due to Boserup (for a formalization see Dairty) which turns Malthus on its head. It shows that historically it is communities confronted with declining per capita food output, as a result of population growth, which have switched to more intensive techniques of production. So that instead of the classical view, with rising output per head leading to population growth,

Boserup argues it is (exogenously) rising population growth which leads to rising output per head. (Also, see Simon for a growth model in which population growth is associated with long-run increasing returns to scale.)

Nor is there any historical evidence to suggest that per capita income has declined in any economy with population growth — quite the contrary (see Kuznets and Simon for a judicious survey of the evidence). It is true that within the conventional neo-classical growth models a higher population growth rate will, *ceteris paribus*, raise capital requirements (and hence entail lower consumption per head). But the resulting belt-tightening doesn't seem to be too great as Kuznets shows through some simple numerical simulations based on historically plausible estimates of the models' parameters. Thus

with a growth in per capita production of 2.0% per year a rise in the rate of population growth as large as that from 1 to 3% per year can be met by a reduction in consumption of about 16% — which means that the sacrifice of half the long-term increase of 2% in per unit consumption for about a decade and a half would bring the country to the high level of per capita product that it would have achieved with only 1/3 of the population growth rate — and thereafter the growth in per capita product would continue at 2% (Kuznets, p. 17).

Lest it be thought that the per capita consumption cut during the transition reflects a pure social loss and no social gain, it should be remembered that there are many ethical systems (such as the Utilitarian and the Catholic) which would include the number of heads together with consumption per head as positive arguments in a society's welfare function! Thus, though there may be various social, ecological, or aesthetic reasons for population control, it is by no means firmly established that population growth is necessarily harmful for development, or even more narrowly for the levels of labour incomes — a consideration of some importance in our study of the Kenyan labour markets where population growth has and continues to be very rapid.

This should not be taken to imply that a growing population does not pose any economic problems. But those problems are concerned with adjusting to a new rate of growth (and thence level) of population, and are similar to those we cited in discussing the 'unemployment' associated with any large dislocating economic change. In particular, given the spread of the concerns associated with the modern welfare state, a rise in the population growth rate will make the public provision of various social services (like education) and infrastructure (housing, roads, etc.) that much more onerous. This may worsen planners' headaches, but whether their pain should axiomatically be treated as representing a social welfare loss is more debatable!

(3) Determinants of the Wage Structure

The third class of questions in the study of labour in development concerns the determinants of the structure of wages in an economy and its evolution over time during the development process. Adam Smith's chapters on labour in *The Wealth of Nations* are the precursors of the currently dominant set of theories (broadly labelled as 'neo-classical'). These theories were given a more rigorous formulation after the 'marginalist revolution', in the writings of J. B. Clark, Alfred Marshall's *Principles*, and Hicks's *Theory of Wages*. But there has always been an undercurrent of discontent against these misleadingly labelled 'marginal productivity theories' of wages. Though Marx and his followers were more concerned with questions about trends in real wages and the functional distribution of income during a capitalist growth process — our first two problem areas — Marxists have generally repudiated 'marginal productivity' type explanations for the structure of wages. This is part of their general rejection of 'neo-classical' economics, which is seen as an apologia for the existing liberal, bourgeois, capitalist system they seek to bury.

But not all those who have had doubts about the realism or relevance of neo-classical explanations of wage-structures have been Marxists. There was an influential school of American institutionalist economists — particularly Veblen and Commons — who emphasized so called institutional and customary factors in wage determination. Nor were the classicists and neo-classicists such as Cairnes, Marshall, or Hicks insensitive to the importance of such factors. But in their theories such aspects were taken into account by what amounted to tautologies, such as Cairnes' notion of non-competing groups. It is only more recently, as a result of the modern variant of the institutionalist challenge presented to conventional theory by the 'dual economy' or 'segmented labour market' theorists such as Doeringer and Piore and L. Thurow, that systematic attempts have been made to incorporate these 'institutionalist' aspects into neo-classical theories of wage determination. These extensions essentially take account of problems concerned with imperfect information and uncertainty in a market where many of the characteristics of heterogeneous labour are unobservable. Cost minimizing and utility maximizing behaviour in this context can produce rigidities in both the structure of wages and the level of real wages in the economy in the face of exogenous changes in the demand and supply of labour. We shall have more to say about these theories, and their relevance in explaining formal sector wage structures in developing countries in Part Two.

II   On Method

Hence, in answering policy-related questions concerning resource allocation, poverty redressal, and income distribution, a view on the functioning of a country's labour market must be taken, at least implicitly if not explicitly. The series of country studies, of which this book forms a part, are expressly concerned with delineating the functioning of labour markets in particular countries over as long a period of time for which relevant data are available. Their major aim is to analyse the historical evidence from each country to see what particular 'view' on the functioning of labour markets is consistent with the available evidence in the country. In addition it is hoped that they will also provide the basis for developing a more general theory of the evolution of labour markets in the course of development.

The method employed in this study is a composite of the characteristics identified by Hicks (1965) of two different types of economic history.

One of the standard ways of writing economic history (much practised by political historians in their economic chapters) survey the state of the economy under consideration, as it was in various historical periods, comparing one state with another. This is comparative statics. It is when the economic historian tries to throw his work into the form of a narrative that it becomes, in our sense, dynamic (p. 11).

Whilst the comparative statics method is a useful and powerful one for analysing questions related to static and contemporaneous causation,[9] it is not designed to answer questions relating to sequential causality, that is those concerning processes. In explaining these processes — say of the evolution of different types of labour markets, or particular trade cycles, or the nature of unemployment — the differences between the phenomena studied by economists and natural scientists (that economic processes are irrevocable and irreversible and involve human agency and actions) cannot be ignored.[10] As is well-known from the debates in capital theory, deep problems arise if we attempt to string along a series of static equilibria into a growth model. There is no way in which the essential elements of a process (how one gets from here to there) can be shown in such models which do not (and cannot) move in historical time. To do so it is necessary to trace out the chains of causation in the form of a narrative, much in the way of a historian. In this chain of causation, human agents and their actions enter as important intermediate steps in the chain between certain events (causes) which trigger certain actions which in turn lead to certain other events which are the ultimate effects. Thus, as Hicks notes, each link in the chain 'of sequential causation in economics has two steps in it: a prior step, from the objective cause to the decisions that are based on it, or influenced by it, and a posterior step, from the decisions to their (objective) effects' (Hicks 1979, p. 88).

These two steps in the process, as seen from the viewpoint of what is distinctive about these economic as opposed to material processes, namely the human agent, can be labelled the *recognition* lag (between the occurrence of the initial event, and the receipt of the accompanying 'signal' by the human agent) and the *reaction* lag (between the action taken by the human agent and the ensuing final events which are the effects). But unless the 'signal' compels *immediate* action by the agent after the recognition lag, there may still be yet a third lag, which may be labelled the *decision* lag between the recognition and reaction lags.

These lags will not only determine the speed of the adjustment process in an economy, but also its nature. For broadly speaking most economic changes (the objective causes) are changes in prices or quantities. Similarly, most of the actions human agents undertake in response to these signals will affect either prices or quantities. The larger are the reserves or cushions available to the human agent to ignore the signals associated with some particular 'shock', the more likely is it that the final effect of the initiating change will be on quantities rather than prices. In labour market analysis this is of particular importance in understanding and explaining the nature of unemployment (the first of the cluster issues outlined in the last section).

Suppose the derived demand for a particular type of labour falls. There are two sets of decisions which will now impinge upon the likelihood of the final effects being open unemployment rather than a fall in the real wage of this group. The immediate effect of the fall in output demand will be to raise the stocks of the concerned commodity of the producer. If the fall in demand for output is not temporary, at some stage the producer will realize that this piling up of stocks at unchanged prices is leading to a loss of profits, and his financial reserves (which he must have had, to tide him over the temporary loss of profits during this unexpected rise in stockholding) are not unlimited. He will then seek to both reduce his prices and cut his output. Only at this stage will he try to lay off workers.

Suppose, however, that there is enough flexibility in production methods for the producer to employ all his workers, but at a lower wage. The workers now, like the producer, are faced with a fall in the demand for their services and they will have to make a decision on whether to accept a wage cut or else look for employment elsewhere at a lower wage. Whether they can even consider the second option will depend upon their 'reserves' (available to them from either past saving, family contributions, or social provision) to tide them over the period of job-search. Depending upon one or the other of the decisions made by the workers, the effects will be a rise in unemployment or a fall in their wages.

Thus in describing an actual process we will have to identify not merely the three lags between the objective effects of a particular event (cause), but also determine the likely responses of the human agents involved. But precisely because these human responses *need not be automatic* they cannot be taken for granted in the same way that we can the automatic shuffling of molecules in a gas container. They cannot be reduced to a mechanical analogue.

This, however, implies that the empirical knowledge we may obtain about these processes, from studying the past or current occurrence of various events, must necessarily be imperfect by comparison with that in the experimental natural sciences. Though it may be useful to use the techniques of statistical inference in 'estimating' these various lags for a particular period of time and location, where there is reason to believe that human agents could have been *expected* to act in a particular way in the face of exogenous shocks, it would be inappropriate to place too much faith on the resulting numerical estimates in making 'predictions' about the future course of historical processes which involve time and the human agent in an essential way.

It is essentially for this reason that we have relied in this book on the method of analytical economic history, where we use our judgement to split up the process into 'periods', during which there are certain common characteristics of human 'sorters', and the process of 'sorting' can be taken to be relatively uniform over the period.[11] We can then discuss various issues concerning the determinants of the wage structure and some of the issues about the course of average labour incomes during the period in terms of comparative statics. But, equally important, we will have to identify the 'events' and the changed responses of the 'sorters' to them (in, for instance, any of the three lag dimensions distinguished above), which moved a particular economy from one 'period' to the next. Finally, it is the particular characteristics of the 'sorters' and the decisions taken by them (namely various economic agents) within each of our 'periods' which will provide the explanations for the various issues concerning unemployment and poverty identified in the previous section. The resulting narrative or 'dynamic' story can only be judged by its plausibility. If this study can tell an intelligible *analytical* story of the evolution of Kenya's labour markets which is not inconsistent with the available evidence, that will be enough, but more it is hoped than if it had been confined to mere statistical hypothesis testing. It should be emphasized this does not mean that this is a work of economic history. We are only interested in the history because of the *analytical* reasons discussed above.

III   Plan of the Book

The book is divided into two parts. The chapters in the first part follow the sub-division of the period under study into three periods. The first, covering 1800–1948, concerns the evolution of the Kenyan labour market from its pre-colonial forms to a particular form of coercive monopsonistic organization under the colonial impact. The second covers the period from 1948–68, during which under the pressures of rising nationalism various humanitarian impulses moderated the coercive features of the earlier forms of labour organization. The third covers the more recent period from 1968–80, when some of the policy-induced distortions in the labour mrket of the previous period were corrected. These distortions had led to both an uneconomic wage structure and a rise in urban unemployment and rural–urban migration. A greater reliance on market forces corrected many of these distortions.

In each chapter of Part One a more or less descriptive narrative highlights the salient events and decisions which shaped the major determinants of labour market behaviour in the period. This is followed by an analytical chapter which attempts to explain wage and employment trends and structures during the period in terms of the comparative statics 'neo-classical' method discussed above.

In the late 1960s and 1970s many 'experts' on Kenya were obsessed with the effects of the policy-induced distortions during the second of our periods on (i) the structure of wages (and thence income distribution), (ii) the levels of urban unemployment and the growth of supposedly low income urban informal sector employment, and (iii) the failure of the fruits of growth to 'trickle down' to the poor. Various models were constructed to 'explain' these outcomes. The second part of this book shows how and why many of the predictions of these models have proved to be false in the light of subsequent history.

It may be useful for the reader to have a brief preview of our argument. From the viewpoint of efficient poverty-redressing growth, there are two processes which are vital in the Kenyan context. One is the efficient growth of smallholder agriculture; the other is efficient skill formation for the growing urban labour force. These processes have been attenuated in Kenya because (*a*) rural factor markets — in particular those for land and credit — are truncated, and (*b*) the compassionate wage policies of our second period distorted the urban wage structure by penalizing efficient skill formation.

However, against this the large urban–rural wage differentials that were created in the compassionate period did have mitigating beneficial effects on rural smallholder development. They promoted rural–urban migration. But, in contrast to the conventional view, this migration did not lead to an increase in poverty or, once the policy-induced sectoral wage distortion was cured, to rising unemployment. Instead it provided rural smallholders with the financial means to overcome the limitations of the rural credit and land markets.

These remittances from relatives who had succeeded in finding jobs in the growing urban labour market provided a major source of finance for smallholder innovation and an associated reversal of the poverty of both smallholders and landless labourers. Furthermore, as the government over time reversed the compassionate wage policies of the late colonial and early post-independence periods, the reduction in rural–urban wage differentials meant that the access of unskilled rural labour surplus households to the urban labour market improved. For in the high urban wage period, as the rural élites were better at obtaining educational credentials which urban employers used as a criterion in their hiring, they probably acquired a larger share of urban employment. As these rural–urban wage differentials narrowed, the returns to education fell — to the advantage of the unskilled and relatively less well educated rural 'poor'.

The reduction in the rural–urban wage differential in the third of our periods also had salutory effects on the efficient formation of skills in the urban labour force. The rise in minimum wages in the compassionate period and the accompanying narrowing of the seniority-based urban wage structure reduced the incentives for employers and employees to invest in firm-specific skills. The reduction in the wage rate for unskilled recruits enabled a partial restoration of seniority and skill differentials which probably enhanced skill formation.

In developing this story of two-way rural–urban interactions and how they are affected by public wage policies, we provide an implicit, and in Chapter 6 explicit, critique of many fashionable interpretations of Kenyan labour markets and the resulting prognosis of growing poverty, unemployment, and worsening income distribution that many past observers have seen as being endemic in the Kenyan growth process.

The resulting analytical exorcism it is hoped will provide both a justification for the longer historical view taken in this book, as well as provide a sounder basis for future prognostications on the likely evolution of Kenyan labour markets.

A final chapter briefly summarizes our conclusions.

As labour incomes are unavoidably the subject of much passion, it is not surprising that political factors impinge fairly directly on their pattern and growth. The interaction of politics and economics is thus of particular importance in the type of study we have undertaken. Hence there is no apology for our combining political with labour market evolution in this work, as these are (as we hope to show) intertwined. For those uninterested in politics, or history, the purely technical chapters should suffice to give an outline of the stages in the story we are reconstructing. But for the reasons given in the previous sections of this Introduction this gives too 'static' a view of the evolution of the Kenyan labour market. To understand how it got from 'there' to 'here', the narrative chapters are of equal importance. If nothing else they provide a cautionary tale, which also happens to be (in our view) an engrossing story!

Notes

1 This is the implicit model of the labour market underlying various monetarist challenges to Keynesianism (see Lal 1977, 1980).

2 Though in countries where government (or paternalistic) interventions in the labour market are pervasive, and 'wages' are fixed (as in socialist or in slave societies), involuntary unemployment of the Keynesian type may occur.

3 Though the general lay public has been bamboozled by many simple-minded projections which include these elements, as in the Club of Rome's 'Limits to growth' study (see Beckerman, Leontief, *et al.* for critiques showing the empirical irrelevance of these models).

4 That this view of optimal employment in a planning framework is closely related to the theories of the wage fund can be seen from Sen (1975), pp. 85–6, and Hicks (1973), p. 52.

5 These comparisons are altered if the terms of trade are variable, see Jorgenson and Zarembaka.

6 There are some other differing implications which are not as sharply focused distinguishing the two approaches, which need not concern us, but see Jorgenson (1967a) for a fuller discussion.

7 Except of course in India!

8 Whilst Hicks (1936) in reviewing the General Theory stated: 'It does become very evident when one thinks of it, that the expectation of a continually expanding market, made possible by increasing population, is a fine thing for keeping up the spirits of entrepreneurs. With increasing population, investment can go roaring ahead, even if invention is rather stupid; increasing population is therefore actually favourable to employment. It is actually easier to employ an expanding population than a contracting one, whatever arithmetic might suggest — at least that is so when the expansion or contraction is expected, as we may suppose to be the case' (p. 252).

9 Hicks (1979) too distinguishes between three types of causality in relationship to time: 'Sequential (in which cause precedes effect), contemporaneous (in which both relate to the same period) and static (in which both are permanencies)' (Hicks, 1979). Much economic analysis, including most of the theories outlined in the previous section are concerned with contemporaneous and static causation. Whilst this is useful and illuminating in many areas — demand analysis, welfare economics, international trade theory — it is not much use in answering the type of questions about the evolution of labour markets in the process of development which are concerned with sequential causation.

10 See Georgescu-Roegen.

11 The importance of 'sorters' in economic as opposed to natural processes is best illustrated in terms of Georgescu-Roegen's distinction between 'shuffling' and 'sorting'. He illustrates this distinction, and its relevance for distinguishing the natural from the social sciences, by the fable of Maxwell's demon in thermodynamics. J. Clarke Maxwell 'imagined a miniscule demon posted near a microscopic swinging door in a wall separating two gases, *A* and *B*, of equal temperature. The demon is instructed to open and close the door "so as to allow only the swifter molecules to pass from *B* to *A*". Clearly the demon can in this way make the gas in *B* hotter than *A*' (Georgescu-Roegen, p. 80).

   In the gas molecules surrounding Maxwell's demon, *automatic shuffling* of molecules is going on in line with the laws of thermodynamics. What the demon does is to *sort* some of these out, and if he succeeds he defeats the entropy law of statistical thermodynamics! It should be emphasized that whereas the shuffling in the material environment is automatic in that it goes on by itself, sorting requires a human agency. Hence Maxwell invented a demon, not a mechanical device for this sorting.

Part One

HISTORY

1

COERCION (1800–1948)

I The Pre-colonial Economy and Labour Organization

The physical environment was the major determinant of the various forms of economic organization that evolved in the pre-colonial period in the part of East Africa now known as Kenya. These forms of economic organization represented both adaptations to and manipulations of the extant physical environment. Broadly speaking, by the time of the colonial impact four broad groups of African people can be classified by economic organization — settled agriculturalists, nomadic pastoralists, small craftsmen, and traders. In addition there were Arab traders, slavers and plantation owners, and Indian money lenders (particularly in the coastal region), who also determined the forms of economic organization that evolved in pre-colonial Kenya. In this chapter we describe the evolution of these various economic groups, though it should be emphasized that for the Africans these categories should not be used to distinguish any rigid occupational categories or 'classes' of people. For the African it was tribes and clans which were the basic associative groups, these being differentiated more by their spatial location than by purely economic characteristics flowing from specialization and inter-tribal trade.

The most important feature of the pre-colonial economy from our viewpoint is that it was a labour deficit one and that anything approaching wage labour as we know it was absent. Men either worked for themselves or were slaves.

(1) Agriculturalists

The first notable aspect of the physical environment was that taking the area as a whole, till the end of the nineteenth century, there was an abundance of land relative to men. Not all of this land was suitable for settled agriculture. That depended upon adequate rainfall (around forty-five inches per annum) and good soils. The latter were not uniformly distributed over the area, but were to be found chiefly in the Highlands and some parts of Western Kenya on the shores of Lake Victoria. The rest of the country was semi-arid.

Given the abundance of land, and the resulting high land–man ratio, it would be rational (see Boserup) for the peoples of this area to adopt a form of shifting cultivation in which the period over which a particular piece of land was left fallow (as the relevant groups moved to a more fertile plot) would be

determined both by the natural fertility of the land and the population size of
the relevant groups.

Virtually nothing is known of the size and rates of growth of the Kenyan
population before 1890. The little evidence available is summarized by
Zwanenberg and King, who conclude that the population was likely to have
been small (probably less than one to two million by the mid- and late
nineteenth century) though not stable.[1] Certainly, it would seem 'that land,
the major factor of production for the agriculturalists, was not in short supply
overall' (p. 6).

This meant that natural fertility and rainfall would be the major determinants of the length of fallow in different parts of the country as well as of
the varying population densities. The usual period of cultivation ranged from
two to four years for each piece of land. In fertile areas with regular rainfall
population densities may have been 100 to 150 people, but were generally
lower. A great variety of agricultural practices existed in the area, based on
intimate local knowledge of climate, soils, and vegetation, which was passed
down over generations. The repositories of this knowledge were the old men
of a clan.

(a) Land Tenure   The resulting pattern of land use and land rights was thus
intimately related to its availability. The pre-coloial land tenure system has
been researched most thoroughly for the Kikuyu tribe, and the following
details from Muriuki's reconstruction based on a a collection of oral traditions
covering three Kikuyu districts will be used as an illustration.

Kikuyuland has good rainfall, moderate temperatures, and deep red soils
which are rich in humus from the cleared primeval forest. This highly
productive land, and the hard working Kikuyu, 'made it the granary of their
neighbours as well as for the European and Swahili caravans which passed
by or through their country, especially in the nineteenth century' (Muriuki,
p. 33).

Kikuyuland is an area of ridges and valleys. This has influenced both the
pattern of settlement and land tenure in the area. The pioneers originally
staked their claim (by clearing forests) to particular ridges, and were subsequently joined by their kinsmen. In the Southern regions they bought their
land from the Athi. This land was 'owned' by the *mbari*, which was a lineage
or sub-clan, depending on the numbers, tracing its origin to a common male
ancestor a few generations back. Someone outside the *mbari* without lands
became a *muhoi* (tenant at will) on someone else's land, with the assurance
that, save for misconduct, his tenancy would be secure (Muriuki, p. 35). The
resulting system of land tenure amongst the Kikuyu could not however be
described as communal ownership, as Kenyatta's account of the creation of a
mbari in *Facing Mount Kenya* makes clear.

Little is known about whether the same land tenure systems also applied
to the other peoples of Kenya, though the Luo certainly recognized claims to

newly cleared land. However, given the general situation of a land surplus in the pre-colonial era every individual could expect to have some right to occupy and use land. This right arose either from his position within a kinship group or from his own entrepreneurial abilities in opening up new tracts of land. Every large agricultural group had rules governing, firstly, the forms of land ownership, which were usually based on kinship with the founder who first claimed the area for cultivation; secondly the distribution of land to wives, sons, and daughters; and, thirdly, the distribution of lands to friends and outsiders for the temporary cultivation of a plot (Zwanenberg and King, p. 28).

Two general principles of land tenure seem to have been that, *within* clans land was relatively equally divided

so that all sons could expect an equal share of part of their mothers' property. Another common practice was to allow acquaintances to look after a piece of land for a while in return for a fee of goats or food. The plot could be redeemed by the clan elders by repayment of the original fee. The principles of equal division of inheritance and redeemability have become important in the 20th century when land is in short supply (Zwanenberg and King, p. 29).

(b) Labour Organization   Descriptions of the forms of labour organization on the farms in the area of settled agriculture are also only available for the Kikuyus.

As labour was scarce relative to land, the need for extra labour could arise for a household or group of households which found themselves short of 'family' labour at some periods of the agricultural cycle. Various communal labour-sharing arrangements arose to meet this need. Some of these traditional forms of labour organization still coexist side by side with wage employment, and Cowen and Murage have provided a description of these traditional organizational forms on the basis of oral histories from three districts in Central Province.

There were three basic forms of obtaining labour from outside the farms. The first was *Ngwatio*, which usually covered between three and ten women who would move as a group, from day to day, from plot to plot, until the required task of all the participants had been completed. *Ngwatio* is still used in such tasks as tea plucking, when family labour is inadequate and working capital insufficient to hire wage labour to meet a tea growers plucking requirements.

The second form was *wira*, in which a man or woman asked a number of participants (up to eighty) on a specific day to complete a specific task, such as digging up permanent grass (men) or weeding (women). It was obligatory under *wira*, but not in *ngwatio*, for the host to provide either beer or food. Neither the *ngwatio* nor *wira* groups were necessarily clan based. Though *wira* has not disappeared, it has become increasingly uncommon.

The third from was *ndungata*, in which a man without livestock (but not necessarily a kinsman) would be taken into a household to herd for his host, who had sheep or goats. The *ndungata* would be paid a sheep or a goat depending upon the regularity of their births. Many of these *ndungata* became wage labourers when the institution of a wage system replaced payment by livestock with payment by wages (Cowen and Murage, pp. 39–40).

These various forms of 'communal' labour practices designed to meet excess demand for labour on particular farms can be looked upon as forms of bartering labour for labour, or else for the only available asset — cattle. Thus Kenyatta states, 'In the Kikuyu country before the introduction of the European monetary system, sheep and goats were regarded as the standard currency of the Kikuyu people. The price of almost everything was determined in terms of sheep and goats (*mbori*)' (Kenyatta, p. 66).

The first two systems of bartering for labour may be looked upon as the only rational response given the relative indivisibility of the available currency, namely sheep and goats, into units sufficiently small to pay for temporary and relatively minor shortages of labour. Under the third system labourers were close to being permanent labourers, and hence payments in the indivisible currency were feasible. But this *ndungata* form of labour use did not represent wage labour but a partnership where one party contributed capital (livestock) and the other labour, and the two had established shares of the profits (sharing the bovine progeny). The important point to be noted is that there was no wage labour or even an employer–employee relationship before colonialism, except for slavery. A modern wage system did not evolve on the African farms until 1916. It began with the spread of a European monetary system and the emergence of a class of absentee African smallholders who earned sufficient money income to pay for the hiring of labour on their farms with cash.

(2) Nomadic Pastoralists

In the semi-arid regions of much of Kenya the environment did not favour settled agriculture. The dominant economic mode in these regions (which cover over 75 per cent of the total land area of the country) was (as it has to a large extent remained) what has been termed nomadic pastoralism, based on livestock production. Moreover, whereas today the picture of a nomadic pastoralist is of someone close to the bottom of the economic heap, this was not always the case. In fact, in the early part of the nineteenth century the pastoralists had become the militarily predominant force in East Africa as pastoral tribes like the Turkana, Somali, and Masai expanded their pastoral preserves over wide areas of the country.

Not much is known about the way of life and economic organization of these pastoralist peoples, beyond some obvious general features which we can briefly summarize. First, the form of shifting settlements of the pastoralists were determined by the changing water supplies and grazing available for their livestock during the various seasons. Thus the Masai lived in areas which were relatively better watered than the Turkana. But by the end of the nineteenth century there were already signs of a waning of pastoralist fortunes. First, the expanding pastoralists came increasingly into conflict with expanding agriculturalists over land control in contiguous areas. These conflicts were no longer invariably won by the pastoralists. Moreover, the agriculturalists were also able to take advantage of the weaknesses emerging in some pastoralist societies such as the Masai, which were due as much to natural causes such as new diseases like rinderpest as to internal political and social problems in their clans. Finally, where the environment proved fruitful some groups amongst the pastoralists in the Luo and Masai tribes switched from primarily pastoralist towards predominantly agricultural pursuits. But it was the establishment of colonial rule which sounded the death knell for the relative dominance of pastoralists and their way of life and values in Kenya.

(3) Crafts and Trade

The major traditional industries in pre-colonial Kenya were iron, salt, and textiles. African traders and trade pre-dated the penetration of Arab traders into the interior. Famine was the major cause of this internal trade. The traditional picture of self-sufficient peasant or pastoralist societies, supposedly typical of pre-colonial Africa, does not apply to East Africa. Thus Marris and Somerset have.documented trade between the Southern and Northern Kikuyu and the Masai, who had complementary economies. The Kikuyu imported sheep and goats from the Masai and exported flour, honey, ochre, and tobacco goods which were not available in Masai country. Similarly, the agricultural Gusii (who lived in the south-western part of the Highlands) traded iron instruments, grain during droughts, and leopard and baboon skins with the pastoralists for cattle, pots, and poisons.

Finally the Akamba entered foreign trade well before the large demand for ivory in the nineteenth century might have been expected to stimulate such trade. During the second half of the eighteenth century, as population outgrew the available resources of the area, entire villges began to pioneer homesteads in uninhabited areas, particularly in the Kitui region which however was less fertile. As standards of living dropped, people began looking to local trade to supplement the local resources in Kitui. Thus by the beginning of the nineteenth century the Kitui Akamba had penetrated Kikuyu, Embu, Mwimbe, and the Taita Hills, and large well-armed parties of Akamba traders, participating in the coastal ivory trade, had reached the coast.

These African trading caravans in the early nineteenth century were the precursors of the Arab caravans which were to introduce an alien presence into the interior of East Africa for the first time and lead to the eventual establishment of colonialism.

(4) Slaves, Ivory, and Arabs

In their attempts to safeguard the sea lanes to India, the British sought to secure the coastal regions of East Africa from falling into unfriendly hands. Between 1838 and 1841 Lord Palmerston encouraged and protected the Imam of Muscat in securing his authority along the East African coast.

By this time Zanzibar was already the entrepôt of a flourishing slave trade which was in the hands of the Omanis. In the early part of the nineteenth century, as a result of a rise in demand for ivory in Britain and the US, the ivory trade became an even more valuable business than slavery for Omani traders. About the same time there was a great demand for cloves in international markets. This led to the establishment of clove plantations under Arab ownership in Zanzibar, Pemba, and in the Kenyan regions of Mombasa, Malindi, and Lamu.

These various factors gave rise to certain patterns of trade and a widening of the division of labour in East Africa. Arab caravans, financed by 1840 by Indian money lenders, brought ivory and slaves from the interior to the coast. Whilst the ivory and some of the slaves were exported, a fair proportion of the latter were required for the Arab clove plantations (which suffered from an inadequate supply of cheap labour — a problem that was to bedevil their erstwhile successors in the white Highlands nearly a century later). It was the abolition of slavery (whose extent and dismal conditions were greatly exaggerated by missionaries: see Zwanenberg and King, pp. 176–81) which destroyed the Arab trading and plantation economy.

The British colonial system was to arise in its place. Its origins lay in the emergence of British traders in East Africa in the late nineteenth century as a result of the granting of a Royal Charter in 1888 to the Imperial British East Africa Company (IBEAC). In turn the IBEAC paved the way for the subsequent establishment of British administration in the area from 1895. This was to have long-lasting effects on the way the Africans were to earn their living for the next three quarters of a century.

II The Colonial Impact

The incorporation of the area now called Kenya into the British Empire marked the beginning of profound changes in the functioning of the Kenyan labour market. Many of these changes were the result of the compulsions arising from what were, in the context of overall British colonial policy, a series of historical accidents. The genesis of British colonialism in the region was the establishment of the East Africa Protectorate under the suzerainty of the Sultan of Zanzibar in 1895. This was to subserve the larger interests of the UK in securing the trade and supply routes to India, which remained the focus of imperial interests and passions, rather than any desire to exploit the natural resources of these new territories (see Robinson and Gallagher).

Unlike other parts of Africa, the tract that was to be renamed Kenya in 1920 possessed little mineral wealth or other natural resources capable of easy exploitation. Its economic development and 'exploitation' was the by-product of the decision taken in 1895 to construct the Uganda railway from the coast at Mombasa to the fertile belt around Lake Victoria.

It was soon apparent that the railway, opened in 1902 and built at a capital cost of £5½ million, could not be expected to make any profits. This was not surprising, for there were no exportable goods produced by the natives of East Africa, nor any minerals whose exploitation required a railway; whilst the ivory and timber trades were too specialized or too limited to support the railway on their own. The search for customers for the railway became a major preoccupation of the Empire builders. It was sugested that East Africa become the 'America of the Hindu', a national home for the Jews, or that Persians or Finns be imported to improve native farming. Ultimately white settlement to develop the area's resources was seen as the only way to make the railway commercially viable. The tail had wagged the dog!

(1) The Settlers

Once it had been decided to introduce settlers into Kenya, it was necessary to make settlement attractive enough for potential settlers who had attractive alternative areas in Southern Africa, Canada, Australia, and New Zealand open to them. Compared with the Africans, the settlers had no superior specialized agricultural skills. They had to be given implicit or explicit subsidies to make farming and settlement in the White Highlands attractive enough to ensure that a sufficient number of potential settlers bound for Australia and Canada were diverted to Kenya. Despite these subsidies the number of white settlers grew only very slowly, from only about 100 in 1903 to about 4,000 in 1953.

The first implicit subsidy to the original settlers was the provision of 'alienated' land at virtually throwaway prices. The UK authorities were not happy with the large land grants made by the Governor, Sir Charles Eliot (1901–5), because of their justifiable fear that this would fuel land speculation, but the settlers' views prevailed. By 1915 they had received large concessions of high quality land on 999-year leases with little obligation to develop it. Eight thousand two hundred and forty-two square miles of land had been alienated on behalf of about 1,000 settlers. The distribution of alienated land was however very unequal: 20 per cent was held by five individuals or groups and thirteen individuals or groups had control of 894,434 acres of land out of a total of 4,500,000 acres granted to settlers (Zwanenberg and King, p. 37). The early land speculators were able to earn large profits at the expense of the new settlers; thus land values in the Rift Valley rose from 6*d.* an acre in 1908 to 240*d.* an acre by 1914 (ibid, p. 38; see also Ghai and McAuslan).

Having got the land, albeit at an inflated price from the earlier large landholders, the relatively small white settler farmers faced two sets of interrelated problems in becoming economically viable. The first was in the choice of the appropriate crops to be grown on their newly acquired land. The second was the availability of complementary factors of production, in particular labour, at a wage which would enable them to price their produce competitively in either the domestic or world markets and still earn a living which was roughly comparable to those of their fellow settlers in the other white dominions.

As these small white settlers were unlikely to have a comparative advantage in producing for the domestic market, in which they would have to compete with the output of subsistence crops of the African smallholders on the 'reserves', they naturally searched for viable export crops. They first concentrated on familiar products such as wheat, wool, meat, and dairy products. By 1914 it was apparent that these were not viable as exportable commodities, though coffee and sisal proved more successful. By 1914 the export market for them was growing, and coffee became the premier export to Europe. It was on coffee and sisal that the settlers were to found a viable economy for themselves.

However, even in these crops the white settlers were unlikely to have had a comparative advantage over the African smallholders. This was firstly because there are no economies of scale in the production of these crops, as can be gleaned from the fact that in Tanzania, where African smallholders were allowed to grow coffee, their produce was of a higher quality than estate coffee and earned a premium (see Brett). Secondly, as these are labour-intensive crops the cost of labour would be of importance in determining their viability in world markets where the output price was determined by world rather than domestic market conditions. As the real cost of labour to an African smallholder would be determined by the supply price of family labour, the wage-based white settler farms (under competitive labour market conditions) would have had to pay a wage which was higher than this supply price of labour on African farms.

Given their desire to make estate agriculture viable, the white settlers and the colonial officials were thus compelled by this logic to devise methods to drive Africans into labour on European farms at wages below the competitive level. A variety of mechanisms were used to achieve this purpose — outright compulsion, cash taxes, restrictions on African cash-crop production, and the manipulation of African access to land (see Brett, and Ghai and McAuslan for a historical account of the evolution of these policies).

Though about 18 per cent of Kenya's cultivable land had been alienated for the white settlers (Zwanenberg and King, p. 30), there was still sufficient land left for the Africans to become viable commercial cash-crop farmers if they had been provided with the requisite complementary factors of production. Moreover, as the available land relative to the African population was still sufficient to provide more than a subsistence income, the supply price of African wage labour to the white settlers' estates would probably have been too high to make their export agriculture commercially viable. The settlers and the Kenyan government they dominated, therefore moved towards various statutory measures to provide the settlers with wage labour below its competitive supply price.

The management of land was central in the resulting coercion of African labour. European settlement began at a time when the Kikuyu population had been depleted by the Rinderpest. The white settlers absorbed all the available land, and then as the Kikuyu population began to recover they started trading access to land for agricultural labour. Until 1918 this was in the form of 'Kaffir farming', which was a kind of feudal relationship (see Ghai and McAuslan), and thereafter in the form of 'squatting rights' on the white estates, for which the Africans were required to pay rent. Initially, as most of these Africans were engaged in subsistence agriculture, the only form in which they could pay their rents was through labour on the white farms. However, as they saw the advantages of cash-crop agriculture they attempted to grow these crops, and to switch their rent payments from labour into money. This led the government to pass the Resident Native Ordinance in 1918, which required future payments to be made in labour and not in cash. This turned the relationship of the African squatters with the white settlers from tenancy into serfdom (Brett, p. 172). As Kikuyu access to land became more and more difficult, the labour supply turned from a deficit to a surplus in the 1930s, and the seeds of the Mau Mau rebellion were sown.

In 1921 the Registration Ordinance instituted the *kipande*, which was a certificate all Africans were required to carry. Its aim was to track down individuals who broke their employment contracts and therefore became liable under the newly instituted employers charter, the Masters and Servants Ordinance (Brett, p. 187). In 1920, through various official circulars, district officers were allowed to use compulsion to recruit labour for public works. But care was taken to see that this was not labour for which the settlers were competing. More directly, labour circulars issued by the authorities in 1919 and 1920 asked the district officers in labour-supplying areas to coerce labour to work for the settlers. This, however, drew the ire of the missionaries and the Colonial Office, and subsequent circulars made it clear that 'no pressure should be brought to bear on those cultivating their own crops [but] nevertheless reiterated that "it is in the interests of the natives themselves for the young men to become wage-earners and not to remain idle in the reserves" ' (Brett, p. 189).

Apart from these coercive measures, the native hut and poll tax was also seen as an indirect incentive for the Africans to work on the white estates. In 1919 this tax was raised from 10s. to 16s., and the authorities were in no doubt about the persuasive value of this tax in providing increased cheap labour to the estates. To prevent the development of competing African commercial cash crops the settlers persuaded the authorities to ban Africans from growing coffee and pyrethrum.

Finally, as Brett has documented, though the Africans bore nearly 70 per cent of the tax burden in the early 1920s the benefits from the resulting public expenditure were virtually monopolized by the settlers. Thus in transport, marketing, and extension services — all of which were essential for the viability of cash-crop export agriculture — the white settlers had a monopoly of public provision.

The net effect of these policies was to create a monopsonistic market for African labour on the white estates.

(2) Employment and Labour Force

We have no reliable estimates of the labour force before 1948. However, if the basis of the official estimates of population till 1948 are recalled, it is possible to reconstruct the numbers of adult males (over fifteen years of age) on whom the Poll Tax was levied. This probably understates the actual male labour force in these years. The estimates are given in Table 1.1. This Table also provides estimates of the average number of African males in wage employment. These too are likely to be underestimates.[2] If the trends in the male labour force and wage employment are roughly correct, there was a large rise in the share of the male labour force in wage employment over the first half of this century. By 1948 some 22 per cent of the labour force was so employed. It appears that there were three periods: 1920–1, 1923–4, and 1929–31 when wage employment fell. After surveying the available data on real wages for this period we will provide an explanation of these trends (in the next section) in terms of changing world demand for Kenyan agricultural exports which shifted the demand curve, and changing degrees of coercion which shifted the supply curve for African labour.

Despite its large size, the African wage labour force was confined to a very narrow range of occupations centring upon agriculture and domestic service (see Table 1.2). The labour market was further racially segmented between Asians, who predominated in industry and commerce, and Europeans who predominated in agriculture and the public sector. This segmentation became more pronounced over the period, as can be seen by comparing the snapshots of 1921 and 1948 detailed in Table 1.2.

The best wage data available for the period to 1948 are probably those compiled by Cowen. This is based on labour histories of current workers in Central Kenya, mainly from Nyeri district. He has compared the trends which emerge from this oral record with the few estimates on agricultural wages of unskilled labourers available from the official Blue Books. This comparison suggests that the method is not seriously unreliable. Cowen's own estimates of the real wages between 1924–48 for workers in agricultural estates are given in the right-hand column of Table 1.1. From this it is

Table 1.1
Wage Employment and the Labour Force 1902–1948

Year	African adult male employment ('000s)	African males aged over 15 ('000s)	Wage employment as a percentage of male labour force	Real wages of agricultural workers[a] (1924 = 100)
1902	—	1,240		
1911	—	820		
1919	45[b]			
1920	56[b]			
1921	52[b]	770		
1922	*54[b]*			
1922	119[c]	780	15.3	
1923	138			
1924	134			100
1925	152			102
1926	*169*	830	20.4	102
1927	148			105
1928	152			105
1929	160			107
1930	157			111
1931	·141	920	15.3	115
1932	132			115
1933	141			115
1934	—			115
1935	—			110
1936	173			113
1937	183			117
1938	183			118
1939	—			116
1940	—			113
1941	251			104
1942	281			107
1943	286			98
1944	291			115
1945	296			111
1946	287			113
1947	301			111
1948	310	1,399[d]	22.2	108

[a] Cowen (mimeo).
[b] Employed on a monthly basis in agriculture only.
[c] Native Affairs Department Annual Report.
[d] 1948 Census not comparable with earlier figures based on Poll Tax.

Table 1.2

The Occupational Structure of Employment by Race

Year	Agriculture		Industry and commerce		Public	
	Indian	European	Indian	European	Indian	European
1921	498	1,893	9,765	1,496	3,390	1,082
1948	502	3,411	25,056	5,406	4,674	4,764
Increase						
1921–48	4	1,518	15,291	3,910	1,284	3,682

African (males) 1927 (per cent)

Agriculture	48
Railways	10
Government Departments	8
Domestic Service	14
Other	20
Total	100

apparent that real wages rose during the 1924–38 period, falling during the Second World War period. This decline continued until 1953. Though Cowen does not provide any data on real wage trends before 1924, he nevertheless states that:

our evidence for the period 1918–1924 and earlier indicates that we have caught the point of upturn of a U-shaped real wage cycle. From 1910/1912 to 1922, real wages had in all probability been falling, but from 1923/4, the rise of African political organisation prevented the use of widespread physical coercion in assisting a fall in money wage rates (Cowen mimeo (n.d.), p. 3).

Summarizing the scanty wage evidence therefore, until 1922/3 there is likely to have been a fall in the real wages of Africans; from 1924 to 1938 there was a marked rise in real wages for all types of African wage labour; whilst from 1939 to 1953 real wages of unskilled agricultural workers and of artisans probably fell.

The effect of the various coercive measures undertaken during the period was to increase the supply of African labour to the settler farms. If the employers nevertheless had acted individually the competitive wage would have been depressed by this coercion. But with collusion amongst employers, and hence monopsony, the wage rate was further depressed, whilst the marginal product of labour on the settler farms was above the wage. It was this latter divergence which gave the appearance of a labour shortage on the estates.

It remains to provide evidence of collusive behaviour on the part of the estate employers. Given the small number of white settlers and their desire as bearers of the White Man's Burden to stick together, it is plausible to assume that they would have tended to collude in setting wages. By the 1940s, moreover, we have direct evidence of such collusion. In a press interview in 1950 Mr E. M. Hyde Clark, Kenya's labour commissioner, said that the way the problem was tackled in rural-agricultural areas at the moment was that, with the assistance of the Kenya National Farmers Union, farmers' associations, and production sub-committees, area wage discussions took place at which the Labour Department on the whole represented the African (Singh, p. 290).

The subsequent history of wages and employment levels in the settler estates can be explained in the interplay in the shifts over time in the demand and supply curves for African labour. The former were largely dependent upon the changing world demand for Kenya's agricultural exports. The latter were determined by both demographic changes as well as the changing levels of coercion of African labour.

The African labour market during this period was characterized by government intervention to raise labour supply, employer monopsony power, dependence upon world markets, and racial stratification. Movements of employment and earnings can be seen to have been responsive to changes in these factors. The behaviour of African agricultural employment and earnings can be divided into the periods summarized below:

	Employment	*Wages*
1910–22	Generally rising	Generally falling
1922–24	Falling	Rising
1924–30	Rising	Rising
1930–32	Falling	Falling
1933–38	Rising	Rising
1939–48	Rising	Falling

In the first of these periods the explanation for the juxtaposition of rising employment and falling wages probably lies in the mounting repression documented in the previous section. The settler newspaper *Leader*, commenting upon African unrest in 1921, noted: 'this as we have predicted, is the direct outcome of the recent much debated and more or less efficient action of the Kenya employer.' The cumulative effect of land alienation, crop restrictions, forced labour, taxation, and biased public expenditure was a rightward shift in the labour supply schedule.

However, by 1922 repression had gone so far that the Colonial Office was provoked into demanding liberalization in the Devonshire White Paper of 1923. The Hut and Poll Tax was reduced and Singh (not an observer prone to see signs of colonial liberalization) noted that 'forced labour became less intense' (Singh, p. 20). This sudden leftward shift in the labour supply curve produced the expected combination of falling employment and rising wages.

The third period, 1924–30, is the heyday of the settler economy, supported by rising world prices for sisal and the other export crops. Employment increased by 50 per cent in five years, and in order to attract this extra labour real wages rose more rapidly than any other part of the whole period. The process went into reverse following the collapse in the sisal price in 1930–2. The demand for labour contracted and so employment and wages fell.

The fifth sub-period, 1933–8, is characterized by a slow recovery of the demand for labour combined with the emergence of African smallholder commercial cultivation, chiefly for the domestic market. This is perhaps best seen not as the result of deliberate liberalization but rather the growing ability of Africans to circumvent a fairly consistent set of colonial regulatory obstacles. Hence, rising demand and a gradual reduction in supply induced slowly growing employment and rapidly rising wages.

The final sub-period, in which the demand for labour grew rapidly because of the war, was marked by a substantial increase in the extent of official repression. In 1938 the Native Lands Trust Ordinance and the Crown Lands Ordinance introduced further land alienation and was combined with forced sales of African cattle. At the onset of the war forced labour was introduced and this was rapidly extended to cover the agricultural estates. Finally, during the war, the composition of output was skewed against African foodstuffs, and much of this output was pre-empted by the military. Africans thus faced very unfavourable movements in relative prices (see Cowen, mimeo (n.d., pp. 7–8). Hence, large increases in both the demand and supply of labour resulted in an expansion of employment and falling real wages.

This flexibility and responsiveness of the estates labour market meant that the earnings of unskilled labour on the estates did not rise significantly above incomes in smallholder agriculture. Indeed, if anything, mean smallholder incomes were probably above those on the estates. For example, the 1935 Nyeri District Annual Report noted 'any person of average industry can earn more by cultivation in the native reserve than by seeking outside employment'.

Further, since the estates were fundamentally uncompetitive vis-à-vis smallholder agriculture, they could not attract the full labour supply of an African household on a permanent basis. Even the combined effect of all the labour supply increasing policies was only to make the estates competitive with smallholder agriculture for the use of the temporary labour of single household members, generally male.

The corollary of this combination of flexibility and economic marginality of the estates labour market was that there were large short-term migration flows and a corresponding high rate of turnover of unskilled labour. This had consequences for the use of labour in smallholder agriculture since it encouraged the sexual division of labour (which still persists in Kenya) whereby the woman was responsible for the day-to-day work whilst the man would add his labour only at peak periods of labour input.

Whilst the unskilled estates labour market was characterized by high turnover, the estates were able to retain for longer periods labour in which they had invested training by paying higher wages. The emergence of this group of skilled and semi-skilled wage labour also had a profound impact upon smallholder agriculture. Possessing land which they could not sell but unable to supply their own labour, and having a relatively high cash income, this group found it profitable to hire labour and introduce cash crops. Hence, skill differentiation among the estates labour force rapidly induced differentiation into absentee commercial farmers and labourers within smallholder agriculture.

In the national labour market the supply of trained, educated, and cheap Asian labour proved a more economic alternative than providing African labour with extensive means of skill acquisition. Hence Africans were confined to the lower ranges of the skill hierarchy. In order to prevent the competition of skilled Asian labour from depressing European incomes the occupational distribution of employment became increasingly arranged on racial lines. The alienated land was confined exclusively to Europeans so that Asians were excluded from the array of implicit and explicit subsidies provided to settler agriculture. Similarly, public sector employment opportunities were increasingly reserved for Europeans. This left the Asians to dominate commerce and industry. Hence, both skills and sectoral divisions coincided with racial divisions.

(3) African Agriculture

The resulting labour market system of the estates also provoked profound and long-lasting effects on labour organization within the African smallholder reserves. We outline these effects in this section.

The first effect of the enforced migration of African male labourers to work on the settler estates was to convert many Africans into non-resident cultivators. Their farms were managed most often by their women folk, a practice which continues to this day. Some idea of the impact of the coercive migration of male African labour to the estates can be gleaned from the following figures:

By the end of the 1920s, the Native Affairs Department estimated that some 69 to 77 per cent of the able-bodied Kikuyu males of Kiambu, 35 to 45 per cent of the Kikuyu of Fort Hall and Nyeri, 60 to 75 per cent of the Nandi, 44 to 54 per cent of the Kipsigis, 35 to 45 per cent of the Luhya, about 36 per cent of the Luo in Central Kavirondo and 26 to 36 per cent of the Taita were employed [on the estates] in any given month (Stichter, 1975, p. 50).

Total African employment on the estates increased from 62,000 in 1921/2 to 126,000 in 1929/30.

Moreover, with this large scale migration of male labour, the non-resident owners of land on the reserves could not practice the traditional forms of communal labour-sharing. The more skilled amongst them, who earned higher wages on the estates, could, hoever, afford to hire labour to work their farms on the reserves. Cowen estimates, 'the first recorded wage rate (for such labour), in 1922, at 20 cents a day, . . . bears a marked resemblance to the then monthly wage rate of six shillings on the Nanyuki estates' (mimeo n.d., p. 41).

Because of this coercive labour system, which was established to provide a cheap labour supply for the estates, the African smallholder responded in ways which have had a continuing impact on the evolution of the rural labour market in Kenya. Thus the importance of the relative size of non-farm income in determining agricultural innovation was probably established during this period, as was the practice of leaving their women folk as managers on the farms. The importance of these features in explaining the incidence of current smallholder poverty is developed in Chapter 8.

Despite colonial policies to discourage African smallholders from switching to cash crops, and their reluctance to provide them with the necessary marketing and transport infrastructure, African smallholders did succeed in moving from subsistence to cash crops. The settler farms and the building of towns, particularly Nairobi, led to the growth of the domestic market for foodstuffs, in particular maize. European vegetables such as beans and potatoes and fruit were marketed. Given the indifference of the government the Africans themselves provided transport and traders to take the goods to the market places. 'Pack horses, donkeys and cart-owner associations and a large number of traders' groups sprang up everywhere. It is clear from the writing of contemporaries that there was a thriving peasant commercial activity based on the internal market' (Zwanenberg and King, pp. 40–1).[3]

(4) The Asians

Between the Africans and the whites were the Indians. Indian traders had been trading along the coast for many years, and had become established as the money lenders for the caravans and exporters to India from Zanzibar, from around the 1840s. The Uganda railway was built almost entirely by Indian coolies and serviced by Indian craftsmen, clerks, and technicians. There were nerly 20,000 Indians involved. After the completion of the railway a majority of the coolies returned to India under the terms of their original contracts, but a large number remained in Nairobi and Mombasa.

The growth of the Indian population in Kenya relative to that of the European and African is shown in Table 1.3. Just as the majority of Europeans (over 5,000 in 1931, and twice the number of farmers) were involved in trade and professions to service the settlers, the Indians too provided the essential professional and commercial skills to service both the white settlers and the

Table 1.3
Population 1911–1962
('000s)

Year	Indian[a]	European[a]	African[b]
1911	12.0	3.2	—
1921	23.0	9.7	3,700
1926	41.1	12.5	—
1931	57.1	16.8	4,000
1948	97.5	29.7	5,600
1962	176.6	55.8	8,600

[a] From Zwanenberg and King, p. 14.
[b] From Lury (1966).

African smallholders. Over 3,000 Asians in Kenya and Uganda were employed in government services by 1921. Though in Kenya, as government jobs became the preserve of the whites, this number decreased. First industry and commerce and later the professions provided the major occupations for the Asians.

The white settlers were adamant that the Indians were not to be allowed to buy land. They feared that as Indians in Kenya outnumbered Europeans by almost four to one, Kenya would soon become an Indian colony if they were given equal rights to buy land (Murray-Brown, p. 81), and the reality of this fear is borne out by Table 1.3.

The conflict between the Indians and the settlers was not easily resolved. The UK Colonial Office frankly looked to India for the development of East Africa. But with the Indians of East Africa looking to the Viceroy in Delhi for moral support, and the white settlers to South Africa and General Smuts, it was not clear who would win, as both Smuts and the India Office carried weight in the Imperial cabinet.

Whilst the settlers used arguments (against the Indian claims) from 'nature, stock breeding, Darwin and the Bible', the Indians in May 1921 began to attack the settler bias of the colonial government from the viewpoint of the Africans rather than their own (Murray-Brown, p. 82). They promoted the agitation, organized by Harry Thuku, against the *kipande* and a proposed cut in money wages on the estates. Though, from now on, the Indians were to use African nationalism against the Europeans, they were to lose this particular battle. For there was another interest group in Kenya — the missionaries — which proved most influential in the drafting of the 1923 White Paper, *Indians in Kenya*, on the question of white settlement and its relationship with the other communities in Kenya. This document laid down the principle of paramountcy, namely that it was His Majesty's 'considered opinion that the interests of the African natives must be paramount, and that if, and when, those interests and the interests of the immigrant races should conflict the former should prevail'.

However, despite these high-sounding sentiments, by the middle of the 1920s in effect a three class society stratified on racial lines had emerged in Kenya, with the whites monopolizing export-crop agriculture, the higher administrative posts, and the professions; the Asians trade, commerce, and the middle reaches of the bureaucracy; and the Africans left with unskilled wage employment, smallholder farming (but within which they were excluded from cultivating the cash crops grown by the white settlers), petty trade at the village level, and (with the gradual spread of literacy as a result of the mission schools) the lower-level clerical posts in the administration.

Notes

1 H. Kjekshus argues that the Great Rinderpest of 1888 was particularly devastating to the pastoralists and perhaps mixed farmers too. By contrast, the mid-nineteenth century was a period of great prosperity for Africans, and the colonial penetration at the end of the century came at a particularly low ebb for these societies.

2 Kitching has suggested that employment is more seriously underestimated than population so that the percentage of adult males in wage employment was around 20 per cent in 1922 and 33 per cent by 1948. See Kitching (1980) Table IX:1, p. 249.

3 Furthermore, it should be noted that up until 1913 the African smallholder farms also provided the bulk of exports. These were first, 'grain and pulses, mostly maize, simsim, beans and peas . . . [which] for the year ending March 31, 1913, [had] a value of £131,258, more than four times the amount exported just 3 years before. These were primarily from African farms and were not European produce. Likewise, the second item on the list, hides and skins valued at £86,673, was also mainly African produce; the same is true of the third item, copra valued at £31,956. European produce, coffee, fibers, potatoes, wheat, livestock and so forth all showed gains of two to four times over 1910, but they were still at pretty low levels. Total exports were £421,084 in 1913' (Hickman in Lewis (ed.), p. 187). Thus in the period when there was relatively pure competition amongst the estates and African reserves, clearly the latter made better use of the opportunities offered and outperformed the white settlers.

2

COMPASSION (1948–1968)

I The Colonial Government's Interventions in the Labour Market: 1945–1952

Institutional interventions are of some importance in explaining relatively new trends in the functioning of the Kenyan labour market in the post World War Two period. This period saw the official recognition of African trade unions as well as the introduction of minimum wage laws, and the institution of a protective labour code.

There were a number of reasons why the government's stance changed from repressing the fledging organized labour movement in the country towards at least some minimum accommodation of its demands. The first of these reasons was the growing feeling in the UK that legalizing trade unions, besides promoting 'the prosperity and happiness' of colonial peoples in the words of the 1940 Colonial Development and Welfare Act, would also act as a therapeutic safety valve for the expression of grievances. This was pointed out as early as 1930 in a dispatch from the Colonial Office (when Sidney Webb was Secretary of State for the Colonies) to Colonial governors and reiterated by the Conservative goverment in 1937. The latter's despatch made clear that the Colonial Office's major worry was political — namely that the suppression of trade unions would lead to political extremism which could threaten colonial domination.

The second reason for the emergence of a policy of accommodating labour's demands was the growth of the urban labour force during the inter-war period and its increasing militancy, as reflected in a number of strikes in the 1930s. Though these strikes failed to generate any significant labour organization, and were primarily concerned with raising wages (e.g. the 1937 Nairobi strike of Asian artisans was for a 25 per cent rise in wages; the 1939 Mombasa African workers general strike was about wages and conditions of employment), they were nevertheless also looked upon by the authorities as incipient seditious movements. These fears were not completely paranoid. It is now commonly recognized that the first expression of African nationalism in Kenya was the demonstration by Harry Thuku's Young Kikuyu Association in 1922 against the white settler European Convention Association's proposal to cut the salaries of their African employees by a third. The veteran trade union leader, Makhan Singh, says of the 1937 Nairobi strike that 'the unity and solidarity of workers frightened the employers and the colonial authorities (Singh, p. 63).

To accommodate London's increasing humanitarian concern for trade union rights, as well as to exorcise their fears of domestic subversion, the Kenyan government (still dominated by white settler interests) instituted a set of formal regulations which provided the window dressing for what remained a policy of holding down African real wages. Thus in 1937 a Trade Union Ordinance was published legalizing trade unions. Nevertheless attempts to register a trade union were thwarted by the stipulation that 'before a trade union could be registered, the founders of such a union had to get consent from the government by establishing that they would not indulge in offensive conspiracies' (Lubembe, p. 56). As a result the first African trade union was not recognized until 1947. A slightly less illiberal ordinance to regulate trade unions and trade disputes was issued by the Governor in 1943. This was in response to pressure by MPs in the UK, as well as the stipulation that

a colony's eligibility for financial assistance under the terms of the 1940 Colonial Welfare and Development Act was contingent upon the legalization of trade unions. The European leader on the Legislative Council commented in the press that the settler community had accepted the Ordinance only by *force majeur*. Soon, relations between the government and the white farmers worsened on this score . . . For a short while the '43 ordinance was a sterile document, for no new African trade union presented itself (Amsden, p. 30).

In 1944 a Labour Advisory Board was set up. Being dominated by European employers it was unlikely to serve the interests of the African workers (Lumbembe, p. 61).

From 1946 onwards a protective Labour code was enacted for the African worker. Except for 'desertion' (for which there were reduced sanctions), other penal sanctions for breach of contract were abolished. There was stricter government surveillance of labour recruitment. There were improvements in the recommended standards of medical treatment, housing, and rations. Protection was offered to women in night work and children in municipal employment, and a ceiling was imposed on the hours worked by juveniles in agriculture. A workman's compensation ordinance was passed in 1946 and a comprehensive factories ordinance in 1950. There was some tightening of labour inspection, which helped in ensuring some compliance with Kenya's labour code (Amsden, p. 7). However, the *kipande*, a work certificate containing their fingerprints which all African males were required to carry, was not abolished. In 1948, as a result of an agitation by the only African member of the Legislative Council, it was extended to all races, but with the storm of protest from settler quarters (who said it 'made Europeans feel like criminals and smacked of totalitarianism' (Amsden, p. 8)), it was limited by the goverment in 1949 to those African men who could not fill in and sign a work card in English.

In 1946 a Central Minimum Wage Advisory Bord was set up to recommend such wages for two urban areas — Nairobi and Kisumu. Its stated objective was to devise a wage which 'while covering the cost of living of a single adult male employee working at unskilled labour would not give him the feeling of complacent satisfaction in which he would make no effort at self-improvement' (Kenya, Report of Committee on African Wages, p. 54).

Thus by 1947 the UK Colonial Office had succeeded in forcing the Kenyan government to institute the formal structure for granting the supposed rights of labour as embodied in the ILOs Philadelphia convention. Even though the settlers had succeeded in thwarting the liberal intentions of the promoters of these institutions, their worst fears were soon to be realized.

In October 1946 there was a squatters' protest in Kijabe, culminating in a demonstration on the lawns of Government House, Nairobi, in January 1947. The squatters' struggle was now gathering strength, and so was the struggle of other workers in Kenya. This led to the Mombasa general strike for higher wages.

The Mombasa strike gave rise to a new militancy, which increasingly complemented the political agitation of Kenyatta's political party — the Kenya African Union. With strikes becoming more numerous and strike demands more radical, the climax came when the East African Trade Union Congress (EATUC), spearheaded a campaign against the granting of a Royal Charter to Nairobi in 1950. When the leaders of the resulting boycott were arrested, a general strike — the biggest ever in Nairobi — began. In addition to the usual demands on pay and working conditions there was one new demand: self government for the East African territories. The link between worker's grievances and political independence, which both the colonial authorities and the white settlers had feared for so long, was now an established fact.

The remaining reasons for the evolving intervention by the authorities in the Kenyan labour market arose from their attempts to break this link. They adopted the twin poilicy of accommodating perceived grievances of moderate Kenyan labour while at the same time repressing the extremists. This use of the carrot and the stick was to continue until the coming of Kenyan independence in 1963.

The attempt to divert the emerging Kenyan labour movement away from political agitation towards a concern for pay and working conditions, was reflected in the authorities' new willingness to see minimum wages rise. Thus the immediate response to the 1947 Mombasa strike was to raise the minimum wage from 31 to 38 shillings in Nairobi, and from 22 to 28 shillings in Kisumu, and from 33 to 40 shillings in Mombasa. But the stick was also used: after the same strike the EATUC was proscribed and its leader banished. After the demand for 'complete independence and sovereignty' made during the 1950 general strike, Makhan Singh, the trade union leader who had moved the crucial resolution at a meeting convened by KAU and the East

African Indian National Congress, was placed under detention and not released for eleven years.

The last of the *dramatis personae* to be introduced in our story is the Association of Commercial and Industrial Employers (ACIE) which was formed as an association of industrial employers in 1956. Its origins, however, go back to the Mombasa strike of 1947. Until then European business men in Kenya had not questioned the incompatibility of their interests with the settler dominated colonial government's policies. They had been willing to accept the government's paternalism regarding African wages, but the labour tribunal's award at the end of the 1947 Mombasa strike, and in the water-front strike in 1955, made an appreciable increase in the labour costs of many firms. This gave rise to their growing antipathy to arbitration and increasing support for a system of collective bargaining. The emerging nation-alism and its expression, in part through the growing trade union movement, also gave a fillip to combinations of employers.

Thus by the end of 1952 the formal apparatus for protecting labour rights had been established, albeit reluctantly. It had not, however, led to any marked improvement in either African real wages or working conditions, as the continuing confluence of interests of the white settlers, industrial em-ployers, and the colonial officials was successful in large part in sabotaging the spirit of the new reforms.[1]

Cracks in this homogeneity of interests began to appear as the trade union movement increasingly came to link political with economic demands. The settlers and the officials were willing to concede the economic demands (which hurt the industrial employers). They hoped thereby to break the link between what were seen as politically seditious demands and those concerning pay and working conditions by the labour movement. By accommodating the latter, and repressing the proponents of the former, they hoped to channel the trade union movement into what were less dangerous areas from their point of view. The industrial employers, however, saw the concessions on economic demands as being as seditious as any accommodation of the demands for self-government. This conflict of interests and the resulting policy responses towards labour emerged more clearly when the political repression and the failure of the newly established labour market intervention to raise real wages, the simmering discontent amongst the Kikuyus arising from the alienation of their lands, and the accompanying increase in the pressure of population on the reserves as well as the removal of the squatters from European farms once a 'labour surplus' had been achieved, fuelled the long-feared open rebellion, which goes by the name of Mau Mau.

II The Emergency, Uhuru, and After: 1952–1968

(1) Mau Mau, the Emergency, and Political Repression

On 7 October 1952 Chief Waruhhiu who had openly opposed the oathing movement amongst the Kikuyu known as Mau Mau was murdered in broad daylight on an open road. On 20 October the new Governor, Sir Evelyn Baring, signed the Emergency proclamation, to enable him to arrest Kenyatta and other African leaders and to restore 'law and order'.

There was a violent Kikuyu reaction to the arrests. African collaborators of the colonial government were brutally murdered, as were many white settlers. For them Africa seemed to have become the savage place they had always feared it was.

The repression of African nationalism and nationalists, which followed, left the Kenya Federation of Labour (KFL) as the only channel for expressing African nationalism. However, it should be noted that the previous policy of channelling trade union protest into economic rather than political areas had not been altogether unsuccessful (see Sandbrook, p. 38).

(2) Accommodation of Labour Demands

The repression of African nationalism was accompanied by attempts at accommodating what were perceived to be the legitimate economic demands of the loyalist Africans. It was thereby hoped to divide the Africans and preserve colonial and white settler interests. Two wage commissions, for rural labour in 1955, and for urban labour in 1954, were set up. The former clearly reflected the continuing desire of settlers to obtain a cheap supply of African labour through coercive means, but the latter reflected the new desire to accommodate African grievances on low wages.

The Report of the Rural Wages Committee saw the main problem as alleviating the perceived acute labour shortage on plantations and other European rural enterprises. The major problem was of 'desertion',[2] to prevent which they recommended the institution of what amounted to South African style pass laws. (*Report of Rural Wages Committee*, p. 19 and 21).

On wages they recommended a minimum wage of 19 cents an hour, for workers contracting to work a 48-hour week for at least six months. This minimum wage was less than the average wage rates in rural employment which the Committee in a survey found to be 21 cents an hour for an average of 38 hours a week.

By contrast the *Report of the Committee on African Wages* 1955 saw the need to raise wages of urban African labour in order to stabilize the urban work force. They suggested a system of positive incentives, to counteract the 'enervating and retarding influences of his economic and cultural background'. They were concerned with 'stabilizing the labour force', an objective which continued to dominate East African wage policy into the 1960s. The transitory and migratory pattern of wage employment which they sought to redress was blamed on the fact that a worker could not earn a sufficient wage to support his family in the city. The report recommended an immediate change in the basis of the statutory minimum wage — 'from one which takes account only of the needs of a single man to one based on the needs of a family unit'. This family wage was to be buttressed by regular employment, improved urban housing, and a security programme for old age. The report also accused employers of *'reckless* extravagance in the use of labour', and rejected the argument 'that increases in wages must wait upon increased productivity' by declaring that 'in Kenya, low wages are *a cause* rather than an effect of the low productivity of labour'.

On the basis of these recommendations the government committed itself to raising urban minimum wages by two thirds over a five-year period. But instead of agreeing to different rates for married and single workers, it granted different rates to youths (below twenty-one years old) and adults. This was of some long-term importance for it meant that the incentive to bring families into the urban areas, which would have been created by different rates for single or married workers, did not operate.

(3) Uhuru and the Demise of the White Settlers

With the countryside still in flames as the result of the Mau Mau, the government was naturally reluctant to accept the recommendations of the Rural Wages Committee. In fact this report was the swan song of the settler interest in obtaining labour through coercion. For in the 1950s, despite their protests about labour shortages, the White Highland farmers had become efficient enough to withstand competition from peasant agriculture. Furthermore, by the mid-fifties the colonial government had radically altered its discriminatory strategy and begun to support African peasants in competition with European large-scale farming.

The Swynnerton plan of 1954 and the East Africa Royal Commission of 1955 gave dramatic expression to this changed colonial policy. Swynnerton's proposals amounted to a complete reversal of earlier government policies on African agriculture. He recommended that all high-quality African land be surveyed and enclosed; that the policy of maintaining 'traditional' or tribal systems of land tenure be reversed; and that all the thousands of fragmented holdings be consolidated and enclosed. The 'progressive' farmers would thereby be able to obtain credit, which had been previously denied them, whilst the new title deeds would create security of tenure which would lead to investment and rural development. Furthermore, he recommended that African farmers be allowed to grow cash crops, be given a major increase in technical assistance, and have access to all marketing facilities.

The Royal Commission accepted all Swynnerton's proposals and went even further, by recommending the removal of all racial and political barriers inhibiting the free movement of land, labour, and capital. These twin policies of land consolidation and removal of all barriers to the functioning of a land market were put into practice by 1960. They enabled a reconciliation between the departing colonial authority and the leaders of independent Kenya, who have followed the same policies since. Consolidation measures were forced through between 1954 and 1960 in Kikuyu land, and in 1959 the White Highlands were at last thrown open to all races in the colony.

Meanwhile political events were moving rapidly. Following Harold Macmillan's 'winds of change' speech, the Colonial Secretary Ian Macleod made it clear at the Lancaster House Conference on Kenya's future in January 1960 that African majority rule was to be granted as soon as possible. With Uhuru now legitimized the white settlers had finally lost the game.

On 1 June 1963 Jomo Kenyatta, who had been reviled by the settlers and gaoled by the colonial authorities as the organizer of the Mau Mau rebellion, became Prime Minister of independent Kenya. Born as the step children of an Empire which sought to salvage the mistake of a nineteenth-century equivalent of the Concorde, the settlers had never been able to gain the same sympathy and place in the counsels of the Colonial Office that their brethren, in other parts of the Empire, had enjoyed. When at last they seemed to have become economically viable, the changed historical circumstances nevertheless made their demise inevitable. However, the system of labour relations they (and their European urban counterparts) had created was to continue to have far-reaching effects on the economy of independent Kenya.

(4) New Institutional Developments in the Urban Labour Market

The structure of industry had also been changing rapidly in Kenya in the post World War Two period. In the earlier periods there was a commonality of perceived interests amongst the settlers and European businessmen. Often there were Europeans who combined farming with business (see Amsden, p. 47). But by 1945 a great number of firms registered in Kenya were (what would nowadays be called) British multinational companies. Besides expanding the areas of Kenyan industry from its previously narrow base in building and construction, these firms also increasingly catered for (or whetted the appetites) of African consumers, unlike their pre-1940 predecessors which were mostly secondary industries geared to the demands of the settlers. There was also a 70 per cent increase in the net output of firms in commerce, finance, and insurance between 1948 and 1952 (Amsden, p. 50).

Moreover, most of these new enterprises were of a fairly large size. Even though as late as 1967 most firms employed less than fifty workers, nevertheless the large enterprises dominated employment: by 1957 approximately 75 per cent of the labour force was employed in factories with more than fifty workers (Amsden, p. 51).

Finally, whereas much of pre-war Kenyan industry was located in rural areas (based as it was on agricultural processing), the new post-war industries conglomerated in Nairobi and Mombasa. This facilitated the growth of a more coherent urban working class.

The horrors of Mau Mau led private industry to reassemble its forces and recast its policies. For the emergency discredited both businessmen and the settler community in the eyes of the Africans as belonging to the ruling class. As the government sought to make reparations to African workers at management's expense, industry could no longer rely on the colonial administration to look after its interests. As we have seen, following the raising of minimum wages and the various arbitration awards after the Mombasa strike, the employers organized themselves into the ACIE. Their main aim in the next few years was to set up, in their own words, 'a system of voluntary negotiations in Kenya, which it was envisioned would be supplementary to and would gradually supersede the paternal industrial regulations set up by the government'.

The details of the meandering negotiations between the ACIE and the KFL need not concern us (but see Amsden, pp. 67–82, for a summary account). Generally speaking the ACIE was successful in carrying its viewpoint on both the trade union structure as well as the form that collective bargaining should take. Thus on 8 May 1958 a *Demarcation Agreement* between the ACIE and KFL was drafted, which on the whole embodied the principle of industry-wide unions favoured by the ACIE who feared a duplication of the perceived chaos in British industrial relations due to the co-existence of craft, general, and industrial unions. The Demarcation Agreement, whilst setting precise limits on the scope of existing unions, also called for the creation of new unions with carefully delimited spheres of influence.

There were proposals mooted by an organizer of the Plantation Workers International Federation — a part of the international ICFTU — to organize agricultural trade unions. The PWIF organizer, Bevin, wanted to help the KFL organize one union for all agricultural workers. This, not surprisingly, met stiff resistance from the ACIE, who feared that an omnibus agricultural union would be able to play one sector of employers off against another, because of the peculiar characteristics of each crop. Thus, as coffee must be picked as soon as it ripens, coffee growers were in a vulnerable position as compared with sisal growers. The employers were afraid that an omnibus union could threaten a strike just when the coffee crop was ready to be picked, and any concessions they made would then be transmitted to other industries within the coffee growers' bargaining unit. The ACIE therefore demanded separate unions in the hope that thereby it would not be feasible to have sympathetic strikes. Though they were successful, the PWIF official in asking the KFL to acquiesce with the ACIE noted that once sectoral unions were organized, they would prove easy enough to amalgamate (Amsden, p. 70–1).

In order to provide countervailing power to the employers the ACIE also successfully promoted the development of industry-wide employers' associations which were amalgamated into the Federation of Kenya Employers (FKE), which replaced the ACIE in 1959.

The ACIE also successfully replaced the existing system of compulsory arbitration of industrial disputes by collective bargaining agreements, the details of which need not concern us. What is of importance is to note that roughly 150 collective agreements (embracing a large number of firms) were being drafted each year, by the end of 1963.

Approximately 60 per cent of all employees within the private industrial sector (or 100,000 workers) were covered by collective bargaining agreements. Negotiations were also under way in the plantations. The unions demarcated in 1958 materialised quickly and were poised for the fight. Whilst 9 predominately African unions existed in 1956, approximately 30 unions were operative by 1962. Whilst union membership totalled 17,000 in 1956, it reached 100,000 by 1963 (Amsden, p. 74).

(5) Rising Industrial Unrest and the Emasculation of Trade Unions: 1960–1968

If the employers had hoped to buy industrial peace as a result of the new institutional developments they promoted, and which were outlined in the previous section, these hopes were soon belied. Table 2.1 shows the number of man days lost as a result of strikes from 1962 to 1974. 'In 1962 alone, the number of man days lost from strikes was greater than the cumulative record for 1948–59' (Amsden, p. 74). By June 1962 a coalition government (with Tom Mboya as Labour minister) which was to be the precursor of an independent government had been in power for only two months. The new government was weakened by the wave of strikes in June 1962. The fear of

Table 2.1
Annual Number of Strikes, Employees Involved, and Man-Days Lost,
1962–1974

Year	Number of strikes	Employees involved	Man-days lost
1962	285	132,433	745,799
1963	230	54,428	235,349
1964	294	67,155	167,767
1965	200	105,602	345,855
1966	155	39,123	114,254
1967	138	29,985	109,128
1968	93	20,508	47,979
1969	124	37,641	87,516
1970	84	18,945	60,761
1971	72	17,300	162,108
1972	110	26,000	141,000
1973	83	15,834	449,053
1974	132	23,157	101,241

Source: R. Kombo, p. 47, cited in Damachi *et al.*

African self-government led to a cessation of capital formation and rising unemployment. Even Mboya, however, could not push the unions too far, as the KFL's leadership had passed to Peter Kibisu, who was unlikely to fully acquiesce to Mboya's desires. An Industrial Relations Charter was issued in October 1962, as a result of consultations between the FKE and the KFL. There was little new in the Charter, which was merely a statement of hope by the government and the two sides of industry that tensions could be relieved and the economy rebuilt. There were no coercive means laid down.

With independence in 1963 Kenyatta's new government showed that it sought central control of the labour movement, much in the same way as its predecessor colonial regime. It wanted, as the colonial government had, 'both political subordination and economic responsibility' on the part of unions, and it wielded a number of sanctions to obtain the acquiescence of workers' leaders. The KFL split in 1964 into rival factions vying with each other over accusations of each rival having received funds from foreign sources. The conflict climaxed in 1965 when, as part of the jurisdictional battles for workers' loyalties, three workers were killed and over 100 injured in Mombasa.

The government stepped in by deregistering the KFL and the rival Kenya African Workers' Congress (KAWC), and forming the Central Organization of Trade Unions (COTU) with exclusive rights to represent industry-wide unions. The government had control over the federation's internal affairs through its control over appointments of the top officials of the union, through its firm control over the power of the purse, and through its supervision of union elections. Finally the rule was laid down that the failure of a national union to gain COTU's sanction for strike action would constitute an offence.

Clearly, these changes, taken together, represent a significant increment in centralised, government control. The object seemed to be to obtain a strong voice in COTU for public officials, and then to provide COTU with more authority over its supposedly autonomous affiliates. The proposed rule requiring unions to obtain COTU's permission before undertaking strike action is a case in point (Sandbrook, p. 40).

Thus, 'with the coming of autumn 1965, labour saw the last of its freedoms to politicise, at least on paper. With the coming of autumn 1966, it saw more. From now on mixing national politics and trade union affairs became a dangerous business in Kenya' (Amsden, p. 112).

Furthermore, a series of Trade Disputes Acts, beginning with that of 1964, of 1965, and the Amendment of 1971, have progressively limited unions' right to strike. The first of these acts set up an Industrial Court. The 1965 Act, recalling an earlier colonial measure, prohibited strikes in essential services, with numerous industries scheduled as being essential. If the Minister of Labour fails to take action on industrial disputes reported to him in an essential service, after twenty-one days he may refer such a dispute to the

Industrial Court. In all cases, awards of the Court are binding. The penalties were relatively severe both for inciting an employee to break his contract of service in an essential service and for wilfully breaking a contract of service (Amsden, pp. 122–3).

In an amendment in 1969, though in principle the right to strike was preserved, the unions were however obliged to exhaust all voluntary disputes machinery, and also secure COTU's endorsement for strike action (Sandbrook, p. 45). Whilst under the Act of 1971 the definition of a strike was expanded to include a 'go-slow', the definition of what were acceptable trade disputes were narrowed, and the 'cooling-off' period of strike notice was extended. Thus by the early 1970s many of the rights of labour that had been institutionalized by a reluctant colonial government under pressure from the new humanitarian sensibilities of the UK Colonial Office had been greatly circumscribed, if not eliminated, by its first African government.[3]

(6) Minimum Wages and Emerging Unemployment

In a previous section we have documented the introduction of the minimum wage ordinance of 1946, which laid down statutory minimum wages with the object of raising urban African real wages. To serve the same purpose wage councils were established in 1951, on the British pattern. They were to be the first step in the introduction of collective bargaining. Finally, the government hoped to influence post-war pay rates through public sector pay, which was considered to be a policy tool as the government was the largest single employer and its wage scales were emulated in the private sector (Amsden, p. 16).

We have seen how the Carpenter report on African Wages in 1954 recommended a family minimum wage and a bachelor minimum wage to stabilize the urban labour force. The government whilst accepting the need to raise the minimum wages, chose the categories of 'youth' and 'adult' instead of the Carpenter report's categories of 'bachelor' and 'family' in setting up its dual minimum wage structure.

As a result of these policies, by 1960 the Nairobi minimum wage was double its level in 1954, but mean earnings of Nairobi African wage earners rose less substantially (by 38 per cent). There are two reasons for this large discrepancy. First, prior to the Carpenter Report the minimum wage was to some extent a slack constraint. Amsden, promoting this argument, cites the evidence of a Labour Department survey of 1952 which found that only 10 per cent of wage earners received as little as the minimum wage. However, it is dangerous to conclude from this that the minimum wage was substantially below the rate at which firms engaged unskilled labour. We argue that there is a second, and more significant, reason for the more rapid increase in the minimum wage than in mean earnings: namely, the wage rate at which workers were engaged rose relative to mean earnings, thus altering the wage structure. Between 1954 and 1960 the mean engagement rate for all workers rose by 64 per cent, by which time it was only 9 per cent above the minimum wage. That the mean engagement rate was even 9 per cent above the minimum wage might suggest that it was still slack, but this would be false for mean engagements include both skilled and unskilled workers. When the mean engagement rate of unskilled workers is considered separately, by 1960 it stands less than 2 per cent above the minimum wage. This suggests that the engagement rate for unskilled workers in 1954 (on which we have no data) might not have been very far above the minimum wage.

Thus, though it is not possible conclusively to prove whether the rising statutory minimum wages merely reflected or caused the explosion in average African urban earnings, there would be a presumption (lacking any other reason for so large an autonomous rise in African wages) that the minimum wage caused the real wage rise. We return to the effects of the rising minimum wages on the wage structure in our analysis of the Kenyan labour market during this period in the final section of this chapter.

Whatever the reasons for the rise in urban real wages, the spectre of hardcore unemployment evoked by Governor Mitchell as a counter-argument to a 'family' minimum wage in the early 1950s soon came to haunt the authorities.

By 1959 the government was worried about what was perceived as an emerging unemployment problem amongst the African population. The Dagleish report of 1960 was the result. Its general prognosis and conclusions bear quoting, as they seem more perspicacious in some respects than much of the subsequent *obiter dicta* on this problem, and also illustrate the underlying concerns that have continued to this day. The report stated:

During recent years there has been considerable public comment on the subject of unemployment in Kenya. Much of this comment had tended to suggest that the problem of unemployment amongst Africans is new, that it is basically a problem of the settled areas (or of the wage-earning sector of the economy), and that it can be resolved, or at least be substantially alleviated by special relief measures designed to increase temporarily the numbers in wage-earning employment. In the following paragraphs, arguments are presented to show that this assessment of the nature of Kenya's unemployment problem is fundamentally incorrect; that the problem is not new, although some of its present manifestations are; that its root cause lies in the undeveloped state of the economy as a whole; and that, generally speaking, it is not amenable to short-term measures of the type adopted from time to time in more advanced countries (*Unemployment*, Sessional Paper No. 10 of 1959/60, Colony and Protectorate of Kenya, 1960, p. 1).

Dagleish accepts the notions of underemployment current at that time, and cites with approval an extract from an ILO report of 1950 entitled *Action against Unemployment*: namely

the phenomenon of underemployment in the less developed countries consists of two major elements, the first and most obvious is the long period of seasonal unemployment peculiar to agricultural production in these countries, the second element is the redundance of labour on the land — redundance in the sense that the present supply of agricultural labour exceeds the supply required to produce the existing volume of agricultural output with the existing methods of production and organisation (ibid., p. 3).

Dagleish however makes two qualifications to the ILO's definition of under-employment:

(*a*) a state of widespread underemployment is objectionable only to the extent that it fails to meet the economic, social, and other needs and aspirations of the people associated with it. Were this not the case and were full employment accepted as an end in itself, there would be little merit in the trend, now evident in most western economies, towards shorter working hours and greater leisure to enjoy the fruits of labour . . . (*b*) a second point which needs emphasis is that, for the individual worker, it takes little to change underemployment into full employment — no more for example, than that a smallholder should decide to farm his land by his own and his womenfolk's efforts than rely, as in the past, on the assistance of other male members of his family or tribe. Summarising the position, therefore, as it exists today in the African land units, one may say *that there is in these areas, chronic and widespread underemployment; that, unless remedial action is taken the problem is likely to grow as a result of population increase; and that, with the growing desire of many Africans for improved living standards, there is also a very real danger of much of this underemployment developing into manifested full unemployment.* This last trend — from underemployment to full un-employment — is already in evidence and is one cause of the mounting demand for wage-earning employment in the settled areas. (Ibid., p. 3.)

Dagleish is rightly wary of any statistical measurement of this notion of underemployment. But he fully supports the Swynnerton proposals as 'the ultimate and only real solution to Kenya's unemployment problem lies in the full economic development of the African land units' (ibid., p. 9).

Dagleish also saw the possible frustrations of increasing numbers of educated unemployed, and that increasing employment in Nairobi ahead of its infrastructure 'would add to rather than diminish the problems of the Police Department' (ibid., p. 8).

The biggest danger inherent in the present situation is that the raising of living standards and the provision of employment opportunities in the African land units will not keep pace with the demands of a population rapidly becoming more educated, more socially and politically conscious, and more impatient of the tempo of advance. Education poses special problems in this regard. With increasing education, Africans will not be content with the standard, or way, of living at present open to them in their land units; yet, even today, wage-earning employment is not available for all those school leavers who are not absorbed into farming life in their own areas. The economy must, therefore be expanded to provide worthwhile employment for the products of education both on the land and in that wider economic life that accompanies a more developed agriculture. Unless this is done, real danger must exist of producing a large number of frustrated and embittered persons posing social problems far bigger than any experienced to date (ibid., p. 10).

The worst fears aroused by Dagleish appeared to be confirmed when only forty-three days after Uhuru there was an uprising in a small division of Kenya's army and the government sent out a call for UK troops. The Kenyan government responded to the crisis with immediate relief for the jobless. A tripartite Agreement on Unemployment between the employers, trade unions, and the government was signed. Whilst private employers pledged to increase their labour force by 10 per cent, the trade unions agreed to a twelve-month wage freeze after the expiry of existing agreements. No strikes or go-slows were permitted during the freeze. Some price controls were instituted, and the government undertook to increase employment in the public service by 15 per cent. An Industrial Court was proposed to settle disputes which were unresolved by voluntary negotiating machinery. However, Amsden argues that

additions to total employment appear to have been no greater than what would normally have been experienced. Whereas 28,000 workers obtained employment soon after the Agreement was drafted, the Labour Department estimated in 1964 that annual attrition amounted to 20,000 in the wage-paying sector. Whereas commercial agriculture was bound by the 10 per cent figure, annual labour turnover in most agricultural undertakings is easily 10 per cent (Amsden, p. 101).

But the problem of urban unemployment and its perceived link with domestic disorder was to continue to haunt the independent government. Besides attempting to restrain urban wages through the means described in the last few sections, the government concluded another tripartite agreement in 1970 to increase employment by 10 per cent.

Earlier, in 1967, it had also recognized the link between the rising levels of public sector pay, its effects on the general wage structure, and hence on overall levels of employment. Thus the Salaries Review Commission of 1967 emphasized the need for public sector pay restraint.

By 1970 the unemployment problem appeared chronic to the government, and a Select Committee of Parliament reported on the subject. Their perception of the problem had moved in ways that were to become fashionable fairly soon.

In specific terms, the Committee identified the following as the major causal factors of unemployment in Kenya:

(i) Increased population pressure on land leads to poverty and increased rural–urban migration
(ii) fuelled by a large urban–rural income gap
(iii) which in turn is due to the high urban wages maintained by trade union activities.
(iv) These high urban wages have led an excessive capital intensity in industry which has been at the expense of industrial employment.
(v) The capital intensive bias in industrial technology is also due to the inappropriate factor proportions of much imported technology.

(vi) Inappropriate school curricula leading to a problem of unemployed school-leavers.

(vii) Inappropriate agricultural policies which have discouraged agricultural production.

(*Report of the Select Committee on Unemployment*, Republic of Kenya, National Assembly, December 1970, pp. 2–3.)

These were themes which were to be picked up by the ILO team of experts that the government called in to study the continuing unemployment problem in 1972.

(7) 'Kenyanization'

Towards the end of 1967 the Kenyanization of Personnel Bureau was set up to service the Immigration Office in providing work-permits for non-Kenyans, as a result of the Immigration Act that was passed in April 1967. While part of the African nationalist demands for ending the racial segmentation of the land and labour market had been met by the policy in the 1950s of throwing the whole of the Highlands open to all races, there were still the perceived grievances of the Africans against Asian traders and the desire amongst educated blacks to obtain better jobs in both the urban private and public sectors.

The main brunt of the new immigration policies, however, was borne by the large Asian community. The aim of the 1967 Act was to fill the jobs of expatriates with Kenyan citizens, irrespective of colour. But as Amsden noted in 1970, 'there is little ground for optimism that Asians will be guaranteed fair chances of employment even if they become Kenyan citizens (and roughly 70,000 have done so)' (Amsden, p. 29).

For the Asian trader, along with the white settler, was looked upon by African nationalists as 'a potent symbol of African subordination in colonial society'. The important issue was succinctly put in the 1966–7 Development Plan:

No other economic activity is in direct contact with so many people as commerce. As long as the people as consumers depend on retail shops that are eventually owned or operated by non-Africans, they will conclude that, although Africans have gained control over the political and administrative machinery of the country the economic life of the nation is still in the hands of non-Africans (Hazlewood, p. 89).

Under the Trade Licensing Act of 1968 lists were prepared of non-Kenyan businesses which had to be sold to Kenyans. The work permits instituted for non-Kenyans also hit the Asians, nearly 100,000 of whom had declined to become Kenyan citizens by December 1965. Their jobs were now jeopardized.

Thus Kenyanization was essentially a policy of Africanization 'and it may be thought that this is a well justified policy of "reverse discrimination" '[4] (Hazlewood, p. 188). The policy of Africanization of both the public sector (though not as we shall see of the private sector), and trade and commerce progressed rapidly in the late 1960s. Thus a 1971 survey of distribution showed that the proportion of establishments in retail and wholesale trade owned wholly or mainly by Kenyans increased from 48 per cent in 1966 to 80 per cent in 1971, and in retail trade alone from 55 to 89 per cent (Hazlewood, p. 90).

By the late 1960s, therefore, the most obvious racial segmentation of the colonial period's labour market had ended.

III The Growth of Education

Modern education of Africans in Kenya is the product of missionary zeal. The first mission school was established at Rabai, near Mombasa, in 1844. But it was not till the building of the Uganda railway that missionary activity could spread into the interior of Africa.

David Livingstone had aroused British public opinion to the 'great social evils of African society'. The missionaries, seen as the vanguard of the colonial power, thus found favour with the British government in attempts to spread Christian civilization. The missions were soon seen as performing another essential function in furtherance of the Imperial cause by training 'interpreters and policemen . . . builders and joiners . . . messengers, orderlies and domestic servants' (R. Oliver, p. 177). Their educational function thus became paramount in their contribution to the colonial society. In 1911 the government set up an Educational Department which made financial grants for every pupil who passed a government departmental exam. This was the first official help the missions received from the government, apart from land grants to set up their missions.

In addition there were separate (and better) schools set up for the two ethnic minorities in Kenya, the Europeans and the Asians. The European School established in 1904 in Nairobi, and an Indian school founded by the Uganda Railway Authority in 1906, were the first major schools for ethnic minorities. After 1911 other European and Indian schools were started in areas where these minorities predominated. However, even for Europeans and Asians, it was not till 1942 that primary education was made compulsory for 'European children between 7 and 15 years and Indian boys in Nairobi, Mombasa and Kisumu of the same age group' (Thias and Carnoy, p. 9).

In this racially segregated educational system the number of Africans who were able to obtain any education at all remained fairly small for a long time. Thus in a 1919 census it was estimated that '30,000 Africans out of a 2.7 million population were attending 410 mission schools. The entire budget of the Education Department was £636' (Sheffield (1973) p. 12). Whilst Thias and Carnoy estimate that 'some 80,000–100,000 Africans had received some schooling by 1924/25' (op. cit., p. 10).

In 1919 an Education Commission was appointed. Its recommendations amounted in practice to 'academic education for Europeans and for Africans industrial training after an academic primary education, based on the model established for American negroes by Booker T. Washington among others' (Sheffield (1973) p. 18). Underlying this vocational bias in African education was (as is clear from the Education Department's 1926 *Annual Report*, p. 17) a racist assumption about the African's intellectual potential.

In addition there were to be two smaller tiers on the official educational pyramid for Africans. An artisan class for the territory as a whole was sought to be created by the establishment of the technical school at Machakos and the Native Industrial Training Depot established at Kabete in 1925. Further technical training was said to be unsuitable because of the low mental development of the Africans (Sheffield, p. 24).

At the top of the pyramid the Alliance High School, Kikuyu, established in 1926 by an alliance of Protestant missions, was said to meet 'the demand of the state and of commerce for a more highly educated class of individuals who can take their place as leaders among the Africans or within the ranks of the community as thinkers and professional workers' (Education Department, *Annual Report*, 1926, op. cit., p. 14).

Thus a three-tier pattern of African education emerged in Kenya: community development for the majority, technical training for a minority, and academic secondary education for a tiny fraction of the population.

The Africans, quite rightly, saw this emphasis on vocational training as providing them with a second-rate education designed to keep them in their place. The missionary educators' attempts to introduce school gardens with an emphasis on 'traditional' agriculture met widespread opposition from Africans, who saw this as further emphasizing the political and racial basis of the educational system.

The inequitable expenditure on education is borne out by the data in Table 2.2 on the Education Department's expenditure by race in 1926. The Africans, however, had by the inter-war years come to see education, and missionary co-operation in acquiring it, as the key to economic and social progress.

At the same time the Kikuyus had reacted violently against the prohibition by the Church of Scotland and several other missions of the traditional rite of female circumcision. They formed the Kikuyu Independent School Association (KISA) in 1929, which wanted to reconcile Christianity with some aspects of their traditional culture such as female circumcision. They developed an entire school system independent of the missions, and established a teacher training college at Githunguri, which rejected the government syllabus and examinations, and substituted its own.

But the numbers in the independent schools were not large. The government estimated that by 1936 only 5 per cent of the total African student population was in the independent schools, with the overwhelming majority of these being in Kikuyu areas (Sheffield, 1973, p. 29). The government then

Table 2.2

Education Department Expenditure by Race[a]

Race	Pupils[b]	Expenditure £	Expenditure per pupil £
African[c]	6,948	47,800	6.88
Asian	1,900	14,500	7.63
European	776	28,800	37.11

[a] Excluding 'administrative' and 'extraordinary' expenditure.
[b] State and state-aided schools only.
[c] Including Arabs.
Source: Kenya, Education Department, *Annual Report*, 1930 (Nairobi, Government Printer, 1931), pp. 9–10.

made various attempts to gain control over the growth of the independent schools, at which they were not very successful as these schools expanded rapidly in 1937 and 1938. However, once the KISA had agreed to use the government syllabus, in 1937 an Inspector of Schools for the independent schools was appointed.

But the African school system despite its expansion was still low quality at the end of the Second World War. The Education Department's *Annual Report* for 1949 noted that more than one third of the roughly 25 per cent of the primary school aged population enrolled in schools were in unaided institutions without regulated standards. About 60 per cent of all students completed only two years of school, only 5 per cent received more than six years of schooling, and less than 1 per cent went beyond the eighth year. Girls formed 30 per cent of total enrolment in the first year and less than 7 per cent at the end of the fourteenth (Sheffield, 1973, p. 32).

After the war, with African nationalism becoming more strident and increasingly being accommodated by the authorities, there was a rising clamour for greater educational opportunity for Africans. This meant both more African primary and secondary schools as well as an upgrading in their quality. In 1949 the Beecher Committee had prepared a plan which wanted to achieve four years of primary schooling for all who wanted it by 1961. Beecher also recommended improvements in the teaching profession and generally substituting qualitative control for quantitative expansion in African education. By 1960 there were more than twice as many African primary schools and three times as many intermediate and secondary schools than forecast by Beecher. Table 2.3 gives the 1948 enrolment as well as Beecher's projections.

By the 1960s there had been a dramatic increase in primary and secondary school pupils (see Table 2.5 below). The explosion in secondary schools was

Table 2.3

School Enrolments

Standard (grade)	1948 Enrolment	1957 on Ten-year Plan	1957 on Beecher plan
1	113,987	60,000	180,000
2	51,160	60,000	110,000
3	36,849	60,000	70,000
4	26,018	60,000	60,000
5	21,578	40,000	13,600
6	6,983	40,000	13,600
7	3,046	4,200	11,050
8	2,204	4,200	11,050
Form			
I	278	800	960
II	194	800	960
III	57	400	480
IV	39	400	480

due to a dramatic resurgence of independent schools in the 1960s as the private demand for education outstripped public provision. Though it was illegal to establish any school without the approval of the Ministry of Education, with politicians vying with each other to open self-help schools such legalities were brushed aside. Adopting the Kiswahili phrase meaning 'Let's all pull together' from the KANU slogan, *Harambee* or self-help schools have become an important part of Kenya's secondary school system.

Meanwhile, as a result of two commissions (the de la Ware Commissions of 1937 and the Asquith Commission in 1943), Makerere College, in Uganda, which was initially established in 1922 as a school for skilled trades, was developed into a university. With the changing perception of the requirements of African education, the 1937 Commission stressed vocational and technical education whereas the 1943 Commission stressed the need for academic training. In 1958 the Lockwood Commission urged that the Royal Technical College in Nairobi be reorganized as a federated university college within an East African University (the other colleges being Makerere in Uganda, and the University College of Dar es Salaam in Tanzania, established in 1962).

But even these growing opportunities for African higher education were less than the demand. So thousands of promising students went abroad, often without the official knowledge of the government. Once again politicians responded promptly to the demand. Tom Mboya, for example, organized several airlifts of students to the United States. 'Although exact figures are unavailable, Kenya at the time of independence probably had more students overseas in proportion to the total population than any other African country' (Sheffield (1973) p. 86).

IV Labour Force, Employment, and Wages: 1948–1968

(1) The Labour Force and Education

The natural rate of increase of the African population was tentatively estimated as being in the region of one per cent per annum around the time of
the 1948 census. Over the whole period 1948–69 this had increased to 3 per
cent per annum. Birth rates remained very high throughout the period.
Goldthorpe, on the basis of the 1948 census, estimated that the birth rate was
at that time 49–50 per thousand, and by 1962 it was still in the range 47–51.
The rising growth rate is accounted for by a sharp fall in mortality rates from
extraordinarily high levels. In the 1920s infant mortality was around 500 per
1000 births. By 1948 40 per cent of all children born were dead by fifteen
whilst by 1962 this had fallen to about 31 per cent. The effect of this rapid fall
in infant mortality was not merely to produce a rapid increase in the total
labour force but to produce a bulge in the population around a particular age
cohort. Thus, while the male population over the age of fifteen increased by
54 per cent between 1948–62, the increase in males aged fifteen to nineteen
was 186 per cent. In the period 1962–9 the bulge had moved up to the cohort
aged twenty to twenty-four, which increased by 55 per cent while the total
male population over fifteen increased by 26 per cent (see Table 2.4). The
proportion of males aged between fifteen and twenty-four in the total male
population aged over fifteen rose from 20 per cent in 1948 to 32 per cent in
1962 and 36 per cent in 1969. 1948–68 was also the period of the urbanization of
the African labour force. The African population of Nairobi for various years
was:

1938	48,500
1948	64,400
1957	115,000
1962	156,200
1969	421,100

These figures have to be treated with some caution because of boundary
changes. However, since the boundaries changed because the city was growing,
to a large extent the figures reflect a genuine increase in the urban population.
Not only did the total size of the African Nairobi population increase, but the
age and sex composition changed. In 1948 out of a total African population
of 64,400 some 50,000 (50,900 in 1949 according to the EES 1954) were male
wage earners so that at a maximum women and children made up 21 per
cent of the population (in Nairobi). By 1969 37 per cent of the African
population was female and 42 per cent were children under fifteen. Women
and children combined had increased from something below 21 per cent in
1949 to 58 per cent.

Table 2.4
The African Male Labour Force by Age Group
('000s)

	1948	1962	1969
all males over 15	1,399	2,162.2	2,722.2
males 15–19	148.3	424.1	549.9
males 20–24	132.9	271.6	420.0
African employment	376.8[a]	523.9	589.7[b]
employment as percentage of males over 15	26.9	24.2	21.7

[a] 1946.
[b] Citizens.
Source: Censuses 1948, 1962, and 1969. The proportion in the age group 15–19 and 20–24 in 1948 have been estimated from the 1962 census. From the 1948 Census we know only the number in the age group 15–45. The male population aged 30–34 and 35–39 as a proportion of the male population 30–60 in 1962 is taken as applying to the 1948 figures for the age group 15–45.

As we have seen in the last section, during the post-war period the colonial government gradually took over the control and finance of African education from the missions. Education expenditure was increased rapidly, but right up to independence this was confined to primary education. Although proportionately African secondary school enrolment increased more rapidly than any other educational group, since the absolute quantity in the base year was so tiny proportional increases could not help but be high. The details of enrolment by race and educational level are shown in Table 2.5. The period 1938–61 saw the Asianization rather than the Africanization of the secondary school. Whilst Africans increased their share in enrolment from 21 per cent in 1938 to 31 per cent by 1961, the share of Asians increased from 42 per cent to 55 per cent over the same period. Between 1945 and Independence the total output of African secondary schools must have been slightly less than 8,000. This contrasts with primary school output approaching 27,000 per annum in the immediate post-war period and around 100,000 per annum just before Independence.

One of the major acts of the new government was to reverse these extraordinary priorities and expand secondary education very rapidly. This abrupt change in the rates of expansion of education of different levels produced corresponding lagged changes in the supply of labour of different types. The stock and flow implications for the labour force are estimated in Chapter 6 (Tables 6.14 and 6.15). They form a key element in assessing the extraordinary nature of the adjustment process during the 1960s. For example, the stock of Africans with Form IV education increased fourfold in the period 1963–9.

Table 2.5

Enrolment in Schools by Race, 1938–1968

| | Secondary | | | | Primary |
	European	Asian	African	Africans as percentage of total	African ('000s)
1938	326	375	184	20.8	128.8
1946	772	809	395	20.0	218.2
1947	1,262	1,059	450	16.2	226.5
1948	1,306	1,306	600	18.7	256.5
1949	1,502	3,023	1,450	24.3	300.0
1950	1,945	3,484	1,500	21.6	337.1
1951	1,744	4,584	1,643	20.6	358.3
1952	1,991	4,301	1,624	20.5	330.5
1953	2,009	4,401	1,729	21.2	330.2
1954	2,061	4,882	2,099	23.2	347.9
1955	2,283	5,448	2,167	21.9	392.9
1956	2,559	5,570	2,586	30.7	442.9
1957	2,783	5,188	3,134	28.2	500.3
1958	2,949	8,023	3,922	26.3	601.4
1959	3,189	9,568	4,894	27.7	667.1
1960	3,507	10,156	5,409	28.4	726.9
1961	3,069	11,507	6,422	30.6	817.8
1962	3,369	13,141	9,055	35.4	884.8
1963[a]	n.a.	n.a.	30,100		891.6
1964	n.a.	n.a.	35,900		1,010.9
1965	n.a.	n.a.	48,000		1,014.7
1966	n.a.	n.a.	63,200		1,043.4
1967	n.a.	n.a.	88,800		1,133.2
1968	n.a.	n.a.	101,300		1,209.7

[a] From 1963 the series is for all races.

Whilst around 1960 the annual output of Form IV was about 3,500 by 1969 annual output was around 15,000, this being nearly 30 per cent of the stock. Thus, the stock was expanding so rapidly that the flow during the late 1960s was not merely enormously increased in absolute terms but became a very high proportion of the stock. The burden of adjustment imposed upon the labour market for Form IV leavers as a consequence of the necessary reversal of colonial policy was massive.

(2) Racial Segmentation, Skill Acquisition, and Africanization

Racial segmentation extended beyond education into the labour market

Table 2.6

Skill Composition of Nairobi African Wage Labour Force
(percentages)

	1953[a]	1956/7[b]	1968[c]
Professional, executive, and supervisory	1.0[d]	4.0	7.2
Clerical	16.3	20.2	17.2
Semi-skilled and skilled	26.7	46.9[e]	22.5
Unskilled	56.0	28.9	53.6
All	100.0	100.0	100.5

[a] *Report of the Committee on African Wages* (Carpenter Report), Table 3(1).
[b] Forrester (1962).
[c] Thias and Carnoy (1972) T.4.11.
[d] Headmen only.
[e] The Forrester Survey was a household survey while the other two surveys were workplace surveys. This probably accounts for the higher proportion of workers classifying themselves as 'skilled'.

Table 2.7

Africanization of the Private Sector, 1964–1968

Skill	African Citizens ('000s)		Others ('000s)		Percentage African	
	1964	1968	1964	1968	1964	1968
Professional and senior managerial	0.4	1.3	3.5	8.0	10	14
Executive and middle managerial	3.1	1.1	10.1	5.7	23	16
Supervisory and technical[a]	—	3.8	—	4.8	—	44
Clerical and secretarial	8.4	11.0	13.6	7.7	38	59
Sales	5.0	2.8	4.0	1.7	56	62

Note: [a] This was not a category in 1964, but from the 1968 earnings data this category would appear most likely to be the higher clerical sector in 1964. This would also fit with the fall in employment in the clerical sector 1964–8.

itself. Occupational profiles of the Nairobi African labour force are available for 1953, 1957, and 1968 (Table 2.6). These indicate that in the early 1950s Africans were heavily concentrated in unskilled occupations. More striking, however, is the very slow pace at which Africans moved up into more skilled occupations. In 1953 some 56 per cent of workers were unskilled, while by 1968 still 54 per cent were unskilled. Proximately, part of the explanation for this was the slow pace at which the private sector Africanized skilled jobs. Table 2.7 charts the progress of Africanization in the private sector for the sub-period 1964–8 (the data not being available for earlier periods). Surprisingly, in the managerial, professional, and executive grades the private sector tended to de-Africanize from an initial level of Africanization which was rather modest. Thus, whilst non-African employment increased from 13,600 to 13,700, African citizen employment fell from 3,500 to 2,400.

The de-Africanization of the private sector was the result of the unwillingness of the private sector to resist the desire of the public sector to Africanize. Between 1964 and 1968, whilst the private sector lost 1,100 Africans in the two highest skill categories and gained only 2,600 in the clerical category, the public sector employed an additional 4,400 Africans in the two highest skill categories and an additional 13,800 clerks.

The public sector, which of course had to Africanize, succeeded in bidding workers away from the private sector by a massive increase in wages. Between 1963 and 1965 real wages of African public employees rose by an average of 48 per cent against an increase of 6 per cent in the private sector. As a result not only did the public sector attract more Africans, but it was able to attract the best. By January 1968 in each of six categories of skilled African workers the public sector had better educated workers than the private sector (see Table 2.8). Even by 1968, when the private sector had belatedly responded to the public sector wage increases, wages by skill were higher in the public sector than in the private sector (see Table 2.9). In 1968 Europeans with Form VI education were paid on average 150 per cent more than Africans, and European graduates 40 per cent more.[5] Thus it might have been economic for the private sector to defend its African staff by raising wages in line with the public sector rather than de-Africanize. Instead, it was not until 1966 that the private sector raised wages rapidly. By 1968, controlling for changes in the skill of African employees, real wages had risen by 58 per cent from their levels in 1964. Whether the belated response of the private sector reflected a market response to the market changes in the public sector, or an ability to see the writing on the wall, anticipating the enforced Africanization of the private sector through the Kenyanization of the Personnel Bureau, founded in 1967, is hard to say.

These transfers of the relatively few skilled Africans between the private and the public sectors clearly do not address the prior question of why the urban labour market as a whole was so slow to upgrade the skill level of Africans. Our answer to this question must wait until Chapter 6, however.

Table 2.8

Years of Education of African Male Urban Employees, 1968

Skill	Sector		
	Private manufacturing	Private commerce	Public
Professional scientific	10.1	7.2	17.0
Other professional	—	—	16.2
Technicians	7.3	—	7.8
Supervisors/foremen	7.0	5.0	11.0
Administrative and managerial	9.0	11.0	13.3
Clerical	7.8	7.5	10.3

Source: Thias and Connoy (1969) Table 4.7

Table 2.9

African Earnings by Skill, 1968
(shillings per month)

Skill	Private Sector	Public Sector
Professional and senior management	1,627	1,984
Executive and middle management	1,985	2,043
Supervisory and technical	1,101	1,235

That analysis relies upon the major changes which occurred in wage levels and structures, to which we now turn.

(3) Wages and Employment

The changes in African real wages by sector over the whole period 1949–68 is shown in Table 2.10. In 1949 non-agricultural wages were some 60 per cent above agricultural wages. This offset the higher cost of living in urban areas (see page 213). Following the recommendations of the Carpenter Committee in 1954, non-agricultural wages rose sharply. 1954 is not an ideal base year because there was a temporary urban labour shortage following operation Anvil, but by 1959 public sector wages were 88 per cent higher and private sector wages 73 per cent higher than in 1949. We have no satisfactory data on the skill composition of the two sectors prior to 1964, but both the slightly faster rise in and the slightly higher level of public earnings might well reflect

Table 2.10
African Real Wages by Sector
(Shillings per month at 1959 prices)

Year	Public Sector	Private agriculture	Private non-agriculture
1949	83.6	49.1	85.5
1954	111.1	47.8	108.9
1959	157.0	57.0	148.0
1960	166.7	60.8	150.0
1961	180.8	62.5	161.5
1962	198.8	60.7	175.7
1963	216.8	71.0	197.2
1964	276.6	78.5	200.9
1965	320.8	85.8	209.4
1966	329.4	87.2	267.0
1967	329.7	82.0	282.0
1968	343.8	85.7	300.9

changes in public sector skill composition; for example, by 1957 there were 10,300 African school teachers.

Real wages in estates agriculture rose by 16 per cent between 1949 and 1959, having fallen in the sub-period 1949–54. This probably reflects the increase in the supply price of rural labour following the policy change in favour of smallholder agriculture enshrined in the Swynnerton Plan. Real wages rose by a further 50 per cent between 1959 and 1968, again probably reflecting the growing commercialization of smallholder agriculture. It is extremely difficult to estimate changes in smallholder incomes. Over the period 1954–77 per capital real incomes rose by around 2½ per cent per annum, slightly less than the rate of increase for estate wages over the same period (see page 213). It is not unlikely that improved rural transport and the diminishing share of total unskilled wage employment provided by the estates was progressively weakening their monopsony power and therefore forcing up their wages faster than smallholder incomes.

The outcome of the colonial intervention in the urban wage labour market was that by 1962 the gap between agricultural and non-agricultural wages had risen from 35 shillings in 1949 to 125 shillings (in constant 1959 prices). This rural–urban income gap was further widened by the post-Independence government. By 1968 it had risen from 125 to 238 shillings. About half of this gap was explained by the different skill compositions of the agricultural and non-agricultural sectors, but the mean wage of African non-agricultural unskilled workers was 117 shillings higher than the mean wage of African agricultural workers. We have already noted that part of this second non-agricultural wages explosion was due to the need of the public sector to Africanize upon Independence. Additionally, there was a natural inclination to raise minimum wages upon independence so as to be seen to spread the financial rewards of independence more widely than just among the educated élite. This policy did not persist after 1964. In the period 1964–8 most of the real wage rise in the public sector was due to changes in skill composition (15.6 per cent). Holding skill constant, real wages rose by only 7 per cent.

Prior to 1965 the private non-agricultural sector did not participate in this wage explosion. Between 1959 and 1965 real wages in the private sector rose by only 41 per cent compared with a 104 per cent increase in the public sector. This ranking was reversed between 1965 and 1968. The loss of skilled Africans to the public sector during this sub-period meant that changes in skill composition tended to lower real wages by 5 per cent, but holding skill constant real wages rose by 58 per cent.

To summarize the movements in the level of African wages by sector: in agriculture there was a steady rise during 1954–68 caused by smallholder commercialization and a decline in monopsony power of the estates. In the public sector there was a large rise between 1954 and 1959 following the Carpenter Report and another between 1963 and 1965 upon Independence given the needs for Africanization and a sharing of rewards. Private non-agriculture shares the Carpenter boom between 1954 and 1959 but lags behind the public sector in the second boom which occurs between 1966 and 1967. Whether the restoration of differentials with the public sector which occurred in the late 1960s was due to enforced Africanization or a delayed perception of profit maximizing strategies is an open question.

Information on the development of the African wage structure over the period is limited. By 1968 the wage structure by seniority appears to have been virtually flat for less skilled African workers. A rough proxy for this is the relationship between earnings and age for urban African male wage earners with nought to two years of education, reported by Thias and Carnoy (1969) (see Table 2.11). This probably overstates the extent of the age scale for unskilled workers since some older uneducated workers will be skilled and thus have higher earnings. However, it suggests that by 1968 seniority was scarcely rewarded among less skilled workers.

This had not always been the case. During the 1950s seniority scales flattened considerably. The gap between the engagement rate (that rate at which on average African workers were recruited by the firm) and mean African earnings narrowed in the private non-agricultural sector from 36 per cent to 14 per cent between 1954 and 1960 (see Table 2.12). The real minimum wage rose by 92 per cent, the engagement rate rose by 64 per cent, and mean earnings by only 38 per cent. The engagement rate for the unskilled was scarcely above the minimum wage. Thus, the increase in the

Table 2.11
Earnings by Age for the Uneducated, 1968

Age Group	Mean Wage (sh. per month)
20–24	285
25–29	288
30–34	325
35–44	335
45–54	326
55+	314
mean	321

Source: Thias and Carnoy (1969).

minimum wage appears to have coincided with a change in the wage structure. We investigate the interaction between the minimum wage and the wage structure in the context of a theory of labour turnover in Chapter 6.

The process begun in 1954 whereby a rise in the urban minimum wage squeezed skill and seniority differentials while the occupational profile of the African labour force remained heavily skewed towards the unskilled continued until around 1964. The period 1964–8 reaped this harvest. The economy expanded, employment grew, the public sector outbid the private sector for skilled African labour and then legislated that the private sector should Africanize skilled jobs. The result was a wage explosion for skilled African labour. Table 2.13 documents this for teaching and the civil service.

African and non-African employment by sector over the period is shown in Table 2.14. In the pre-Carpenter phase, African employment in private non-agriculture increased by 40 per cent (1946–54) and in the public sector by 66 per cent. The proportion of non-Africans stayed constant in the public sector at around 12 per cent over the whole period from 1946 until Independence. The private sector increased its proportion of non-Africans from 12.6 per cent in 1946 to 17.6 per cent in 1954. Post-Carpenter African employment in the private non-agricultural sector fell continuously so that the 1963 employment level was nearly 20 per cent below the 1955 figure. Between 1963 and 1964 there is a change in coverage for the African private sector so no employment change can be calculated, but in 1965 employment fell slightly below the 1964 level. By no means all of this decline in employment can be attributed to the wage rises, for the political uncertainty prior to Independence led to a virtual halt in investment and a severe recession. However, it is significant that the trend in the employment of non-Africans does not follow that of Africans: during the period 1955–65 employment grew by 10 per cent. The proportion of non-Africans had risen from 12.6 per cent in 1946 to 22.5 per cent by Independence.

Table 2.12

African Wages in Private Industry and Commerce (at 1959 prices)

Year	Nairobi minimum wage	Mean earnings (all)	Mean engagement rate (all)	(unskilled)	Minimum wage as percentage of mean earnings	Mean earnings/ engagement rate (all)	(unskilled)	Real wages 1954=100 Minimum wage	Mean earnings	Engagement rate (all)
1954	61	109	80	n.a.	56	1.36	n.a.	1.0	1.0	1.0
1960	120	150	131	122	78	1.14	1.23	1.92	1.38	1.64
1961	128	162	140	133	79	1.15	1.22	2.10	1.49	1.75
1962	132	176	n.a.	133	75	n.a.	1.32	2.15	1.61	n.a.

Source: Ministry of Labour *Annual Reports*.

Table 2.13
Wage Differentials in Teaching and the Civil Service

	(A) Teaching by Grade (Untrained CPE Teachers = 1)			
	P 3	P 1	S 1	Graduates
1955–62	1.2	2.5	5.5	—
1963–69	1.8	3.8	6.9	8.4
1970–75	2.0	3.2	5.4	6.7

	(B) Civil Service (Subordinate Staff = 1)			
	Clerical	Executive	Administrative	Superscale
1961–64	2.8	10.5	12.4	22.5
1964–67	3.6	7.5	10.4	24.5
1967–71	2.6	5.1	11.4	14.8
1971–75	2.4	5.9	9.8	14.2
1975–76	2.1	4.7	7.4	—

Source: Smock (1978).

The public sector, post-Carpenter, shared the experience of African employment decline, though less sharply. Between 1955–63 employment fell by 9 per cent. On Independence there was a once-and-for-all fall in the number of non-African employees in 1963–4 of 25 per cent and a 19 per cent increase in African employment. In the period 1964–8 African employment rose by a further 24 per cent. Of this expansion the largest single skill group was clerical and secretarial workers, which comprised 34 per cent of the total.

The pre-Swynnerton performance of private agriculture was reasonable. The settlers had a combination of rising prices (culminating in the sisal boom of 1951) and cropping switches, chiefly to tea. Between 1946 and 1955 African employment grew by 25 per cent. Post-Swynnerton, for a few years (1955–60) continued economic success enabled the rising supply price of African labour to be more than offset by rising demand. But from 1960 to 1968 employment fell continuously. After 1963 this was partly due to the break-up of some estates. However, an indication that the higher supply price was also important was the fall in the number of workers per acre from 0.311 in 1964 to 0.287 in 1968 (*Agricultural Census* 1964 and 1968). By 1968 private agriculture had become the smallest of the three sectors as a provider of African employment, whilst as late as 1966 it had been the largest.

(4) Education, Migration, and Unemployment

As noted in Section I the African urban population grew rapidly and changed

Table 2.14
Employment by Sector, 1951–1968
('000s)

Year	Private agriculture		Public sector		Private non-agriculture	
	All African	All non-African	All African	All non-African	All African	All non-African
1951	203.2	1.9	93.4	13.4	115.8	24.2
1952	202.7	1.8	101.6	14.0	130.3	25.3
1953	211.3	1.8	118.0	16.5	123.7	27.0
1954	220.8	2.3	130.5	17.9	141.6	30.3
1955	245.7	2.2	155.0	20.6	157.4	34.2
1956	233.1	2.1	148.7	19.3	158.3	35.2
1957	251.1	2.3	146.9	20.1	156.8	37.2
1958	247.2	2.3	137.9	19.8	149.6	36.4
1959	249.4	2.3	140.0	20.1	148.0	37.1
1960	269.1	2.7	140.7	20.7	151.1	37.9
1961	249.8	2.2	145.9	21.1	134.1	36.7
1962	243.5	2.0	147.2	19.8	133.2	34.1
1963	213.7	2.0	141.3	18.2	127.1	37.0
1964	200.2	1.9	168.2	13.7	154.0	37.3
1965	200.7	1.8	173.3	14.9	153.8	37.6
1966	186.1	2.0	184.5	15.9	158.4	39.4
1967	170.7	2.0	198.3	13.8	178.3	37.6
1968	171.1	1.9	208.8	13.0	177.3	36.7

its character from being composed almost exclusively of adult male wage earners in 1948 to having a substantial proportion of women and children by 1968. Three stylized facts have dominated past perceptions of this period: the educational selectivity of migration, the growth of unemployment, and the growth of the informal sector. These views developed during the late 1960s when the evidence for them appeared compelling.

Considering first the educational selectivity of migration, between 1964 and 1968 secondary school leavers comprised 34 per cent of the gross male migration flow into Nairobi, whilst only between 3 and 5 per cent of young males were attaining Form IV education. Table 2.15 gives details of the educational composition of the male migrant flow to Nairobi over this period. We have estimated that the propensity of non-Nairobi male Form IV leavers to migrate to Nairobi during this period was 0.79, against approximately 0.05 for primary school leavers. Such educational selectivity of rural-to-urban migration was not just a feature of the late 1960s. Forrester had noted the same thing in 1957 and that this must have been true for many years

Table 2.15

Educational Qualifications of Male Migrants to Nairobi, 1964–1968

	Percentage
None	10.8
Primary	55.2
Secondary I–III	11.1
Secondary IV–VI	22.9

Source: See Table 7.3.

Table 2.16

Educational Qualifications of the Nairobi African Labour Force, 1957

Education	Nairobi African Work force[a]	All Kenya males[b] aged over 18
None	32	69
Primary 1–4	25	10
Above primary 4	43	21
All	100	100

[a] From Forrester.

[b] From 1969 *Census*, Table 1, males aged over 30.

before 1957 can be seen from the educational distribution of the stock of the African Nairobi work force in 1957 (Table 2.16).

Rapid rural-to-urban migration by the educated had, by the late 1960s, become juxtaposed with open urban unemployment. By 1969 the male unemployment rate in Nairobi was 10.3 per cent: that is about 20,000 people. Further, the unemployed were heavily skewed towards being young and dependent. Of the male unemployed, 30 per cent were below the age of 20, while the unemployment rate among male dependents was almost four times that of male heads of households. The link from educational expansion to migration and from migration to unemployment seemed so compelling that almost an entire intellectual community made it an article of faith.

The apparently dismal performance of the wage sector as a source of employment growth was also noted by economists. African wage employment as a percentage of the African male population over the age of fifteen fell from 27 per cent in 1948 to 22 per cent by 1969. The only bright part of the employment scenario appeared to be the growth of the urban informal sector. The ILO estimated that by 1969 the size of the Nairobi informal sector was 30,000 people. This would have been equivalent to about 16 per cent of the male labour force. By way of comparison, in 1957 Forrester had found self-employment formed only 3 per cent of the Nairobi African labour force. The dynamism of the 'informal' sector contrasted with the stagnation of the formal sector became a second article of faith. We will see how these articles of faith have been borne out by subsequent trends in Chapters 6 and 7 which provide an analytical examination of the whole 'Weltanschuang' which came to characterize economists' views on the Kenyan 'employment' problem in the 1970s. We hope to show that economists no less than generals are often fighting the last war!

Notes

1 As was noted in the previous chapter, this period was one where real wages at best stagnated and could (as argued by Cowen) have fallen.

2 'The shortage of labour on the sisal plantations was not a failure of recruitment, but because 10,000 workers had "illegally left employment" during the year. These "deserters" far exceeded the industry's estimated labour shortage of 6,651' (Weeks, pp. 24–5).

3 However, as Sandbrook has emphasized, internal conflict has been rife amongst unions, and as a result 'Kenyan unions have not, on the whole, been "pliable and responsive to party pressure", though . . . the trade union federation often has been' (Sandbrook, p. 182). Furthermore, 'in political terms, one must doubt whether a country like Kenya possesses the requisite means of coercion to impose sacrifices on a strategically located working class, as the European countries did in the 19th century' (ibid., p. 161). Finally, it should also be noted that over time 'as wages have increased and the number of people seeking employment has escalated, the union's main task has become the protection of the jobs of the employed' (ibid., p. 175).

4 However, not all observers have been as sanguine of the moral implications of this policy. Thus Guy Hunter remarked in 1963: 'The other main grudge of Africans against Asians is that Asians with a longer tradition of craft, commercial and clerical skills, have occupied just that middle level of technical, clerical and administrative posts to which thousands of African school leavers now aspire. In a word, there is jealousy which can be focussed on an "other" group which is distinguishable by physique and culture, a culture not native to the African continent. This is plain, straight-forward racialism, however it is disguised or rationalised' (Hunter, 1963, p. xvi).

5 Thias and Carnoy.

3

COMPETITION (1968–1980)

I The Policy Environment

Despite large external shocks, the period 1968–80 was one of quite rapid growth. Real GDP grew on average at 4.9 per cent p.a., though subject to large fluctuations; GDP per capita grew at around one per cent p.a. Government intervention in the labour market was not abandoned, but the formal apparatus of regulation gradually became a validation of market forces rather than a constraint upon them. Interventions in agriculture and industry, however, had powerful effects upon income distribution and, indirectly, upon the labour market. We consider these three policy interventions in turn.

(1) Intervention in the Labour Market

The unwinding of the post-war policy-induced distortions in the labour market, which had begun in the immediate post-Independence period, continued in the 1970s. The major government intervention in the 1970s was to lay down wage guidelines for the formal private sector under the 1971 Trade Disputes Act amendment. These guidelines, however, even if effective were designed only to cover a limited proportion of the Kenyan labour force, within the modern private sector. Thus by the end of the period, of a total labour force of about 6 million, the modern sector provided roughly 1 million jobs, of which 580,000 were in the private sector. The first Guidelines were issued in August 1973. They laid down that (a) all collective agreements had to be registered with the Industrial Court (on whose genesis see Chapter 2) to ensure their conformity with the Guidelines; (b) while increases in wages and salaries should not exceed the overall rate of income growth in the economy, workers were entitled to a basic minimum standard of living, and to have their real purchasing power protected from inflation. As Oduor-Otieno noted

the main problem with the Wages Guidelines is the harmonisation of its three fundamental principles: adopt a ceiling for wage increases, ensure a basic minimum standard of living and ensure stable purchasing power. This equation has no easy solution and requires a continuous and careful study of all its parts especially because the minimum standard of living is not defined (Oduor-Otieno, 1979, p. 116).

In the 1970s the Kenyan economy, which had had relative price stability in the 1960s, found itself caught up in the world-wide inflation following the oil price rise. In view of this deteriorating price situation as well as the effects of the adverse shift in the terms of trade that accompanied it in 1975, the Wage Guidelines were amended. From then on productivity increases could not be used to justify wage increases. Furthermore,

compensation for cost of living increases would be allowed in full only for the lowest paid groups (those earning shs. 250/= or less) while workers earning over sh. 2000/= were not to get any increases, with a uniformly declining rate of compensation between shs. 250–2000/=. Quantitatively, there was even a restriction of increases in wage and salaries which put the upper limit as shs. 50/= per month. (Oduor-Otieno, 1979, p. 38.)

But as a result of protests from the COTU, and the threat of a general strike, these amended guidelines were eased in August 1975 with increases over and above the ceilings laid down in January 1975 being permitted. In May 1975 the President announced increases in the statutory minimum wages above those recommended by the General Wages Advisory Board. But though these measures reduced the political tensions caused by the new inflationary conjunction they did not lead to any marked upward pressures on real wages. Thus the higher statutory minimum wages did not mean any increase in their real value as compared with 1972 (Oduor-Otieno, 1979, p. 41 and pp. 47–88). With improvements in Kenya's terms of trade and thence the economy in 1976 and 1977, the Guidelines were further relaxed in August 1977 to allow wage increases based on productivity increases.

   Thus, motivated partly out of concern for urban unemployment, partly by a desire to curb inflation, and partly as an imitation of 'Incomes Policies' in advanced economies, labour market intervention shifted direction. Instead of attempting to raise wages, the wage guidelines attempted to reduce them in real terms. Naturally such a major policy shift did not occur abruptly; indeed the new policy co-existed with the old throughout the period, an example of conflict being the 1975 Presidential decree discussed above. However, the apparatus of wage control has to be sophisticated if it is to frustrate a mutual desire of employers and employees to maintain real wages. The Kenyan Ministry of Labour was in general in no position to enforce a reduction in real wages had employers and employees colluded to frustrate the policy. Rather, the change in policy direction liberalized the labour market in that should market forces generate a reduction in real wages, such a change became permissible within limits. Hence, in effect, public policy on formal sector wages shifted towards validating changes due to underlying economic forces, rather than acting as an independent source of wage inflation.

(2) Developments in Agricultural Policy

Following the Swynnerton Plan, and the demise of the white settlers (outlined in Chapter 2), the twin policies of Africanization of the white settler Highlands and of adjudication and regisrtation of individual titles to replace traditional communal land tenures amongst Africans, proceeded apace. The large farms in the scheduled areas under European ownership covered 3.1 million hectares at the height of white settlement. By 1976 1.25 million hectares had passed into African ownership. Of this about 581,500 hectares were settled as small farms by individual families through a number of settlement schemes. Even the high-density settlement schemes, however, established holdings which were substantially larger than in the traditional African small-farm sector. (The average holding on the high-density settlements was about 12 hectares, as compared with about one hectare on the traditional small farms — see Hazlewood, Chapter 4). However, by 1978 there was still substantial non-African ownership of estates and ranches. Thus in 1975 some 40 per cent of the coffee estates, accounting for some 60 per cent of the area under coffee estates, were non-African (Hazlewood, p. 207). But of the non-estate, non-ranch area in the old white settler scheduled areas, only 60,000 hectares in thirty-five 'mixed' farms were in European hands (Hazlewood, p. 32). This massive land reform (financed in large part through UK aid) was achieved without any loss in productivity and output and represents one of the most successful and socially profitable examples of land reform in the world (see the social cost-benefit study of the settlement schemes by J. MacArthur, contained in Scott *et al.*).

As a result of this land reform, Hazlewood has estimated that current land use in Kenya is approximated by the data given in Table 3.1. Two points need to be made about this table. The 'mixed farms' sub-category amongst large farms contains much land that is being cultivated as smallholdings

Table 3.1
Estimated Land Use in Kenya
(million hectares)

Recorded small farm	3.5	
Recorded large farms	2.7	
of which: Mixed Farms		1.1
Estates		0.4
Ranches		1.2
'Gap' farms	1.0	
Forest land	1.8	
Other use	1.9	
Range land and other unsuited to cultivation	46.0	
Total land area	56.9	

Source: Hazlewood, Tables 4.3 and 4.4

either by squatters or by (in effect) co-operatives which are collections of small farms. Secondly, the 'gap' farms are farms larger than 20 hectares and hence not included as small farms, and as they are outside the old white settler scheduled areas not also in the 'large farm' category. Hazlewood (p. 32) estimates that there are maybe 40,000 of these 'gap farms' on a land area of about one million hectares, which would yield an average sized farm of about 25 hectares. Thus, if we add the 'mixed' and 'gap' farms to the recorded small farm area, we find that only about 22 per cent of the available agricultural area is likely to be currently in truly large farms in the form of estates and ranches.

The second part of the land reform process, namely the adjudication and registration of land titles, has also proceeded apace in some regions (such as Central, Nyanza, and Rift provinces) though not others (such as Eastern Coast and North Eastern provinces) (see Hazlewood, p. 34). Nevertheless, it was never the objective of the agricultural policies following Swynnerton to freeze the pattern of land holdings. The Africanization and commercialization of land Swynnerton foresaw would lead 'able, energetic or rich Africans . . . to acquire more land and bad or poor farmers less, creating a landed and a landless class' (*A Plan to Intensify the Development of African Agriculture in Kenya*, Government Printer, Nairobi, 1955).

We will see in Section II that the combination of land reform and the emergence of a land market (of limited extent, as is discussed in Chapter 5) had the net effect of substantially increasing land concentration in the smallholder sector. Swynnerton's 'rich Africans' were buying land. First, however, we consider a policy intervention which may be germane to the origin of these households' riches.

(3) Protection and the Structure and Growth of Manufacturing

There has been a rapid increase in manufacturing output in Kenya during the post-Independence period. The quantity index of manufacturing production stood at 345 in 1977 as compared with its 1963 base level (see Hazlewood, Table 5.1). Food, drink, and tobacco and chemicals have accounted for the bulk of manufacturing (nearly 70 per cent) during the period, with some increase in the share of the latter at the expense of the former (though a large part of this change in shares is explained by the rise in the value of petrochemicals following the oil price rise).

By 1977 manufacturing provided 13 per cent of total wage employment. Much of this was in large firms. Eighty per cent of total manufacturing employment was in firms with fifty or more employees, and 70 per cent in firms with more than 100 employees. The latter large-sized firms accounted for nearly three-quarters of manufacturing value added.

Finally, Kenya has been the recipient of a large amount of private foreign investment (see Lal, 1975, for a survey and social evaluation of private foreign investment in Kenya), roughly 60 per cent of total value added in manufacturing being by foreign firms in 1972. Much of this foreign investment was of the import-substituting 'tariff-jumping' variety, whereby foreign firms sought to maintain access to Kenyan markets by substituting domestic production for exports from the home country of their products. As a result of this 'hothouse' development of Kenyan industry under tariffs and import controls, a fair proportion of the foreign investment is not likely to have been as socially profitable as it could have been.

In fact, the high level (and differentiated degree) of effective protection granted by the Kenyan trade control system (see Phelps and Wasow for estimates of effective protection in Kenya) has been a major source of the 'rents' which were generated in the urban economy for producers of import-substitutes at the expense of both agriculture in general and of exporters in particular. Apart from the resulting inefficiency in resource allocation resulting from this differentiated protective system, the effects on income distribution and poverty alleviation have also been inimical. It is likely that the resulting urban 'rents' have been a major source of the rural land concentration which reduced demand for rural labour and is a major source of landlessness, and the attendant rural poverty which we discuss in Chapter 8.

Much of the protection to domestic industry since the early 1970s has been through import licensing. This licensing system has been tightened whenever the economy ran into balance of payments problems, as in 1972 and 1975. This has imparted further variability in the effective protection and thence the private profitability of different industries. As this resulting relative private profitability bears little relationship to social profitability, the resulting structure of Kenyan industry may be inferred to have impaired both efficiency and equity in the economy (see Scott *et. al.*).

II Poverty, Income and Land Distribution

In 1971, worried by what seemed to be mounting problems of employment and poverty, the Kenyan Government asked an inter-agency team of experts under the banner of the International Labour Organization (ILO) to investigate and report on the nature and solutions of these problems. In the subsequent report the cause of the employment problem was diagnosed as 'the poverty level . . . of incomes obtained by many producers and their families as the return on their work, whether in self- or family-employment or in wage employment.' Like many other observers of the Kenyan scene, the ILO investigators assumed that people and resources in a supposedly capitalist economy such as Kenya's always flowed from countryside to cities. The investigators also assumed that flows reflected imbalances: 'the imbalance between the growth of the labour force, the urban population, and education and overall growth of the economy and the imbalance between people's aspirations and expectations of work and the structure of incomes and opportunities available' (ILO, p. 1).

This section gives a summary account of trends in poverty, income distribution, and growth in Kenya between 1963 and 1974. The year 1974 was selected as the reference point because data on it are the most comprehensive or reliable of those available. By adding bits of information on earlier and later years we try to discover how the pattern of poverty was drawn. Nevertheless, it must be stressed that the data base will support only broad approximations. While Tables 3.2 and 3.5 of necessity contain specific numbers, these must be interpreted as means of a range which is sometimes wide. This caveat applies with even greater force to Table 3.6, which describes changes in income distribution. Considerable care has been devoted to making intertemporal data precisely comparable, but the data are still subject to unquantifiable errors of sampling and ennumeration.

(1) Poverty

Any measure of absolute poverty is sensitive to the poverty line chosen. We have taken 2,000 Kenyan shillings a year (at 1974 prices) as the rural poverty level for a smallholder household. The primary purpose of this poverty line is not to reveal how many people are poor, because all Kenyan smallholders are poor by Western standards, but rather to enable comparison of one rural group with another, better-off, group. Two revealing questions can then be asked: why some localities have a far higher incidence of poverty than others, and why, within a locality, some households have incomes higher than the poverty group's. Setting a poverty income line enables a sufficiently large sample to be taken on either side of the line to identify a viable but significant group for the purposes of policy formulation.

An alternative approach to the poverty line used in this study is one that identifies a minimum standard of nutrition and sets the poverty line at the income level necessary to purchase food meeting this standard (Thorbecke and Crawford). In Kenya the poverty lines suggested by these two approaches almost coincide. The rural household income level of 2,000 shillings a year is a class limit in Integrated Rural Survey I (IRS I) (Kenya, Republic of, 1977). It thus yields adequate sample sizes and poses no data problems. Crawford and Thorbecke's nutritional approach results in a critical level of household income of 2,050 shillings a year at 1974 rural prices.

Our rural household income level of 2,000 shillings a year consigns 30 per cent of the smallholder rural population to poverty but only a small percentage of urban households, allowing for differences in price levels and household size. To make intra-urban comparisons a much higher poverty line had to be used to obtain a reasonable sample size. This urban poverty line was set at roughly twice the national poverty line. (A detailed discussion of our statistical methods may be found in Appendix A of Collier and Lal, 1980).

Table 3.2 shows that 4 million people were 'poor' in Kenya in 1974 out of a total population of 14.3 million. The majority of the poor were smallholders. There were relatively few urban poor (60,000).

Table 3.2

Poverty in Kenya, 1974

	Below poverty line ('000s of people)	Above poverty line ('000s of people)	Total ('000s)	Household poverty line (shillings a year)
Pure pastoralists	615	110	725	4,285
Pastoralists who farm	25	50	75	2,700
Migrant farmers	110	90	200	2,000
Landless with poor occupations	210	210	420	1,900
Landless with good occupations	n.a.	245	245	—
Smallholder population	2,990	7,350	10,340	2,000
Nairobi population	20	680	700	2,150
Other urban population	40	660	700	2,150
Large farm squatters	200	400	600	2,000
'Gap' farms	n.a.	270	270	—
Large farms	n.a.	20	20	—
	4,210	10,085	14,295	

n.a. not available

— not applicable

For sources and methods see Collier and Lal (1980), Table 1.

The population of pastoral areas is estimated at 1,000,000. Based on guesswork, we divided this population into 75,000 pastoralists who also farm, 200,000 migrant farmers, and 725,000 pure pastoralists. (The appendix to Chapter 1 of Collier and Lal, 1980, further explains our methodology.) The pastoralists who also farm have a mean per capita income close to the Kenya smallholder average, so we assumed that the percentage of all households below the poverty line is the same as the Kenyan smallholder average (34 per cent). The mean income of migrant farmers is 30 per cent above the poverty line, but the median is slightly below it. Of the 190,000 landless households in rural Kenya in 1976, 120,000 were in the potentially poor subset which excludes government and urban workers and shopkeepers. Perhaps 50 per cent of this potentially poor subset of the landless have per capita incomes below the poverty line of 2,000 shillings a year.

Available data does not allow presentation of as complete a picture of the extent or of the composition of poverty in earlier years. However, there are data which enable a charting of trends in the incidence of poverty for two sub-groups of the Kenyan poulation: smallholders in Central Province, and residents of Nairobi. The former constitutes nearly a quarter of the small-holder population in 1974; the latter constitutes about half of the urban population in 1974. Table 3.3 contains our estimates of the proportion of the relevant population in poverty for earlier years (1963 for Central Province smallholders, 1969 for Nairobi) and the relevant proportions for 1974 (derived from Table 3.2). This table shows that the proportion of the relevant population in absolute poverty declined substantially in Central Province. In Nairobi, using the same poverty line (adjusted upwards by 60 per cent to allow for a higher cost of living) the incidence of absolute poverty has been negligible.

(2) Income, Consumption, and Land Distribution

Tables 3.4 and 3.5 contain our estimates of the national distribution of income in 1974. Trends in distribution cannot be derived at the national level with existing data. For rural income distribution, trends can be derived only for Central Province, and there only for the period 1963–74, the basis for our estimates being a comparison of two smallholder household budget surveys. Our comparison is handicapped by the fact that the raw data from the 1963 survey are no longer available so we are restricted to published information. In their published versions the two surveys are not comparable due to large

Table 3.3
Trends in Absolute Poverty, 1963–1974
(percentages of population below poverty line)

Sub-group	1963	1969	1974
Smallholders (Central Province[a])	49.8	n.a.	22.4
Nairobi[b]	n.a.	3.2	<3

n.a. not available
[a] See Table 3.6 and the associated text for a discussion of the sources and the comparability of these figures.
[b] See Table 3.8 for sources.

Table 3.4

Distribution of Income in Kenya by Economic Status of Households, 1974

Group	Rich (>8,000 sh. p.a.)		Middle Income		Poor (<2,000 sh. p.a.)		Total	
	Population	Income (m. sh.)	Population	Income (m. sh.)	Population	Income (m. sh.)	Population	Income (m. sh.)
Smallholders	1,998,000	2,400	5,352,000	3,158	2,990,000	642	10,340,000	6,200
Nairobi	525,000	3,580	155,000	210	20,000	10	700,000	3,800
Other urban	448,000	2,680	212,000	300	40,000	20	700,000	3,000
Landless (poor occupations)	n.a.	n.a.	210,000	180	210,000	90	420,000	270
Landless (good occupations)	245,000	1,030	n.a.	n.a.	n.a.	n.a.	245,000	1,030
Pure pastoralists	n.a.	n.a.	110,000	48	615,000	112	725,000	160
Pastoralists who farm	n.a.	n.a.	50,000	33	25,000	7	75,000	40
Migrant farmers (dry lands)	n.a.	n.a.	90,000	42	110,000	28	200,000	70
Squatters	n.a.	n.a.	400,000	314	200,000	36	600,000	350
Large farms	20,000	170	n.a.	n.a.	n.a.	n.a.	20,000	170
'Gap' farms	270,000	800	n.a.	n.a.	n.a.	n.a.	270,000	800
	3,506,000	10,660	6,579,000	4,285	4,210,000	945	14,295,000	15,890
Percentages of totals	24.53	67.09	46.02	26.97	29.45	5.95	100	100

n.a. not available

For sources and methods see Collier and Lal (1980), Table 4.

Table 3.5
Distribution of Income in Kenya, 1974

Smallholder household income equivalent (sh. p.a.)	Percentage of population	Percentage of income
Above 8,000	25	67
2,000–8,000	46	27
Below 2,000	29	6

Source: Derived from Table 3.4.

changes in provincial boundaries and radically different definitions of income. To correct for this the 1974 data was analysed again on the 1963 boundaries and income definition.[1]

An unsatisfactory feature of the published results of the 1963 survey is that in the distribution of income the measure is total household income. Clearly, large households need more income than small ones for a common living standard. Being restricted to published data, we can only partially correct for this by dividing the mean total household income of each of sixteen income groups by the mean number of 'adult equivalents' in that group (where an adult equivalent is either one adult or two children). This is unsatisfactory since the ranking of households by total income will differ from that by income per adult equivalent, so that our identification of 'poor' households is inaccurate. The best that can be done, however, is to apply precisely the same (unsatisfactory) methodology to both surveys. Budget surveys measure income in the previous year. In the risky conditions of smallholder agriculture, this is a poor guide to permanent income which should be better reflected by consumption. Again, no ranking of the 1963 data by consumption is published, but we are able to calculate consumption per adult equivalent for the previously identified income groups.

The results, reported in Table 3.6, are not easy to interpret. On the criterion of current income, there has been a fairly substantial loss of share of the poorest 40 per cent of the population to the other income groups. The poorest 40 per cent were not immiserized, for their real per capita[2] income rose by 9 per cent in eleven years; but this was far short of the 60 per cent increases of other income groups. However, this picture of deteriorating distribution is not supported by the data on consumption. Over the period, the poorest 40 per cent of the population maintained their share of consumption while the richest 30 per cent lost a share to the middle income group. If the data are credible, an explanation for the divergent trends in income and consumption may be that the adoption of innovations has involved smallholders in an objectively greater degree of annual crop risk.[3] This would have the effect of increasing the dispersion of current income more than that of permanent income, so that snapshots of annual income would show a worsening of distribution even if the true distribution, reflected by consumption, was unaltered. On this account the apparent deterioration in income distribution is entirely spurious because the distribution of consumption has not deteriorated. Evidence that the increased risk involved in innovation had by 1974 indeed generated a large component of transient income is presented in Chapter 8 (pp. 256–7). A further indication that the permanent income of poorer smallholders broadly kept pace with the change in the mean is that the real wages of labourers hired on smallholdings in Central Province rose by around 50 per cent over the period (see Chapter 5). Since, as we will show in Chapter 5, many of these labourers were themselves poor smallholders, we expect real wages to change in line with the permanent incomes of poor smallholders which is indeed implied by the consumption data of Table 3.6. Perhaps the safest conclusion is that no definite statement can be made on the basis of Table 3.6 as to whether or not the poorest 40 per cent of smallholders experienced a slower growth of income than the average. What

Table 3.6.

Changes in the Distribution of Income and Consumption in Central Province, 1963–1974

percentage of 'population'[a]		percentage of income		percentage of consumption		Transient income[d]		1974 real income per adult equivalent (1963=100)	
		1963	1974	1963	1974	1963	1974	Current[e] income	Permanent income
poorest[b]	40	25.2	18.2	32.0	32.9	−6.8	−14.7	109	155
middle[b]	30	24.5	26.2	26.4	32.4	−1.9	− 6.2	162	185
richest[b]	30	50.3	55.6	41.5	34.7	+8.8	+20.9	167	126
all	100	100	100	100	100	0	0	151	151

[a] The 'population' is measured in adult equivalent units (see text), *not* households or people.
[b] The 'population' is ranked by total household income into these three bands.
[c] Income is annual receipts from wages, crops (including subsistence), milk sales, and own businesses, less all input costs.
[d] The share of income minus the share of consumption.
[e] On the above definition, total household income rose from 1,238 sh. to 4,139 sh. This is deflated by the low income urban cost of living index reweighted to correspond to the typical smallholder consumption bundle in 1974, and corrected for the increase in the number of adult equivalents per household.
Sources: Economic Survey of Central Province 1963/4, Kenya, Republic of (1968); Kmietowicz and Webley; *IRS I 1974/5*, Kenya, Republic of (1977).

seems unambiguous is that the middle income group of smallholders increased its share of permanent income (since it increased its share of both current income and consumption). No conclusion can be reached on whether the highest income group increased or decreased its share of permanent income.

The possibility of some deterioration in the distribution of permanent income is increased when evidence of changes in the ownership of land is considered, although causal interconnections may be rather weak (as is argued in Chapter 8). Table 3.7 charts changes in the distribution of land holdings among smallholders in Central and Nyanza provinces between 1960 and 1974. It shows an increase in concentration of land holdings in both regions over time. Concentration in land is greater among smallholders in both regions than the concentration of consumption, but similar to that of current income.

Table 3.7

Landholdings of Cultivators of Land on Smallholdings
(percentage of land owned)

	Percentage of population[a] (by land size)	Central Province			Nyanza	
		1961	1963	1974	1961	1974
Poorest[b]	40	23.9	26.3	18.3	15.6	12.9
Middle[b]	30	30.9	29.7	27.9	29.5	28.0
Richest[b]	30	45.2	44.0	53.8	54.9	59.1
All	100	100	100	100	100	100

[a] Here the 'population' is in units of persons, not adult equivalents.
[b] The population is ranked by total household acreage (not per capita) into these three bands.
Sources: IRS I, Kenya, Republic of (1977); *African Agricultural Census 1960–61*, Kenya, Republic of; *Economic Survey of Central Province 1963/4*, Kenya, Republic of (1968); *Rural Household Survey of Nyanza Province 1970/71*, Kenya, Republic of (1977).

Trends in the distribution of urban income can only be estimated from snapshots of income distribution in Nairobi in 1969 and 1974. Urban income is far less problematic to measure than smallholder income. However, the distribution of that income is much more sensitive to sample selection because residential zoning by income level is more pronounced in urban than in rural areas. The comparison of the two surveys, reported in Table 3.8, suggests that the richest 30 per cent of households benefited much more than other

Table 3.8
Distribution of Income in Nairobi, 1969 and 1974

	Population[a] (by income)	Percentage of income		Percentage change in share	Percentage change in per capita real income
		1969	1974		
Poorest[b]	40	17.2	15.1	−12.2	+ 7.0
Middle[b]	30	28.8	21.8	−24.3	− 7.7
Richest[b]	30	54.0	63.1	+16.9	+42.5
All	100	100	100	0	+21.9

[a] 'Population' is in persons.
[b] The population is ranked by total household income into these three bands.
Sources: Urban household budget surveys conducted by the Central Bureau of Statistics in 1969 and 1974. Data for 1969 were published in ILO (1972). Data for 1974 were compiled by Gunning (1979) in collaboration with Collier.

households from the growth in urban incomes. We will suggest that this had powerful repercussions for the rural economy (see Chapter 8).

It should be stressed that all these figures reflect situations prevailing at two distinct points of time, not trends. This is important because changes might not be part of a steady, continuing process but rather the result of a single event. The changes might also be the outcome of transient or random events. The first possibility applies to all the previously cited distributional changes, but might be particularly true of land since the Africanization of the White Highlands was a once-only event. The second possibility applies mainly to changes in income distribution: consumption should approximately reflect permanent income and therefore be subject to smaller transient variations. We would not expect significant transient variations in the distribution of land.

III   Wages and Employment

(1) Labour force

The 1979 Census indicates that between 1969 and 1979 the population was growing at 3.9 per cent p.a. compared with 3.4 per cent during the period 1962–9. The bulging cohort of the population was in the age group 15–29, with a growth rate of 4.3 per cent, compared with a growth rate of 2.8 per cent for the population aged 30–59. Hence, whilst the population explosion which began in the post-war period had stabilized, it was skewing the population towards the younger end of the labour force. The total population aged over fifteen increased at the same rate as for the entire population. However, the expansion of education reduced the rate of growth of the labour force slightly below this level, and in particular reduced the growth of the *young* labour force.

Total primary school enrolment grew from 1.2 million in 1968 to 3 million in 1978, so that by 1978 83 per cent of the age cohort 6–12 was in school. In January 1974 school fees were abolished for all children attending standards 1 up to 4. This caused an explosion in primary school enrolment: whereas over the period 1969 to 1973 the annual increases in primary school enrolment ranged from 7–11 per cent per annum, in 1974 the rise in enrolment was 51 per cent.

The pupil/teacher ratio averaged 33 between 1968 and 1973. Even with the explosion of primary school enrolments the pupil/teacher ratio only rose to 36 in 1974, and by 1975 had reverted to 33. This meant that by 1977 the total number of primary school teachers had grown to 90,000, some 60 per cent more than in 1973.

By contrast with its priorities in the 1960s, during the 1970s the government became concerned to restrict the growth of secondary education which was commonly perceived to lead to an actual or incipient problem of educated unemployed. The government's wishes were, however, thwarted by an explosion in unaided (particularly Harambee) schools. In 1966 approximately half of all Kenya's schools were in the aided sector; by 1974 the proportion had declined to 39 per cent; by 1977 it had declined further to 29 per cent. Total secondary school enrolments expanded from 100,000 in 1968 to 360,000 in 1978.

This expansion enabled a greater proportion of children in primary schools to continue their education at the secondary level. By 1977 the entry to Form I of secondary schools was some 44 per cent of the total enrolments in Standard 7 of primary schools. However, this considerably understates the proportion of children who were going on to secondary education because of the extent of repeating in the last year of primary school so as to attempt entry to the government financed schools, these being both free and of higher quality.[4] African Form IV enrolment, having doubled in 1967–8, increased a further 3.2 times between 1968–78.

In Table 3.9 we present estimates of the distribution of educational attainment of African boys for the age cohort of which some members were in the 1977 Form IV, and for the age cohort of which some members were in the 1964 Form IV. The figures for 'the percentage Form IV and above' are probably accurate, though the division between 'primary' and 'none' is very unreliable and almost certainly underestimates the proportion of boys with no education. The implication of the table is that the chances of an African boy gaining a Form IV secondary education increased sixfold in just thirteen

Table 3.9

The Distribution of Educational Attainment

Total number of males aged 20	1977	1964
in 1977 and 1964	125,000[a]	76,000[a]
Form IV enrolment 1977 and 1964	34,800[b]	3,345[b]
Form I enrolment 1974	40,000[b]	n.a.
Primary enrolement of males, Standard 7, in		
1973 and 1960	122,700[d]	45,400[e]
Percentage Form IV or above	27.8	4.4
Percentage completed primary, or Forms I–III	70.4	55.3
Percentage none, or incomplete primary	1.8	40.3

[a] From 1969 Census.

[b] Includes non-Africans and non-citizens. Taken from *Educational Trends 1973–77*, Tables 46 and 49.

[c] Thias and Carnoy (1969), Tables 3–6.

[d] This overstates the number of sixteen-year olds in primary school. Standard 7 would have contained many repeaters, though to some extent this is offset by repeating lower down the school. *Source: Educational Trends*, Table 7.

[e] This is only an approximation, being one seventh of total 1960 African primary enrolment.

years, from something less than one-in-twenty, to something better than one-in-four.

Post-form IV education experienced in the 1970s the same rapid growth from a very small base which Form IV education had experienced in the 1960s. Candidates for Higher School Certificate (including non-Africans) increased from twelve hundred in 1968 to five thousand in 1977. Kenya students at the universities of East Africa increased from thirteen hundred in 1967/8 to nearly six thousand in 1977/8.

The pace of urbanization slowed. The growth of Nairobi was 6.9 per cent between 1969 and 1973, 3.4 per cent between 1973 and 1977, and 4.5 per cent between 1977 and 1979. Since the natural rate of growth of the urban population was around 2.8 per cent, the rate of net migration must have dropped sharply to a very low level. This is substantiated, and its implications developed, in Chapter 7.

(2) Employment

Trends in employment by sector are shown in Table 3.10. Over the period 1968–78 African wage employment increased by 61 per cent. However, the private non-agricultural sector grew by 83 per cent, the public sector by 84 per cent, and private agriculture by only 10 per cent (though 1978 was a poor year for wage employment in large-scale agriculture, for over the period

Table 3.10
Employment by Sector, 1968–1978
('000s)

Year	Public		Private non-agriculture		Private agriculture	
	Citizen	Non-citizen	Citizen	Non-citizen	Citizen	Non-citizen
1968	*208.8*[a]	*13.0*	*177.3*[a]	*36.7*[a]	*171.1*[a]	*1.9*[a]
1969	226.0	11.5	188.3	23.1	175.4	3.3
1970	236.1	11.1	194.6	19.0	180.3	3.4
1971	256.8	10.7	217.0	17.1	187.4	2.2
1972	276.7	10.3	220.6	14.3	196.4	1.5
1973	289.9	9.0	232.0	9.9	219.8	0.8
1974	322.4	7.7	272.6	9.9	212.7	1.0
1975	335.7	6.4	269.7	11.2	194.8	1.0
1976	351.3	5.1	291.6	11.8	196.8	0.9
1977	371.3	5.1	307.7	12.4	205.5	0.9
1978	385.0	5.0	324.2	8.4	188.1	0.9

[a] African

1968–77 employment grew by 20 per cent). The trend of a decline in the ratio of African wage employment to adult males, which had persisted over the period 1948–69, was reversed quite sharply. Had the trend continued at its average rate for that period, by 1978 the ratio would have been only 0.192 (wage job per adult male) while in fact it was 0.244. Not only had wage employment kept pace with one of the fastest population growth rates in the world, but the setbacks experienced between 1962 and 1969 had been more than recouped.

Table 3.11 shows the occupational distribution of the wage labour force by sector and citizenship. Perhaps the most striking feature is the growth in the number of teachers. While in the immediate post-Independence period, 1964–8, the major occupational expansion of public sector citizen employment had been clerical, in 1968–78 it was teachers. Excluding teachers, public sector employment grew by around 60 per cent, substantially less than private, non-agricultural employment.

The skill composition of the citizen labour force changed in favour of the higher range of occupations. Whilst manual (non-agricultural) employment grew by 45 per cent between 1968 and 1977, technical and supervisory employment grew by over 70 per cent, clerical and secretarial employment doubled, executive and middle managerial employment grew by 140 per cent, and top level employment more than tripled. Unfortunately, because of a change in the definition of skilled manual workers it is not possible to obtain time series figures for this category.

The notion of the public sector as being dominated by low-level bureaucratic employment which expanded to meet the supply of qualified people is not supported by the evidence. Public sector citizen clerical and secretarial employment expanded by around 40 per cent between 1968 and 1977 compared with an expansion of 240 per cent in the private sector. By 1977 the bulk of citizen employment in the category was private, and of the incremental employment during the period over 70 per cent was in the private sector. While the productivity of public sector clerical employees is inherently difficult to measure, the 43 per cent increase in clerical employment should be compared with an 84 per cent increase in total public employment and a 94 per cent increase in real public expenditure, so that any thesis of falling labour productivity looks *prima facie* unlikely.

The decline in the monopsonistic role of the public sector for African skilled manpower was not confined to the clerical sector. In the case of technical and supervisory staff, over 90 per cent of incremental citizen employment was in the private sector, for executive and middle level managements nearly 70 per cent of incremental citizen employment was private, and for top-level posts 60 per cent was private. Hence, the dominance which the public sector had briefly held around Independence in the skilled African labour market rapidly passed to the private sector.

Part of this was due to the Africanization of the private sector which,

Table 3.11
Employment by Skill
('000s)

(A) By Skill

Year	Project and senior manager	Executive and middle manager	Technical and supervisor	Clerical and secretarial	Sales	Teachers	Manual skilled and semi-skilled	Unskilled regular	Unskilled casual	Agriculture All Africans
1964	7.4	17.1	n.a.	34.0	9.0	33.3	113.9	118.0	34.2	200.2
1968	15.5	13.4	18.4	45.6	5.0	41.7	115.8	127.5	49.7	171.1
1969	17.3	16.0	21.1	56.5	5.0	47.8	114.5	119.2	65.5	175.4
1970	18.4	16.6	27.5	67.0	6.9	50.8	119.2	104.6	16.7	180.3
1972	21.3				7.0	64.1	193.8	113.5	35.4	196.4
1975	20.2	12.7	21.4	68.7	6.6	98.0	134.3	203.6	36.8	194.8
1976	20.2	17.8	21.6	71.7	6.2	100.6	59.7	266.6	62.0	196.8
1977	20.5	18.1	21.7	74.5	7.2	105.4	65.1	265.2	81.4	205.5
1978	21.6					101.9	86.3			188.1

(B) By Public and Private

Year	Project and senior manager		Executive and middle manager		Technical and supervisor		Clerical and secretarial		Sales		Teachers		Manual skilled and semi-skilled		Unskilled regular		Unskilled casual		Agriculture All Africans
	Public	Private	Public	Private	Public	Private	Public	Private	Public	Private	Public	Private	Public	Private	Public	Private	Public	Private	
1964	3.5	3.9	3.9	13.2	n.a.	n.a.	16.0	18.0	0.0	9.0	30.7	2.6	42.8	71.1	35.9	82.1	29.5	4.7	200.2
1968	6.2	9.3	6.6	6.8	9.8	8.6	26.9	18.7	0.5	4.5	33.9	7.8	59.8	56.0	43.8	83.7	24.9	24.8	171.1
1969	5.1	12.2	8.7	7.3	11.5	9.6	36.2	20.3	0.5	4.5	41.8	6.0	55.8	58.7	39.6	79.6	32.8	32.7	175.4
1970	6.3	12.1	10.8	5.8	18.1	9.4	45.7	21.3	1.6	5.3	45.2	5.6	63.0	56.2	6.7	97.9	8.4	8.3	180.3
1972	3.0	18.3									40.6		56.2		40.6	72.9	25.2	10.2	196.4

Year	Project and senior manager		Executive and middle manager		Technical and supervisor		Clerical and secretarial		Sales		Teachers		Manual skilled and semi-skilled		Unskilled regular		Unskilled casual		Agriculture
	Citizen	Non-cit	Citizen	Non-cit	Citizen	Non-cit	Citizen	Non-cit	Citizen	Non-cit	Citizen	Non-cit	Citizen	Non-cit	Citizen	Non-cit	Citizen	Non-cit	All Africans
1975	11.5	8.7	6.1	6.6	13.4	8.0	42.8	25.9	0.4	6.2	94.4	3.6	69.7	64.6	66.6	137.0	7.2	29.6	194.8
1976	9.3	10.9	8.9	8.9	9.6	12.0	35.2	36.5	0.3	5.9	96.6	4.0	19.8	39.9	121.2	145.4	12.3	49.7	196.8
1977	8.3	12.2	9.1	9.0	9.7	12.0	36.7	37.8	0.4	6.8	100.8	4.6	22.1	43.0	114.9	150.3	16.1	65.3	205.5
1978	10.0	11.6									97.3	4.6	31.4	54.9					188.1

(C) By Citizenship

Year	Project and senior manager		Executive and middle manager		Technical and supervisor		Clerical and secretarial		Sales		Teachers		Manual skilled and semi-skilled		Unskilled regular		Unskilled casual		Agriculture
	Citizen	Non-cit	Citizen	Non-cit	Citizen	Non-cit	Citizen	Non-cit	Citizen	Non-cit	Citizen	Non-cit	Citizen	Non-cit	Citizen	Non-cit	Non-cit	All Africans	All Africans
1964	1.8	5.6	5.7	11.4	n.a.	n.a.	19.8	18.2	5.0	4.0	30.4	2.9	106.7	7.2				171.1	200.2
1968	4.3	11.2	6.5	6.9	11.9	6.5	36.2	9.4	3.1	1.9	37.0	4.7	105.6	10.2	127.5	49.7		175.4	
1969	6.0	11.3	7.0	9.0	14.3	6.8	45.0	11.5	3.4	1.6	43.8	4.0	110.2	4.3				180.3	
1970	6.9	11.5	8.1	8.5	21.0	6.5	57.3	9.7	5.1	1.8	47.2	3.6	118.2	3.7				196.4	
1972	11.8	9.5							6.7	0.3	61.6	2.5	191.3	2.5				194.8	
1975	13.8	6.4	11.3	1.4	18.6	2.8	67.2	1.5	6.4	0.2	95.8	2.2	132.5	1.8				196.8	
1976	14.2	6.0	15.3	2.5	20.2	1.4	70.4	1.3	6.0	0.2	98.4	2.2	58.3	1.4				205.5	
1977	13.4	7.1	15.6	2.5	20.3	1.4	73.2	1.3	7.0	0.2	103.1	2.3	62.1	3.0	265.2	81.4		188.1	
1978																			

Sources: Employment and Earnings Surveys, Kenya, Republic of (various years); Ray in Sheffield (ed.).

History

except for top-level jobs, occurred mainly during the period 1967–72. In the private sector the contribution of Africanization to incremental skilled employment was more substantial than in the public sector, which had Africanized before 1968. Forty-five per cent of top level incremental employment, 50 per cent of both executive and technical incremental employment, and around 30 per cent of clerical incremental employment in the private sector between 1968 and 1977 was accounted for by the fall in non-citizen employment. This process was concentrated in the earlier part of the period and appears to have ended by 1975. Non-citizen skilled employment in 1977 was higher than in 1975 in four of the seven categories of skilled labour.

(3) Wages

Our estimates of African real wages by sector between 1968 and 1978 are given in Table 3.12. Whilst agricultural wages rose by 32 per cent over the period, non-agricultural earnings fell sharply in both the public and private sectors.

Table 3.12
African Real Wages by Sector
(shillings per month at 1959 prices)

Year	Public Sector	Private agriculture	Private non-agriculture
1968	343.8	85.7	300.9
1972	368.0	108.0	348.0
1976	326.2	120.9	255.8
1977	290.4	109.6	244.9
1978	234.0	113.2	220.2

Source: Employment and Earnings Survey (various years); and *Statistical Abstract* (various years).

Changes in mean earnings could be due to changes in wage levels, or the wage structure by skill, changes in citizen/non-citizen differentials, or changes in the skill and racial composition of the labour force. Using the 1968 wages structure and citizen/non-citizen differential, that part of the total earnings change attributable to changes in the composition of the labour force by race and skill was identified, leaving as a residual the change in earnings due to changes in skill- and race-specific real wages. Recall from Chapter 2 that between 1964 and 1968, excluding composition effects, real wages rose by 7.5 per cent in the public sector and by 58 per cent in the private sector, these rises being due to large wage increases for the skilled. Between 1968 and 1972 in the entire non-agricultural sector real wages were constant once the composition changes are removed. Over the whole period 1968–77 skill- and race-specific real wages fell by 18 per cent in the public sector and 11 per cent in the private sector. There were further large falls of at least 10 per cent in each sector between 1977 and 1978.

Disaggregating by skill, real wages fell in all but top-level jobs. The trend in the unskilled wage is problematic to measure because of data inconsistencies for private sector earnings in 1968. In that year the public sector unskilled wage was 253 sh. per month, and since House and Rempel found that in 1968 there was no significant difference between public and private sector unskilled earnings (House and Rempel, 1978, Table 5.7, regression 5.23), this figure has some degree of validity as a measure of the private sector unskilled wage. If this is the case, then unskilled wages would have fallen by 4 per cent between 1968 and 1972 and by 24 per cent over the whole period 1968–77. However, no measurement problems arise in confirming the sharp fall in unskilled real wages between 1972 and 1977 of 20 per cent.

For citizen and non-citizen skilled earnings during the 1970s our best source is not the Employment and Earnings Surveys (which do not distinguish between citizen and non-citizen earnings) but a series of private sector surveys made by Inbucon for 1972, 1977, and 1979. Between 1972 and 1977, when unskilled real wages fell by 20 per cent, the real wages of skilled citizens fell by between 7 per cent and 19 per cent, depending upon the skill level (see Table 3.13). With the single exception of the rather loosely defined bottom

Table 3.13
Median Salary for Citizens

Occupation	Real salary 1972=100			Salary of citizens relative to non-citizens	
	1972	1977	1979	1972	1979
(1) Director	100	93	85	0.84	0.77
(2) Division head below director	100	87	80	0.77	0.74
(3) Senior manager responsible to (1) or (2)	100	81	77	0.71	0.79
(4) Middle manager responsible to (3)	100	77	75	0.61	0.67
(5) Middle manager below (4)	100	92	87	0.70	0.77

Source: Inbucon (1973, 1978, 1979).

grade, there is a clear tendency for skill differentials to have widened between 1972 and 1977. Further, the skilled–unskilled wage differential must have widened. The trend of falling real wages for the skilled continued through to September 1979, the date of our most recent data. The trend is confirmed when the five groups are disaggregated further into twenty-two well-defined jobs. The citizen/non-citizen earnings differential within a skill category remained fairly constant at a high level (see Table 3.13). There was some tendency for the differential to widen in the highest category and narrow in the lower categories. The persistence of this differential is analysed in Chapter 6, section II.

The choice between citizens and non-citizens among skilled workers has as its counterpart among unskilled workers the decision whether to hire on a regular or a casual basis. This decision will be influenced by several factors. First, the casual worker will tend to be cheaper than the regular worker because casuals are exempted from National Social Security Fund contributions and certain other benefits. In 1977 mean earnings per month of regular unskilled workers were 42 per cent above mean earnings of employed[5] casual workers. Second, casual workers are much easier to dismiss than regular workers. We have noted that in the 1970s unions placed greatest emphasis upon employment protection of the regular work force. We return to reasons for hiring casual workers in Chapter 6, section IV. The two main costs of casual labour are the greater transactions costs associated with more frequent recruitment and the loss to the firm from any investment in the worker associated with the higher quit rate likely among casual workers.

Government intervention in the form of the Tripartite Agreements of 1970 and 1979 has had a major impact upon this decision. The intention of the Agreements, to increase employment, did not materialize. Stewart demonstrated that no evidence could be found for an increase in total wage employment as a result of the 1970 Agreement. What has not been noticed, however, is the very sharp switch from casual to regular labour which occurred as a result of the Agreement.[6] Between 1969 and 1970 the non-agricultural casual labour force fell from 65,500 to 16,700. This is very likely to have been a cost-minimizing response to the Agreement, which required a 10 per cent increase in regular employment with casual employment exempted. The Agreement thus had the consequence of regularizing the casual labour force rather than that of expanding employment. The economic implications of this will be explored in the context of our analysis of recruitment.

Most unskilled labour in Kenya is self-employed on smallholdings. Since Independence smallholder per capita real incomes have been rising quite rapidly. For example, Table 3.6 suggests that in Central Province between 1963 and 1974 mean real incomes increased by 50 per cent, while nationally (over a longer period) they have grown at around 2½ per cent p.a. (see page 213). Further, hired labour increased among smallholdings from 5 per cent to 10 per cent of total labour input. These factors raised the supply price of labour to the estates and reduced their monopsony power. Real wages on the estates rose by 32 per cent between 1968 and 1978. However, the Annual Labour Reports indicate some continued monopsony power — for example, in 1975 the Report noted that job seekers would not take estate wage employment because wages were too low. Notified vacancies for 600 tea pluckers in Kisumu and 1,000 in Kericho drew a combined response of 20 applicants. This feature of massive excess demand for labour at the existing wage rate without a tendency to increase the wage rate is, of course, the classic characteristic of monopsony power. We have noted its persistence in Kenyan estates agriculture from its inception.

A study by COTU suggested that, by the late 1970s, the cost-of-living differential for an unskilled worker between urban and estates employment was 60 per cent (see Oduor-Otieno, 1979). This corresponds closely to the estimate made by Scott for the late 1960s. On this basis, by the late 1970s there was little difference between the unskilled estates and the unskilled non-agricultural wage. The issue of monopsony behaviour by the estates is revisited in Chapter 5, section III. The issue of rural urban wage differentials and wage adjustment, a central theme of our study, is revisited in Chapter 6.

Notes

1 Two different definitions of income were used in published results of the 1963 survey. We adopt that of Kmietowicz and Webley as being the more coherent.

2 Strictly, per adult equivalent.

3 An example would be the greater use of purchased inputs which raise mean yield but do not reduce the climate-related risk of crop failure. Net income has a higher variance as a result.

4 The figures given include non-Africans. For primary schooling the proportion of non-Africans is so trivial as to be unimportant. In Form IV, the numbers of non-Africans probably lie in the range of two to six thousand.

5 Those in employment during one month. To a limited extent this may reflect a shorter number of days worked during the month by employed casuals. However, most casuals seem *de facto* to be hired on a monthly rather than a daily basis.

6 Stewart's figures miss this because the casual labour reported included agricultural estates, where the casual labour force expanded.

Part Two

ANALYSIS

4

SOME SIMPLE THEORY

I. The Experts and the Kenyan Employment Problem

In the late 1960s and early 1970s Kenya attracted a number of visiting development economists who constructed analytic models explaining the labour market of the 1960s. Several of these models have gained an acceptance beyond their local application and are now among the orthodoxies of development economics. The predominant view of these models, which might be termed 'institutionalist', was systematized by the ILO's comprehensive employment strategy mission which visited Kenya in 1972 in a highly influential report. The stylized facts which these writers were seeking to reconcile were the by-product of the compassionate twist in colonial policies after the Second World War, and accentuated by the independent government's minimum wage policy, which led directly to the first stylized fact: the wage explosion for skilled African labour in the late 1960s (see Chapter 2). The other stylized facts were: a very rapid expansion of education; an increase in rural–urban migration, and in open urban unemployment; stagnation in formal sector urban employment, and a rise in urban 'informal' sector employment.

First on the scene were Harris and Todaro who provided an elegant model of a dual economy in which rural–urban migration and the level of 'equilibrium' urban unemployment were jointly determined by an exogenously given gap between a fixed wage in the formal sector, and the substantially lower alternative value marginal product and/or supply price of rural–urban migrants. The latter would in this model seek to equate their income foregone in agriculture with the higher expected income in the formal urban sector. This expected income in turn being a function of the ratio of the number of unemployed seeking formal sector jobs to the number of vacancies opened up, in each time period. The model thus predicted, at least in its simplest version, that, with an urban–rural wage differential of two, the open urban unemployment rate would be 50 per cent.[1] Moreover, expanding industrial jobs would paradoxically (by improving the probability of finding an urban job for the existing urban labour force) increase rural–urban migration, as well as the equilibrium level of open urban unemployment.

The Harris–Todaro model was refined by Fields, who incorporated the screening of job applicants by the number of years for which they had been educated, while retaining the assumption of an institutionally rigid wage structure. Thus consider the urban sector as made up of jobs to which particular 'tags' are attached. Initially, each of these 'jobs' which can be ranked in terms of their corresponding wages also have accompanying educational qualifications which are used by employers as a screen. But employers will always prefer a worker with an educational level higher than that which they are currently using as a screen. Thus job seekers educated beyond the level currently used as a screen on a particular rung in the job ladder will have a high probability of being hired at that rung. With the expansion of education, the 'excess' of workers who meet the educational requirements at each rung in the ladder will have to apply for jobs at the next rung down, where their prospects of finding jobs still remain high. As this realization sinks in, more and more 'excess' workers with the requisite educational status at each rung will apply for jobs lower and lower down the ladder. In the process, better-educated workers will 'bump' their less-educated cohorts off each rung of the ladder.

The resulting composition of the unemployed and the rate of unemployment over time will then be determined by three sets of interrelated factors. First, the relative imbalance between the jobs offered and job seekers at each educationally differentiated rung in the job ladder will determine how many people are in 'excess' on that rung at any moment. Next, some of this 'excess' will decide to remain temporarily unemployed, to try their luck later at the same rung in the ladder. Others, lowering their sights, will seek and almost certainly obtain jobs at the next rung down. This latter choice will be determined in part by the speed with which job seekers lower their expectations and by their access to some means of financing their unemployment while deciding whether or not to lower their sights. As the major source of financing is likely to come from relatives and, considering the costs of education, the more educated are likely to belong to richer families, the less-educated are also less likely to be able to ride out a prolonged period of unemployment while lowering their job expectations. For these reasons, a heavy bias in unemployment rates toward the more educated should be expected. With the expansion of education, the bumping process should force more and more of the less-educated to choose low-income employment rather than continued job search. Though this model would seem to fit the stylized facts of the 1970s better than the Harris–Todaro model, it still carries the connotation that the educational screening is an inefficient and unproductive method of reducing real urban wages in the formal sector. We question this implicit assumption by providing an alternative and subtler explanation of the relationship of education to unemployment in Chapter 6.

The apotheosis of these institutionalist explanations of the behaviour of urban labour markets in Kenya (and by extension in many other LDCs) is the book by House and Rempel for the ILO. They attempt to explain, through various econometric tests, the observed rigidity of the modern sector wage structure in the face of growing labour supply pressures, by the influence of a few large foreign firms (whose wages are determined by their ability to pay) on the whole modern sector wage structure.

The hallmark of the institutionalist thesis was the assumption of permanent institutionally determined wage rigidity. A counter-thesis proposed by Stiglitz, also a visitor to Kenya in the period, suggested that the rural–urban wage gap was the outcome of rational wage setting by employers. This explanation relied upon differential costs of labour turnover in the two sectors (rural and urban). He showed that if there were no such costs attached to the use of labour in agriculture, but they were positive for urban formal sector labour, then it could be in the interests of profit maximizing urban producers to influence these costs by providing higher wages to their employees. These, together with the accompanying open urban unemployment, would lower quits by their workers. Thus there would be an optimum rural–urban wage differential and an accompanying open unemployment rate, at which the costs of turnover would be minimized.

We will argue that none of these models fit the evidence of the 1970s. The Stiglitz model 'explains' and the institutionalist models assert a rigidity of wages which did not characterize the period. However, we go beyond this to claim that none of the models offers an adequate account of the labour market even in the 1960s when there was undoubtedly a rural–urban wage gap.

In order to provide an alternative explanation of the evolution of the labour market it is useful first to set out the logic of modern 'neo-classical' theories of industrial wage structures.

II   Determinants of the Wage Structure

(1) The Competitive Model

To fix ideas it is best to begin with the purest case of a perfectly competitive world, in which *homogenous* labour inputs enter into the production process, which is characterized by a convex production set. Then given a convex preference structure which includes the labour–leisure choice of individuals, profit maximization by producers and utility maximization by consumers will yield a general equilibrium in which a competitive wage will emerge for the labour input, which will be uniform in all the industries, and which will entail the equality of value marginal product (VMP) of labour with the wage (W), which will also equal the labourers' marginal rate of substitution between income and leisure (MRS_{yl}) (or $VMP = W = MRS_{yl}$).

As is well known, in this perfectly competitive world there are no problems of (*a*) information (given the assumption of perfect information on both sides of every market), or (*b*) uncertainty (if, as in the Arrow–Debreu framework, there are contingent claims markets for future contingent 'commodities'). Hence there are no transaction costs given the assumption of a costless

Walrasian tatonment process, in which, moreover, there is no false trading at non-equilibrium prices in any market.

In such a world, clearly, there would be no wage differentials. However, the assumption of *homogenous* labour is particularly unrealistic. Various reasons for this non-homogeneity may be cited. The most important (within this tradition which goes back to Adam Smith) are differences in the level of skills amongst different members of the labour force. These skills, which are acquired either through education and formal or informal 'on the job' training, are the human capital acquired by raw labour and give rise to differentials in the productivity of different labourers. Moreover, as in the case of physical capital, the acquisition of human capital also entails costs in terms of fore-gone earnings (consumption, output) during the period the capital is being accumulated. Hence it will only be profitable to invest in human capital (as in physical capital) if the returns to such investment are equal to (or greater than) those from alternative forms of investment. This entails that the discounted value of the expected earnings stream from the date the skills are acquired till the end of the labourers working life must at least equal the discounted costs of the earnings foregone from the sale of raw labour during the period the skills are being acquired. For any given positive rate of discount this must mean the requisite skills will only be acquired if their skilled wage is higher than that for unskilled (raw) labour, with the differential being greater the longer the required period of training (and hence dis-counted costs of foregone earnings). The actual differential is determined by these supply considerations and the relative value marginal productivities of different skills which are given by the derived demand for these different labour services within a general equilibrium framework.

Clearly, the introduction of human capital considerations which led to the non-homogeneity of labour inputs will yield inter-industry average earnings differentials, for different industries will be combining different skills in different proportions. Moreover, to the extent that different occupations embody different skill mixes there will also be occupational earnings differentials.

An important question in this context (as we shall see below), is whether the *long-run* supply curve for labour with specific skills, or that in particular occupations with a given skill composition, is perfectly elastic or upward sloping? If workers had (*a*) *the same tastes* and (*b*) *discounted the future at the same rate*,[2] then the different skills (or occupations with given skill compositions) could be ordered in terms of their wage (earnings) differentials (with raw unskilled labour at the bottom), and the supply of labour would be perfectly elastic at a wage rate for a particular skill (occupation) which would be determined in relation to that for unskilled (raw) labour by the costs of training, pecuniary advantages or disadvantages attaching to different occu-pations (skills), as well as any rents that accrue to natural abilities. It being noted that, given our assumption of identical tastes of workers, the valuation of these non-pecuniary aspects of different jobs would also be identical amongst workers.[3] In this case demand considerations will be redundant in determining wage differentials, which will be purely dependent on supply considerations. Changes in the demand for different levels of skills will determine the *level* of employment in each skill category, but the wage differentials between different skills and occupational categories should be explicable purely in terms of the relative costs of skill acquisition (and some common evaluations of the non-pecuniary aspects of jobs). Moreover, in this case changes in earning differentials over time should be explicable purely in terms of changes in the relative costs of acquiring the skills required for particular occupations, and any changes in the common evaluation of the relative non-pecuniary valuation of different jobs.

Clearly, however, workers are unlikely to have identical tastes. Then, even assuming that workers' evaluations of the costs of training and their discount rates are the same, if they value the non-pecuniary characteristics of jobs differentially, the long-run supply curve of labour in each skill (occupation) group will not be perfectly elastic but upward sloping. This implies that, given differentials in tastes, the workers who value the non-pecuniary advantages (disadvantages) of particular occupations most (least) highly will require a smaller wage (earnings) differential to accept the 'job' than those who value these aspects less (more) highly.[4]

Furthermore, if training costs and discount rates differ between workers this will provide further reasons for the long-run supply curve of labour for particular skills (occupations) to be upward sloping. In these more realistic circumstances the demand for different types of skilled labour will once again be a determinant (together with the upward-sloping supply curves) of the relative wages (earnings) of different skills and occupations, and hence changes in earnings differentials will need to be explained in terms of changes in *both* the supply and the demand for labour. We would therefore not expect that explanations of wage differentials within the simple unicasual human capital approach (which would only be valid with identical tastes and training costs for workers) could explain the whole of the variance in earnings. Most studies of wage differentials in both developed and developing countries, based on estimating so-called earnings functions, however, have tried to explain these differentials within the simple human capital approach, and not surprisingly because of either a neglect of demand influences or difficulties in finding good statistical proxies for them, have found that the human capital variables *do not* explain a large part of the variance in earnings.[5]

The reintroduction of the second blade of Marshall's scissors — demand — in the determination of skill (occupational) differentials, when there are upward-sloping supply curves for different skills (occupations), is also of importance because the market conditions in both product and labour markets now become important. Within the strictly competitive framework, within which the arguments above have been couched, both product and labour markets are assumed to be perfect. If, however, the long-run supply curves to different skills were perfectly elastic then, as we have argued, irrespective of the assumptions about the nature of product and factor markets, relative wages could be explained purely in terms of the human capital approach. Moreover, in equilibrium, irrespective of imperfections in product and labour markets, the equality of the wage and value marginal product for any occupation (skill) would be maintained.

With upward-sloping supply curves for different skills (occupations), how-ever, market conditions are of some importance. If perfect competition prevails in both product and factor markets, then clearly even with upward-sloping supply curves for different skills their earnings would be equal to their private and social value marginal products. If, however, there are imperfections in either the product or factor markets this equality will no longer hold. In the case of product market imperfections (monopoly), though the wage would still equal the private value marginal product it would be less than the social value marginal product of that type of skill. (Note that this distortion would also exist if the supply curve of that type of skill was perfectly elastic.) More importantly, if there is *monopsony* in the labour market then, as with an upward-sloping supply curve of a particular type of labour, its marginal wage cost is greater than the average cost to the producer: the value marginal product of that type of labour will be equal to the higher marginal cost of labour, which will be greater than the wage paid. As the competitive model usually quite clearly rules out monopsony, the equality of wages and value marginal products for different skills would also be an important prediction of the model, but if monopsony exists then this equality will no longer hold.

There is one other source of occupational wage differentials which should be introduced within this competitive framework, and that is the existence of differences 'in scarce natural talents which are more important in some occupations than in others',[6] and which give rise to intra-occupational rents accruing to the more talented members of the occupation above the average earnings in that occupation. This would be a factor which could be used to explain intra-occupational earnings differentials. However, as Rees empha-sizes, within the competitive framework it is not clear why the average earnings within such occupations should involve rents above those in other occupations which need less native ability but as much training. For if in these occupations

new entrants overrate their own chances of winning the large prizes of if they place higher value on the non-pecuniary attractions of such a career, many people of modest talent will enter. As their hopes of success fade, some of these people will not leave the occupation immediately because of the sunk costs of their investment in training. The result can be low rates of pay or frequent periods of unemployment, that drive the average earnings of people in these occupations below those of skilled occupations in which native ability is less important. (Rees, op. cit., pp. 169–70.)

Thus the competitive model would lay most emphasis on the human capital component in explaining wage and earnings differentials between occupations, and because of the differing occupational mixes in different industries also for inter-industrial differentials. There are various additional features which could be grafted on to the model, for instance by differentiating between different components and cost structures of human capital — namely formal training and general and specific on-the-job training. However, as these aspects (for instance specific on-the-job training, of which more below) and others which we shall consider later usually involve the introduction of non-convexities in either the production or consumption sets, they are incompatible (if important) with the existence of a competitive general equilibrium. So they are best considered as neoclassical extensions of the competitive-type model which we will discuss later in this chapter.

The two major predictions of the competitive model would therefore be (*a*) that most of the earning differentials in an economy should be explicable in terms of the differentials in the supply and demand conditions for human capital, and (*b*) that average wages (earnings) of different groups should be equal to their marginal value products.

Also within this model (as so far expounded) there should be no reason why employers should prefer one worker with a given mix of skills over another similar worker at the same wage rate. The model would also predict a fairly rapid adjustment through changes in relative wages to any sectoral disequilibria in particular occupational labour markets, with the adjustments taking place through rapid price (wage) adjustments and hence with little quantity (unemployment) adjustment (except of course for any frictional elements due to immobilities of labour over space, and changing expectations through the process of job search).

(2) Neoclassical Theories

Thus, though the competitive theory can take account of some of the factors leading to the heterogeneity of labour (primarily on the supply side of the market), there are others (mainly on the demand side) which it cannot. These missing aspects concern various (often non-observable) characteristics of workers which are important determinants of workers' productivity and hence in the demand for labour. They were aptly summarized by Samuelson as being

the tremendous differentiation of abilities and attitudes as between workers, so that no two are alike — and so that no person can accurately ascertain their differences. This, plus the fact that the performance you get from a man is not something that exists independently of his wage, the wages of others, his past employment experience, and the performance of others, pulverizes the labour market into separate but highly interrelated segments. If each morning people could be hired in an organised auction market the world would be a very different one. (Samuelson, p. 1567.)

It is the existence of many of these non-observable or non-measurable aspects of work performance, along with the self-consciousness of the phenomena being studied, which makes the labour market inherently different from those for capital or commodities. It means that exclusive reliance on the competitive model will be misleading in explaining the structure of wages.

In fact the competitive model implicitly assumes that *all* labour contracts are in the form of sequential spot contracts. In each period, given the extant demand and supply conditions in the particular labour market, the market for all types of labour is like that for casual labour, with spot rates being set (including recontracting if necessary) at the 'new equilibrium' rates for already employed workers. But even the most casual empiricism will show that casual labour is only one, and by no means the most important, of the labour contractual modes to be found in developed or developing countries. Institutionalist writers impressed by this multiplicity of contractual modes, ranging from various forms of tenancy in agriculture to the highly structured and hierarchical internal labour markets in much of modern industry, have concluded that politics, sociology, and anthropology are the determinants of the existing contractual modes rather than any coherent economic factors.

By contrast, modern neoclassical theorists are seeking to understand the departures from the perfectly competitive conditions, in particular environmental circumstances, which would justify the development of particular types of labour contracts as a 'second best' cost-efficient and utility-maximizing response on the part of producers and workers. In particular three fundamental assumptions of the competitive model which we have hitherto maintained — namely, perfect information on both sides of the market, no uncertainty (or else perfect future markets), and no transactions costs in achieving a competitive market equilibrium — need to be questioned.

Most of the emerging neoclassical literature of labour markets is based on recognizing the importance of imperfect information on both sides of the market, the absence of perfect future markets, and the relevance of differential transactions costs in determining whether or not a competitive market solution to a particular allocation problem will be viable.

Imperfect information about the 'ability' of the worker, and of the working conditions and future prospects of the employer, are both a source of uncertainty on the two sides of the labour market. If it were possible to establish markets in contingent claims (as, for instance, if there were universal futures markets) such that trades could be made for *all conceivable* future states of the world for different 'commodities', differentiated not only by physical and temporal characteristics but also by whether or not certain states of the world obtain at particular dates, then it would still be possible to achieve a Pareto-efficient competitive equilibrium. Economic agents would then be able to maximize their expected utilities according to their own subjective probability distributions about the various future unknown states of the world (Arrow and Hahn).

However, universal contingent commodity markets are not found because in many cases, particularly concerning the determinants of labour incomes, it is not possible to delineate at all precisely the various future outcomes, nor the 'states of nature' which are their determinants, except at prohibitive cost. It is these latter transactions costs which make it infeasible to establish universal futures markets. A market for a particular 'good' (for instance a future (contingent) commodity) may then fail to exist if transactions costs drive a large enough wedge between the buyer's and seller's price, so that the lowest price at which anyone is willing to sell the commodity is above the highest price anyone is willing to pay for it.

Various 'non-market' forms of allocation may then represent second-best efficient adaptions to this ubiquitous incompleteness of markets. Dreze has characterized the economic risks causing uncertain labour incomes as being either endogenous or exogenous.

The endogenous uncertainties concern an individual's proficiency at work: qualifications, creativity, drive, sociability. The exogenous uncertainties concern the demand for the labour services offered by an individual: high demand at times of full employment, but low demand at times of under-employment; a demand which assigns to a particular type of labour a higher or lower value, depending upon business conditions and industrial structures. (Dreze, p. 6.)

(a) Risks Associated with Labour Supply We cite a few cases on the risks associated in the supply of labour which are relevant in explaining why the sequential spot contracting mode of competitive casual labour markets may not be a feasible alternative when due to particular types of imperfect information there are risks which cannot be shed because of prohibitive transactions costs.

(i) *Firm-specific training* Consider the case of on-the-job firm-specific training which is of importance in much of modern large-scale industry. It is usual to distinguish general training which imparts skills which are of the same value to all firms from specific training which yields firm-specific skills of greater value to the firm imparting the skills than other firms. It is well known that, in the case of general training, the worker will (within the framework of the competitive model) receive his net marginal product both during the training period *and* after he is trained. He will thus bear the cost of his training. With specific training, however, as the worker cannot command an equal premium for such training outside the firm training him it would be possible for the employer to bear the initial costs of specific training by paying the worker a wage greater than his net marginal produce during the training period, and recouping this investment by paying a wage less than the worker's marginal product after he is trained.

However, if for some reason the worker leaves the firm before the employer has recouped his specific training costs then the employer will suffer a loss on his investment. It may be thought that the employer should offer a worker being imparted firm-specific training a long-term contract, which ensures that the employer will be able to recoup his specific training costs. But in practice such long-term contracts are rarely observed. Why? There is nothing within the competitive framework to prevent such long-term contracts from arising. They are usually infeasible, because for certain types of on-the-job training the transactions costs of writing, negotiating, and enforcing such contracts are prohibitive.

For instance, some forms of on-the-job training require the transmission of valuable information from one employee to another. Thus

> both individually and as a group, incumbents are in possession of a valuable resource (knowledge) and can be expected to reveal it fully and candidly only in exchange for value. The way the employment relationship is structured turns out to be important, in this connection. The danger is that incumbent employees will hoard information to their personal advantage and engage in a series of bilateral monopolistic exchanges with the management — to the detriment of both the firm and other employees as well.[7]

Promotional ladders and seniority rules of the internal labour market variety are then seen as an alternative contractual form (for that of sequential spot transactions) in the labour market to overcome these problems.

> Access to higher level positions on internal promotional ladders is not open to all comers on an unrestricted basis. Rather, as part of the internal incentive system, high level positions (of the prescribed kinds) are filled by promotion from within, whenever this is feasible. This practice, particularly if it is followed by other enterprises to which the worker might otherwise turn for upgrading opportunities, ties the interests of the worker to the firm in a continuing way. Given these ties, the worker looks to internal promotion as the principal means of improving his position. (Ibid., p. 273.)

Promotional ladders within a collective organization where wage rates attach mainly to jobs rather than workers, mean that 'the incentives to behave opportunistically, which infect individual bargaining schemes . . . [are] correspondingly attenuated'.[8] This enables both the transmission of task-specific training by one employee to another, and also enables the 'tying in' of the trained worker to the firm.

(ii) *Monitoring job performance and providing incentives*   The superiority of the internal labour market type of wage structure over the sequential spot contracting of casual labour markets for many industries is further strengthened when we take account of the informational imperfections concerned with the monitoring of job performance by workers with the same level of skills, but who differ in their abilities and hence productivities.

This problem of monitoring arises particularly for what Williamson *et al.* label 'idiosyncratic jobs, or tasks'. The characteristics of these idiosyncratic jobs are that they involve specific skills, whose specificity often depends upon specific environmental features of the work-place.

The apparently routine operation of standard machines can be importantly aided by familiarity with the particular piece of operating equipment . . . Moreover, performance in some production or managerial jobs involves a team element, and a critical skill is the ability to operate effectively with the given members of the team. This ability is dependent upon the interaction skills of the personalities of the members, and the individuals work 'skills' are specific in the sense that skills necessary to work on one team are never the same as those required on another. (Doeringer and Piore, pp. 15–16.)

Given these differences in 'ability', whether natural or acquired, clearly it will be in the interest of employers to screen workers. If screening costs are low (that is, there are negligible transactions costs), individuals know their own abilities, and they and firms are risk neutral, then if a competitive equilibrium exists it must involve screening.[9] Clearly it is in the firm's interests to screen as it can then tailor remuneration exactly to the specific value marginal products of its heterogenous labour force. But would it be in the interests of workers to accept screening, in this case; for their co-operation is required if they are to be screened. There is an obvious incentive for a 'high-ability' person, who *ex hypothesi* knows his own ability, to be identified as he will then receive a higher wage than the mean wage he would receive if there were no screening. But then it must be in the interest of the next most 'able' person to identify himself from those less able than him, and so on until we reach the least 'able' person in the group, for whom there is no incentive to be identified, but because all the others more able than him have been identified in practice he too has been screened.[10]

But let us now relax the assumptions that (i) screening costs are negligible, (ii) that individual workers know their own 'ability', and (iii) that they are risk neutral.

If screening costs are positive then they imply a fixed cost of employing particular workers. In a competitive world (as in the case of general on-the-job training), given that workers are mobile, and that if one firm screens workers this screening information is equally valuable to its competitors, clearly it will not be able to appropriate the returns from its screening. For all firms will now bid for the workers who have been screened to be the most (next most . . .) able, and they will receive their value marginal product, but the firm which has undertaken the initial fixed screening costs will obviously have made a loss. Thus, in a competitive equilibrium with positive screening costs, these must be borne by the workers if there is to be any screening.

But if workers do not know their 'abilities' and are not risk neutral, they will never be willing to bear this cost of screening. For suppose the worker is risk averse, and 'say at an extreme he thinks his probability of being a low risk (high ability person) is equal to the proportion of low risk (high ability) individuals in the population, then screening simply increases the variance of his income and lowers the mean (if he bears the costs): he will never be willing to pay for it.'[11]

Thus if screening costs are positive, if workers are not certain of their abilities, and are not risk neutral, then a competitive equilibrium with screening will not exist. Or in other words, in a world of imperfect information, and where information on individual characteristics is of value, with positive transaction costs and risk aversion, the class of competitive labour contracts will not exist, but will tend to be substituted by other contractual modes.

For idiosyncratic jobs where these individual characteristics may be of importance, the internal labour market structure may be the most efficient feasible system of labour allocation. This is equally important in 'team-type' idiosyncratic jobs, where it may be impossible, except at prohibitive cost, to monitor *individual* performance.

If group but not individual performance is monitorable at reasonable cost, then the group that is being monitored has a public goods problem. If the members of the group monitor each other more easily than the supervisory personnel, then it may be rational for supervisors to contract with the group, not with individuals. The group will then require some internal structure that maintains incentives for individual performance. (Spence, p. 165.)

Moreover, even in the absence of the 'joint goods' type problem involved in team work, if individual screening is prohibitive, and monitoring is still desirable, then the particular structuring of wage incentives may be important. 'When the individual employee knows more about the job than supervisors, the best strategy may be to structure incentives so that the information is partially or completely revealed in the course of the performance of the job.'[12] Thus there are likely to be optimum payment systems (for instance combinations of piece and time rates),[13] and hierarchical authority systems, given the differing attitudes to risk of workers and employers, and the nature of the uncertainties faced.

(iii) *Experience rating and port-of-entry restrictions*   Finally, imperfections of information and the costs of acquiring them could also explain the practice of restricting entry within promotion ladders of many industries with internal labour markets to lower-level jobs.

It permits firms to protect themselves against low productivity types, who might otherwise successfully represent themselves to be high productivity applicants by bringing employees in at low level positions and then upgrading them as experience warrants. Restricting access to low level positions serves to protect the firm against exploitation by opportunistic types who would, if they could, change jobs strategically for the purpose of compounding errors between successive independent organisations. (Williamson *et al.*, p. 274.)

The reason why markets do not handle this experience rating function too well is not merely because it may not be in the interests of competitive firms to make their ratings public, but also because these experience ratings being partly subjective may not easily be communicable.

The advantages of hierarchy in these circumstances are especially great if those who are most familiar with an agent's characteristics, usually his immediate supervisor, also do the experience rating. The need to rationalize subjective assessments that are confidently held but, by reason of bounded rationality difficult to articulate, is reduced. (Williamson *et al.*)

The 'port of entry' restriction to lower-level jobs in these industries implies that labour turnover will be highest at these levels (rather than for more 'senior' personnel). Furthermore, it would suggest that it is the rate of remuneration for these port-of-entry jobs (the lowest 'skills') which would tend to be inversely correlated with quit rates for different firms and industries.

(iv) *Summary* Thus, largely dependent upon the technological conditions of particular industries, the informational requirements connected with different tasks, the need for task-specific training, the nature of the uncertainties attaching to different activities, and the relative degrees of risk aversion of various economic agents, there is likely to be a whole continuum of labour contracts in any economy, stretching from the sequential spot contracting of casual labour markets to the highly structured labour contracts associated with promotional ladders and restricted job-entry points of the hierarchical internal labour market in modern industry. The competitive model best provides an explanation of wage differentials where contracts are of the sequential spot contracting variety. But the emerging neoclassical analysis of internal labour markets would seem to provide the explanations for the wage structure in those industries where idiosyncratic tasks are of importance. We would expect to find promotion ladders within such industries since, in the context of imperfect information and the importance of task-specific on-the-job training costs, (*a*) such promotion ladders 'serve to reward meritorious performance and to reduce turnover . . . As a worker moves up a promotion ladder, the gap between his opportunity wage, at the entry point of an alternative firm and his actual wage widens'; (*b*) promotion ladders may be advantageous because 'workers may acquire not only specific information about their own jobs, but also specific training for higher level jobs in the firm'; (*c*) 'promotion ladders also provide a screening mechanism' (with the twin function of monitoring and providing incentives for job performance).[14]

Most of the above problems arise because of the imperfect information of employers about the 'ability' of their work force, and hence concern risks associated with the supply of labour. Most of the internal labour market solutions can thus be viewed as non-market institutional forms which provide second-best cost-minimizing contractual modes in the face of these uncertainties, when the first-best solution is infeasible because of the prohibitive transactions costs of delineating and enforcing sequential spot contracting competitive contracts.

(*b*) *Risks Associated with Labour Demand* However, there are equally important risks which employees face due to imperfect information about their em-

ployers behaviour and prospects which affect both their current and future
working conditions as well as the demand for their labour services.

(i) *Non-pecuniary chracteristics of the work environment*   There are important
risks which employees face due to imperfect information about their employers
behaviour and prospects which affect both their current and future working
conditions as well as the demand for their labour services.

Thus different firms are likely to have many non-pecuniary characteristics,
which workers can only discover after the individual works for the firm. Risk-
averse workers will then find that the 'effective wage' attached to a new job
must be sufficiently above that in his old job to compensate him for this risk.
Once again it is difficulties in communicating these non-pecuniary characteristics which mean that markets may not be good avenues for channelling this
information. This would also explain why a common feature of hiring practices in industries with idiosyncratic jobs, in both developed and developing
countries, are informal hiring procedures, with new workers (particularly
production workers) being hired through existing members of the firm's
labour force. The existing worker will be able to provide a better assessment
of these subjective elements of jobs in the firm to the potential recruit, whilst
the employer, who 'knows' his own employees abilities and judgement, may
also be able to rely on their judgement in screening potential workers for the
characteristics on which markets cannot provide enough information. Moreover, at least in developing countries where family or other group (caste,
tribal) ties are strong, for idiosyncratic tasks which involve team or group
effort, and hence pose the problems connected with non-separabilities,[15] it
may be efficient for firms to hire additional workers from those with family or
other existing group ties with their current work force. This would tend to
minimize some of the transaction costs connected with monitoring performance and providing individual incentives for work within team-type tasks.

(ii) *Uncertain labour demand, implicit contracts, and the cyclical rigidity of real
wages*   Another case concerns the observed downward rigidity of real wages
in much of the industrial sector in fact of cyclical changes in the demand for
labour. The 'implicit contracts' model (see Azariadis and Stiglitz, and Dreze)
seeks to explain this phenomenon in terms of the different degrees of risk
aversion of firms and workers, and the problems of moral hazard involved in
monitoring the changing value marginal product of labour over the trade
cycle which would make a competitive insurance-type contractual mode
infeasible for shifting the worker's risks.

Thus if a firm's demand curve and hence price of its output is subject to
random fluctuations, the value marginal product of labour for any given level
of employment will also be random. If workers are risk averse and are faced
with a choice of either a fluctuating wage equal to the random value of their
marginal product or a fixed wage lower than their expected value marginal
product, they will prefer the latter. This is because the higher risk associated
with the fluctuating earnings entails an additional utility loss for risk averse

workers, as compared with a fixed wage. For if they were risk neutral they would be indifferent between the fluctuating random wage and a fixed wage equal to the expected value of the random wage. As they are risk averse, however, they would be indifferent between a fixed wage lower than the expected value of their random marginal value product and the associated random wage.

Employers who are *ex hypothesi* less risk averse than their workers would also prefer to pay a wage lower than a random wage equal to the fluctuating value marginal product of labour. For suppose they were risk neutral: they would be indifferent between paying labour a wage equal to the expected value of the value marginal product or the random wage, and would then clearly be better off if they could get away with paying a fixed wage which was lower than this expected wage. Thus

both parties have incentives to sign a contract specifying a fixed wage unaffected by demand fluctuations. It is an employment contract coupled with an implicit insurance contract. The worker earns a wage equal to the marginal value product of his labour plus an insurance benefit in case of adverse business conditions, but minus an insurance premium in case of favourable business conditions. The insurance contract is underwritten by the firm itself and not by an insurance company because the firm has immediate access to the information required in order to monitor the contract (the marginal value product of labour). The insurance company would be confronted with a moral hazard problem (Dreze, p. 10).[16]

III Summary

Enough has been said, it is hoped to show how these emerging neoclassical theories can provide cost-minimizing and utility-maximizing rationales for various aspects of labour market behaviour which have hitherto been assumed to be the result of vaguely specified and unilluminating 'institutional' characteristics or 'customary' features of labour market behaviour. However, as these theories are based on deriving the second-best optimal responses for dealing with uncertainties due to imperfect information regarding both the demand and supply of labour, it is difficult to see how they can be 'tested'. For if, as these theories assert, it is the non-measurable and non-observable characteristics of work and workers which are the source of uncertainty, statistical proxies for these characteristics cannot be defined. If such proxies were available we would find employers using them in their labour allocation decisions, and we would then not observe these 'non-market' allocation processes.

In the remaining chapters of this book we seek to use these thoughts to exorcise the analytical demons which have imprisoned thought on labour markets and poverty in Kenya.

Notes

1 Thus in the simplest versions of the model it was implicitly assumed that the whole of the industrial labour force (N) was randomly rehired in each period from a pool consisting of the total urban labour force. The probability of finding a high-wage urban job (P) was then simply given by $P=N/L$. If W_a and W_u were the given agricultural and urban wages, the equilibrium condition for rural–urban migration would be $W_a = PW_u = N/L \, W_u = (1-u)W_u$ where, u is the rate of unemployment, and hence $1 - u = W_a/W_u$.

2 Or if there were perfect capital markets.

3 See Rees, p. 166 ff.

4 That this argument can be of some importance in the context of developing countries' labour markets has been pointed out by Scott in his discussion of the unrealistic predictions of the Harris–Todaro-type migration models about the induced level of urban unemployment for any given rural–urban wage differential. See Scott *et al.*

5 See Thurow, Wachter, Blaug. There are also difficulties in finding good proxies for the components of human capital, like on-the-job training. Age and experience are most often used, but are obviously inadequate. Also, as Wachter notes: 'Other variables in the skill array such as quality of schooling and manual dexterity, are omitted because they cannot be measured; hence the coefficients on the human capital term may be biased and any scalar measure of skill is severely limited and incomplete' (op. cit., p. 653.)

6 Rees, op. cit., p. 169.

7 Williamson *et al.*, p. 257.

8 Ibid., p. 271.

9 See Stiglitz (1975a).

10 Stiglitz, ibid., labels this the Walras law of screening.

11 Stiglitz, ibid., p. 35.

12 Spence, p. 166.

13 For an analysis of these see Stiglitz (1975) and Mirrlees.

14 Williamson, *et al.*

15 See Alchian and Demestz.

16 For a fuller discussion of implicit contract theory, and its implications for Keynesian demand management policies, see Lal (1982).

5

THE FUNCTIONING OF THE LABOUR
MARKET: AGRICULTURE

I Introduction

Underlying our discussion of labour market theory has been the theme that a transaction in the labour market is a complex undertaking. Employers are involved in selecting uncertain quality, supervising, and investing in skill accumulation. As a consequence behaviour which might superficially appear irrational might in fact be an optimizing contractual response to such an environment. In agricultural labour markets some of these considerations are less applicable than in industrial labour markets. In general skill acquisition is less important if only because basic skills are learned within the household. Similarly, quality variation between hired workers might be less significant and also better known by employers, the latter frequently being close neighbours of their potential employees. However, the supervision problem is potentially far more severe in agriculture than in industry. First, the consequences for production of variable performance by hired labour, often instantly noticeable on a factory production line, may be drowned by the combination of the long lags in the agricultural production function and the large random variations in productivity due to climate and disease. Poor work may often be undetectable just by means of its consequences. Second, specialization and the division of labour is generally less exploited, especially in smallholder agriculture, than in industry. Hence a single hired worker may perform a wide range of tasks, complicating the monitoring process. Third, agricultural work by its nature is not conducted in a fixed location, making a given level of supervision more expensive. As the Labour Department summarized the problem: 'In rural areas, the raising of individual productivity presents special problems not associated with urban employment—in particular, that of maintaining close supervision over widely dispersed labour forces' (Labour Department *Annual Report*, 1955, p. 10).

Because of the problems of enforcement of agricultural labour contracts it would be erroneous to assume that the Kenyan market for casual unskilled smallholder labour is an unproblematic efficient spot market. In fact, we will argue that smallholders have been markedly less successful than either plantation or industrial employers in surmounting the problem of contract enforcement. The inefficiency of the smallholder casual wage labour contract is studied in section II. Section III contrasts smallholder labour hiring with the plantations but suggests that despite large wage differentials the two sets of employers are operating in a common labour market subject only to geographic segmentation. Section IV investigates changes in this market over time, in particular focusing upon changes in contractual inefficiency within the smallholder labour market and changes in real wages.

II Smallholder Labour Allocation[1]

(*1*) *Introduction*

In the non-agricultural sector the predominant means by which factors are combined is through the labour market; that is, labour is hired to work with capital. In the agricultural sector no one factor market dominates the process of factor combination. Only on the plantations and very large farms is labour hiring the exclusive method of combination. Within the smallholder sector there is also substantial scope for factor exchange due to substantial differences in both absolute and relative factor endowments among households. Such differences have arisen partly because households are at different stages in the life-cycle and thus have different labour endowments (see Sen, 1975), and partly because of underlying endowment differentiation resulting from demographic, ecological, or economic processes. Thus, cross-section descriptions of household endowments reveal widely different proportions of land, labour, fixed capital, material inputs, and finance. If all households have access to the same production functions, then these different proportions generate differences in marginal products prior to market transactions. In turn these differences in marginal products create the opportunity for mutually profitable transactions in either factor or commodity markets.

If market transactions were unconstrained, costless, certain, and enforceable, then the particular form of the transaction would be undetermined. It would make no difference whether landowners hired labour or workers rented land, whether capitalists rented land and hired labour, or acted as money lenders. A further alternative would be for some degree of specialization in commodity production which could remove the need for any factor market transactions. In a world of such markets, poverty would be related directly to a lack of endowments. The ability to convert given endowments into income would be the same for all households.

In practice, rural factor and commodity markets are not characterized by costless, certain, and enforceable possibilities for exchange. Labour transactions involve an uncertain quantity of 'effort' on the part of the worker, and land transactions may involve uncertainty over changes in land quality due to cultivation practices, or in the possibility of repossession at the end of the contract, both viewed from the perspective of the landlord, and an uncertain land fertility as viewed by the tenant. Credit transactions may involve uncertainty concerning repayment. In addition to these contract-specific risks and uncertainties which arise from the conflicting interests of the parties to a contract, both parties operate in an environment of objective uncertainty concerning climate and crop prices and so may wish to enter into insurance or hedging transactions.

Because exchanges in rural markets potentially involve these elements of risk, quality uncertainty, and enforcement difficulties, the contractual form needed to overcome these obstacles to efficient transactions can be complex. A contract confined to a single transaction in a single market to be undertaken now at a specified price and quantity—the ideal–typical 'spot' contract —is often inappropriate. Sharecropping is an instance of a single contract blending transaction in the labour, land, credit, and insurance markets. Recent theoretical work has established that sharecropping is an economically rational contract superior to other forms of contract in environments in which there are multiple risks or limited information about labour quality. Empirical work on Asia has established that sharecropping is generally efficient in the sense that output per acre is not lower than on owner-operated farms.[2] Many labour transactions in rural Asia are now understood to be only part of multi-transaction contracts which include credit transactions (see Bardhan, 1980; and Bardhan and Rudra 1980). Such packaging of transactions into a single contract can be seen as attempts to overcome the obstacles which make 'spot' contracts unattractive.

In some circumstances there may be no feasible contract which enables efficient transactions to take place in a particular market. However, this need not upset the attainment of allocative efficiency and the direct connection between poverty and endowments. These appear robust because they are only broken if *all* of the possible mechanisms for preserving a common mapping from endowments to income fail simultaneously. The marginal products of land and labour will be equalized in all households if the hired labour market or tenancy or commodity specialization works efficiently. Any one of these processes is sufficient. Initial differences in land/labour ratios between households will give rise to differences in marginal products only if neither specialization in commodity production nor efficient exchange in land or labour markets is feasible. In the event of such a global failure of markets, poverty is not determined purely by the same process which determines endowments. The complex of market failures results in both a generalized loss in efficiency and in a different distribution of income compared with the case of efficient exchange. To understand poverty it becomes necessary to understand the constraints which confine feasible contracts to inefficient exchanges in all markets.

Factor and commodity markets in rural Kenya are unusual for the absence of contractual complexity in transactions. In contrast to rural Asia there is no sharecropping nor any linking of labour and credit transactions into single contracts. It will be argued that this is not because Kenyan circumstances are such that risk, quality, and enforcement problems do not render 'spot' contracts unattractive. Rather, it will be suggested, there are in Kenya additional constraints which preclude certain modes of contract. The roots of these constraints are a non-capitalist conception of property rights over land, combined with widespread absenteeism among landowners. In this environment landowners cannot monitor labour input, making labour hiring inefficient, but land hiring is precluded by the limited nature of the rights of land holders. Because of these contractual constraints upon transactions no market exchange mechanism remains by which a common mapping from endowments to income is generated. The consequence of this market failure is that rural poverty becomes a compound of low endowments and an unfavourable mapping from endowments to incomes.

In order to substantiate this thesis we need first to show that efficient transactions in Kenyan factor and commodity markets are contractually feasible. This is undertaken in sub-sections 2 (the labour market), 3 (the land market), 4 (the commodity market), and 5 (the credit market). Sub-section 6 brings together the analysis of the causes of these market failures and assesses their consequences.

(2) *Labour Transactions*

In sub-sub-section (*a*) data are compiled on the malfunctioning of the Kenyan rural labour market. For readers prepared to take stylized facts on trust, findings are summarized at the beginning of sub-sub-section (*b*).

(*a*) *Evidence* The most striking fact about labour utilization in Kenyan smallholder agriculture is that hired labour forms only a small component of total labour input, of the order of 10 per cent. Even in the most commercialized area of rural Kenya, Central Province, only some 11.3 per cent of the days worked on smallholdings (and 10 per cent of the hours) were done by hired labour.[3] Further, much of this hired labour was used to meet seasonal labour requirements as opposed to offsetting permanent differences in land/labour ratios between households. Hired labour in the slackest four-week cycle contributed only 6 per cent of total labour input. Of the hired labour used during the year on smallholdings, two-thirds had contracts as casual day-labour and one third as regular (monthly-based) labour. However, even the regular labour force was largely seasonal, only 30 per cent of the regular hired labour force being employed in the slackest cycle. The theory of multi-transaction contracts which include a labour transaction predicts that, if regularly hired labour was employed through such contracts, there would commonly be a differential between the wage rates of casual and regular hired labour. There is no evidence of such segmentation between the casual and regular smallholder hired labour markets in Kenya. Mean daily earnings for the two groups were virtually identical.

While segmentation by type of employment contract does not appear to be present, the smallholder labour market is segmented geographically. Cross-section surveys reveal wide variations in wages between different regions. For example, in the SPSCP Survey of 1975/6 the mean wage in Eastern Province was 40 per cent higher than in Western Province. In 1982 wage rates in Central Province were approximately double those in Nyanza. That the smallholder hired labour market should be geographically differentiated is not surprising. Much hired labour is casual labour hired by the day in the immediate locality of the holding. Tribal barriers and lack of accommodation preclude long-distance speculative migration for work on smallholdings. Long-distance intra-rural migration is confined to the employment on estates which, enjoying recruitment economies of scale, enter into contracts in the locality of origin of the potential migrant.

However, of more significance than the failure of market processes to equalize the marginal product of hired labour between localities, is the failure to do so within localities. Table 5.1 analyses the contribution that hiring of labour by smallholders makes towards reducing *ex ante* differences in factor proportions among smallholdings. In part *A* of the table the data base is the *Integrated Rural Survey I* (*IRS I*) which provides the closest approximation to national coverage currently available. *Ex ante* differences in factor endowments are large; for example, land per household member[4] on holdings above 5 hectares is nineteen times greater than that on holdings of less than 0.5 hectares. The rows of the table show the percentages of the population, land, and hired labour distributed over holdings divided into four size classes. Thus, 13.5 per cent of the total smallholder population is resident on holdings of below 0.5 hectares. The same holding size group accounts for 1.5 per cent of the total smallholder land area and for 5 per cent of the total amount of labour hired by smallholders. The paradoxical finding of Table 5.1*A* is that there is a clear inverse relationship between farm size class and labour hiring per hectare. Normalized on hired labour per hectare on holdings of 5 hectares and over, holdings in the size class 2.0–4.9 hectares use 48 per cent more hired labour per hectare, holdings in the size class 0.5–1.9 hectares use 175 per cent more hired labour per hectare, and holdings in the smallest size class use 450 per cent more hired labour per hectare.

The hiring of labour by smallholders tends therefore to widen the absolute gap in the amount of labour used per hectare between larger and smaller holdings. Since, however, smaller holdings hire less labour *per household member*, the gap between labour/land ratios is narrowed. A priori, it is ambiguous whether this widening of the absolute difference in labour input and narrowing of the difference between labour/land ratios reduces or further widens both the absolute and relative difference between the marginal product of labour on large and small farms.

One possible explanation for this result is that the national data on land area used in Table 5.1 make no allowance for differences in land quality. It might be that the larger holdings are tracts of inferior land which can only

Analysis

Table 5.1

The Hiring In and Out of Labour by Farm Size

	Farm size class (hectares)				
A. National data	<0.5 ha	0.5–1.9	2–4.9	5+	All
per cent population	13.5	42.0	27.4	17.1	100
per cent land—by area	1.5	21.0	41.2	36.3	100
—by value	1.5	16.4	41.8	40.3	100
per cent hired-in labour[a]	5	35.0	37.0	22.0	100
hired-in labour per hectare (5 + class = 1)	5.50	2.75	1.48	1.0	
per cent hired-out labour[b]	14.0	45.0	29.0	12.0	100
hired-out labour per hectare (5 + class = 1)	28.23	6.48	2.13	1.0	
hired-out labour per household member (5 + class = 1)	1.48	1.53	1.51	1.0	

B. Murogeto sub-location	0–4	4+	All
per cent population	76.5	23.5	100
per cent land area	38.0	62.0	100
per cent hired-in labour	57.8	42.2	100
hired-in labour per hectare (4 + class = 1)	2.23	1.0	
per cent hired-out labour	86.3	13.7	
hired-out labour per hectare (4 + class = 1)	10.28	1.0	
hired-out labour per household member (4 + class = 1)	1.94	1.0	

[a] The data in *IRS* I are the farm wages bill. We assume here that the mean wage rate paid does not differ between size classes in order to convert the data into labour quantities.

[b] The data in *IRS* I are for earnings from casual and regular employment. We assume here that the mean wage rate earned does not differ between size classes in order to convert the data into labour quantities. In support of this assumption, there are no significant differences between size classes in the ratio of casual to regular earnings. The assumption is reconsidered below.

Sources: For A, *IRS* I; for B, derived from Bager (1980), Table 14.

sustain low labour/land ratios. Whilst a priori this has some plausibility it is not confirmed by other data. First, *IRS* I also collected estimates of land market values. To the extent that market value is a proxy for land quality we can check to see whether there is a discrepancy between land shares by area and shares by value. In fact, as Table 5.1*A* reveals, there is a close correspondence between shares by value and shares by area with a tendency for the larger holdings to have a *higher* value per hectare. This suggests that explanations which rely upon differences in land quality lack credence. The same relationship is also found when the *IRS* data are disaggregated to the regional level. Further evidence that large holdings hire less labour per hectare than smaller holdings is provided in Table 5.1*B*. Here the data base, is that of a single sub-location with a uniform quality of land. Holdings below 4 hectares use 123 per cent more hired labour per hectare than holdings above 4 hectares. Finally, a survey conducted for US Aid in three provinces during 1975/6 (ATAC 1977) found the same relationship in each province. Holdings with less than 5 acres used 76 per cent more hired labour per acre than those with 5 acres or more in Western Province, 55 per cent more in Eastern, and 51 per cent more in South Nyanza.

We conclude that labour hiring by smallholders does not make any substantial contribution towards equalizing the marginal productivity of factors and may well be disequalizing. We next consider whether labour sales by smallholders serve as an effective alternative. Sales of labour by smallholders can be divided into that labour which is sold to other smallholders and that which is sold on the non-smallholder labour market.

We have seen that some 10 per cent of labour used on holdings is hired. There is no accurate data on the proportion of this hired labour provided by smallholders as opposed to that provided by landless labourers. Using indirect estimates based on the *IRS* I and the *1978 Labour Force Survey* (Government of Kenya, forthcoming), approximately 60 per cent (within a range of 50 per cent to 75 per cent) of hired labour appears to be landless, the remainder owning some holdings, generally of below average size. Thus, only some 4 per cent of total smallholder labour input is provided by smallholders working for other smallholders, and much of this is merely seasonal interchange. This sale by itself is clearly inadequate to even out the large differences in factor proportions between farms.

The non-smallholder labour market provides more important opportunities for smallholders to sell their labour. Again, there is no direct data on how much smallholder labour is sold on this market. Using indirect procedures[5] our best estimate is that 15 per cent of total smallholder labour is sold on markets other than the smallholder hired labour market.

Our estimates of the allocation of labour resulting from labour transactions is set out in Table 5.2.

Some 18 per cent of the smallholder labour endowment is therefore hired out. The distribution of these labour sales by farm size category is presented in the last three rows of Table 5.1*A*. In each size class under 5 hectares some 50 per cent more labour per household member is hired out than on holdings over 5 hectares. Naturally, this fairly uniform selling of labour per person represents radically different labour sales per hectare. Labour sales therefore narrow the absolute differences in labour input per hectare but only modestly reduce differences in labour/land ratios, leaving the differences among the first three size categories unchanged.

Unlike labour hiring transactions, labour sales do unambiguously tend to equalize marginal products of factors on farms of differing sizes. It is note-

Table 5.2

The Allocation of Smallholder Labour

	Best Estimate	Probable Range
Total smallholder labour of which:	100	
hired to other holdings	3	1.5–3.5
hired to non-shamba employment	15	10–20
work on shamba	82	76.5–88.5
Labour hired from landless for smallholdings	5	4–7.5

worthy that over 80 per cent of smallholder labour sales are in the non-smallholder labour market. The pressure of enormous differences in factor proportions appears to be insufficient to enable mutually profitable transactions to be contracted in the smallholder labour market. Rather, the pressure leads to differential sales of labour on other markets. Even so, the combined effect of all labour market transactions by smallholder households may increase differences between marginal products of factors on farms of differing sizes. In Table 5.3 the data of Table 5.1*A* are combined with our estimates of the magnitudes of labour transactions to calculate the net change in farm factor proportions in different size classes resulting from labour transactions.

Each size category is a net seller of labour, but the net sales of the largest holdings are close to zero, while those of the smallest are around 16 per cent of the total labour endowment. However, the contribution which labour markets make towards an equalization of factor proportions is small, and their contribution towards the equalization of the marginal product of labour is ambiguous. From row (8); of Table 5.3 we find that the absolute differences in land per worker between size classes is generally increased. For example, holdings in the smallest farm size class experience an increase in land per worker of only 0.007 hectares compared with a mean increase for all holdings of 0.037 hectares. The difference in factor proportions between the smallest and the largest size class is reduced from 19:1 to 16:1, but the absolute difference in land per unit of labour-input actually widens.

While the figures used in Table 5.3 represent only orders of magnitude, the central conclusion which we draw from the analysis is quite robust. This is that participation in rural labour markets by smallholders has failed to be of a magnitude or of a direction such that it could be regarded as making a substantial contribution towards reducing the poverty and the inefficiency consequences of inequalities in initial endowments of the land and labour. It is indeed striking that such equalizing tendencies as the labour market

Table 5.3

The Contribution of Labour Transactions to Smallholder Factor Proportions

	Farm size (hectares				
	<0.5 ha	0.5–1.9	2.0–4.9	5.0 +	All
(1) percentage of household labour which is hired out	18.7	19.3	19.1	12.6	18
(2) percentage of household labour remaining for use on holding (100—(1))	81.3	80.7	80.9	87.4	82
(3) labour hired in as percentage of household labour	3.0	6.7	10.8	10.3	8
(4) net market effect per cent on labour used on holding ((3)—(1))	−15.7	−12.6	−8.3	−2.3	−10
(5) labour used on holding as percentage of household labour (100—(4))	84.3	87.4	91.7	97.7	90
(6) hectares per family member before labour market transactions	0.037	0.183	0.502	0.703	0.334
(7) hectares per worker on the holding after labour market transactions	0.044	0.209	0.548	0.719	0.371
(8) change in hectares per worker on the holding due to labour market transactions	+0.007	+0.026	−0.046	+0.016	+0.037

Sources: Table 1, *IRS* I, and previous text.

provides come predominantly through the indirect effect of differential sales of labour to non-smallholder labour markets rather than through the direct exchange of labour among smallholders. There are, of course, smallholders who own small plots working for those who own larger ones, but the extent of this is limited.

(*b*) *Analysis* The preceding compendium of data has sought to establish four stylized facts of the rural labour market in Kenya. First, there is our initial paradox: an inverse relationship is found between hired labour per hectare and farm size. Second, the extent of labour hiring by smallholders is very limited despite large differences in factor proportions. Third, the extent of sales of smallholder labour on the non-smallholder rural labour market is also very limited, so that such transactions do not provide an alternative mechanism of equalizing factor proportions used on farms. Finally, the net effect of rural labour transactions by smallholders may well be to amplify rather than to reduce initial differences in acreage per cultivator.

These stylized facts generate three puzzles to be explained. First, *given existing modes of contract* in the smallholder hired labour market, an explanation is required for the limited extent of transactions and for the paradoxical pattern of those transactions. Secondly, why are smallholder labour sales on the non-smallholder rural labour market so limited? Finally, the most general problem to be explained is why transactions in the smallholder labour market are limited to a mode of contract which both theory and the experience of Asian rural labour markets suggests is inappropriate. Are there, in fact, constraints upon the formulation of contracts which are at the root of the manifest failure of the Kenyan labour market to cope with endowment differentiation? We defer consideration of this last question; the two former questions we take in turn.

There is a standard argument that hired farm labour is expensive relative to family labour because of a combination of supervision costs and the low incentive for unmonitored effort. Some indication of the lower productivity of hired labour in Kenya is provided by the effect upon the productivity of hired labour of the introduction of piece rates. Piece-rate contracts are only feasible in a limited range of agricultural activities and so cannot be adopted as a general solution to the problem of variable labour effort, but they permit a demonstration of the sensitivity of labour input to the mode of contract. Cowen and Murage (1974) give two instances of a change from day rates to piece rates. In 1962 tea picking switched to piece-rate contracts and mean output per person per day rose by 275 per cent. In the late 1930s, when contracts for land digging changed to piece rates, productivity more than doubled.

The lower productivity of hired labour provides an explanation for its limited use in the face of large differences in factor proportions on farms, an explanation well established in the literature (see Sen, 1975). In the limiting case, hired labour transactions would not occur and farms would be cultivated entirely by family labour.

In order to generate an explanation for the differential use of hired labour on large and small holdings the simple model of hired labour inefficiency must be modified. One approach is to introduce some seasonal variation in the demand for farm labour. Consider, for example, a two-season model in which labour is used first for planting and subsequently for harvesting. Labour inputs in the two seasons are thus complementary factors. Suppose that planting requires less labour than harvesting to the extent that all households use only family labour for planting. Finally, for simplicity assume that the family labour input is the same in the two periods. Formally, agricultural production per hectare is a function of family labour used in planting (F_1) and total labour used in harvesting (L_2):

$$Q = Q(F_1, L_2) \tag{1}$$

L_2 is the sum of family labour (F_2) and hired labourers (H) weighted by their lower efficiency (h) to convert them into equivalent units of family labour:

$$L_2 = F_2 + h.H. \tag{2}$$

The marginal product of a hired labourer is therefore:

$$Q_H = h.Q_{F2}. \tag{3}$$

For a given number of hired labourers per hectare an increase in family labour input per hectare will change this marginal product according to (4):

$$Q_{HF} = h.Q_{F2F2} + h.Q_{F2F1}. \tag{4}$$

Diminishing marginal productivity makes the first term negative, and complementarity of factor inputs makes the second term positive. It is therefore possible that more family labour input per hectare, such as will occur on smaller farms given that h is less than unity, will imply a higher marginal product of a given quantity of hired labour per hectare and hence a greater use of hired labour per hectare. This result is preserved when the model is generalized to many periods and a variable family labour supply. However, one prediction of the model is that in the slackest period of labour demand either no labour is hired or larger farms hire more labour per hectare than smaller farms. We have no Kenyan data with which to test this prediction. However, whilst the annual differences in hired labour use by farm size reported in Table 5.1A are very large, the monthly variations in the use of hired labour are not (the trough being around half of the peak). It therefore seems unlikely, if farms over 5 hectares use more labour per hectare in the trough month than farms below 0.5 hectares, that over the year the latter should use 450 per cent more than the former. Whilst the seasonal variation model may provide part of the explanation for our opening paradox, it appears to be inadequate as the only explanation.

An alternative (or additional) explanation is provided by regarding the inefficiency of hired labour (h) as a variable. Family labour may provide a supervisory role as well as being directly productive, so that the efficiency of hired labour may be a function of the quantity of family labour input on the farm. This is likely to be a particularly powerful consideration in the event of absentee ownership. On holdings where the owner is not generally present the unit cost of hired labour in efficiency units may indeed be so high as to encourage a very land-intensive form of cultivation.

Little evidence is available about the extent of absentee ownership in Kenya. The *IRS* I found that nationally 20 per cent of holders[6] both lived away from the holding and were not in charge of day-to-day decisions about operating the holdings. In Central Province, the most commercially advanced region, this rose to 31 per cent.[7] A small survey conducted by Cowen and Murage found that 90 per cent of the smallholdings over 7 acres were owned by absentee heads of households such as teachers and businessmen.

In Kenya absenteeism generally takes the form of the husband working away while the wife remains on the holding. Social mores restrict hired agricultural labour almost entirely to males so that on absentee holdings hired labour involves males being supervized by females. Some researchers have suggested that in a male-dominated society female supervision is liable to be less effective than male supervision.

The explanation can be stated formally. Given the land and capital endowments, agricultural production per hectare (Q) is a function of labour input per hectare (L):

$$Q = Q(L), \ Q_L > 0, \ Q_{LL} < 0. \tag{5}$$

Labour input per hectare in efficiency units normalized on family labour is the sum of family labour (F) and the number of hired labourers (H) deflated by their relatively lower efficiency (h):

$$L = F + hH. \tag{6}$$

The efficiency of hired labour is a function of the intensity of supervision provided by family labour:

$$h = h(F), \ h_F > 0, \ 0 \leq h \leq 1. \tag{7}$$

The marginal product of a hired labourer is therefore:

$$Q_H = h(F).Q_L \tag{8}$$

For a given number of hired labourers per hectare an increase in family labour will change this marginal product according to (9):

$$Q_{HF} = h.Q_{LL} + Q_L.h_F. \tag{9}$$

If $Q_{HF} > 0$ then an increase in family labour per hectare, by raising the productivity of hired labourers, will make the marginal labourer intra-marginal and thus increase the optimal number of labourers hired. In the absence of any relationship between the number of family workers per hectare and the efficiency of hired labourers, h_F is zero and so Q_{HF} is strictly negative: farms with a high input of family labour per hectare would use less hired labour per hectare. However, with h_F positive the sign of Q_{HF} is a priori ambiguous and it is quite possible that over some range of family labour input Q_{HF} is positive.

A further possible explanation of the differential use of hired labour is if larger farms have access to labour-saving technologies denied to small farms due to scale economies. In Kenya the major instance of this is the use of tractors for land preparation, a process which is likely to involve scale economies. However, we must reject this as the dominant explanation for it entails that larger holdings, having a technological advantage over smaller holdings, would be more productive. In fact it will be shown that they are drastically less productive, supporting our previous explanation which rested on supervision diseconomies of scale.

The above explanations have both focused upon influences on the marginal product of hired labour. We now turn to a second possible variable, namely a divergence between the marginal product of hired labour and the wage rate. In simple models of household income maximization hired labour will be employed up to the point at which its marginal product equals the wage rate. However, since the wages of hired labour must be paid before output is either known or sold, this equality will not survive the introduction of costs of borrowing, financing constraints, or uninsurable risks. In such situations the hiring of labour will be restricted to a level at which its marginal product is above the wage.

In Kenya, the hiring of agricultural labour involves a substantial cash-flow burden. In 1975 to hire a full-time labourer would have cost around 2,000 shillings per annum.Since the output of most crops runs at least annually in arrears, this is the order of magnitude of the financing problem per worker hired. But mean household income per annum was only 3,650 shillings, and mean asset value per household only 6,900 shillings. This asset value was largely in illiquid form, such as land, buildings, and planted crops. Paradoxically, an important way of financing hired labour might well be the possession of an income from wage employment. In this case the same household might both hire in and hire out labour. For example, households in the size range 2–4.9 hectares both hire in and hire out more labour than those with holdings above 5 hectares. It might be that households with large holdings never experience the pressure of population which gives an incentive for non-shamba employment, whereas those in the lower-size category are first pushed off their land but are then able to finance a labour intensive form of cultivation.

Whist a financial constraint upon labour hiring can help to explain why so little labour is hired, it cannot explain why smaller holdings hire more labour per hectare unless it is maintained that financial constraints *per hectare* are more severe for larger holdings. In some rural factor markets such conditions might apply; for example, Griffin (1977) postulated an inverse relationship between capital per hectare and farm size in Colombia on these grounds. In Kenya, however, credit to the smaller farms is so attenuated that such a thesis is less likely. The issue is taken up again when the credit market is examined.

The remaining aspect of the rural labour market to be considered is the failure of the non-smallholder sector to hire sufficient smallholder labour to equalize factor proportions on holdings. A priori it might be expected that the opportunity of smallholders to sell their labour to this sector would establish a common rate of return to labour, and hence common factor proportions, on all but the largest holdings. We argue that in fact the more attractive employment opportunities are not freely accessible to small-holders, whilst those opportunities which are accessible offer returns too low to be worthwhile for most smallholders.

The major hirers of rural labour other than smallholders are the estates.

This labour market is considered in the next section where we argue that monopsonistic practices on the part of employers tends to depress earnings throughout the rural labour market, and that apparent opportunities for earnings above those offered by smallholdings only reflect the greater disutility attached to plantation labour contracts.

Two other major employment sectors, non-agricultural formal sector wage employment and self-employment, may not provide opportunities for the rural near-landless. To some extent access to jobs in the formal wage sector has been rationed by educational credentials, whilst access to self-employment opportunities commonly requires both skills and finance. The remaining accessible sector is therefore wage employment in the informal non-agricultural sector. In the urban component of this sector wage rates have been bid down to very low levels, partly because of the ability of young single male migrants to survive on very little whilst living as dependents in the households of wage employees. These migrants may be learning skills, or simply waiting for something better to turn up. Wage rates in the sector are frequently below the level at which a worker could support a family so that the sector provides only limited income opportunities for near-landless households. Currently, too little is known about wage employment in the rural non-agricultural informal sector to ascertain whether it shares the characteristics of the urban sector.

Rural wage rates are generally low. *IRS* I data reveal that if all the family labour available to the mean smallholder household were sold on the smallholder hired-labour market it would generate an income of some 1,950 shillings per annum.[8] This then must have been approximately the income level of landless households with the same demographic structure as smallholder households but dependent upon selling their labour to smallholders. The mean income of smallholder households was 3,650 shillings per annum, nearly double that of labouring households. A small survey by Cowen and Murage found an even wider differential of 190 per cent, though part of this was accounted for by a smaller household size.

To summarize the above discussion of the rural labour market, we have sought to establish that it does not provide an effective mechanism whereby factor proportions are equalized across holdings of differing size. This is primarily because of a failure in the smallholder hired labour market. Given the existing model of contract by which smallholders hire in labour, the productivity of additional hired labour is potentially very low, especially on the larger holdings, and this is compounded by financial constraints which restrict labour hiring to a level at which the marginal product of hired labour is probably well above the wage. However, a second labour market mechanism which potentially might equalize factor proportions, namely the sale of smallholder labour to other sectors, fails to do so because a combination of monopsony and entry barriers depress earning opportunities for smallholders.

Of itself, the failure of the labour market mechanism to equalize factor returns is of little consequence: either transactions in the land market or specialization in commodity production can achieve the equalization of factor returns even in the absence of a labour market. The failure in the labour market acquires significance through its conjunction with the failure of both of the alternative mechanisms. It is to these that we now turn.

(3) Land Transactions

Land exchange may occur in a variety of contractual modes. The length of contract can range from seasonal rental to the infinite rental period which constitutes a permanent transfer of ownership. Payments can precede or lag the flow of use of land, thus forming an inter-linked land and credit contract. Payments can be fixed in advance or be dependent upon the output from the land, thus forming an inter-linked land, labour, and insurance contract. In none of these forms is there an extensive land market in Kenya: most holdings are acquired through inheritance.

Bager's survey of Kisii in 1978 (Bager 1980) found that only 3 per cent of the total land area farmed by smallholders in his sample had been acquired by purchase, and a further 6 per cent of land was 'rented'. This 6 per cent included land that had been left with a relative whilst the household was outside the district, although rent was not usually paid in such cases. Carlsen's survey in Nyanza and Coast provinces found that 9 per cent of smallholder households were renting some land and 10 per cent had purchased some land. The SPSCP survey (ATAC 1977) in Western, Eastern, and South Nyanza provinces found only 1 per cent of the land area held by smallholders to be hired in, a further 2 per cent being borrowed without payment. Sharecropping contracts were found on only two holdings in a sample of nearly 800. Finally, in the national *Integrated Rural Survey IV* of 1978/9 only 5 per cent of rural households were found to be renting in any land, the total area being rented accounting for only 0.9 per cent of the smallholder land area. Sharecropping contracts were again vanishingly rare, being found in less than one per cent of all tenancies; that is in less than 0.05 per cent of all households. There is little evidence on the relationship between land rental and land size. Carlsen reports survey data for Kisii showing some tendency for smaller holdings to rent more land than larger holdings: those with holdings below 2½ acres were renting twice as much as those with over 5 acres, and the same amount as those with 2½–5 acres. The land rental market thus probably tends to equalize factor proportions, but its effect is slight because the extent of tenancy is limited. The failure of the land rental market to equalize factor proportions can, in fact, be deduced from Tables 5.1 and 5.3. The land distributions shown in these tables (wherein large differences in factor proportions are revealed) already allow for land rentals.

The concept of a holding used in *IRS* I included any land rented in or borrowed by the household and excluded any land rented out.

Typically, Kenyan land rental contracts display the reverse of the normal inter-linkage between land and credit transactions. Bager notes that all the rental is paid at the start of the contract, the normal renting period being for one, two, or three years. Since those who rent land are generally poorer than those who lease it, and also have a cash-flow problem generated by the cultivation of the rented land, it is normal for tenants to be in net receipt of credit. It is a pointer to some powerful obstacle to factor market transactions that in Kenya the inter-linkage runs the 'wrong' way. Why, for example, is the rental not paid as a flow contemporaneous with the use of the land?

Whilst the land rental market is so small as to have had only a negligible equalizing effect, land purchase appears to have effected a net transfer of land from smaller to larger holdings. Migot-Adholla (1977), Livingstone (1981), Carlsen (1980), and our own data from Table 3.7 all suggest that there has been some increase in land concentration through purchases and sales in the land market. Carlsen shows that, stratifying by income, it was the poor who were making land sales and the higher income groups who were making purchses. Our own data shows that in Central Province over the period 1963–74 there was a substantial increase in the concentration of holdings. This gives the combined effect of rentals, sales, inheritance, and settlement. Whilst the data base for land market transactions is not adequate to support a quantification of the effect upon factor proportions and marginal products, the qualitative inferences to be drawn are disturbing. It appears that land market transactions are inadequate in scale and quite probably perverse in direction as a mechanism for equalizing factor proportions between larger and smaller holdings.

The foregoing description of land transactions poses three puzzling features: the limited extent of land rental, the perverse land and credit inter-linking, and the inability of land-scarce households to purchase land. Our explanation for the limited extent of tenancy parallels that of the failure of the hired labour market, namely that the contractual mode of the transaction involves the parties to the contract in enforcement problems. Probably the most important constraint upon tenancy is that in the absence of any tradition of tenancy there is no social value system enforcing the contract. As a consequence, the landlord sees himself as risking a permanent loss of property rights becaues of the difficulty of ensuring physical repossession of the land. Traditional East African land law is complex and variable.[9] However, a universal feature is the absence of a capitalist concept of individual property rights over land. The structure of traditional rights and obligations were generally specific to a particular function of the land, such as grazing. As noted in Chapter 1, control of some rights might be exercised at the level of the extended family, of others at the level of the clan, administration sometimes being by the chief. The individual household had *usage* rather than *ownership* rights to the land. In such a system tenancy contracts are invalid because, by definition, the landlord is not using his land and therefore forfeits his rights over the land. The present state of Kenyan land practice is a limbo world between this traditional system and capitalist property rights. At the time of *IRS* I (1974) some 25 per cent of the smallholder acreage has been legally registered as belonging to individuals, although the register is not always up-to-date. The remaining 75 per cent is gradually being registered. However, even on registered holdings there must be considerable uncertainty for a potential landlord. It is clearly perceived in rural Kenya that land law and land policy remain in a state of flux. In particular, there are many thousands of 'squatters' on large farms, and also large farms which have been unofficially sub-divided by their multiple owners. At some stage the position of these groups will be regularized and at such a time usage may again become the criterion by which property rights are assigned. The present state of land rights is therefore rather unsatisfactory, for it precludes usage-enhancing exchanges which would occur either under the traditional tenure system or under a capitalist system.

The absence of a social value system enforcing tenancy contracts may also explain the paradox of the perverse inter-linking of land and credit transactions. Landlords may fear that they will be unable to ensure regular payment of rent except by getting all the rent initially. This will be compounded in the case of absentee owners, for whom the monitoring and enforcing of payments is more difficult.

While the potential property rights of tenants might account for the attenuated form of the rental market, they do not provide any explanation for the limited extent of land sales. Since those with little land relative to their labour cannot rent land and cannot effect an offsetting exchange through labour markets, why do they not purchase land? We develop an answer by way of a discussion of asset pricing, wealth composition, and credit; land values are high relative to the non-land-based wealth of smallholders, so that purchases of land would have to be financed by credit. To substantiate this, first we review evidence on land values.

The average value per hectare reported in the 1974 *IRS* was 780 shillings. This conceals substantial variations. In densely populated areas the land price is very much higher: Bager reports a land price in Kisii in 1972 of 23,000 shillings per hectare and a rental of 400 shillings. The price of 780 shillings thus radically understates the cost of land in land-scarce areas. Overwhelmingly the most important realizable smallholder asset (other than land itself) is livestock. Livestock ownership is correlated with land ownership, partly because private grazing is often required. Those holdings with less than 0.5 hectares of land owned 1,500 shillings of livestock, and those with 0.5–20 hectares owned 1,900 shillings. Using the *IRS* data, at the Kenyan average land price sale of this livestock would enable the purchase of some two hectares of additional land, at the land price prevailing in Central

Province it would purchase one hectare, and if Bager's figure is correct then in Kisii it would purchase less than 0.1 hectares. In buying land the household would also commit itself to the purchase of inputs necessary for cultivation, which are approximately 100 shillings per hectare. In addition, the household would lose the income formerly generated by its livestock. For holdings of below 2 hectares the average annual income from livestock was 257 shillings. This must be set in the context of annual cash consumption for households operating holdings of less than 2 hectares of around 1,700 shillings. To summarize, land purchase other than by means of credit would involve either the elimination of a household's liquid assets or a drastic curtailment in expenditure. The amount of land which households in the bottom land size categories could purchase, even were they prepared to realize all their liquid assets, would merely raise them to the next smallest size category. Thus, land purchase financed by assets could not make a major contribution to equalizing factor proportions.

In fact, since land is a lucrative asset even as a speculative proposition, there is evidence to suggest that a considerable amount of land purchase has been undertaken by absentee urban high-income groups. Directly, this leads to an increase in concentration and worsens the imbalance in factor proportions between larger and smaller holdings. Indirectly, by raising land values relative to other assets it inhibits the intra-smallholder exchange of land whereby land-scarce households could purchase land from land-plentiful households. The inability of land-scarce households to finance land purchases out of liquid wealth would not matter were they able to borrow. This they cannot do. The analysis of this constraint is deferred until a fuller treatment of the rural credit market is made.

Having established that factor proportions are not equalized across farms either through labour market exchanges or through land exchanges, we turn to the pattern of commodity production to investigate whether this acts as a substitute for factor markets.

(4) Commodity Specialization

The remaining degree of freedom in the system whereby an initially skewed distribution of endowments would not additionally lead to an inferior return on endowments for the poor, thus compounding their poverty, is through specialization in the commodity market. Indeed, it is one of the standard theorems of international trade that differences in factor proportions will not lead to differences in factor returns if appropriate specialization occurs. In the Kenyan context 'appropriate' specialization in production would be for the land-abundant larger holdings to be planted disproportionately to land-intensive crops (predominantly the food crops) whilst the smaller holdings were planted to the labour-intensive crops (predominantly pyrethrum, coffee, and tea).[10]

In Table 5.4*A IRS* data are arranged by size class for the three major food crops and the three major cash crops. There is some evidence for commodity specialization, *but the direction is perverse.* The smaller holders tend to specialize in land-intensive crops and the larger holdings in labour-intensive crops. Table 5.4*B* investigates the same relationship but at the sub-location level, using data derived from Carlsen. With the exception of the largest size category the same finding emerges strongly.

Table 5.4

Commodity Specialization

A. *IRS* Data

	Farm size class (hectares)				
	<0.5	0.5–1.9	2.0–4.9	5+	All
Percentage of total acreage of local maize, hybrid maize, and beans	6.1	35.8	36.8	21.3	100
Percentage of total land area	1.5	21.0	41.2	36.3	100
Propensity to use land for major food crops (5+ size class = 1)	6.93	2.91	1.52	1.0	1.70
Percentage of holdings in size class growing:[a]					
Pyrethrum	6.2	8.8	8.6	16.2	
Coffee	10.2	32.9	30.7	10.9	
Tea	8.3	26.9	32.1	11.7	
Total[b]	24.7	68.6	71.4	38.8	

[a] *IRS* I does not publish data on the area of these major cash crops broken down by size of holding.
[b] This total will include some double counting of holdings which grow more than one of the three crops.
Source: *IRS* I.

B. Three Sub-locations

		Farm size class (hectares)			
Sub-location		<2.4	2.5–4.9	5.0–7.4	7.5+
Murogeto	major food crops[a] area (%)	47	40	37	37
	major cash crops[b] area (%)	24	32	37	24
	other land uses (%)	29	28	26	39
	total land (%)	100	100	100	100
	ratio cash area/food area	0.51	0.80	1.0	0.65

Table 4.5 *B.* (*cont.*):

Sub-location	Farm size class (hectares)			
	< 2.4	2.5–4.9	5.0–7.4	7.5+
Werugha major food crops[c] area (%)	57	47	33	17
major cash crops[d] area (%)	19	19	13	5
other land uses (%)	24	34	54	78
total land (%)	100	100	100	100
ratio cash area/food area	0.33	0.40	0.39	0.29

	Farm size class (acres)			
	0–3.9	4.0–6.9	7.0–13.9	14+
Kikonerii major food crops[c] area (%)	92	77	59	56
major cash crops[f] area (%)	8	21	37	23
other land uses (%)	0	2	4	21
total land (%)	100	100	100	100
ratio cash area/food area	0.09	0.27	0.63	0.41

[a] Maize, millet.
[b] Pyrethrum, tea, coffee.
[c] Maize, beans.
[d] Onions, potatoes, tomatoes, coffee.
[e] Maize.
[f] Sugar, tree crops.
Source: Derived from Carlsen (1980).

It is clear that in Kenya commodity specialization has not provided a mechanism for preventing the unfavourable entitlements of the poor from leading to an additionally unfavourable exchange-entitlement mapping. Again we attempt to explain a paradox in rural factor utilization, in this case the paradox being perverse commodity specialization. There are two power-ful forces, risk and cash flow, both inducing a specialization directly opposing the factor proportions influence. Unfortunately, the land-intensive crops are generally food crops. It is a risk-averting strategy for the household to grow at least a proportion of its own food crops since this eliminates one element of risk, the relative price of food and the cash crop. This risk argument is less powerful if the holding is diversified into many cash crops, if income is high, or if liquid wealth is substantial, but all these mitigating factors are them-selves correlated with land size.[11] In Kenya there is also an additional element of risk since sometimes the maize market is rationed so that reliance upon purchased food involves the risk that none will be available. The combination of uncertain price and uncertain availability makes subsistence cultivation a rational choice for those with little land even though it reduces the returns to household labour.

While the labour-extensive crops are generally food crops, the major labour-intensive crops are tree crops with long gestation periods. This is particularly true of coffee and tea, the major smallholder cash crops, there being no yield from coffee for the first four years, while tea yields take eleven years to reach their mature maximum. The labour-intensive crops therefore pose severe problems of cash flow for smallholder households. In addition to the financing of inputs needed during the gestation period, there is the output foregone by diverting land to tree crops. Since, as will be shown, the smaller holdings have considerably higher yields per hectare than the larger hold-ings, not only are the households with smaller holdings at least able to finance this gestation period, but their financing problem is considerably greater per hectare diverted. As with the hiring of labour and the purchase of land, therefore, the problem can be traced back, at least in part, to an unsatisfied demand upon the credit market. It is necessary, therefore, to consider why the rural credit market does not cater adequately for the needs of land-scarce households.

(5) *Contractual Constraints upon Credit*

Smallholder credit, by its nature, is a market which will tend not to be cleared through price adjustment alone (the interest rate). Because the default risk increases with the interest rate, rationing among applicants for credit will generally occur in equilibrium (see Stiglitz and Weiss, 1981). The criteria for rationing will clearly be to select applicants with the lowest risk of default. In Kenya three characteristics have tended to be favoured as indi-cating a low default risk. David and Wyeth (1978) have shown that the commercial banks, which now provide considerable flows of credit in rural Kenya, favour applicants with collateral or those with secure wage employ-ment in the formal sector. The most common form of collateral is land presently owned, which clearly works to the disadvantage of those with little land. This leaves as a means of access to the commercial banks for the near landless the possession of a secure formal sector wage employment. It is, for example, quite common for secretaries in Nairobi to borrow from banks to finance land purchase. This pushes the problem for the landless one stage further back: namely, to the acquisition of appropriate wage employment. Here the near-landless might appear to have an advantage over those with land since, from Table 5.1, we find that they get a disproportionately high share of the wage income which is generated by sales of smallholder labour. However, this would be to ignore differences in the type of employment obtained. National data are not available on this issue so we must rely upon the sub-location data collected by Bager. He disaggregated wage employ-ment into 'qualified', 'unqualified', and casual. A qualified job is defined as a job where a person cannot be accepted without some previous education. Table 5.5 reveals that, whilst households with large holdings earn considerably less in total from wage income, they earn more from wages for qualified employment than households with smaller holdings.

Table 5.5
Wage Income by Type of Job, Murogeto Sub-Location

Wage income (mean shillings per household)	Farm size (hectares)		
	0–1.0	1.1–4.0	4.1+
Qualified jobs	574	1,014	1,133
Unqualified jobs	857	232	0
Casual jobs	129	28	29
Total	1,560	1,274	1,162

Source: Bager (1980), Table 14.

Both the criteria employed by commercial banks tend to favour those who already possess larger holdings. Banks could lend to the landless simply on the collateral of the land to be purchased, but they do not, presumably because they are worried about a high likelihood of default and subsequent recovery problems. To the extent that the landless would devote a greater proportion of their new acreage to subsistence cultivation it might be anticipated that sales per hectare would be lower on smallholdings, making repayments more difficult. Such an anticipation would, in fact, be false.[12] However, it appears to have been a widely held view in official circles, having been influential in the decision to retain the larger farms. Banks might also anticipate difficulties in repossessing land especially if it is the only homestead. Finally, repossessed land once sold might not cover debts, so that banks might feel the need to require additional forms of collateral. For whatever reason, the commercial banks have failed to provide finance for land acquisition by the near landless. The definitive study of the subject concludes:

Credit standards employed by commercial banks largely restrict their rural lending to businessmen who can provide reasonable security and a reasonable assurance of repayment, and to part-time farmers who have modern sector jobs, in the civil service, for example, in addition to title deeds to land. (Von Pischke, p. 307.)

The commercial banks are not the main channel of smallholder finance (though they may be a major source of funding for land purchases). Marketing co-operatives are the most common method by which smallholders gain access to finance, the co-operatives themselves generally being funded by the aid agencies.[13] There is generally excess demand for loans and so the co-operative societies also ration loans. In their case the collateral used is not land but is a direct deduction from future crops marketed through the co-operatives. Future crop marketings are typically estimated on the basis of the sales over the previous three years. This system clearly favours those already growing cash crops. The main loan programme, the Integrated Agricultural Development Programme, concentrates on loans with a duration of twelve months only, loans for the purchase of land being expressly precluded. Whilst the marketing co-operatives do provide a mechanism for financing the expansion of cash-crop production, the rules of fund allocation appear likely to preserve rather than to remove differences in incomes. Thus, in Central Province, where loan financing is most developed, *IRS* I found that the value of loans outstanding differed markedly between income classes. Smallholders earning below 2,000 shillings per annum on average had loans of only 200 shillings compared to loans of over 1,000 shillings for smallholders with incomes above 4,000 shillings.

Between them, the commercial banks and the marketing co-operatives account for nearly all smallholder credit. Money lenders, common in rural Asia and West Africa, are almost entirely absent. This is presumably related to fears of a very high default rate because informal debts other than within the extended family would lack the enforcement of social sanction.[14]

(6) Constraints on Contracts: a Summary of the Argument

The cumulative empirical conclusion of the preceding sections has been that none of the potential market mechanisms by which factor returns might be equalized despite differences in initial factor proportions in fact operates. The proximate explanations for this disturbing result have been identified as the inadequacies of existing contractual modes. Transactions are being attempted within a contractual framework in which major elements of the transaction are either unenforceable or unknown. As a result, actual transactions are so much less efficient than they potentially might be that they are curtailed to a rump of their expected magnitude. This pushes the analysis to a deeper level of social explanation, for the question which naturally arises is why has it not proved possible in Kenya to devise different modes of contract which circumvent these inefficiencies. In rural Asia complex contracts have been devised which appear to have overcome the inefficiencies encountered in Kenya. For example, in the study by Bliss and Stern one quarter of all farm land was cultivated under contracts of share tenancy. Productivity was as high on tenanted as on owned land, and there was no relationship between farm size and productivity per hectare. Why, for example, is there no share-tenancy in Kenya?

One explanation might be that in the absence of a tradition of market relationships, complex contracts have not had sufficient time to develop. Such an explanation can almost certainly be rejected because one complex contract, share-ploughing, is relatively common. In the share-ploughing contract, in exchange for ploughing a field the plough-owner retains part of the field for his own cultivation for the duration of a single crop. This differs from share-cropping in three key respects. First, the landowner gets all the payment for his land rental in advance (by way of his land being ploughed) instead of in arrears, thus eliminating default risk. Second, the landowner himself cultivates a substantial part of the field so the plough-owner does not become the sole user of an integral unit of land, thus reducing the difficulties of repossession. Third, the landowner is able to gain access to a scarce and powerfully labour-saving capital good, overcoming the financial constraints upon plough purchase or cash rental.

If Kenyan smallholders are sufficiently ingenious to devise the plough-sharing contract then it is reasonable to conclude that what inhibits share-cropping and other modes of contract is not a lack of ingenuity; rather, smallholders are constrained to inefficient contracts because other modes are not feasible. The roots of these constraints we have suggested are a combination of a non-capitalist conception of land rights and widespread absenteeism of landowners. In such an environment landowners cannot monitor labour input, which makes labour hiring inefficient,[15] but land hiring is precluded by the limited nature of the rights of land holders. Thus, the ability to monitor performance and the structure of property rights operate as constraints which delineate the set of feasible contracts. Many potentially mutually profitable transactions may be impossible to accommodate in feasible contracts. Even as a general proposition in economics this statement has received relatively little attention. As a proposition in developing country agriculture, it has been largely neglected (except tangentially in the Asian sharecropping literature and that on the provision of smallholder credit). As a proposition explaining the near-total failure of factor markets in rural Kenya it appears to be new. If so, it is surprising because the consequences of that failure are calamitous. It is to this that we now turn.

The major prediction of a proposition which accounts for differences in factor proportions in terms of contractual constraints is that factor returns will not be equalized across farm size groups. Specifically, the expectation is that smaller holdings will have lower marginal and average returns to labour but higher returns to land than larger holdings. This is indeed the case. From *IRS* data the value of output per unit of labour rises systematically with size of holding. Compared with the smallest of the four holding sizes the second size group has a 13 per cent higher return on labour, the third size group a 38 per cent higher return, and those with the largest holdings a 62 per cent higher return. Conversely, output per hectare is radically lower on the larger holdings. This is the case for the value of total output, for the value of marketed output, and for the volume yield of specific crops. For example, total output per hectare on holdings over 8 hectares is only one twentieth of that on holdings below half a hectare.

The failure to equalize factor returns has important corollaries for output, for income distribution, and for poverty, which are developed in Chapter 8.

III The Plantation Labour Market

An apparently puzzling feature of the Kenyan rural labour market is the juxtaposition of the small and very low-wage smallholder hired labour market with a considerably higher wage plantation labour market which is characterized by persistent labour shortage. Wage rates on plantations were, for the historical reasons discussed in Part One, not subject to the minimum wage legislation which applied in the urban formal labour market. During the 1960s, when minimum wages had a substantial effect in the urban labour market, plantation wages were in real terms significantly below those of the urban unskilled. However, they have always been considerably above those prevailing in the smallholder sector, typically by 20–30 per cent. For example, the hourly smallholder wage identified in *IRS* I (1974) was 0.74 shillings (see page 149 of this book), compared with 0.9 shillings paid on estates,[16] a 21 per cent premium.Evidence on the persistence of labour shortage comes from a series of Government-commissioned reports (see also Livingstone, 1981). The questions to be answered are, first, why do the estates pay above the wage offered by smallholders and, second, given that they do, why is there a labour shortage rather than a labour surplus? Kenyan plantations are distinct from smallholder farms in three key respects. First they are mono-crop whilst the typical smallholding is diversified into multiple crops and indeed several non-crop income sources. This difference in choices reflects the ability of financially large, limited-liability companies to entertain a degree of income risk quite inappropriate for a smallholding. Second, the plantations are confined to a very limited range in the spectrum of agricultural activities both in terms of the crops grown and the quality of output which they choose to produce. Third, the plantations, being very large units of employment relative to smallholdings, will benefit from any economies of scale. In general there is no evidence to suggest economies of scale in Kenyan agriculture. Fitted production functions on smallholder data show exponents summing to unity or significantly less. Our previous discussion has emphasized that because larger holdings have a higher ratio of hired to family labour they will be subject to the diseconomies of reliance upon inefficient hired labour contracts worsened by a deteriorating ability to supervize hired labour. However, when account is taken of the first two points, there is reason to believe that plantations indeed enjoy economies of scale in enforcing hired labour contracts. Mono-crop agriculture in particular crops enables them to reduce the tasks of agricultural labour to a very narrow range of activities which simulates the conditions of labour activity in manufacturing processes. The crops selected by the plantations, principally coffee and tea, are tree crops with a high ratio of picking activities to soil preparation, planting, and weeding activities. This is important because picking is a more clearly defined activity in which productivity is easier to monitor. Even with picking there is a range in which quality is variable. It is notable that in tea, for example, the quality of pickings optimal for plantations is lower than that adopted by smallholders: quality monitoring is more difficult (and hence more costly) than quantity monitoring.

Piecework rates of pay for picking activities are similar on plantations to those prevailing on smallholdings for the same activities. The slightly higher rate on the estates probably reflects the extra transport costs, the more hierarchical employment structure, and the necessity of living away from home associated with plantation agriculture as compared with working for close neighbours. The main component in the wage differential between smallholder hired labour and that employed on the estates is therefore a reflection of the wage differential between readily monitored and unmonitorable activities, since smallholdings and estates employ labour in a different mix of these two types of activity. Evidence on the very considerable difference in labour productivity under piece-rate and day-rate contracts has already been set out above (page 124). Since labour-supplying households may choose to supply their labour to either type of contract, their marginal decisions will equate the earnings of one unit of labour disutility across the two contracts. A unit of labour disutility will reflect disutilities attached to both time spent at work and effort expended per time period. Hence, disutility differentials between contracts need not equal labour efficiency differentials. For example, a piece-rate contract which doubles labour effort per time period (and hence doubles labour productivity) may require a differential in hourly earnings of less than 2 : 1 because the worker prefers one hour of intensive effort to two hours of less-intensive effort. The analysis is depicted in Figure 5.1.

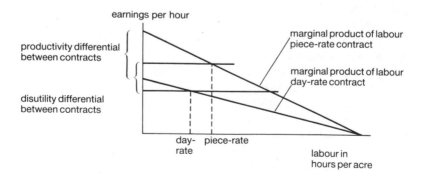

Fig. 5.1

In the absence of any disutility differential between contracts, a productivity differential would result not in an earnings differential but only in a differential between the land/labour ratios adopted under the two contracts. Estates, using piece-rates, would be more labour-intensive than smallholdings using day-rates but would not offer higher earnings. If there is a disutility differential which is positive but less than the productivity differential then higher earnings on the estates will co-exist with greater labour intensity.

Data availability is not yet adequate for the proper testing of this hypothesis. However, present evidence on the overall relative labour intensity of estates and smallholdings shows that the estates are some 30 per cent more labour-intensive than the average smallholding.[17] Recall from section II that among smallholdings, as dependence upon hired rather than family labour increased, the labour intensity of cultivation was reduced. Thus, the estates appear to be considerably more labour-intensive than those smallholdings which use predominantly hired labour.

It should be noted that the greater efficiency of hired labour on plantations reflects their ability to use closely monitored contracts rather than more generalized scale economies in agricultural technology. The large mixed farms, which unlike plantations are multi-activity enterprises in which labour monitoring is difficult, operate on extremely high land/labour ratios. Such farms appear to suffer from the same diseconomies of scale involved in using poorly-monitored hired labour which we have postulated as applying within the smallholder sector. Indeed, this is why, were market forces allowed to operate, the large mixed farms would be broken up into smaller units. The legislation which has preserved large farms intact is both damaging and illogical. It is damaging because the rationale for the legislation, namely that economies of scale exist which make it imperative to retain production in large units, is completely false. It is irrational because were the rationale for the legislation correct, that is were economies of scale indeed present, then market forces would themselves prevent the break-up of large units, and so the legislation would be unnecessary.

The second feature of the plantation labour market which requires explanation is the persistence of labour shortage (see Chapter 1). Labour shortage, which has been a persistent complaint of the estates, means definitionally that they wish to hire more workers than they can get at the wage which they choose to pay. Thus the wage must be below the marginal product of labour. This is the classic characterization of monopsony behaviour in the labour market. Facing an upward-sloping supply curve of labour, the enterprise would choose to equate the marginal product of labour with its marginal cost, the latter being above the wage (Figure 5.2).

The plantations have clearly possessed such monopsony power in the labour market for they set wages collectively, and collectively they employ a significant proportion of the rural landless wage labour force. Currently, employment on the estates is around 260,000, which is probably somewhat

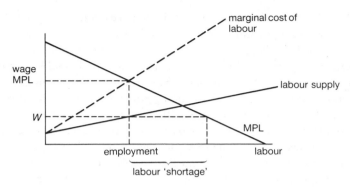

Fig. 5.2

less than the number of the landless working for smallholders. The *IRS* I estimated 1,480,000 smallholdings with on average around four people working on each holding, 10 per cent of this being hired. This would give an estimate of around 590,000 man-years of wage employment on smallholdings. Combined with our previous estimate that around 40 per cent of this hired labour was supplied by smallholders, this would imply total employment of the landless of around 350,000 man-years. In aggregate, the estates are therefore not in a dominant position in the hired agricultural labour market, the bulk of hiring (some 70 per cent) being done by smallholders.

However, the hired agricultural labour market appears to be geographically segmented for reasons of tribe, limited information, and limited housing. Labour shortage in Coast Province coexists with labour surplus in Western Kenya. Even within Western Kenya some estates have considerable difficulty in hiring labour. The existence of monopsony power on the part of the estates is made consistent with their low overall share of hired agricultural labour by the geographic segmentation noted above. Regulation of the estates is made difficult by their use of casual labour contracts for one third of their employees, and by the practice of sub-contracting employment, recruitment, and supervision to agents outside the scope of official regulation. In part, the practice of sub-contracting may be a response to the inefficiencies of the 'spot' labour hiring contract, replacing the 'spot' contract with an implicitly longer-term contract subject to close monitoring of performance. In part, it is probably an explicit means of avoiding such limited regulation as is currently enforced.

However, there is a strong case for some government intervention to raise wages in the plantations. Any minimum wage between the current wage rate and the current marginal product of labour (*W* and MPL in Figure 5.2) would increase employment and improve allocative efficiency as well as increasing the earnings of the existing employees. We have argued that, through the marginal decisions of some households concerning the allocation of their labour supply, the estates and smallholder labour markets are integrated despite a disutility-compensating earnings differential. Hence, raising earnings and employment on the estates would raise the wage rates of hired labourers on smallholdings. Conversely, the exercise of monopsony power by the estates depresses the earnings of all agricultural wage labourers who, we will argue, form a significant category of the poor.

It is ironic that during the 1950s and 1960s, when the monopsony power of the estates was substantial and there was a clear case on the combined grounds of employment generation, efficiency, and equity for legislated minimum wages on the estates, that in fact they were exempted from the minimum wage laws which were applied in urban areas. The monopsony argument did not apply to urban employers as hirers of unskilled labour, and so the employment and efficiency gains which would have occurred in the agricultural labour market became employment and efficiency losses in the urban labour market. Further, the greater equity which would have occurred in rural areas became the greater inequity of a temporarily legislatively-segmented urban labour market. In short, the coverage of the minimum wage legislation was precisely counter to economic rationale.

IV Adjustment Processes in the Agricultural Labour Market

In Section II we suggested that rural factor transactions are severely curtailed due to a failure to overcome the problem of contract enforcement. Our brief history of urban labour markets has, however, emphasized that temporary institutional aberrations, such as the high urban wages of the mid-1960s, should not be mistaken for permanent structural characteristics of an economy. We therefore turn to a dynamic analysis, starting with the issue of contract enforcement. In particular, we investigate whether present constraints upon contracts can be interpreted as a temporary learning phase during which factor markets are in transition towards a pattern of transactions comparable to that found in rural Asia. We then investigate changes in agricultural wage rates in the context of changes in labour supply and demand. This contributes to an understanding of how the market works and provides evidence on changes in the living standards of the rural landless.

(1) Changes in Contractual Efficiency

Our analysis of smallholder factor markets has relied upon evidence which relates only to the mid-1970s. The structure of the analysis is of a particular system of rights combined with absenteeism constraining contractual feasibility to a limited range of inefficient transactions, resulting in resource misallocation and accentuated poverty. The dynamic counterpart to this static analysis is that changes in rights and in the extent of absenteeism should lead to changes in the volume and contractual mode of factor market transactions.

In practice, quantitative information upon past changes in the process of factor exchange is limited because of the lack of suitable survey data prior to the *IRS* I in 1974/5. The only comparison which can be made reliably is for Central Province where the *IRS* data can be matched against a survey of 1963 (Government of Kenya, 1968). Between 1963 and 1974 the major change in the constraints upon contracts was probably an increase in absentee ownership resulting from cumulative rural-to-urban migration. Whilst survey data are not available for the extent of absenteeism in 1963, by 1974 in Central Province the owner was neither living on nor himself operating[18] the holding on 31 per cent of all holdings. During the period 1963 to 1974 there hada been substantial rural-to-urban migration, in particular from Central Province to the nearby city of Nairobi, the African population of which grew from 156,000 in 1962 to 421,000 in 1969.[19] To put this in context, the total population of Central Province in 1969 was only 1.6 million. We might expect that this increase in absenteeism would make labour hiring both a more necessary and less efficient as supervision became more difficult; the net effect upon labour hiring being a priori ambiguous. In fact, over the period reliance upon hired labour doubled from 5 per cent to 10 per cent of the total labour used on holdings. It is tempting to interpret this increased penetration of labour transactions as indicating that labour allocation was gradually improving. However, the opposite appears to be the case. Table 5.6 repeats the analysis of Table 5.1 for five districts of Central Province,[20] focusing specifically upon hired labour per acre. Recall that in 1974 the smallholder hired labour market both nationally, regionally, and in one sub-location where separate analysis was possible, had the effect of increasing the absolute difference in labour use per hectare. Small farms hired more labour per hectare than large ones. No such pattern emerges in any of the five districts of Central Province in 1963. Larger farms clearly tended to hire more labour than smaller farms. This is not to suggest that the hired labour

Table 5.6

Hired Labour per Acre: Central Province 1963

(days per acre)

District	Farm size (acres)		
	0–4	4–8	8+
Kiambu	10.0	10.7	16.2
Fort Hall	6.2	4.9	9.2
Embu	1.8	5.9	4.8
Nyeri	8.4	8.4	16.9
Meru	3.7	6.5	9.1

Source: Government of Kenya (1968), Tables 18 and 28.

market was making a significant contribution to equalizing factor proportions in 1963. Man/land ratios were between two and three times higher, depending upon district, on farms below four acres than on farms above eight acres.

The doubling in the proportion of hired labour used over the eleven years cannot, therefore, be represented as an indication of a reduction in contractual constraints. It appears that the allocation of hired labour among holdings of different sizes was more efficient in 1963 than in 1974, which is consistent with the hypothesis that the growth in absenteeism differentially lowered the efficiency of hired labour on the larger holdings. Rather the explanation for the increased use of hired labour is to be found partly in a greater need for hired labour and partly in a probable cheapening in hired labour relative to family labour. The intensification in the need for hired labour came about through migration of family labour and an increase in land concentration.[21] Because larger farms use a much greater proportion of hired/family labour than smaller farms, the increase in land concentration which occurred over the period *ceteris paribus* would greatly have increased the share of hired labour. The land share of the 40 per cent of the population with least land fell by nearly a third, while that of the most land-abundant 30 per cent of the population increased by nearly a quarter (see Table 3.7). If the ratio of hired/family labour had stayed constant for each holding size group, this increase in land concentration would have raised the average share of hired/family labour from 5 per cent to 9 per cent. Over the same period the poorest 40 per cent of the smallholder population of Central Province possibly suffered a fall in their share of total household income, their real incomes rising less rapidly than the better-off 60 per cent of smallholders (see Table 3.6 and the discussion on page 000). Since the poorer households form a major part of the pool of labour sellers while the better off 60 per cent of households constitute the vast majority of hired labour demand, such a change in relative incomes would probably generate a consequential change in factor prices. The opportunity cost of family labour in the labour-hiring households may therefore have risen relative to the wage rate needed to attract hired labour. Such a change would have induced a further substitution into hired labour and away from family labour. Hence, the observed doubling of the hired/family labour proportion from 5 per cent to 10 per cent appears to indicate not a greater degree of efficiency in the labour market, but rather a response to a widening disparity in relative endowments not offset by a declining degree of contractual efficiency brought about by absenteeism.

Looking to the future, there seems little reason to expect that the hired labour contract can be developed so as to surmount the inefficiencies which have prevented direct labour exchange from generating a common return to endowments. Although hired labour may expand further as a proportion of total agricultural labour, this may again be a response to a widening gap in labour productivity rather than a process of reducing a given gap.

Differential sales of smallholder labour on other labour markets are also unlikely to become a powerful means of equalizing factor proportions because of the development of the private education system in rural Kenya. The higher-income smallholder households have been able to buy a higher level of education for their children and this should afford them better access to wage employment opportunities, and through that to credit.

Our conclusion is that at present there is little reason to believe that within a reasonably short period smallholder factor exchange will develop to the extent required to overcome the current losses through allocative inefficiency and the unfortunate distributive consequences of this inefficiency.

(2) Change in Wage Rates

The investigation of changes over time in rural wages is important both as a guide to understanding how the labour market works and as an indicator of changes in the living standards of the rural landless. Evidence on earnings series on the estates and the limited data available on trends in smallholder wage rates have been presented in Part One. However, to be useful as a guide to how the labour market works, wage series need to be combined with series on labour demand and supply. For the smallholder labour market this data combination is seldom available. Further, because of the geographic segmentation noted in Section II, trends in the smallholder labour market are best investigated at the level of a locality rather than from national data which are the aggregation of distinct markets. As with the preceding study on changes in contractual constraints, the only comparable survey data which includes changes in wages together with labour supply and demand is for Central Province between 1961–3 and 1974/5. We investigate what changes occurred in labour supply and demand and wage rates during this period to determine whether the former are qualitatively compatible with the latter.

Our estimate of changes in the supply of agricultural labour between 1963 and 1974 is set out in Table 5.7. Despite rapid population growth the labour force available for agriculture aged 15–60 stayed roughly constant, and may even have fallen slightly.

Changes in the demand for family and hired labour are estimated as follows. Using survey data for 1963 and 1964 the utilization of family and hired labour per acre is calculated by holding size and by crop. Had these crop and size-specific utilization rates of labour stayed constant, labour demand would have altered due to an expansion in land area, a change in the size distribution of holdings, and a change in the mix of crops. Consider first the expansion in land area. Between 1963 and 1974 there was a 9.4 per cent growth in the area of land per person on smallholdings from 0.35 ha to 0.38 ha according to the two surveys. The rural population grew by some 29.5 per cent over this period and the proportion of rural households which

Table 5.7

Smallholder Labour Force, 1963–1974

	1962	1963	1969	1974
Population of Region	1,234,200[a]	1,264,014[b]	1,458,649[c]	1,643,551[d]
urban	27,866	28,971	36,419	43,826
rural	1,206,334	1,235,043[b]	1,422,230	1,599,725[d]
Percentage adults of working age	48.6[e]			41.3[f]
Participation rates	0.75[g]			0.75[g]
Regional labour force		460,733		509,090
Wage employment		65,818[h]		122,894[i]
Rural agricultural labour force		394,915		386,196
Normalized		1.0		0.9779

[a] *Statistical Abstract* (1964), Table 13.
[b] Interpolated 1962–9.
[c] *Statistical Abstract* (1976).
[d] Extrapolated 1962–9.
[e] *Statistical Abstract* (1964), Table 17, African population of Kenya.
[f] *Demographic baseline Survey 1973*, Table II.3, rural population of Baseline area.
[g] Assumed, though the growth rate is not sensitive within the plausible range of values.
[h] *Employment and Earnings 1963–67*.
[i] *Employment and Earnings 1976*.

were landless, and hence not part of the smallholder population, fell from some 23 per cent to 15 per cent.[22] Combining these elements yields an estimated increase in total smallholder acreage of 57 per cent. This is broadly in line with the 64 per cent increase in acreage deducible from large-scale land-use surveys.[23]

Second, consider the effect of changes in land distribution. In 1963 labour utilization differed markedly by holding size as is shown in Table 5.8. Between 1963 and 1974 there was a substantial increase in land concentration, as was shown in Table 3.7 Because large holdings use radically less labour per acre than smaller holdings this increase in concentration would have reduced the total demand for labour had the relationship between holding size and labour use been constant. The data permit alternative methods of quantifying this effect; using different procedures Gunning (1980) estimated that the reduction in labour demand was 20 per cent and Collier (1980) that it was 17 per cent. The net effect of land-area expansion and land concentration was therefore to raise the demand for labour by around 30 per cent.

Table 5.8

Labour Use by Man/Land Ratios, 1963

Per cent population (by land size)	Hectares per household member	Propensity to use Labour per hectare	
		family	hired
40	0.231	1.56	0.70
30	0.347	0.73	1.07
30	0.515	0.52	1.32
All	0.351	1.0	1.0

Source: Economic Survey of Central Province 1963/4.

Third, consider the effects of the changes in the cropping pattern documented in Table 5.9. Data on crop-specific labour inputs in Central Province during the early 1960s are taken from the Nyeri Survey, 1964. Had these labour inputs applied throughout Central Province in both 1961 and 1974, then the change in the cropping pattern (treating land area cropped as a

Table 5.9

Distribution of Cropping Area by Major Crops, 1961–1974

Crop	Percentage cropping area			Change in relative area 1961–74	
	1961[a]	1969[b]	1974[c]	Absolute percentage	Relative percentage
traditional maize	39.2	39.9	26.3	−12.9	−32.9
hybrid maize	0	1.9	10.3	+10.3	+∞
total maize	39.2	41.8	36.6	−2.6	−6.6
pulses	33.3	31.4	26.3	−7.0	−21.0
potatoes	6.4	1.8	12.2	+5.8	+90.6
sweet potatoes	5.6	1.6	1.4	−4.2	−75.0
vegetables	0.8	0.7	4.0	+3.2	+400.0
coffee	1.2	7.1	3.6	+2.4	−200.0
tea	0.2	1.7	4.4	+4.2	+2,100.0
All	100	100	100	0	0

[a] *African Agricultural Census 1960–61.*
[b] *Statistical Abstract* (1976), Table 91.
[c] *IRS* I.

constant) would have raised the demand for crop labour by 28 per cent. Changes in the composition of livestock can similarly be incorporated, the most significant change being an increase in the proportion of cattle which were of improved breed from 7 per cent to 70 per cent. This and other changes would have increased the labour input per hectare of cattle by some 23 per cent.

The combined effect of the expansion of land area, the increase in land concentration, and changes in the cropping pattern and the composition of livestock was to raise the demand for labour by around 63 per cent had activity and size-specific labour coefficients stayed constant. Since the labour force available for smallholdings was roughly constant, activity-specific labour coefficients must by 1974 have fallen to some 60 per cent (1/1.63) of their level in the early 1960s. This is confirmed by survey data, the 1964 Nyeri survey recording labour input per hectare of crops as 188 days per annum and the 1974/5 *IRS* I recording 112 days, this being 60 per cent of the 1964 figure.

This large fall in activity-specific labour inputs must have substantially raised the marginal product of labour, which in turn would have raised the real wage to hired labour. Offsetting this would be the decline in the efficiency of hired labour relative to family labour suggested in (1) above.

Two independent estimates of the change in the agricultural real wage are available. From the *Economic Survey of Central Province*, Table 43, mean wage payments per smallholding were 56.3 shillings per year in 1963, and from *IRS* I, Table 8.24, mean payments in 1974 were 227.7 shillings. The increase in the number of households can be estimated from the increase in the rural population (29.5 per cent), the increase in household size (21.4 per cent), and the reduction in the proportion of rural households which were landless, to have been 18.2 per cent. So nominal aggregate payments to hired labour rose by 378 per cent ([1.182 × 227.7/56.3] − 1). To convert this into nominal earnings per labourer we require the change in the number of labourers hired. The proportion of shamba labour hired rose from 5.32 per cent to 9.82 per cent, the total shamba labour force falling by 2.2 per cent (Table 5.7). Thus, the number of hired labourers increased by 81 per cent ((9.82/5.32) × 0.978). Hence, nominal earnings per labourer increased by 165 per cent (4.78/1.81), which represents a real wage increase of 57 per cent. Additional evidence for the rise in real wages come from hourly and daily wage rates. The *Economic Survey of Central Province* cites the daily wage rate as 2.13 shillings (Table 21) and *IRS* I shows hourly wages to have been 0.7425 shillings in 1974 (Figure 11.9 and Table 8.24). The typical working day for smallholder hired labour is around seven hours, giving a daily wage rate of 5.2 shillings. This would suggest an increase in real wages of 44 per cent.

Hence, the evidence on wage rates paid by smallholders indicates a real increase of 57 per cent or 44 per cent depending upon the method used to make the calculation. The analysis of section III suggested that the smallholder- and estates-hired labour markets were integrated despite a persistent wage differential due to the differential disutility of work. Hence, the real earnings of workers on estates should change in line with those on smallholdings rather than in line with urban wages, the trajectory of which we will argue was the result of temporary non-market effects. From Tables 2.10 and 3.12 this is indeed confirmed, for over the period 1963–74 real wages on the estates rose by around 52 per cent.

Consider, now, the implications of this evidence for the interpretation of how the smallholder labour market works. Various studies have suggested that in some rural areas of developing countries wage rates are subject to long-term rigidities determined either by tradition, the implicit collusion of labourers, or the nutritional relationship underpinning an 'efficiency wage'. None of these hypotheses of wage rigidity appear applicable in rural Kenya. The wide differences in wage rates between regions would, to be consistent with the efficiency wage hypothesis, require radically different region-specific relationships between wages and effort which is implausible. Further, the real wage change identified in Central Province, namely a 50 per cent increase between 1963 and 1974, implies that even if wages were at some non-market-clearing floor level at the start of the period (for which there is little evidence) this could not have applied by 1974. The increase in real wages between 1963 and 1974 is qualitatively compatible with a competitive market framework of demand and supply.

In section III we suggested that the agricultural labour market was not, in fact, entirely competitive since we postulated monopsony power on the part of the estates. Two factors indicate that monopsony power has been reduced over time. First, the growth in the smallholder hired labour market has reduced the proportion of all agricultural wage labour hired by the estates. For 1974 we have estimated this share at 30 per cent. In 1963 employment on the estates was virtually the same as in 1974 (see Tables 2.14 and 3.10), while smallholder labour hiring was half of its 1974 level in Central Province, the only area for which this comparison can be made. Hence, in 1963 the proportion of all agricultural hired labour employed by the estates was probably close to 50 per cent. Second, the improvement in rural transport networks must have reduced the localized monopsony of the estates. The resulting reduction in monopsony power should, according to our previous analysis, yield an increase in the level of estates employment at any given wage rate, or alternatively stated, an increase in the wage rate at any given employment level. This is indeed what occurred. Despite a real wage increase of some 50 per cent employment was no lower in 1974 than in 1963, suggesting that the potential for a legislative counterweight to the earlier monopsony power of the estates might have had the effects predicted in section III.

The changing monopsony position of the estates aside, the framework of a competitive market appears applicable for the study of changes in agricultural wage rates. However, the implications of this framework may well be less encouraging than any direct inference from the sharp increase in real wages observed in Central Province between 1963 and 1974, for both the region and the period are atypical. First, Central Province experienced an atypically large increase in the demand for agricultural labour compared with other regions because smallholder agricultural innovation, which as we have seen was strongly labour-using, proceeded more rapidly in Central Province than elsewhere (as will be established when we turn to the smallholder sector in Chapter 8). Further, Central Province experienced atypically low increases in labour supply (indeed on our estimate there was no increase) because of its proximity to Nairobi, the major source of incremental urban employment during the period, which enabled the Kikuyu to gain a disproportionate share of new urban employment opportunities. Second, the period 1963–74 was also atypical since it was one of unusually slow growth in the labour force available for agriculture. This was partly due to demographic factors. Note from Table 5.7 above that there was a sharp fall in the proportion of the population of working age between 1963 and 1974. This resulted from an acceleration in the rate of population growth due chiefly to a fall in infant mortality. Hence, the rate of growth of the labour force was also accelerating though lagging some years behind that of the population. Further, as will be argued in Chapter 7, the rapid growth of the urban population was a temporary phase which did not persist beyond the early 1970s. Net migration to urban areas has been sharply reduced and is therefore making a much smaller contribution towards reducing the rate of growth of the rural labour force available for agricultural work.

Hence, if indeed agricultural wage rates are determined by the interaction of demand and supply, their future trend may well be dismal unless rapid increases in the demand for agricultural labour are forthcoming.

Notes

1 This section is based on Collier (1983) and (1983a).

2 On both the theory and Asian evidence see Binswanger and Rosenzweig (1981).

3 The data source for this and much of the subsequent analysis is the *Integrated Rural Survey I, 1974–5*, Bureau of Statistics, Nairobi, 1977. In this survey, which we refer to as *IRS* I, a smallholding was defined as a holding of less than 20 hectares. Some 97 per cent of surveyed holdings were in fact less than 8 hectares.

4 Ideally it would be better to use land per member of the labour force belonging to the household. Unfortunately, at present the data are not available in this form. However, whilst household size is an inaccurate indicator of household labour force, so in practice would be any measure since the specification of dependency in farm households is problematic. The resulting inaccuracy in our measure of labour force is dwarfed by the large differences in factor proportions between households.

5 One means of estimating from *IRS* data is to take the proportion of the population aged over seventeen employed other than on their own holdings or labouring on other holdings. Eighteen per cent of men and 2 per cent of women are in this category, and 9 per cent of the population as a whole. Since not all persons over seventeen are in the labour force whilst some below seventeen are, 9 per cent is probably an under-estimate of the proportion of the smallholder labour force engaged in non-shamba employment.

6 The holder is defined as the person with overall control over the management and operations of the holding.

7 Derived by means of simultaneous equations from *IRS* I, Table 6.8.

8 The *IRS* I data show hired labour accounting for 10 per cent of total labour input on the holding and costing 160 shillings per annum, some 82 per cent of household labour working on the holding. Thus, at the average wage rate paid by smallholders to hired labourers, the total labour input on the mean holding is worth 1,600 shillings. Since this represents only 82 per cent of the mean household labour endowment, the value of the entire labour endowment at the hired labour wage rate is 1600/82 = 1,951 shillings.

9 For an account of Kenyan land law and land reforms see Okoth-Ogendo.

10 Probably the most accurate measurement of the labour intensity of major crops is Labour Requirement/Availability (Ministry of Agriculture, 1979) which reports results of a detailed survey in Kisii. Single-cropped hybrid maize was found to require 33 per cent of the man hours per hectare required for mature coffee, 37 per cent of that for pyrethrum, and 60 per cent of that for tea.

11 Recent analysis of *IRS* I data has established that the lower is liquid wealth, the more likely are smallholders to sacrifice income maximization for reduced risk. The effect of risk appears to be powerful; controlling for other variables, a halving of liquid wealth is associated with a 16 per cent lower value of crop output. See Collier (1983).

12 Evidence that sales per hectare are negatively correlated with holding size is given in Livingstone (1981).

13 A definitive treatment of the subject is to be found in Von Pischke (1977). See also Livingstone (1981).

14 See Von Pischke (1977), pp. 219–27, on the limited nature of informal credit.

15 It is noteworthy that in the study by Bliss and Stern which found that factor market transactions had eliminated differences in productivity by farm size, there was no absentee land ownership.

16 From *Employment and Earnings, 1974*, Table 32, allowing for paid leave.

17 Mean hectares per worker on coffee and tea plantations was 0.52 in 1977, taking employment data from the 1981 Statistical Abstract Table 239 and area data from *IRS* II–IV Basic Report, Table 14.11. Mean hectares per worker on smallholdings was 0.67 from *IRS* I.

18 The operator is the person in charge of the day-to-day running of the farm.

19 This overstates the true change because of boundary changes.

20 Substantial boundary changes occurred between 1963 and 1974. Allowance is made for these changes in the analysis which follows.

21 Data on crop-specific use of family and hired labour was taken from the *Economic Survey of Nyeri District 1964* (Government of Kenya, 1967), and applied to the cropping patterns for Central Province in 1961 and 1974. The method was to

determine what would have happened to the proportion of labour hired had crop-specific usage been at the 1964 level throughout the period. The analysis is described in Collier (1980).

22 Landlessness in 1963 is based on *Economic Survey of Central Province 1963/4*, Tables 29 and 30. Landlessness in 1976 is based on unpublished data from *IRS* II supplied by the Central Bureau of Statistics. Since the precise definitions of landlessness may have differed, the comparison is to be treated with caution.

23 The land-use survey evidence is set out below:

Small and Large Farm Areas of High and Medium Potential Land ('000 hectares)

Farm type	1963	1970	1975	Percentage change in area
Smallholding	290[a]	458[b]	476[e]	+64
Large farms		203[c]	183[f]	
Total land		661[d]	659[g]	

[a] *Statistical Abstract* (1964), Table 80. We assume that half of the smallholding area of Embu pre-1963 falls within the post-1963 boundaries of Central Province.
[b] *Statistical Abstract* (1976), Table 91.
[c] *Statistical Abstract* (1976), Table 96(a).
[d] Total
[e] Residual
[f] *Statistical Abstract* (1976), Table 96(f).
[g] *Statistical Abstract* (1976), Table 80.

6

THE FUNCTIONING OF THE LABOUR
MARKET: NON-AGRICULTURE

I Introduction

In the previous chapter we suggested that the central problem facing agents
in the agricultural labour market was enforcement of contract. Because
the ability of employers to enforce contracts through supervision differed
radically between smallholders and plantations, contracts were struck at
radically different daily wage rates. In the non-agricultural labour market we
would expect differences between types of firm in the ability to supervise
labour to be less marked. Many of the features which make the supervision of
agricultural labour costly do not apply in other sectors, and the polarization
of enterprises into single-supervisor multi-activity or multi-supervisor single-
activity undertakings is also unique to agriculture. Nevertheless, the supervision problem may differ systematically by some observable firm characteristics. Indeed, in section II we suggest that such a relationship may explain
findings which have previously been interpreted as institutional segmentation of the labour market according to firm size.

The central problem facing agents in the non-agricultural labour market
is likely to relate to the accumulation of firm-specific skills. These are inherently long-term transactions for which no enforceable long-term contract
is available (since labour given modern social constraints cannot be bonded).
In section III we show how the wages structure has been used to overcome
this problem and how the government intervention of minimum wages
disrupted this solution. The optimal use of the wages structure to promote
skill accumulation suggests a role for trades unions which is explored in the
context of possible institutional segmentation in section II.

In section IV we address the core issue of market adjustment to disequilibrium. What happens in response to excess supply of labour at a
particular wage? On this, in both the Kenya literature and the Kenya-
inspired theoretical literature, there is a clearly articulated consensus which
in Chapter 4 we termed the 'institutionalist' view of the 'employment problem'.

We will suggest that the 'institutionalist' view is correct neither as an
account of wage determination, nor as an account of non-wage adjustments
to disequilibrium wage levels. The empirical study of wage and non-wage
adjustments to incipient disequilibria requires the prior estimation of
changes in the supply and demand for labour. These data requirements are

enormously amplified because our thesis on the true adjustment mechanism focuses upon the heterogeneity of labour. Workers differ, and so the recruitment problem is a complex trade-off between wages, the quantity of labour hired, and the selection criteria to be satisfied. Section IV starts, therefore, with an attempt to quantify changes in the supply and demand for non-agricultural labour by educational attainment. This forms a necessary but somewhat tedious precursor to our discussions of wage and non-wage adjustments. The former rehabilitates the notion of wage flexibility in response to disequilibrium. The latter suggests that the absence of full wage adjustment may not be a symptom of market rigidity nor need it have the unemployment consequences postulated in either the Harris–Todaro or the Fields models.

II Institutional Segmentation?

In this section we consider the evidence for segmentation within the formal sector. First, we examine whether firm characteristics such as size or ownership status represent a powerful non-market influence upon wages. Second, we examine whether unions represent such an influence. Third, wage differentials by race are analysed. Finally, we consider the role of government as an employer and as an interventionist agent within the private sector of the labour market.

(1) Segmentation by Firm Type

House and Rempel have stressed the importance of the ability of firms to pay as the major determinant of differences in earnings between firms. The idea is that those firms which make high profits per worker share these with the work-force in a manner which departs from cost minimizing behaviour. To test this they regressed the negotiated wage rate for unskilled workers in each firm on the mean value added of all workers in the various industries to which the firms belonged. Alternatively, profit per worker replaced value added, though the correlation between the two measures was 0.98.

Additionally, House and Rempel suggest that big, capital-intensive foreign firms will form a high-wage subset of the labour market. The idea is that capital-intensive firms do not need to worry about the wages bill and so are not cost-conscious. Large foreign firms are in a position to earn monopsonistic profits. Hence, size and ownership determine pay by raising profits per worker in the firm above the industry average. Finally, industrial concentration is added, presumably as a proxy for ability to pay.

The econometric specification used by House and Rempel is not ideally suited to their purposes. The model is in essence

$$W_f = w_f(P_f) \tag{1}$$

where w = the wage rate, P = mean profit per worker, f denotes a particular firm, and i denotes the industry mean. Since data was not available for P_f but only for P_i we require a function to estimate P_f. Whilst industrial concentration might explain P_i (that is whilst we might have $P_i = P_i(C_i)$) it is hard to see how C_i can be used to tell us anything about individual firm divergence from mean profits per worker in the industry, and since this latter is already observed it is hard to see why C_i and P_i should ever be in the same equation.

If employment is to be used as a proxy for the divergence of a firm's profits per worker from the industry average then the appropriate specification would be

$$\frac{P_f}{P_i} = \frac{P_f}{P_i}\left(\frac{S_f}{S_i}\right) \tag{2}$$

where S = employment
so that the final proxy for P_f would be

$$P_f = P_f\left(P_i, \frac{S_f}{S_i}\right). \tag{3}$$

That is, employment in the firm *relative to employment in the industry* would be the appropriate proxy. Unfortunately, House and Rempel do not use this specification, but instead use

$$P_f = P_f(P_i, S_f). \tag{4}$$

This will only give the same result if all industries have the same mean employment, which is unlikely. If instead mean employment by industry varies substantially, then S_f would be highly correlated with S_i and so would be a very poor indicator of S_f/S_i and hence of P_f/P_i. This latter seems rather likely. Hence, (4) is not the ideal specification of the House and Rempel thesis since S_f is likely to be such a poor estimator of P_f/P_i that if their own thesis is correct it should be insignificant.

The results show both P_i and S_f to be significant at the one per cent level:[1]

$$W_f = 229.5 + 0.04\ P_i + 0.07\ S_f,\ r^2 = 0.26. \tag{5}$$

The link from value added per worker to the unskilled wage cannot be described as powerful. A 20 shilling increase in value added per year for all workers raises the unskilled wage by 0.5 shillings per year. If firms are motivated to share profits they do not appear to do so very generously.

Our own regression of unskilled wages on size and ownership status using data for thirty-three firms in 1974/5[2] shows both to be significant.

$$W = 354.8^{xxx} + 0.18^{xx}S + 75.5^{xxx}F \tag{6}$$
$$r^{-2} = 0.38$$

where xxx = significant at one per cent level, xx = significant at 5 per cent level, F = dummy for multinational ownership, and W = wage (s.p.m. − shillings per month).

Why, then, should firms which employ more people tend to pay higher wages to unskilled workers? An incremental hundred employees were associated with a 7 s.p.m. increase in unskilled wages in 1968 and an 18 s.p.m. increase in 1974/5. In neither case is this a large increase, but why should there be any at all?

There is a generally accepted relationship between size and hierarchy in firms. As firms get larger they require a greater proportion of supervisory and managerial staff. The normal channel of recruitment for the supervision of manual workers is to promote from the ranks of manual workers in the firm. This ensures that supervisors have an intimate knowledge of the job which they are supervising. Hence, in recruiting unskilled workers the firm must recognize that it is at the same time recruiting potential supervisors. It must ensure that its terms of service for unskilled workers are sufficiently attractive for it to meet its requirements for supervisors; namely labour with particular characteristics, such as a certain level of education and leadership qualities. Our thesis is that because larger firms require proportionately more potential supervisors, they must be more selective in recruiting unskilled labour, and therefore must offer slightly better terms than smaller firms.

Relatively few unskilled workers may be promoted to a supervisory or similar skilled position so that it might be thought that even if a larger firm required a greater proportion of supervisory staff, the impact upon the wage of unskilled workers would be minimal. This depends upon the ability of the firm to offer different wages to different unskilled workers and its ability to identify future supervisors upon initial recruitment. If the firm knows that 2 per cent of unskilled workers must be promoted to supervisor, and if it knows that all the supervisors require experience plus the functional literacy associated with secondary education then the firm need only attract secondary school leavers for 2 per cent of its unskilled vacancies, since education is a characteristic which can be identified at the time of recruitment. More likely, however, the requirements for a good supervisor are experience, literacy, and 'x', where 'x' denotes a set of characteristics which cannot be identified upon recruitment, but can only be perceived by observation of the worker over some years. If it is known, however, that few workers (say y per cent) have 'x' and that this is uncorrelated with secondary education, then the proportion of unskilled workers required to have secondary education will rise to 2 per cent $\times \frac{100}{y}$. If the firm can then offer different wages to unskilled workers, depending upon their education, then the wages of the majority of unskilled workers would be unaffected. However, there are two drawbacks to this. First, since secondary education is irrelevant (ex hypothesis) to unskilled work, it might be demoralizing and disruptive to have a wage differential which was unrelated to productivity. Second, it might pay the firm to obscure from its unskilled employees which of them are excluded from prospects of promotion, thereby providing a promotion incentive to greater work effort. Hence, if supervisors are required to possess skills which are in short supply, and cannot be identified at the time of recruitment of unskilled labour, then the wage rate for all unskilled labour may be bid up.

The importance of providing a pool of suitably qualified labour from which to recruit supervisors should not be underestimated. The management of one large multi-national firm in Kenya attributed the bankruptcy of the firm which had previously owned the plant to the failure of the previous management to provide a flow of sufficiently high calibre supervisors.

The notion that firms must be more selective in appointing supervisors than in hiring unskilled labour is sufficiently plausible to stand without empirical support. However, we are able to demonstrate one element of this, namely the imposition of higher educational criteria. From the 1972 High and Middle Level Manpower Survey 48 per cent of all foremen appointed in 1971 had secondary education—a far higher proportion than the proportion of manual workers with secondary education. Using Thias and Carnoy (1968) we are able to provide similar data stratified by firm size (see Table 6.1). The smallest firms do not appear to impose educational selection criteria on the recruitment of supervisors. Perhaps this is because the nature of the supervisor's job is rather different in a small firm, having few of the features of a position in a bureaucratic hierarchy. In both the larger size categories there is a substantial difference between the mean education of foremen and that of unskilled workers. Significantly, the largest size group has to make do with lower mean educational achievements in its foremen (6.2 years against 8.7 years) despite having an unskilled labour force which is as well educated as that of middle-size firms. This is consistent with our hypothesis that larger firms require a greater proportion of supervisors, suggesting that the large firms, because of their greater demand, are unable to impose such high screening criteria. Firms employing fifty or more employees are able to attract better educated unskilled workers than the smallest firms, presumably by paying more.

Further evidence is provided by House and Rempel's own regressions. They find (5.24 and 5.33) that the proportion of the labour force in supervisory and related activities is significant at the 5 per cent level in explaining the unskilled wage rate. An increase of one percentage point in the proportion of the labour force in such activities raised the unskilled wage by between 5 s.p.m. and 10 s.p.m. (the data being for the years 1968 and 1972). House and Rempel explain this as a sort of 'demonstration effect': the presence of highly-paid skilled workers raising the pay of the unskilled out of a charitable desire to reduce perceived skill differentials.

Finally, we need to explain why the multi-national firms in our sample paid about 20 per cent more for unskilled labour than local firms. First, local firms in Kenya are predominantly Asian family businesses, generally rather small. By controlling for size we are therefore contrasting small branches of multi-nationals with small family firms. Our contention is that the process of

Table 6.1

Education, Hierarchy, and Firm Size (Unskilled)
Average years of education (African males, 1968)

	Firm size		
	1–14	50–99	100+
Foremen	4.0	8.7	6.2
Unskilled	4.2	4.8	4.7

Source: Thias and Carnoy.

recruitment to positions in the hierarchy is likely to differ substantially in these two cases. In particular, the family firm is more likely to reserve higher positions for family members, thus requiring fewer recruits from lower down the hierarchy and hence being able to impose less exacting selection criteria upon its recruitment process at the bottom of the hierarchy.

Second, both large firms and multi-national firms tend to be more capital-intensive, partly because they have access to cheaper borrowing. It is likely that the higher the ratio of capital to unskilled workers (and hence the higher the average product per unskilled worker) the more it pays the firm to impose more stringent selection criteria upon unskilled workers at the time of recruitment to the regular labour force. In Figure 6.1 we simplify to a single identifiable characteristic, Z, where S denotes the relationship between the mean 'Z' of selected recruits and the wage offered recruits. Letting the elasticity of the average product of labour with respect to Z be unity throughout (not a necessary assumption), if the capital stock per unskilled worker is

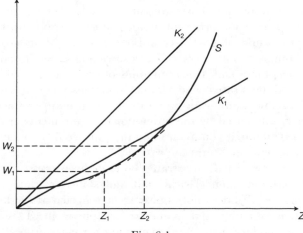

Fig. 6.1

K_1 then the schedule OK_1 denotes the APL with respect to Z. Profits are maximized with respect to Z by maximizing the difference between the APL and the wage. Hence, the firm should choose a wage w_1, and selection criteria Z_1. The more capital-intensive firm, having a capital stock per unskilled worker of K_2, faces a relationship between APL and Z of OK_2, this by assumption having the same elasticity as the other firm. Naturally, for any given Z this firm achieves a higher APL. The firm should therefore impose selection criteria Z_2 and pay an accordingly higher wage, w_2. This then establishes the presumption of a relationship between capital intensity and the wage. Further, this has been based upon the assumption that the elasticity of the APL with respect to Z is invariant with respect to capital intensity. More likely, working with machinery increases the skill content of what is still commonly classified as unskilled labour. This might be because the machinery involves certain numerical operations or requires greater discipline. The type of distinction can be visualized by comparing porterage with assisting a machine operator. If we are correct in believing that mechanization tends to increase the importance of unskilled labour quality, then the elasticity of the APL with respect to Z would increase with capital intensity, and this would further increase the profit-maximizing mean wage.

This relationship between capital intensity and the wage would also explain why P_i was found to be significant in equation (5). That is, industries which are capital intensive will tend to have both a high average value added per worker and high wages. Observed inter-firm wage differentials for unskilled labour are consistent with the hypothesis that the unskilled labour market is not suffering from major imperfections. Differential requirements imposed by hierarchy and capital intensity appear to explain unskilled wage differences at least as well as 'institutional' hypotheses.

Inter-firm wage differences for skilled workers should be more powerfully affected by hierarchy and capital intensity than those of unskilled workers. First, the clerical and administrative hierarchy is likely to involve the promotion of a greater proportion of junior clerical entrants up the hierarchy than the proportion of unskilled workers who rise into positions which require the imposition of characteristics screening at the initial recruitment point. Further, hierarchical diseconomies of scale are probably more pronounced in administrative and clerical functions than in the production process. Hence, we would expect that junior clerical appointments would be more strongly influenced by the promotional requirements of the hierarchy than unskilled labour appointments and that this would be more pronounced in large firms than small firms.

First, in Table 6.2 we demonstrate that large firms impose more stringent educational criteria upon clerical staff and skilled manual workers than smaller firms, yet this does not appear to be reflected at the higher level of administrative executive and managerial employment. This is consistent with the view that large firms need to promote a greater proportion of clerical workers because the upper reaches of the hierarchy are relatively bigger. They would therefore need to attract higher calibre clerical recruits, though this would not lead to higher quality further up the hierarchy than smaller firms.

Second, repeating (6) for junior clerical workers we find that earnings are most sensitive (both absolutely and proportionately) to firm size and ownership than is the case with unskilled labour.

$$W = 461.1^{xxx} + 0.325 \ S^{xx} + 150.7 \ F^{xxx} \tag{7}$$
$$\bar{r}^2 = 0.40$$

Thirdly, the House and Rempel regression of the earnings of skilled workers (5.20, 5.21, 5.22, 5.29, 5.30, 5.31) show that the proportions of workers in four higher-skill categories are significant explanatory variables for mean skilled earnings.

These same regressions show average labour productivity to be a significant explanatory variable. While for unskilled labour a 20 s.p.a. increase in APL (for the whole work-force) is associated with only a 0.5 s.p.a. increase in the wage, for the skilled worker it is associated with an increase of between 2.9 s.p.a. and 5.2 s.p.a. This sixfold to tenfold increase in sensitivity to APL is far in excess of the skilled–unskilled wage differential, so that the skilled wage is proportionately more sensitive to the APL than the unskilled wage. We would suggest that this is because an increase in the overall capital/labour ratio in a firm (and hence an increase in the overall APL) is not uniformly distributed across the skill spectrum within the firm. Increased capital will tend to replace unskilled labour by skilled (or semi-skilled) labour. Additionally, it will tend to raise the amount of capital with which the skilled man works. It will not, however, tend to raise the amount of capital with which the unskilled man works because at very low skill levels human and physical capital are likely to be complementary.

Hence, the introduction of hierarchy and capital intensity affords an explanation of inter-firm wage differentials for both skilled and unskilled labour without relinquishing assumptions of maximizing behaviour. While 'institutional' imperfections can never be eliminated as an alternative explanation of observed behaviour, that explanation can at least be threatened with Occam's razor.

(2) Segmentation by Union Membership

While House and Rempel offer an intsitutionalist account of wage determination based on differences between firms, the dominant institutionalist thesis has rested upon the role of unions. First, let us consider the evidence linking unionization and wage levels.

Three studies provide a snapshot of the impact of unionization around

Table 6.2
Education, Hierarchy, and Firm Size (Skilled)
Average years of education (African males, 1968)

	Firm size			
Occupation	1–14	15–49	50–99	100+
Administrative, Exec., and Managerial	n.a.	12.3	9.4	13.3
Clerical	7.0	7.3	8.0	9.0
Skilled manual	n.a.	5.1	5.9	6.0

Source: As for Table 6.1

1968. Johnson (1971), using a survey of urban African wage earners for 1970, introduced union membership into an earnings function which included age, education, and tribe, but had no data on firm characteristics. The union coefficient was significant and showed a 30 per cent wage premium for union members. Thias and Carnoy (1973), using their 1968 survey, find the union membership coefficient significant for all education levels up to completed primary, though for higher levels of education the coefficient is either based on a small sample, is insignificant, or has a negative sign (see Table 6.3).

Education is correlated with skill. Whilst only 18 per cent of those with 0–2 years education are in skilled manual or white collar occupations, this rises to 29 per cent for those with 3–5 years education and 53 per cent for primary school leavers (Thias and Carnoy, Table 3.6). Hence, it seems likely that union members received a bigger percentage premium in unskilled than in skilled activities. Indeed, the 33 per cent premium for those with 0–2 years education is a good proxy for the premium for unskilled workers. Thias and Carnoy controlled for a large number of personal characteristics but had

Table 6.3
Union Membership and Wages, 1968

	Highest education (years and exam)						
	0–2	3–5	7 (fail)	7 (pass)	9	11	13
Sample size	1079	881	302	496	174	220	n.a.
Percentage unionized	73	75	66	69	67	44	n.a.
Mean wage	321	355	342	439	505	764	1121
Coefficient	86	67	61	80	204	112[a]	−138
Non-union wage	258	305	302	384	368	715	n.a.
Union wage	344	372	368	464	572	827	n.a.
Percentage premium	33	22	22	21	55	16	n.a.

[a] Not significant.
Source: Thias and Carnoy (1973), Tables 3.6 and 3.8.

little information on firms. Firm size was proxied by dummy coefficients for five size bands. Finally, House and Rempel entered unionization as an independent variable in their analysis of wage for 1968 and 1972. Their proxy for union membership was indirect. If a firm had a registered contract with a union it was assumed that all of its employees were union members. If there was no registered contract then union membership was set at zero. Aggregating firms within an industry, the proportion of employees in the industry who were union members then became an independent variable in explaining the mean unskilled wage for each firm. It was found that while unionization was correlated with firm size ($r^2 = 0.38$) and with ability to pay ($r^2 = 0.20$), when entered into wage regressions it was never significant and always had a negative sign (House and Rempel, Tables 5.5 and 5.6). There is then an apparent conflict between the findings of Johnson and Thias and Carnoy on the one hand, who both agree on a wage premium of around 30 per cent and House and Rempel who find no premium at all for the same period. A possible reconciliation might be that the extra firm variables introduced by House and Rempel which are correlated with both wages and unionization explain why the other studies have found a correlation between wages and unionization. Unfortunately, House and Rempel fail to find even a simple partial correlation between wages and unionization. This is not necessarily inconsistent with the reported findings of Johnson and Thias and Carnoy, who do not report simple partial correlations but only regression coefficients in which several personal characteristics are included. Hence, it is not impossible that unions attract disproportionately young and un-educated, and therefore low-wage workers as members; indeed, from Table 6.3 we find this tendency in the case of education.

Alternatively, the proxy for union power against the firm used by House and Rempel might be so poor as to be useless. Support for this view might be that, particularly for unskilled labour, unionization of the industry is of limited significance compared with unionization of a particular firm.

A final possibility, which we would tend towards, is that the observed correlation between unionization and firm size and ability to pay (which we take as a proxy for capital intensity—see sub-section (1)) must sub-stantially understate the true correlation. This is because all the variables are measured very imperfectly. Even firm size is only proxied by dummies for one of five size groups, and that for the year 1970, whilst the wage data are for 1968 and 1972. Hence, the apparent partial correlation of 0.38 might well be considerably higher if the variables were better measured. Similarly, better proxies for union power might establish a partial correlation between it and unskilled wage levels. Suppose, then, we accept that by the late 1960s firms in which unions were strong tended to pay higher unskilled wages. It remains possible that this is explicable in terms of differences in firm charac-teristics—that firms which have particular characteristics are both more amenable to unions and pay more to unskilled labour.

Firms might find unions attractive for two main reasons. First, they offer a hierarchy by which the work-force can be disciplined so that contracts can be made collectively. It is potentially easier to enforce a collective agreement on unskilled labour than several hundred individual ones, partly because of reduced information costs and partly because the union has a contractual continuity which the individual worker lacks and hence has more need to maintain a reputation for sticking to contracts. This is not fanciful. Recall that in Kenya labour unrest, incuding strikes, preceded by many years the formation of unions. The KFE welcomed unions as a means of replacing anarchy by order.

Second, powerful unions can offer the worker some sense of security against dismissal on grounds which fellow workers would perceive as being unfair. Paradoxically, for some firms it is in their own interest to circumscribe their ability to dismiss workers. In particular, this is true of firms which operate seniority scales. In section III(2) we will discuss one reason for this—namely that the use of a seniority scale may entail that all workers reach a level of seniority at which their wage equals their marginal product. Yet the firm needs to assure workers that they will not be dismissed at this stage, for otherwise the seniority scale will fail to attract recruits unless the wage level is bid up. A second reason is that workers are heterogeneous in characteristics which cannot be observed at the time of recruitment. The consequence of this is that only after some years will the firm perceive its good workers (high MPL) from its bad workers (low MPL). Firms in which workers are on seniority scales will, once they identify bad workers, have a greater incentive to dismiss them than firms using constant wage scales. This is because, with identical present values of the wage at the time of recruitment in the two types of firm, at each successive subsequent period the worker in the firm with seniority scales has a future wage stream the present value of which is increasingly greater than that of the worker in the firm with a flat-rate wage. Hence, for a common dispersion of marginal productivities among the work-force, a greater proportion of the work-force will be discovered to have marginal productivities below their wages. Again, unless the firm can assure workers that dismissals will not occur the effect of this increased insecurity is to raise the wage which the firm must offer in order to attract recruits.

Anticipating the result of section III, in which it is demonstrated that where firms wish to accumulate firm-specific skills in their labour force the cost-minimizing wages structure is a seniority scale, we have now suggested that firms with seniority scales will tend to find unions attractive as a means of giving their work-force sufficient power to achieve a sense of security. Contrasted with this, firms which do not accumulate human capital in their work force will have less use for unions. But the more human capital that is accumulated the higher will be the marginal product and the wage level. Hence, high wage levels will tend to be associated with unionization of the work-force even if there is no causal connection from unionization onto the wage level.

These two arguments for unions are consistent with the correlations found by House and Rempel between unionization, firm size, and average productivity. The correlation with firm size is explicable in terms of the mounting costs of hierarchy as firm size increases: the union hierarchy acting as a means of disciplining the work-force and discouraging unofficial disputes means that some of the costs of the hierarchy are in effect born by the work-force.The correlation with average productivity could reflect the predicted correlation between unions and human capital accumulation, especially since human and physical capital are probably complementary at low levels of skill.

Since the late 1960s unions in Kenya have increasingly devoted their efforts towards improving job security rather than wage levels (see, for example, Sandbrook). Note that unions have been unable to prevent the massive falls in both the real and the relative wages of unskilled workers which has occurred since 1968.

(3) Segmentation by Race

In Chapter 2 we noted the persistence of wage differentials by race within quite narrow occupational categories. These differentials may reflect perceived differences in productivity or differences in experience and qualifications. Controlling for the latter, Thias and Carnoy had still found large wage differentials in 1968. An alternative explanation for persistent salary differentials by race is the use of monopsony power by the firm. In Figure 6.2 S_N represents a supply curve facing the representative Kenya firms for non-citizen skilled labour. The firm is assumed to be a price-taker on the world market. The market for Kenyan labour is assumed to be less well integrated than the world market. In this case the firm faces an upward-sloping curve for citizen labour depicted as Sc. The firm will therefore employ Ec citizens at a wage Wc, below the wage W_N for non-citizens. As the supply of citizens expand relative to demand the supply curve will shift to the right. If either the minimum supply price does not fall (being supported by earnings in lower-rank occupations) or the market becomes better integrated, then the supply curve will tend to twist rather than shift. In fact the labour market for skilled citizens did become more integrated over this period, as can be seen from Table 6.4 which identifies a general narrowing of the dispersion among firms in the earnings paid to citizens within most skill categories.

The combination of a flattening of the citizen supply curve with an expansion in supply tends to maintain the citizen/non-citizen wage differential constant while increasing the share of citizens in the total. In the Inbucon survey the share of non-citizens had fallen from 47 per cent in 1972 to 25 per cent in 1979. If indeed the employer is able to act as a discriminating

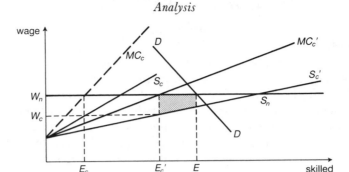

Fig. 6.2

Table 6.4

Upper-Quartile Relative to Lower-Quartile Basic Salary Among Citizens

Occupation	1972	1979
Director	1.47	1.48
Division head	1.70	1.56
Senior manager	1.68	1.47
Middle manager 1	1.80	1.44
Middle manager 2	1.73	1.74

Source: Inbucon (1973, 1979).

monopsonist, then an implication is that Africanization will be delayed beyond the optimum. In Figure 6.2, after the supply increases to $S'c$ the competitive market outcome would be complete Africanization with the earnings of skilled workers starting to fall below the world supply price. Instead, $E–E'_c$ non-citizens are retained in the labour force even though their cost to the economy exceeds that of citizens by the shaded area in Figure 6.2. The accelerated Africanization of the private sector enforced by the Kenyanization of Personnel Bureau can thus be seen to have an economic as well as a social rationale.

(4) Segmentation by Government Intervention

The Government of Kenya has intervened in the labour market in three areas. First, it has attempted to influence wage levels in the private sector; second, it has periodically attempted to influence employment levels in the private sector; and thirdly, as a very large employer of labour, it has needed a policy for wages and employment within the public sector. We consider these in turn.

(a) *Wages Policy* There have been two distinct wage policies. The urban minimum wage was used, especially during the period 1954–63, with the intention of raising wage levels for unskilled workers. This had two un-intended effects. First, the increase in the minimum wage had a powerful effect upon the wage structure, reducing the pace of skill accumulation, especially among manual workers. This mechanism, first suggested in Chapter 2, is formally developed in section III(2). Second, to the extent that the minimum wage increase did succeed in raising the wage level it induced an increase in urban job-search unemployment. The extension in 1967 of the minimum wage to all those aged eighteen and over exacerbated youth unemployment in particular. The unemployment problem is analysed in section IV.

The second wage policy, introduced in 1973 in response to worries about unemployment, has been an 'incomes policy' intended to restrain private firms and unions from raising real wages. The introduction of the incomes policy coincides with the period of falling real wages; we will argue, however, that the fall in real wages was a market-based rather than an institutionally induced phenomenon. The evidence for this is twofold. First, the policy 'guidelines' were changed from year to year, moving in line with market conditions; for example, the guidelines were substantially liberalized during the coffee boom. Second, and most important, the actual bargains concluded bear little relation to the guidelines, sometimes exceeding them, almost invariably falling below them, and in aggregate, as Table 6.5 shows, usually being only one half to three quarters of the maximum permitted increase. The guidelines also attempted to narrow earnings differentials by granting larger increases to the lower paid. We have seen, however, in Chapters 2 and 3 that differentials between skilled and unskilled wage earners tended to widen over the period. Hence, we may conclude that the incomes policy probably contributed little to the sharp fall in real wages. Indeed, to the extent that the guidelines provided unions with both a target and a legal

Table 6.5
Collective Agreements, 1973–1978

Period	Average duration (months)	Average pay increase	Guidelines	Utilization ratio
September				
1973–75	28	18.9	31.2	0.61
1974	29	18.9	28.5	0.66
1975	26	17.9	35.0	0.51
1976	24	28.7	34.7	0.83
1977	25	22.6	28.0	0.81
1978	25	21.2	28.5	0.74

Source: Oduor-Otieno (1979).

means of attaining it (by appeal to the Industrial Court) the policy perhaps tended to raise wages. This conclusion is, of course, quite distinct from the proposition that the legislative initiatives of the government in the mid-1960s, banning strikes and creating COTU, changed the rules of the market place in such a way that unions were never able to establish a position of sufficient power to inhibit significantly competitive labour market pressures.

(*b*) *Employment Policy* On three occasions, 1964, 1970, and 1978, the government has attempted to increase private sector wage employment by directives. Stewart has analysed the 1970 'Tripartite Agreement' and concludes that, whilst some employment opportunities might have been brought forward, the short-term effect was small and the long-term effect negligible. Indeed, whilst regular employment did expand quite rapidly during the agreement, Stewart has shown that much of this was attributable to firms which expanded employment in excess of the agreed target and hence could not have been influenced by it. Further, we have shown in Chapter 3 that the increase in regular employment was matched by a collapse in casual employment, which was excluded from the target. Hence, the effect of the Agreement was to regularize the wage labour force rather than to increase it. We will suggest in section IV(b) that the casual work-force plays an important part in the recruitment policies of firms so that the random enforced regularization of the casual labour force might have significantly damaging unintended effects. As with the impact of minimum wage legislation upon the wages structure rather than the wage level, it is an example of policy not achieving its objective but instead producing unintended and unnoticed negative but unquantifiable side-effects.

(*c*) *The Public Sector* Around Independence we have seen (Chapter 2) that the public sector acted as a wage leader. This was inevitable given the need to Africanize high-level posts. Further, the government needed to spread the visible employment benefits of Independence more widely than this highly-skilled élite so that the public sector also acted as a wage leader in the unskilled labour market. The acute scarcity of top-level African managers encouraged the government to permit civil servants to engage in private enterprise. This has been widely criticized as inducing inefficiency and corruption in the public sector which is undoubtedly the case. However, it has perhaps prevented the emergence of a bureaucratic bourgeoisie with a class interest in inhibiting enterprise.

Since the mid-1960s the public sector has progressively reversed its position as a wage leader. Instead it has tended to exercise its monopsony power in the skilled labour market to depress wages. Recall, however, that the monopsonistic power of the public sector has diminished considerably: its share of new jobs in large occupations such as those of clerks and secretaries fell sharply in the 1970s from the immediate post-Independence level.

The Thias and Carnoy survey (1968) estimated education-specific earnings functions, incorporating a dummy variable for the public sector.[3] For all levels of education below KPE the dummy variable was significantly negative and was only significantly positive for Form IV leavers, perhaps representing the legacy of wage leadership in the high-level African labour market. However, the Thias and Carnoy sampling procedure for the public sector left something to be desired, and no great reliance can be placed upon their findings.

Johnson (1971) found that there was no difference in pay between the public and private sectors for unionized labour, but that the public sector paid a premium of 16 per cent for non-unionized labour. Unfortunately, non-unionized labour categorizes two very different groups of workers: manual workers in small Asian firms and skilled white-collar labour. We have argued above that small firms will tend rationally to pay less than large firms. Hence, it is not possible to infer much from Johnson's results. The 'High and Middle Level Manpower Survey' of January 1972 found that in all but one of fifteen selected narrowly-defined occupations the public sector paid lower salaries (see Table 6.6). This is supported by the much broader occupational classifications used in the Employment and Earnings Survey.

Finally, House and Rempel[4] find that for the two years of their study, 1968 and 1982, the proportion of workers employed by the government is insignificant as an explanation of inter-industry earnings differentials among unskilled workers. The dummy variable was not entered in the regressions for skilled workers.

To conclude, we have questioned whether the non-agricultural labour market has been significantly segmented other than by race. In a recent study using unpublished data from the 1978 National Labourforce Survey, Bigsten (1984) reaches the same conclusion. Fitting a variety of earnings functions, he finds that 'human capital explains a sizable portion of the income variance' (p. 83) whereas 'the introduction of the segmentation variables causes a relatively small increase' in the explained variance (p. 98).

III Skill Acquisition during Employment

(1) Introduction

This section attempts to analyse the process of African skill accumulation in employment, focusing upon the period from the mid-1950s to the late 1960s. Our starting point is from four stylized facts established in Chapter 2:
(1) In the mid-1950s the African urban labour force was largely unskilled (see Table 2.6).
(2) Between the mid-1950s and the late 1960s the urban minimum wage rose very sharply in real terms (Table 2.13).

Table 6.6

Average and Median Monthly Gross Cash Remuneration in Selected Occupations, 1972

Occupation	Average monthly gross cash remuneration (shillings)			Median monthly gross cash remuneration (shillings)	
	private sector	public sector	total	private sector	public sector
Civil engineers	4,519	3,435	4,001	4,300	3,220
Jurists	3,710	2,836	3,300	3,500	2,250
Doctors	3,449	3,169	3,295	2,585	2,490
Semi-professional accountants	3,090	2,377	2,840	2,800	2,206
Clerical and other administrative supervisors	2,588	2,813	2,689	2,136	2,316
Engineering technicians	3,127	1,930	2,282	3,000	1,680
Production supervisors and general foremen	1,962	1,151	1,751	1,600	1,020
Lower level accountants, book-keepers, and cashiers	1,633	1,465	1,591	1,450	1,526
Life science technicians	2,199	1,117	1,506	1,350	850
Professional nurses and midwives	1,539	1,454	1,440	1,450	1,440
Draughtsmen	1,722	1,250	1,434	2,100	1,270
Physical science technicians	1,421	1,000	1,216	1,133	900
Motor-vehicle mechanics	1,124	1,051	1,107	890	1,070
Carpenters and joiners	634	629	633	520	606
Enrolled nurses and midwives	703	546	572	665	500

[a] The private sector includes only large firms.
[b] Total remuneration is calculated as a weighted average of data from private and public sectors.
Source: 'High and Middle Level Manpower Survey of 1971', Central Bureau of Statistics (unpublished).

(3) Over the same period the wages structure changed radically, the premium for seniority falling considerably (Tables 2.12 and 2.13).

(4) The pace of African skill accumulation in the urban private sector was very slow during this period (Tables 2.6 and 2.7).

Our argument starts from the proposition that the low skill content of African employment in the mid-1950s reflected a past history of racial discrimination. However, the easing of discrimination failed to generate a large increase in the skill content of African employment because of the change in the wages structure. In turn, the change in the wages structure was induced by the increase in the minimum wage. The conclusion is that the increase in the minimum wage may indeed have had a more powerful effect on the wages structure than upon the wage level. Further, its distorting effect on labour allocation might have been primarily upon a reduction in the net accumulation of human capital rather than upon the level of employment or, more particularly, upon the level of unemployment.

To establish this argument we first require a theory of the relationship between firm-specific skill accumulation and the wages structure, this being developed in sub-section (2) and stated more formally in an excursus. The consequential relationship between the wages structure and the minimum wage is analysed in (3). The implications for changes in labour turnover and its cost to firms over the period from the early 1950s to the late 1960s are estimated in (4). The accumulation of general skill is considered in (5), where it is shown that, paradoxically, the increase in the minimum wage may have reduced the incentive for workers to acquire skill while at the same time increasing the cost to the firm of skilled workers relative to unskilled. Such a configuration would unambiguously reduce the pace of skill formation. Finally, we turn from the minimum wage to the other powerful government intervention in the labour market, namely the expansion in the education system. Education could be either a complement or a substitute for training by the firm, or it could be entirely irrelevant to work-based skills. In (6) we argue that the evidence suggests that education is complementary to firm-based skill formation, and so its expansion should accelerate the accumulation of skill.

(2) A Theory of Firm-Specific Skill Accumulation and the Wage Structure

Skills acquired in employment can be divided into those which are specific to the firm, and therefore not marketable in other employment, and those which are general to an industry or occupation. The accumulation of general skills will *ceteris paribus* be some positive function of skill-specific wage differentials. This is because, by a well-known result in human capital theory, the firm must raise the wage in line with the accumulation of skill or risk losing the worker to another firm. Hence, the wage will bear a fixed relationship to the marginal product (equality in the perfectly competitive case) so that the firm does not bear any of the costs of training. Since all the investment in training is made by the worker the incentive to make this investment is measured by the skill differential. Should this skill differential fail to respond to market forces then there will be excessive or inadequate investment by workers in general skill acquisition. We consider this in sub-section (3).

The accumulation of firm-specific skills is a more complex matter because the investment will be shared between the worker and the firm. The incentive to invest in skill acquisition is no longer monotonic in skill-specific wage differentials for these merely reflect the returns to the worker on his share of the investment. To discover the returns to the firm we need to analyse the process by which the firm incurs costs and receives benefits.

Consider first the case in which all the cost of skill acquisition is incurred by the firm instantaneously at the time of recruitment, this being the case considered by Stiglitz (1974). As a result, the firm has an incentive to retain the worker in the firm. The cost-minimizing way for the firm to do this is to adopt a wages structure by which the worker also makes an investment which is repaid only if the worker stays in his job. The wage structure which achieves this is a seniority scale whereby the wage rises with the length of experience in the firm. The cost of labour to the firm need be no higher under such a structure than if the firm adopts a flat-rate wage scale in which the wage is unrelated to seniority.

In Figure 6.3 we illustrate the superiority of seniority wage scales over flat-rate wage scales.[5] In Figure 6.3(a) the present value upon recruitment of the two wage scales is equal so that each type of firm is competitive in recruitment. In Figure 6.3(b) we plot the cumulative savings which the worker in a seniority system is implicitly acquiring between time t_0 and t_1, this being equal to the forgone earnings in a firm with a flat-rate wages system. The curve SS denotes these cumulative implicit savings. There are no such savings in a flat-rate wages structure. The effect on the quit rate for each age cohort is shown in Figure 6.3(c). If the wage in the flat-rate firm is a market clearing wage, then the cost of a quit is simply the transaction cost of a job transfer, assumed to be constant over time, so that the rate of quit will be constant (hence FF is horizontal). Only when implicit savings are zero will this be true for the worker under a seniority scale. At all other times the cost of quitting must include the loss of accrued implicit savings, hence the quit rate will be monotonic in implicit savings (SS in Figure 6.3(c)). With a lower quit rate the firm with the seniority scale will need to undertake less recruitment and will therefore incur lower training costs. If the wage is raised above the market clearing wage, so that if the worker gives up his job he may be unable to get another at as high a wage, then, under either wages structure, the worker is additionally locked in as a function of the discounted present value of the future earnings differential which would be foregone by quitting. Clearly this function declines monotonically as the worker approaches retirement, so that for example in a flat-rate wages structure with a wage above the

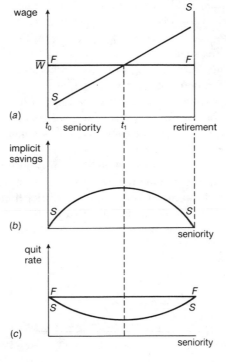

Fig. 6.3

market clearing rate the quit rate will rise with seniority. That is, the schedule *FF* in Figure 6.3(*c*) will be upward-sloping.

The superiority of the seniority wage structure has to be qualified in two respects. First, the wage structure which minimizes training costs would be one in which the worker was only paid for the pre-retirement work period, prior to this working for nothing. In a world of perfect information and perfect capital markets the worker would then borrow to meet consumption needs. In reality the worker faces a combination of quantity limits to borrowing and interest rates above those faced by the firm. This implies that the natural desire of the worker to even out the flow of his consumption rather than have it confined to his retirement should be met by the firm moderating the severity of the seniority scale. Restated, the present value of the discounted wage payments which would enable recruitment to a firm with a wage structure in which all payments were delayed until retirement would clearly be so high as to outweigh the benefits of reduced turnover. The optimal seniority scale must therefore trade off higher wage levels against lower turnover costs. This is examined formally in an excursus to this section.

Second, the seniority scale will generally involve the worker being paid his marginal product in his later years. The MPL is shown in Figure 6.4. The discounted present value of S and F wage structures are equated to that of the MPL. From time t_2 the firm is paying the MPL if it uses a seniority wage structure. The short-run 'profit-snatching' firm is indifferent to sacking workers who achieve seniority t_2 whereas workers still have positive implicit savings. The assymmetry of interests must either be compensated by higher wages, or workers must be assured of tenure as long as conduct is satisfactory. This can be done in a variety of ways: either by an explicit or implicit contract of tenure between the worker and the firm, or by the firm encouraging an institutional framework such as trade unions or labour laws which give the worker confidence that the firm cannot dismiss him unfairly. We have noted that the dominant activity of unions in Kenya since Independence has been in the arena of job protection rather than wage increases. We are here claiming that it might be quite rational for the firm to allow this development. This issue is taken up again in our analysis of the impact of trade unions.

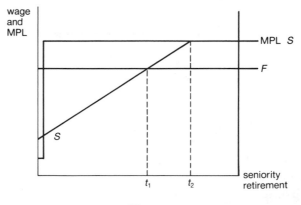

Fig. 6.4

From Figure 6.4 we can derive the cost of labour turnover to the firm as being the difference between the present value of the marginal product and the wage (see Figure 6.5). This demonstrates the second desirable feature of a seniority wage structure: namely that for any particular rate of quit by a seniority cohort, the cost of quitting is lower than in a firm with a flat-rate wage because the employee is bearing some of the investment cost himself.

The overall cost of turnover is the initial cost of training times the total number of quits less the amount of the investment already recouped at the time of the quit. Denoting the net cost of quitting to the firm (SS in Figure 6.5) as a function of seniority as $C(S)$, the total cost of labour turnover in the firm will be:

$$\int_0^n q(S) \cdot C(S) \cdot L(S) ds \tag{1}$$

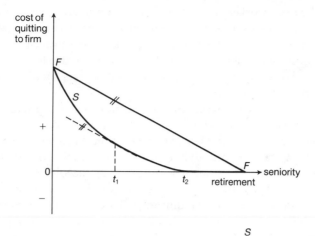

Fig. 6.5

where n denotes the retirement date and $L(S)$ is the labour force in each seniority cohort, this being in zero-growth steady state—a function of the quit rates for all cohorts. For example, $L(3)$ will be $L.(1 - q_1)(1 - q_2)$, L being the total labour force recruited per period.

Now let us relax the assumption that all training costs are incurred instantaneously upon recruitment. Instead, suppose that firm-specific skills are acquired gradually so that the MPL rises over time (see Figure 6.6).

If wages rose in line with the MPL then all the cost of firm-specific human capital acquisition would be borne by the employee and the firm would be indifferent to turnover. If, however, the worker wishes to even out his consumption stream and faces the borrowing constraints discussed pre-

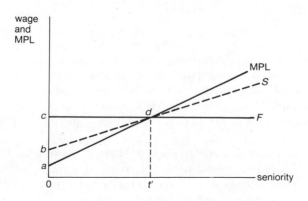

Fig. 6.6

viously, then the worker will accept a lower discounted present value wage upon recruitment in return for a more even wage structure (discounting at the firm's discount rate). However, as before, as the firm flattens the wages structure quit rates increase. Hence, a seniority scale less steep than the MPL is a method by which the firm and the worker share the investment costs and benefits.

From the point of view of the worker, the propensity to quit as a function of the wages structure, depicted in Figure 6.3, is unaffected by the change in the assumption concerning the MPL. However, from the firm's point of view the cost of quitting changes from that depicted in Figure 6.5 to that of Figure 6.7, using the same procedure, namely integrating the difference between the wage and the MPL with respect to seniority. This has the important consequence that the net cost of quitting to the firm becomes an inverted U-shaped function of seniority instead of being a monotonically decreasing function of seniority. But notice from Figure 6.3(c) that a seniority wages structure minimizes quits in precisely the most costly range of quitting—that is the propensity to quit is a U-shaped function.

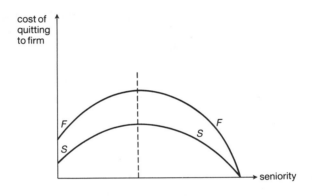

Fig. 6.7

In reality, some costs of training will be associated with the recruitment process, and hence are instantaneous, and others will be incurred gradually while on the job, though this training is unlikely to last throughout the working lifetime. Thus, a plausible MPL schedule and an associated wages structure which approaches optimality will have the features displayed in Figure 6.8.

The implication of this analysis is that the net cost of labour turnover to the firm is a complex function of quit rates and the wage structure. A reduction in total labour turnover may actually increase the *cost* of turnover if low-cost quits are reduced only at the price of an increase in high-cost quits. We will shortly argue that this is probably what happened in Kenya as a

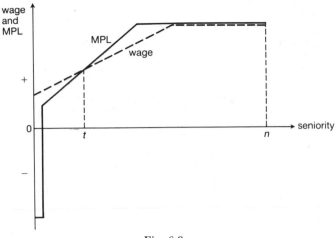

Fig. 6.8

result of the change in the wage structure. First, we must investigate why the wage structure changed.

(3) The Wage Structure and the Minimum Wage

In the previous section we argued that the cost minimizing way of reducing labour turnover is through a seniority wage structure rather than by raising the level of wages. We now suggest that one effect of a minimum wage will be to reduce seniority premiums; that is, to flatten the wage structure. This occurs for two reasons. First, one effect of a minimum wage set above the supply price of labour is to induce job queuing. The resulting excess supply of workers makes quitting perilous for employees and so reduces the rate of labour turnover for any given wage structure. This reduction in quitting, in turn, reduces the benefits associated with expenditure by the firm on its quit-reducing measure, namely its seniority premiums, and so induces a reduction in that expenditure.

Second, a minimum wage raises the cost to the firm of a seniority wage structure compared with a flat-rate wage. This argument is illustrated in Figure 6.9.

Recall that in the early 1950s, prior to the Carpenter Report, the urban minimum wage was so low that only 10 per cent of workers were paid at that rate. In effect, the minimum wage was slack, being at or below that level at which firms with seniority wages structures would engage workers. Firms were free to adopt wage structures with large seniority premiums and appear to have done so:

An employer might employ twenty men nominally labelled 'carpenters', but they would be paid from as little as a shilling or two above the unskilled wage to perhaps

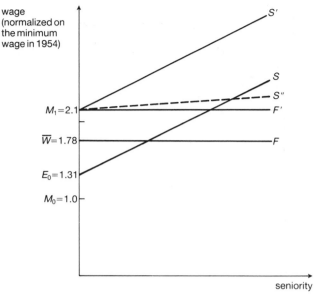

Fig. 6.9

ten or twenty times that figure depending on their level of skill [and] the length of time they had been with their employer . : . This was the case for virtually all occupations from the onset of the colonial period until the emergence of trade unions . . . in the mid-1950s (Kitching, 1980, p. 256).

In Figure 6.9 the minimum wage and the engagement rate prevailing in the early 1950s are represented by M_0 and E_0 respectively. Given that the minimum wage was slack, firms would have adopted seniority wage structures. These propositions are indeed borne out by the evidence of Table 2.12. In 1954, the first year for which data are available, the mean engagement rate was 31 per cent above the minimum wage, thus suggesting that the minimum wage was slack. Mean earnings, $\bar{W}$, were a further 36 per cent above the engagement rate, suggesting that pay rose substantially with seniority (the engagement rate being the wage rate of those with no seniority in the firm).

By 1961 the minimum wage had more than doubled, thus rising above both the engagement rate and mean earnings in 1954. In Figure 6.9 the 1961 minimum wage is shown as M_1, being 2.1 times M_0. The first predicted effect of this increase in the minimum wage is that it would have ceased to be slack, so that the engagement rate should coincide with the minimum wage. This is indeed the case, the mean engagement rate for unskilled workers being less than 4 per cent above the minimum wage (Table 2.12). The second prediction is that the seniority wage structure would flatten. This is because, constrained to pay a common engagement rate by the minimum wage, a firm with the original seniority structure (S' in Figure 6.9) would now pay a higher total wage over the 'lifetime' of the worker than a firm with a flat wage structure (F'). The firm would therefore have an incentive to reduce the impact of the minimum wage increase upon wage levels by reducing the steepness of the seniority scale (to S''). This is indeed confirmed by Table 2.12. The differential between mean earnings and the mean engagement rate fell from 36 per cent in 1934 to only 15 per cent by 1961. As a result, while the minimum wage rose by 110 per cent over this period, mean earnings (of urban Africans) rose by only 49 per cent. Hence, the change in the minimum wage greatly overstates the change in the cost of labour, but conceals a large resultant drop in seniority premiums.

We now investigate what this reduction in seniority premiums would have done to the structure of turnover rates, using the theory developed in sub-section (2) above.

(4) The Structure and the Cost of Labour Turnover

The model developed above predicts that a reduction in seniority premiums would change the structure of labour turnover towards that which would characterize firms with flat wage structures. Namely, the composition of quit rates would change from being U-shaped to being a monotonically increasing function of seniority.

This prediction can be tested for the years 1953, 1957, and 1968. In the first of these the labour market was not affected by minimum wage legislation. The structure of quit rates found by the Carpenter Report was indeed U-shaped (see Table 6.7). By 1957 wage levels had risen somewhat because of the first round of minimum wage increases, but not by enough to wipe out seniority scales. The turnover rates found by the Forrester Survey, 1957, are consistent with the prediction of the model for they retain the U-shaped structure but are uniformly lower than in 1953. However, by 1968 the minimum wage had risen so much that seniority scales had been largely squeezed out of the wage structure. The model predicts that the U-shaped structure of quit rates should now be entirely eliminated. This is indeed the case, for quit rates increase with seniority, so that despite the dramatically higher wage level than that which prevailed in 1953, the quit rate among those with more than seven years' experience is very similar in 1968 to that observed in 1953, while between 1957 and 1968 quits increased.

In 1957 firms had considerably more workers both with under two years' experience (34 per cent against 23 per cent) and over ten years' experience (31 per cent against 23 per cent) than in 1968.[6] Further, the mean length of service fell slightly from 6.7 years in 1957 to 6.4 years in 1968. Thus, despite higher mean real wages, turnover had, it appears, slightly increased between 1957 and 1968. An alternative explanation for the observed fall in the mean

Analysis

Table 6.7

Estimated Quit Rates[a] among Nairobi African Wage Earners

Length of service (years)	1953[b]	1957[c]	1968[d]
< 0	0.48	0.15	0.12
1–2	0.38	0.22	0.10
2–3	0.37	0.20	0.13
3–4	0.30	0.08	0.12
4–5	0.21	0.06	0.15
5–6	0.27	0.07	0.12
6–7	0.25	0.07	0.09
7–8	0.17	0.07	0.14
8–9	0.20	0.08	0.17
9–10	0.25	0.09	0.20

[a] Estimated from distribution of the labour force by years of experience. The quit rate for those with experience t_1 to t_2 is estimated as the percentage of the labour force with at least t_1 experience minus the percentage with at least t_2 experience divided by the percentage with at least t_1 experience.
[b] Carpenter Survey.
[c] Forrester Survey.
[d] Thias and Carnoy Survey.

length of service might be a faster expansion of employment in Nairobi in the 1960s than in the 1950s. However, this does not appear to be the case. Between 1949 and 1957 wage employment of Africans increased by 51 per cent. It is difficult to get a comparable figure for the 1960s because of boundary changes and changes in coverage; however, between 1959 and 1968 African employment probably grew by about 42 per cent[7] thus, the slowing of employment growth should have tended to increase mean seniority.

Recall from sub-section (2) that the overall cost of labour turnover is dependent not just upon the total rate of turnover but upon its composition: the seniority of those workers who quit is very important because the amount of the firm's investment in its workers varies with seniority. We now investigate which of the different quit structures observed in 1953, 1957, and 1968 represented the lowest cost of labour turnover, remembering that these different quit structures reflected different seniority premia which in turn represented responses to the different levels of the minimum wage. Which of these quit strutures generates the lowest cost of labour training is an open question. A given quit structure will generate different costs depending upon the ratio of instantaneous to cumulative training costs and the wage structure. We do not have sufficient data to make more than speculative estimates. These are now made to give some indication of the possible magnitudes involved. Since none of the three periods were times of manual labour shortage in urban areas, it is hard to believe that instantaneous recruitment costs were very high. We will assume that these costs represent 10 per cent of peak total human capital investment (which occurs at t' in Figures 6.6, 6.7, and 6.8). Peak non-instantaneous costs are represented by the area *acd* in Figure 6.6. However, in a seniority system the worker bears *bcd* of this, leaving the training investment of the firm at *abd*. To determine the area *abd* requires information upon the recruitment wage *b*, mean earnings *c*, the marginal product upon recruitment *a*, and the length of time required before the marginal product has risen to equal the wage, t'. While the two former are known, the latter two must be assumed. We arbitrarily set *a* equal to $0.3c$ and t' at five years of seniority. We treat both the wage and the marginal product as linear functions of seniority. The investment by the firm in the worker therefore peaks at five years of seniority and is fully recovered after ten years.

The reduction in seniority premiums alters the cost of training to the firm in two ways. First, by raising *b* it widens the gap between the marginal product and the wage paid and thus increases the peak investment of the firm in a worker who does not quit. Second, it reduces the investment by the worker and thereby lowers the disincentive to quit. Considering the first of these, on the above assumptions Table 6.7 shows the investment by the firm in a worker who stays with the firm for the ten years. The investment, expressed as a percentage of mean earnings, always peaks at the end of the fifth year and is zero at the end of the tenth. However, because seniority premiums were smaller in 1957 and 1968 than in 1953, the peak investment by the firm in the worker is accordingly higher.

Now introducing the second effect, the typical worker had a propensity to quit according to his seniority, summarized in Table 6.6. The quitting losses suffered by a firm result from workers in whom it has an investment quitting. The cost is therefore the product of the firm's investment in the worker (Table 6.8) and his propensity to quit (Table 6.7) summed over all levels of seniority weighted by their proportion of the labour force. This is expressed as a percentage of the mean wage in Table 6.9.

Given the assumptions set out above, and the turnover rates observed in the three years, we arrive at the conclusion that the cost of training as a percentage of the mean wage rose over the period 1953–68. Since the mean wage of manual workers also rose, this compounds the increase in the per capita cost to the firm of training unskilled workers. Clearly, by changing the ratio of instantaneous/non-instantaneous costs and the length of time over which the investment accumulates, these results can be changed, although the assumptions required in order to get the result that the 1968 turnover structure represented lower training costs than the previous years seem to us to be quite implausible. This suggests that the received wisdom that minimum wage increases stabilized the labour force *and thus reduced training costs* may be somewhat cavalier.

Table 6.8

Hypothesized Training Investment of the Firm in a Non-Quitting Worker
(percentage of annual mean wage)

Seniority (years)[a]	1953[b]	1957	1968[c]
< 1	34	39	45
1–2	57	72	87
2–3	75	98	121
3–4	88	116	145
4–5	96	128	159
5–6	96	128	159
6–7	88	116	145
7–8	75	98	121
8–9	57	72	87
9–10	34	39	45

[a] The mid-point is taken. Hence, the investment in training for seniority of 1–2 years is that after 1½ years, namely the instantaneous cost plus 1½ years of accumulated costs.
[b] Applying the 1954 wage structure.
[c] Applying the 1962 wage structure.

Table 6.9

Training Investment of the Firm as a Percentage of the Mean Wage

Seniority (years)	1953	1957	1968
< 1	16.3	5.9	5.4
1–2	11.3	13.5	7.7
2–3	8.9	12.9	12.4
3–4	5.3	4.9	12.0
4–5	2.8	3.8	14.5
5–6	2.9	4.1	9.9
6–7	1.8	3.5	6.0
7–8	0.8	2.7	7.1
8–9	0.6	2.1	5.3
9–10	0.3	1.2	2.7
Total	50.9	54.6	83.1

Instead, we may conclude that the period 1954–68 witnessed the emergence of a serious distortion in the market for firm-specific skill acquisition induced by minimum wage legislation. The large increase in the cost to the firm of investing in such skills must have substantially reduced the rate of skill accumulation from what it would have been in the absence of the distortion.

In the post-1968 period real wages fell and skill differentials widened (see Chapter 3). Presently, data are not available either for developments in the seniority wage structure or for quit rates by seniority. The prediction of our theory is clearly that seniority scales would re-emerge, so that the fall in the wage level would not be associated with either an increase in seniority-specific quit rates or with an increase in training costs per employee. Indeed the 1960s, during which the minimum wage was at its peak relative to mean earnings, may well have been the period of peak costs of labour turnover. By 1968, even though turnover rates had probably fallen from their peak, costs were probably still higher than in 1957. We predict that turnover, and more importantly the costs of turnover, would have fallen during the 1970s.

(5) General Skill Acquisition and the Wage Structure

In the orthodox human capital model general skill acquisition is financed entirely by the employee. In the Kenyan context often this cannot happen because the training costs exceed both the wage and the financial resources of young employees. The problem then arises that either the firm bears part of the cost of the investment or very little general skill formation can take place. But, the firm will only invest in general skill acquisition if it can achieve some subsequent return. The firm can only get a subsequent return if on average, during the post-training stage, the worker receives a wage below his marginal product. But, since the worker possesses a general (that is, marketable) skill, if the firm offers him a wage below his marginal product he can be poached by others: profit maximizing firms will pay him his marginal product. In this case the firm will have made an investment on which the worker acquires all the return. Hence, firms will not invest in the acquisition of general skills unless they can in some way restrict trained workers from quitting. There are two ways by which the firm may achieve this. First, the firm may enter into a contract under which the worker is indentured to the firm for a given number of years at a wage structure whereby the firm will recoup its investment. The public sector bonds all trainees for three years for whom the government has financed more than six months of pre-service or in-service training. Legal provision is also made for an indenture system in the private sector. However, minimum wage scales are laid down at a rather high level for trainees. Such contracts may also be both difficult and expensive to enforce: they are not widespread.

An alternative is for firms which invest in general training to operate a promotion policy which discriminates in favour of workers trained within the firm. Let us assume that prior to recruitment workers are ignorant of their promotion prospects—the promotion policy of the firm can only be observed by experience. Workers once trained can leave the firm and earn their marginal product (W_1). Alternatively they can stay in the firm and receive a lower wage (W_0) plus preferential promotion prospects over trained workers which the firm poaches from other firms at wage W_1. This scenario generates an equilibrium in which some firms invest in general skill acquisition but other firms do not, meeting their needs entirely by poaching. Firms which train also poach off each other but discriminate against those whom they poach in promotion policy. Firms which train must suffer some quits in equilibrium, otherwise promotion prospects for those who stay would not be improved above those which they can expect in other firms to which they might move. Two testable hypotheses generated by this model are that workers once trained would either quit very soon or not at all, and that in the early years after training skilled workers would raise their income by quitting the firm in which they were trained. This is because staying in the knowledge of accelerated future promotion involves making the same implicit savings on the part of the worker which we noted in sub-section (2) occurred under seniority scales in the case of firm-specific skills. It therefore generates the same pattern of quits, high initially and low later.

We now consider two empirical examples of general skill acquisition in Kenya, the first being a white-collar occupation, the second being skilled manual. Our chosen white-collar skilled occupation is that of insurance clerk. Trainees work towards a standard international examination. Once this is passed they are employable in any of a large number of companies and poaching is extensive. The initial training is not provided in all firms. It is quite expensive for the firm, involving much paid leave and examination tuition and entrance fees. The wage whilst training cannot be depressed to the point at which all costs would be borne by the employee. At such a wage the worker would be unable to maintain a standard of appearance considered appropriate. In firms which provide training, the post-training quit rate is very high. However, this is bunched very heavily soon after the completion of training, as indicated in Table 6.10. This is consistent with our hypothesis about the structure of quits.

Our second example is drawn from data collected by Godfrey (1977) in Nairobi in 1973. From a total sample of 446 candidates for Trade Tests, job

Table 6.10
Quitting and Seniority of Trained Insurance Clerks

Years since examination passed	Percentage still employees in the firm
< 1	100
2–5	50
6–10	50
> 10	47

Source: Data collected in 1980 from a large insurance company. Sample size 127.

histories were collected for a sub-sample of 185 workers who had entered the job market within the previous ten years. The occupations covered by the candidates, in descending order of importance, were motor-vehicle mechanics, fitters, welders, plumbers, carpenters, masons, painters, electricians, and tailors; that is, a variety of manual occupations in which general skills can be accumulated. Entry for a Trade Test is voluntary, the candidate having to pay a fee. Once the test is passed the worker is certified as possessing a generally marketable skill to a known standard. The test can be taken at three different grades, III, II, and I, corresponding to ascending difficulty. Candidates for Grades II and I must already have passed Grades III and II respectively. In III(6) we will demonstrate that the Trade Tests are a good and reliable indicator of the possession of skills as perceived by employers.

Using regression analysis Godfrey estimated an earnings function for each of the three groups of candidates: that is, candidates for each of the three grades of test. The number of jobs held since entering wage employment was then entered as an explanatory variable. In each case the coefficient was positive and statistically significant (see Godfrey, 1977, Appendix B, regressions 3, 4, and 5). We now use these estimated coefficients to infer the proportionate premium to earnings accruing to job changes. For candidates for the Grade III test, each job change raised earnings by 12 per cent relatively to mean earnings for the group. For candidates for Grade II, who therefore possessed Grade III and hence had both a greater quantity of human capital and skills which, being certified, could be readily recognized by employers, each job change raised earnings by 28 per cent. Finally, for candidates for Grade I, who therefore possessed Grade II and consequently had a greater level of recognizable general skill, each job change raised earnings by 39 per cent. The full results are set out in Table 6.11.

Table 6.11

Earnings and Job Change by General Skill Level

Skill Level	(1) Mean earnings (s.p.m.)	(2) Increment per job change (s.p.m.)	(3) Percentage increment (2)/(1)
No certificate (taking Grade III)	341	41	12
Grade III (taking Grade II)	513	142	28
Grade II (taking Grade I)	644	254	39

Source: Godfrey (1977).

This supports our hypothesis that even in the case of general skills firms tend to invest in their workers and subsequently attempt to recoup this investment by paying below the marginal product. This would explain why the greater the amount of human capital the greater is the premium upon leaving the firm in which the worker was trained. The greater the amount of human capital the greater will be the firm's investment in the worker. To maintain a uniform rate of return on such investments the wage must therefore be reduced further below the marginal product the greater the investment. Since a worker in which the firm has made no investment will still have a positive wage and marginal product, this entails that the gap between the marginal product and the wage must increase not only absolutely but proportionately to the wage as the skill level increases.

But while the premium upon job change in the early years of employment is high, most workers do not quit their jobs. Of those workers with up to ten years employment experience, 69 per cent were still with their first employer. Nor could this be explained by risks of unemployment. This issue will be taken up in greater detail later, but the unemployment rate subsequent to initial employment was low. Further, Godfrey, although not giving a breakdown by years of seniority, notes that the figure of 69 per cent was 'a proportion varying only slightly with age and length of working life' (Godfrey, 1977, p. 3). Now, if the proportion was invariant with respect to length of working life this must entail that the quit rate was initially high and subsequently low. Indeed, were the proportion completely invariant the quit rate in the first year would have been 31 per cent and in subsequent years zero. This quit profile for general skills, high initially and low subsequently, corresponds to our findings in Table 6.10 on the general skill represented by insurance clerks, and to our predictions concerning the nature of labour turnover for all general skills in which the firm makes an investment.

If the trainee is neither bonded nor induced to stay by prospects of rapid promotion then the firm will not invest in general skills. In the 'informal' sector it is common practice for trainees to pay masters to take them on (see King). This clearly imposes a constraint upon skill acquisition in that only those with assets can finance the training period. In the modern sector this is now overcome to some extent by the operation of training levies imposed on an industry. These finance the payment of firms for approved training courses. The inevitable limitation of this scheme is that it only operates within the confines of formalized institutional processes of skill acquisition which might constitute only a small fraction of the total general skill acquisition which would occur in an optimal system. As a result neither the informal sector fee-paying practice nor the government-administered apprenticeship and indenture schemes constitute major channels of general skill acquisition. An indication of this comes from Godfrey's full sample of 446 workers. While 32 per cent had some full time training, only 4 per cent had been involved in the classic informal sector fee-paying practice, and only 5 per cent had been through the official government training scheme.

So far we have considered general skills from the viewpoint of the firm, given that its employees may be unable to finance all of their skill acquisition. However, since part of skill formation will be financed by the employee, we must also consider the employee's incentive so to acquire skill. Here the effect of the large minimum wage increase between the early 1950s and the mid-1960s was unambiguously to reduce skill differentials. The minimum wage directly increased the unskilled mean wage, but directly only increased the engagement rate for jobs involving skill acquisition as employers flattened seniority scales (as discussed in (3) above). It is possible to construct cases in which, as a result of the minimum wage increase, the premium for skill is reduced for the employee and yet the cost of skilled labour rises relative to unskilled labour from the viewpoint of the firm. Such a case is illustrated in Figure 6.10. Two jobs are considered, one in which there is little skill accumulation (U), and one in which there is a lot of skill accumulation (SK) and hence investment by the firm. The vertical axis shows the wage normalized on the supply prices of labour for these jobs, the horizontal axis showing labour turnover. The higher the wage above the supply price the greater is the excess supply of labour to the occupation, and hence the greater is the disincentive to quit. Because the supply of labour to unskilled occupations will generally be far more elastic than that to the skilled, the turnover rate will be more elastic with respect to the wage in the unskilled occupation,

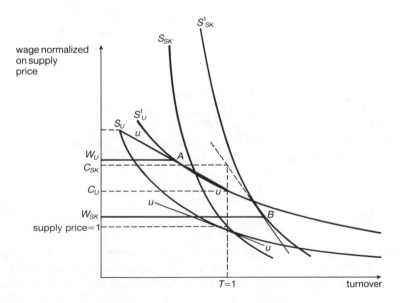

Fig. 6.10

and hence for a given wage structure the schedule relating wages and turnover is flatter.

Prior to minimum wage legislation, firms adopt seniority wage structures for both jobs with resulting wage-turnover schedules S_u and S_{SK}. Each occupation pays the normalized supply price and suffers a normalized rate of labour turnover, T. The slopes of these schedules at this point are equated with, and thus reflect, the cost of turnover relative to the wage. The steeper slope chosen in the skilled occupation thus reflects the greater cost of turnover there.

After the introduction of a minimum wage, the less skilled occupation adopts a flatter wage structure as a cost-minimizing solution. The flatter wage structure increases turnover for any given wage level, so the wage-turnover schedule shifts out to the right to S'_u. Firms optimize by locating on this schedule at A where the slope is the same as that in the initially chosen position, (namely, uu). At A the mean wage in the unskilled occupation has risen to W_u but turnover has fallen so the cost to firms of labour in the occupation is W_u less the value of the reduction in labour turnover. The cost of this labour to the firm thus rises only to C_u.

The skilled occupation similarly adopts a flatter wage structure, the wage-turnover schedule shifting as a result to S'_{SK}. The optimum point at which firms locate is B, at which the mean wage is W_{SK}. However, since turnover has risen the cost of labour in the skilled occupation is C_{SK}.

Hence, the wage in the skilled occupation rises by a smaller proportion than that in the unskilled occupation, thus lowering incentives, yet the cost of labour to firms rises by a greater percentage in the skilled occupation. The corollary of such an effect of the minimum wage increase would be that firms would become less willing to train labour and that workers would have less incentive to acquire skills. The model therefore predicts that the increase in the minimum wage could coincide with a decline in the skill acquisition of the African work-force. Table 2.6 tended to support this as a description of the period 1957–68. Conversely, the decline in the real minimum wage from the late 1960s onwards could have encouraged skill formation in the African labour-force. The data presented in Table 3.11 were certainly consistent with this prediction of the model.

(6) Skill Acquisition and Education

Education can be viewed as itself constituting general skill acquisition, as a training in the method of learning which increases the pace of subsequent skill acquisition, or as a screen by which able people who will naturally tend to have a rapid pace of skill acquisition can be identified. The first characteristic of education would tend to make it a substitute for formal training programmes, the latter two characteristics would tend to make education complementary.

For non-manual workers, we estimate the relationship between education and training using the 1978 survey of high- and middle-level manpower, the sample size being 533. Cross-tabulations of training by education and age suggest that for the younger age groups training was positively correlated with a high level of education: from Table 6.12 we see that, in the age group 25–34, of those with no training only 2 per cent had sixth-form education or better, while nearly 40 per cent of those will full-time training had this education. For all workers under the age of thirty-five, 44 per cent of those with less than Form IV education had received no training at all. This applied to only 28 per cent of Form IV leavers and to only 3 per cent of those with education beyond Form IV. Hence, the net effect of the attributes of education is for training and education to be quite strongly complementary.

Table 6.12

Education and Training of Non-Manual Workers
(percentage educated to sixth form or above)

Age	Training		
	Full-time	In-service	None
Up to 24	40.7	13.5	4.5
25–34	37.5	29.2	1.9
35–44	36.3	17.7	20.7

Source: 'Nairobi High and Middle Level Manpower Survey' (1978), Central Bureau of Statistics (unpublished).

For manual workers, the relationship between skill accumulation and education is investigated through the Trade Test Survey of 1973. As with white-collar workers, there was a tendency for education and training to be complementary. The evidence for this is twofold. First, the proportion of candidates who had full-time pre-service training rose with the level of education, from 9 per cent of those with little or no education to 36 per cent of those with completed primary education, and 37 per cent of those with secondary education. However, pre-service training gives a less complete account of the acquisition of skills than performance on the Trade Tests. Godfrey, who first analysed this data, concluded from it that education is at best of no use for manual skill acquisition by demonstrating that candidates with higher levels of education tended to have lower pass rates on the tests. This inference, however, involves a methodological error. Since entry for a test is both voluntary and costly, the observed pass rate will be a function solely of the gap between candidates' perceptions of their abilities and reality. All that Godfrey's results show is that the educated tend to be more over-ambitious than the less educated, and this tells us nothing about the

Analysis

link between education and skill acquisition. Godfrey's data can, however, be used to address this issue. The appropriate question to pose is whether there is a systematic relationship between the position in the skill hierarchy and the educational composition of the population. That such a relationship exists in a powerful form is shown in Table 6.13.

Table 6.13
Education and Skill Level (Manual Workers)
(percentages)

Skill Level	Education			
	(1) Less than Primary V	(2) Upper primary	(3) Secondary	(4) (3)/(1)
Pass Grade I	8	42	50	6.25
Pass Grade II but fail I	13	51	36	2.76
Pass Grade II not attempted I	13	59	28	2.15
Pass Grade III but fail II	20	45	35	1.75
Pass Grade III not attempted II	21	60	19	0.90
Fail Grade III	22	56	23	1.04
All Nairobi males aged 20 and over (1969)	40	35	25	0.62

Source: Collier and Rosewell.

Ideally, the bottom rung in the skill hierarchy would be those who have not attempted Grade III. Definitionally these were excluded from Godfrey's sample which consisted of those attempting a test, so we use as a proxy the adult male Nairobi population. Since the substantial majority of this group will be manual workers who have never taken a Trade Test, this is a good proxy. Table 6.12 shows that as we move up the skill hierarchy a significantly lower proportion of the population has little or no education and a significantly higher proportion has secondary education. While at the top of the hierarchy the latter group outnumber the uneducated by more than 6 to 1, at the bottom they are outnumbered 0.6 to 1. The intermediate education group is not uncorrelated with skill but the relationship is not monotonic. Completed primary education seems to be most closely associated with success in Grades I and II.

Finally, we need to demonstrate that performance in the Trade Tests is indeed a good indication of the skills which firms value. Godfrey has succeeded in demonstrating this step convincingly. If we accept that workers' productivity is associated with their wages, then a test of the significance of the Trade Tests is to investigate whether performance on the Tests is correlated with the wage immediately prior to the test. This last requirement removes the possibility that higher pay for good test performance merely reflects credentialism. Godfrey ran regressions of earnings functions with test performance as an independent variable for each of the three grades. He found that in each case performance was statistically significant and the coefficient was positive and substantial. This confirms that the Trade Tests are indeed measuring general skills to which firms have already assigned a value.

(7) Conclusion

The process of skill formation at all levels in the skill hierarchy is an important and somewhat neglected aspect of the development of the modern sector in Kenya. We have suggested that to the extent that there is a problem this reflects not a lack of market responsiveness but constraints upon the wage structure. One of these constraints was the minimum wages boom of 1954–64, which probably substantially reduced the incentive for firms to invest in firm-specific skills. A second constraint has been the inability through lack of assets and borrowing power of many workers to finance general skill acquisition. Whether the best response to this is innovation in lending arrangements in the capital market, or in more extensive use of term-based labour contracts, or an extension of training levies, would require a separate study.

Excursus: The Optimal Wage Structure for the Firm[8]

Our analysis contains a series of assumptions, some of which are inherent in the questions we address, some inherent in the techniques we adopt, and some convenient but not fundamental.

1. Skills are firm-specific. The acquisition and possession of general skills of course affect wage structure but we abstract from them throughout.

2. The firm seeks to optimize employment with respect to output and to minimize unit labour cost, defined as the sum of wage and training costs. This objective is implied by many assumptions about firm behaviour, including but not only that of profit maximization. By confining our attention to labour decisions we can avoid the need to specify particular behavioural and production relations of the firm.

3. The analysis is confined to training the cost of which is incurred instantaneously upon recruitment.

4. Quit rates, although endogenously determined, are negligible. This dras-

tic-sounding assumption greatly simplifies the analysis by eliminating terms for earnings in the event of anticipated future quits. As long as workers and firms have common perceptions about the chances of future quits, the analysis is not affected by its withdrawal.

5. The discount rates of both firms and workers are the same and equal to zero.

6. All workers work for the same number of years. If there is a common retirement age then a corollary is a common age of initial recruitment.

7. Each firm is in a steady state with respect to employment and wages. Neither employment nor wage structure changes over time: recruitment is equal to quits, and both occur at a constant rate.

The analysis proceeds by constructing three functions, the propensity of a worker to quit as a function of his wage, termed the 'quit function', the cost to the firm of quitting by a worker, termed the 'cost of quitting function', and the cost to the firm of compensating the worker for any loss of utility involved in his consumption being constrained by a wage structure which incorporates a premium for seniority, the 'compensation function'. The functions are then combined to show how employers may choose to make seniority payments. We show that a seniority wage premium is generally superior to no premium, and that the firm's optimal wage structure consists of a premium which rises with seniority but in general at a diminishing rate.

The Quit Function. The cohort-specific quit rate of a firm (q_i) we define as the proportion of workers with i periods of seniority who quit during the current period. This will be some function of the advantage to be gained by quitting and the chances of finding advantageous quits. In describing workers' quitting behaviour with respect to the wage structure it is necessary to introduce a utility function. We specify the quit function as being dependent on the present value of a flow of utility from a flow of income. This is possible because we assume that the worker can no more borrow for consumption than for training on the basis of future earnings.

We assume that utility is positive in the wage level, and therefore that the cohort-specific quit rate is a monotonically decreasing function of the difference between the expected wage in the firm and the mean expected wage in the economy for a worker with a given number of years before retirement. The analysis refers to a particular firm, and other firms' wage behaviour is assumed to be given. With the discount rate equal to zero:

$$q_i = q_i\left(\sum_{t=i}^{\tau} U(w_t)\right) \tag{1}$$

with $q_i' < 0$

where q_i = the cohort-specific quit rate in the current period

τ = the number of periods between recruitment and retirement

w_t = the wage paid by the firm in period t.

Workers with common seniority have common wage expectations and, by assumption, common quit rates.

The Compensation Function. Suppose that the firm makes no payment for seniority, i.e. the wage is constant at $\bar{w}$. With τ periods between recruitment and retirement, the worker expects upon recruitment $\bar{U} = \tau.U(\bar{w})$. A cost-minimizing firm will choose $\bar{w}$ such that $\bar{U}$ coprresponds to the marginal supply price of the required flow of recruits. Now consider any two consecutive periods, t and $t + 1$, and suppose the firm to lower the wage in t below $\bar{w}$, raising it by the same amount in $t + 1$. An amount of pay $(\frac{x}{2})$ is deferred from t until $t + 1$. Now let us introduce the compensation function, i.e. we consider how much the firm must pay to the worker so that upon recruitment he is indifferent between the two wage structures.

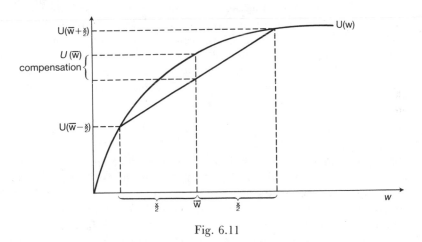

Fig. 6.11

The problem is illustrated in Figure 6.11. We assume diminishing marginal utility of income. The net loss (L) to the worker in utility from receiving $\bar{w} - \frac{x}{2}$ in period t and $\bar{w} + \frac{x}{2}$ in $t + 1$ instead of $\bar{w}$ in both periods is:

$$L = \left[U(\bar{w}) - U\left(\bar{w} - \frac{x}{2}\right) \right] - \left[U\left(\bar{w} + \frac{x}{2}\right) - U(\bar{w}) \right]$$

$$= 2\left[U(\bar{w}) - \tfrac{1}{2}\left(U(\bar{w} + \frac{x}{2}) + U(\bar{w} - \frac{x}{2}) \right) \right] \qquad (2)$$

Series expansion gives

$$L = 2\left\{ U(\bar{w}) - \tfrac{1}{2}\left[U(\bar{w}) + \frac{x}{2}.U'(\bar{w}) + \tfrac{1}{2}\left(\frac{x}{2}\right)^2 U''(\bar{w} + \ldots + u(\bar{w}) - \frac{x}{2}U'(\bar{w}) \right.\right.$$

$$\left.\left. + \tfrac{1}{2}(-^2U''(\bar{w}) - \ldots \right] \right\}$$

$$= -\left(\frac{x}{2}\right)^2 U''(\bar{w}) + \text{ higher powers of } \frac{x}{2} \cdot \qquad (3)$$

By taking sufficiently short time periods, x can be made as small as we like for any given seniority scale. Choosing x to be sufficiently small, the higher powers of $\frac{x}{2}$ can be ignored. L indicates the amount of utility by which the firm must compensate the worker for a transfer of an amount $\frac{x}{2}$ of pay from period t to period $t + 1$. The seniority premium attached to remaining in the firm from period t to period $t + 1$ is x, the wage increment. The larger the seniority premium the larger the compensation required by the worker. Differentiating (3) with respect to x yields:

$$\frac{\partial L}{\partial x} = \frac{x}{2} \, U''(\bar{w}) + \text{higher powers of } \frac{x}{2}. \tag{4}$$

Since $U''(\bar{w})$ is negative by assumption, both (3) and (4) are positive, so that the loss to be compensated increases at an increasing rate with the size of the seniority premium between the two periods. The compensating utility required is thus a strictly convex function of the seniority premium.

Treating the marginal utility of income as constant in the relevant neighbourhood, the compensating utility required can be converted into wage units by dividing through by the marginal utility of the wage, to indicate the required wage compensation (C):[9]

$$C = -\frac{x}{2}\left(\frac{U''(\bar{w})}{U'(\bar{w})}\right). \tag{5}$$

The cost of Quitting Function. In a steady state, with no employment growth, the rate of recruitment will be equal to the rate of attrition of the firm's labour force. The period-specific rate of recruitment $[R_t)$ is defined as the firm's recruitment as a proportion of its employment at the start of period t. R_t is a function of the cohort-specific quit rates, q_i. The labour force of the firm in period t (E_t) consists of those workers recruited at the start of period t, those recruited at the start of the period before less the proportion that quit at the end of that period, and similarly for previous cohorts:

$$E_t = \sum_{i=0}^{\tau} E_{t-i} R_{t-i} (1 - q_0)(1 - q_1) \ldots (1 - q_i) \tag{6}$$

where the cohort recruited at the start of period t is intact $(q_0 = 0)$ and that recruited τ periods before is due to retire $(q_\tau = 1)$. In steady state equilibrium, employment and the recruitment rate are constant, so that E_t and R_t are the same for all t. The recruitment rate in each period can thus be solved as:

$$R = 1/ \sum_{i=0}^{\tau} (1 - q_0)(1 - q_1) \ldots (1 - q_i) \tag{7}$$

The cost of quitting function (Q) shows the effect of introducing a seniority premium on quit rates, on the recruitment rate, and hence on the costs of the firm. Assume that a premium is paid by means of a transfer of $\frac{x}{2}$ from the wage paid at a particular seniority, i, to the wage paid at seniority $i + 1$. The worker is precisely compensated for the disruption to his consumption stream by raising the wage paid. The quit rate of workers with seniority $i - 1$, q_{i-1}, is unaltered because, by assumption, workers in the cohort $i - 1$ face an unaltered present value of their future utility stream. However, the quit rate of workers of seniority i, q_i, falls upon the introduction of the seniority premium because for the cohort i the wage in the next period is now higher. The present value of their utility stream rises and, from (1), this reduces the propensity to quit. Formally,

$$q_i = q_i(x_i), \; q_i < 0 \tag{8}$$

where x_i is the premium by which the wage in seniority $i + 1$ exceeds that in seniority i. Since some voluntary quitting occurs for reasons other than wage, as x_i is increased so q_i approaches a minimum greater than zero; it is therefore plausible to regard q_i'' as positive. In words, the cohort-specific quit rate falls as the seniority scale is made steeper, but there are diminishing returns.

The reduction per employee in the cost period which results from an increase in the seniority premium x_i can be expressed as:

$$\frac{\partial}{\partial x_i} = c_i \cdot \frac{\partial T}{\partial q_i} \cdot \frac{\partial R}{\partial x_i} \tag{9}$$

where c_i is the cost of a worker in cohort i quitting. It is clear that an increase in q_i raises the equilibrium recruitment rate, and it can be proved that it does so at an accelerating rate.[10] Hence the cost of quitting declines at a decelerating rate as the seniority scale is made steeper.

The cost of quitting function (9) can be combined with the compensation function (5) to derive the optimal seniority premium between seniority i and $i + 1$. The value of x_i at which the marginal reduction in the cost of quitting equals the marginal increase in the cost of compensating workers for their uneven consumption pattern is:

$$c_i \cdot \frac{\partial R}{\partial q_i} \cdot \frac{\partial q_i}{\partial x_i} = \frac{x U''(\bar{w})}{2 U'(\bar{w})} . \tag{10}$$

If the result applies to seniority i and $i + 1$, it generalizes to all levels of seniority. For every seniority there is a value x_i which minimizes net costs. For any seniority i with wage w_i, the wage for seniority $i + 1$ will exceed w_i by x_i^* (where w_i^* is the optimal premium and the solution to (10)). Thus the optimal wage structure for the firm is one in which the wage is a monotonically increasing function of seniority, subject only to $c_i > 0$.[11]

Now consider c_i, the cost to the firm of a quit by a worker in cohort i. The firm makes an instantaneous investment in the worker upon recruitment which it precisely recoups during subsequent employment. Since in steady-state equilibrium the firm is optimally adjusted to quitting behaviour, the cost of a quit can be viewed equivalently as the loss of a past investment or of a future opportunity. Thus c_i is the unrecovered investment in the worker, namely $\int_{t=i+1}^{\tau}(m - w_t)dt$, where m is the marginal product of the worker, assumed to remain constant. Initially c_i is positive; while it remains positive the wage rises monotonically with seniority. We now show that there is a potential limit to this rise: it is never optimal for the firm to pay a wage above marginal product.

Consider the value of c_k, where k is that period in which the wage has risen to equal the marginal product. Assume that c_k is positive. It follows from (10) that $w_{k + 1} > w_k = m$, i.e. the wage of cohort $k + 1$ exceeds marginal product. Since $c_{k + 1} - c_k = w_{k + 1} - m$, $c_{k + 1} > c_k$. In that case $c_{k + 1} > 0$, and thus $w_{k + 2} > w_{k + 1}$. By extension, the optimal wage rises in all future periods. However, if in all future periods the wage exceeds marginal product, c_k must be negative, so contradicting our assumption. A precisely analogous argument establishes that c_k cannot be negative. If, however, c_k is zero, then from (10) the optimal wage premium between periods k and $k + 1$ is zero. In that case $w_k = m = w_{k + 1}$, thus $c_{k + 1} = 0$, and $w_{k + 1} = w_{k + 2}$. By extension, the optimal wage in all periods subsequent to k is set equal to m, which indeed generates $c_k = 0$. With $c_i = 0$ for $i \geqslant k$, the firm becomes indifferent to quits from k onwards.

Thus, there is a unique point, k, at which the firm completes the recovery of its investment in the workers; k occurs when the wage rises sufficiently to equal the marginal product. We term this the 'recoupment point'. A seniority wage structure can be characterized by the recoupment point, the marginal product, and the recruitment wage. The optimal wage is a monotonically increasing function of seniority throughout the working life of the worker only if the recoupment point does not occur until period $\tau(k = \tau)$. If the recoupment point occurs before period $\tau(k < \tau)$, from period k onwards the wage equals marginal product, and is constant if marginal product is constant. The optimal wage structure is therefore kinked around k. The size of k relative to τ depends on the factors which govern the steepness of the seniority scale prior to k and on the size of the initial investment in training.

IV Adjustment Processes in Non-Agricultural Labour Markets[12]

In the previous sections on the formal sector non-agricultural labour market we stressed the importance of supervision and of skill accumulation. The third feature of employment which complicates the analysis is differences in labour quality. Labour quality is of particular importance in the context of the adjustment to a disequilibrium in the market since adjustment can be of the form either of a change in the wage rate or of a change in the quality of recruits, or both.

As in our analysis of the agricultural labour market, we begin by estimating changes in the demand and supply of labour, now with the added complication that these data should be quality-specific. We then consider wage and non-wage adjustments, culminating in a discussion of unemployment.

(1) The Supply of Labour

We now convert the education enrolment data into a flow of supplies onto the labour market. This requires some assumptions; in particular, at which age people can be said to enter the labour market. It seems reasonable to think of Form IV and Form VI leavers entering the labour market at once. At the other extreme, someone who never receives education clearly does not enter the labour market at birth. Such a person might work on a shamba from the age of five, but since this chapter focuses upon the formal-wage labour market we need an assumption about the minimum age of entry.

We have good data on the age of entry into the wage labour force from the National Social Security Fund (Bigsten and Collier 1980c). This recorded data for the period 1971–6, approaching total coverage of the formal-wage labour market. Data on entry refers not to entry to a particular job but to entry into the first wage job, which is precisely what we require. The data are not confused by labour turnover within the wage sector. In each of the six years the frequency distribution of age at entry is bimodal. In 1971 the modal ages are nineteen and twenty-two/three, for example. It is not implausible that these reflect different levels of education, namely primary and secondary school leavers. We will return to the NSSF data when we consider the demand for labour. Here we will adopt the age of nineteen as the age of entry to the wage labour force. In each year between 1971 and 1976 the number of recruits aged nineteen exceeded by a wide margin the number of recruits below the age of nineteen. For example, in 1971 3,787 workers were recruited aged nineteen against 2,194 workers below that age (of whom 1,676 were eighteen).

The unofficial practice of repeating some standards of primary education complicates the estimation of labour force flows. Assuming the problem away yields nonsensical results (negative flows of the uneducated). Allowing for repeating makes two differences; first primary output is reduced and secondly the duration of primary education is increased. Official estimates of repeating for 1976 (Ministry of Education Annual Report) shows 6 per cent of total primary enrolments to be repeaters, 14.4 per cent of Standard 7 enrolments, and 6 per cent of Standard 1. This is probably an underestimate. For example, Somerset found that 75 per cent of those going on to secondary school had repeated Standard 7. We will assume that 10 per cent of Standard 1 are repeaters and 20 per cent of Standard 7. In addition to repeating it has been the practice for children to drop out of education for a year if money for school fees was short. We will assume that the combination of repeating and dropping out adds on average three years to primary education. This compares with Moock's estimte from a village study of four years (mean leaving age seventeen), urban areas probably being subject to less dropping out. There is then a three-year lag before entry to the wage labour market is feasible.

The resulting flow estimates together with the underlying assumptions are presented in Table 6.14, rates of change of the stocks of labour being shown in Table 6.15. No allowance has been made for stock attrition through death and retirement, these factors being incorporated subsequently.

Table 6.14
The Flow on to the Labour Force
(corrected for repeating)

Year	Population aged 19 ('000s)	Age 19 no education ('000s)	Age 19 partial primary ('000s)	Age 19 standard 7/8 ('000s)	Age 19 partial secondary ('000s)	Form IV ('000s)	Form VI ('000s)
1961	152[a]	38[b]	104[c]	4[d]	2.0[e]	3.5[f]	283[g]
1962	155	38	106	5	1.5	3.7	359
1963	158	69	75	7	1.6	4.1	445
1964	152	70	72	11	2.3	4.6	563
1965	169	78	68	13	3.1	5.7	721
1966	176	33	*115*	*15*	1.9	5.7	948
1967	183	57	29	78	4.4	9.2	1,124
1968	190	46	42	78	6.8	12.6	1,389
1969	199	31	43	93	12.5	14.7	1,502
1970	210	44	43	87	12.5	16.3	2,010
1971	221	55	44	82	12.4	19.5	2,558
1972	232	60	50	81	12.9	23.5	3,002
1973	243	85	22	90	14.5	24.0	3,581
1974	254	109	0	92	17.4	27.1	3,452
1975	265	97	16	93	13.1	30.8	4,154
1976	276	94	20	97	12.1	40.4	4,523
1977	287	103	4	106	13.9[h]	46.5	5,174
1978	298	71	24	108	17.8[h]	52.8	5,240[h]
1979	319	81	32	100	20.1[h]	68.9	6,000[h]
1980	340		38	83			
	362						

[a] From *1969 Census* interpolated from 5-year age groups. No allowance for death.
[b] Derived residually: output in year i = population aged 19 in year i minus primary output aged 19 in year i, minus Form I in year $i - 2$.
[c] Output in year i = primary Standard 1 × 0.9 in year $i - 11$ − Standard 7 × 0.8 in year $i - 3$.
[d] Output in year i = Standard 7 × 0.8 in year $i - 3$ minus Form 1 in year $i - 2$.
[e] Output in year i = Form I in year $i - 2$ minus Form IV in year $i + 1$.
[f] Output in year i = Form IV in year i minus Form VI in year $i + 2$.
[g] Output in year i = Form VI in year i.
[h] Estimate.

Table 6.15
Rates of Stock Accumulation

Year	No education ('000s)	%	Partial Primary ('000s)	%	Full Primary ('000s)	%	Form I and II ('000s)	%	Secondary Form IV ('000s)	%	Form VI ('000s)	%
1961	2,704[a]	1.4	328[b]	31.7	193[b]	2.1	18.8[c]	10.6	9.3[c]	38.7[5]	4[a]	5.2
1962	2,742	1.4	432	24.5	197	2.5	20.8	7.7	12.9	28.7	5.7	6.3
1963	2,780	2.5	538	13.9	202	3.5	22.4	7.1	16.6	24.7	6.0	7.4
1964	2,849	2.5	613	11.7	209	5.3	24.0	9.6	20.7	22.2	6.5	8.6
1965	2,919	2.7	685	9.9	220	5.9	26.3	11.8	25.3	22.5	7.0	10.2
1966	2,997	1.1	753	15.3	233	6.4	29.4	6.5	31.0	18.4	7.8	12.2
1967	3,030	1.9	868	3.3	248	31.5	31.3	14.1	40.2	29.7	8.7	12.6
1968	3,087	1.5	897	4.7	326	23.9	35.7	19.0	52.8	31.3	9.8	14.3
1969	3,133	1.0	939	4.6	404	23.0	42.5	29.4	67.5	27.8	11.2	14.3
1970	3,164	1.4	982	4.4	497	17.5	55.0	22.7	83.8	24.1	12.8	15.6
1971	3,208	1.7	1,025	4.3	584	14.0	67.5	33.9	103.3	23.3	14.8	17.5
1972	3,263	1.8	1,069	4.7	666	12.2	90.4	14.3	126.8	22.7	17.4	17.2
1973	3,323	2.6	1,119	2.0	747	12.0	103.3	14.0	150.8	18.9	20.4	17.6
1974	3,408	3.2	1,141	0	837	11.0	117.8	14.8	177.9	18.0	24.0	14.6
1975	3,517	2.8	1,141	1.4	929	10.0	135.3	9.7	208.7	17.3	27.5	15.3
1976	3,614	2.6	1,157	1.7	1,022	9.5	148.4	8.2	249.1	19.4	31.7	14.5
1977	3,708	2.8	1,177	0.3	1,119	9.5	160.5	8.7	295.7	18.7	36.3	14.0
1978	3,811	1.9	1,181	2.0	1,225	8.8	174.4	10.2	348.5	17.9	41.4	12.5
1979	3,882	2.1	1,205	2.7	1,333	7.5	192.2	10.5	417.4	19.8	46.6	12.9
1980	3,963		1,237	3.1	1,433	5.8	212.3				52.6	

[a] From Table 6.14 minus output in 1961 and 1962.

[b] Primary dropout occurred throughout standards. Therefore Table 6.14 is not a good guide to the partial/completed distinction. 'Partial primary' is defined as less than Standard 7 and is taken from the 1969 Census (1978 *Statistical Abstract* Table 19(a)) minus output in 1961 and 1962.

[c] From the 1969 Census minus output in 1961 and 1962. Non-citizens and citizens assumed to be split between partial secondary and Form IV in the same proportions. The resulting estimate of the African Form IV stock in 1961, 9,300, can be compared with the cumulative flow of output to 1961 of about 10,200 (Ministry of Education, *Annual Reports*).

Considering, first, those with no education: over the period 1961–79, before allowing for attrition the stock increased by 44 per cent. However, little reliance should be placed on this figures. First, they are derived residually without allowing in our population estimate for attrition between the Census date and the year for which the population is estimated. This tends to raise the rate of flow in later periods and lower it in earlier periods. For example, with a one per cent p.a. attrition rate the 1979 flow onto the labour market would have been 46,000 instead of 81,000, and the 1961 flow would have been 52,000 instead of 38,000. In addition to this bias, which overstates the rate of increase of the flow, the omission leads to a net over-estimate of the 1979 stock, though this is small relative to the overestimate through the absence of stock attrition. While the figures could be improved by appropriate assumptions about attrition, for our study, accurate trends in the supply of the various categories of educated labour are far more important than trends in uneducated labour.

For educated labour our estimates are unaffected by population estimates and so are more reliable. The series are still unadjusted for stock attrition. This is because the age profile of the stock of each category of educated labour was both distinct and changing rapidly over time. The application of age-specific mortality rates estimated from the Census to these changing stocks would be a substantial undertaking. More importantly, attrition through death can be accommodated more accurately, through the analysis of labour turnover which we consider separately.

The stock of labour with partial primary education grew at a decelerating rate. Completed primary education growth was heavily concentrated in the period 1967–71; thereafter the growth rate decelerated continuously from a peak of 31 per cent in 1967 to 5.8 per cent by 1980.

The growth of partial secondary education was also heavily concentrated in the period 1968–72. The growth in the stock of Form IV leavers was never below 17 per cent p.a. and yet again displays peaking in the period 1967–72.

To conclude, the expansion of the Kenyan education system, though rapid throughout the period, was heavily concentrated in the period 1967–72. During this sub-period stocks of educated labour commonly grew at around 30 per cent per annum, which must have placed an enormous burden of adjustment on the labour market. Hence, this sub-period and its aftermath warrants special attention in the analysis of labour demand, to which we now turn.

(2) *The Demand for Labour*

In this sub-section we analyse how the development of the economy changed the demand for educated labour. Ideal estimation would require simultaneous solutions of demand and supply because to some extent observed changes in output occur because of changes in the supply of educated labour.

However, the data requirements of such a procedure are far beyond data availability. We follow instead two alternatives. Each starts by holding constant the educational profile of each occupation as observed at a particular date. The first alternative then takes the observed changes in employment by occupation and derives the changes in demand for types of educated labour which would have resulted had the intra-occupational education profile stayed constant. The second alternative combines the educational profile of each occupation with the occupational profile of each industry at one date, to derive the educational profile of each industry at that date. Observed changes in the employment of labour by industry are then used to derive the changes in demand for types of educated labour which would have occurred had the education profile within each industry been constant over time. Each of these approaches has something in its favour both on theoretical and practical grounds. To some extent the demand for occupations within an industry will change over time exogenously, and to some extent such changes will be an endogenous response to changes in labour supply. If all changes were exogenous to labour supply the first alternative is theoretically appropriate; if all changes were endogenous the second is appropriate. A third possibility would be to treat observed changes in output as exogenous to the changing composition of labour supply and to derive demand for different types of labour from these output changes. This would require the estimation of industry-specific production functions. The problems with this approach in Kenya appear to be insuperable, the issue being considered in our analysis of labour productivity. Fortunately, unpublished material from the *1972 Manpower Survey* provides matrices of education by occupation and of occupation by industry. Assuming the former matrix to apply to each industry, these can be combined to yield an industry by education matrix. In Table 6.16 this matrix is used to calculate the change in the demand for different levels of education arising from the industrial change between 1961 an 1977. The results show that the change in industrial composition was modestly biased away from educated labour. Had the industry by education matrix stayed constant, industrial change would have increased the employment of those with secondary education by around 66 per cent compared to a 75 per cent increase for those without education.

We now turn to the estimation of labour demand by education using trends in employment by occupation instead of in industrial structure. The additional problem posed is that occupational data have not always been collected upon a regular basis. Employment and Earnings surveys, which cover all wage employees, have contained information on occupation only since 1968. Hence, for an adequate time-span we have to resort to the data from intermittently conducted manpower surveys which cover only the skilled labour force.

This restricts comparison to the years 1964 and 1977, for which survey data provide a breakdown by citizenship and occupational group. These

Table 6.16

The Change in the Demand for Labour by Education due to Industrial Change

Industry	Change in Employment 1961–77 ('000s)	Increase in Employment by Education ('000s)				
		None	P1–4	P5–8	SI–IV	SV and above
Agriculture	8.1	n.a.	n.a..	n.a.	n.a.	n.a.
Mining	−0.4	−0.1	−0.1	−0.1	0	0
Manufacturing	59.3	19.6	19.6	16.6	3.0	0.6
Construction	31.0	10.9	12.4	6.8	0.9	0
Electricity	7.2	2.1	2.2	2.2	0.6	0.1
Commerce	24.4	7.1	7.8	6.6	2.7	0.2
Finance	12.9	1.4	2.1	5.2	3.5	0.8
Transport	3.9	1.1	1.3	1.1	0.3	0
Services	125.3	28.8	31.3	40.1	16.3	8.8
Total change in employment (excluding agriculture)		70.9	76.6	78.5	27.3	10.5
	Employment in 1961 ('000s)					
Agriculture	252.0	n.a.	n.a.	n.a.	n.a.	n.a.
Mining	3.8	1.3	1.3	1.0	0.2	0.1
Manufacturing	48.6	16.1	16.1	13.6	2.5	0.5
Construction	17.9	6.3	7.2	3.9	0.5	0
Electricity	2.5	0.7	0.8	0.8	0.2	0
Commerce	38.2	11.1	12.2	10.3	4.2	0.3
Finance	16.8	1.8	2.7	6.8	4.6	1.0
Transport	44.2	12.5	14.7	12.5	3.4	0
Services	197.1	45.3	49.2	63.1	25.6	13.8
Total employment (excluding agriculture)		95.1	104.2	112.0	41.2	15.7
Percentage increase in employment		74.6	73.5	70.1	66.3	66.9

Sources: *1972 Manpower Survey*, Appendix Tables 19, 33, (unpublished); R. S. Ray in Sheffield (ed.), *Statistical Abstract, 1978*.

employment changes are converted into education-specific demands, shown in Table 6.17. This shows a strong bias towards educated labour with secondary education, growing by around 200 per cent against 70 per cent for those without education.

The most interesting step is to compare the industry-based and occu-

Table 6.17

The Change in the Demand for Labour by Education due to Occupational Change

Occupational group	Total	Education				
		None	P 1–4	P 5–8	S I–IV	S V+
Education profile of occupation (percentages)						
Professional and administrative	100	7	15	40	25	13
Managerial and executive	100	18	30	22	20	10
Clerical	100	4	8	9	35	4
Sales	100	32	35	24	8	1
Teachers	100	1	3	47	31	18
Manual and technical	100	35	36	25	3	0.5
Change in Citizen Employment 1964–77 ('000s)						
Professional and administrative	11.6	0.8	1.7	4.6	2.9	1.5
Managerial and executive	9.9	1.8	3.0	2.2	2.0	1.0
Clerical	53.4	2.1	4.3	4.8	18.7	2.1
Sales	2.0	0.6	0.7	0.5	0.2	0
Teachers	72.7	0.7	2.2	34.2	22.6	13.1
Manual and technical	170.6	59.7	61.4	44.4	5.1	0.9
Total change	320.2	65.7	73.3	90.7	51.5	18.6
Citizen Employment in 1964 ('000s)						
Professional and administrative	1.8	0.1	0.3	0.7	0.5	0.2
Managerial and executive	5.7	1.0	1.7	1.3	1.1	0.6
Clerical	19.8	0.8	1.6	1.8	6.9	0.8
Sales	5.0	1.5	1.8	1.2	0.5	0
Teachers	30.4	0.3	0.9	14.3	9.5	5.5
Manual and technical	258.4	90.4	93.0	67.3	7.7	1.4
	321.1	94.1	99.3	86.6	26.2	8.5
Percentage Increase in Employment		69.8	73.8	104.7	196.6	218.8

Sources: as for Table 6.16.

pational-based estimates, though the procedure is subject to qualifications. The time periods covered, 1961–77 and 1964–77, differ, but fortunately for our purposes 1961–4 was a period of employment stagnation. The coverage of the two approaches is different. First, the occupation-based approach relates to citizens and thus captures Africanization. Second, while the industry-based figures exclude agriculture the occupation-based figures exclude only unskilled agricultural workers. This latter coverage is preferable because qualified agricultural workers such as managers can be thought of as part of the formal (non-smallholder) labour market. This difference in coverage is, however, minor.

The comparison of the *stock* estimates in 1961 and 1964 suggests that differences are probably almost entirely accounted for by the omission of non-citizens from the occupation-based estimates. The implied education profile of non-citizens derived in Table 6.18 is plausibly skewed towards the highest education categories. Table 6.19 compares the estimates of the *change* in the demand for educated labour. The estimate based on employment changes by industry yields an increase in the employment of those with completed primary education or beyond which is some 44,500 less than that based on employment changes by occupation. However, some 31,500 of this discrepancy can be accounted for by the decline in the employment of non-citizens and their replacement by citizens, this change having no net effect on the industry-based estimate but increasing the occupation-based estimate due to its omission of non-citizens. Thus, excluding Africanization, the occupation-based estimate of the change in demand for educated manpower is 13,000 above the industry-based estimate. The two methods corrected for Africanization thus estimate the annual growth in demand over the period 1964–77 as being 4.2 per cent (industry-based) and 4.6 per cent (occupation-based), a discrepancy not large enough to warrant further analysis.

Table 6.18

The Educational Profile of the Non-Agricultural Wage Labour Force in the Early 1960s ('000s)

	Education				
	None	P 1–4	P 5–8	S I–IV	S V+
Industry-based	95.1	104.2	112.0	41.2	15.7
Occupation-based (citizens only)	94.1	99.3	86.6	26.2	8.5
Difference	1.0	4.9	25.4	15.0	7.2
Total difference			53.5		
Non-citizen employment			49.3		

Sources: Tables 6.16 and 6.17.

This concludes our analysis of the demand for labour by education as generated by employment expansion. Before combining the demand and supply analyses, however, we must consider a factor which mediates between the net growth of employment and the recruitment of labour, namely labour turnover.

(3) Labour Turnover

The recruitment of labour to wage employment exceeds the growth in

Table 6.19
Changes in Employment by Education, 1961–1977
('000s)

	Education				
	None	P 1–4	P 5–8	S I–IV	S V+
Industry-based	70.9	76.6	78.5	27.3	10.5
Occupation-based (citizens only)	65.7	73.3	90.7	51.5	18.6
Difference	−5.2	−3.3	−12.2	−24.2	−8.1
Differences in P5 and above				−44.5	
Change in non-citizen employment				−31.5	
Residual				−13.0	

Sources: Tables 6.16 and 6.17.

employment by the extent of exits from the wage labour force. This factor may do more than just increase the total recruitment of labour. Just as employment growth can be (and has been) biased with respect to education, so exits can be education-saving or education-using. The total demand bias thus has to take into account both growth and exits.

Labour turnover is a complex phenomenon. We can schematize it at the level of the individual firm as follows:

> *Recruitment* *Exit*
> Replacement (1) Death
> New jobs (2) Retirement (urban)
>   (3) Retirement (rural)
>   (4) Quits (to rural)
>   (5) Quits (to other firms)
>   (6) Quits (to unemployment)
>   (7) Of which due to redundancy

Not all exits generate recruitment because some exits are due to redundancy. Not all replacement recruitment generates employment opportunities for new job seekers because some recruits are previous quitters. We can simplify the analysis somewhat by assuming that the flow of quits into unemployment equals the flow of unemployed former quitters being recruited. Alternatively, we can adopt a time period after which rather few quitters are still unemployed, having either found work or given up search. That is, we can reassign (6) into either (5) or (4). In either case that part of replacement recruitment which generates jobs for new job seekers is:

$$(1) + (2) + (3) + (4) - \max \left| \begin{matrix} (7) - (5) \\ 0 \end{matrix} \right. \tag{i}$$

That is, total exits except those to other firms minus any excess of redundancies over quits to other firms. This can also be expressed as:

$$\text{Replacement} - (5) - \text{max}\left|\begin{array}{l}(7) - (5)\\0\end{array}\right.$$ (ii)

or, finally as:

$$\text{Recruitment} - \text{new jobs} - (5) - \text{max}\left|\begin{array}{l}(7) - (5)\\0\end{array}\right.$$ (iii)

These three versions, although expressions of the same phenomenon require different data, which is important since the data requirements are formidable. Surveys of the urban labour force provide data on quits to other firms, (5), and on recruitment. Necessarily, such surveys miss (1), (2), (3), and (4) since these people are no longer part of the urban labour force.

An ILO survey reported in Nigam and Singer (1974) of Kenyan manufacturing in 1971 found (4) + (5) + (6) to be 9.3 per cent. Whilst these rates are low historically and internationally, they are likely to imply a rate of inter-firm quitting much higher than the redundancy rate. Thus, whilst a few firms may occasionally find that they do not need to recruit as much as (1) + (2) + (3) + (4) we are unlikely to bias the results very greatly by ignoring them. In this case (7) − (5) is negative so that the term $^{\text{max}}|\,^{(7)\,-\,(5)}_{0}$ takes the value zero and drops out.

We are therefore left with needing data on replacement recruitment, or total recruitment and new jobs, or (1), (2), (3), and (4). There are no data which disaggregates recruitment by motivation so the first option is not feasible. Taking the second option, the ILO Survey does not provide data on recruitment, whilst the 1968 IBRD Survey, which does provide recruitment data has no quit data. If the quit data observed in 1971 also applied in 1968 we can estimate recruitment − New Jobs − ((4) + (5) + (6)) as 12 per cent − 1.3 per cent − 9.3 per cent = 1.4 per cent so that the demand for new employees as a result of quitting would be 1.4 per cent + (4). Using approach (i) we have two data sources. The ILO Survey provides data for (1) + (2) + (3) and for (4) + (5) + (6). For manufacturing the former is 2.3 per cent and the latter 9.3 per cent. This merely establishes the broad range 2.3 per cent to 11.6 per cent. Our second source is the National Social Security Fund. In 1971 this had records on some 400,000 people currently in regular wage employment. From this data base Bigsten and Collier have calculated rates of exit from wage employment excluding inter-firm quitting.[13] This yields data on (1) + (2) + (3) + (4) which are precisely the data required. For 1971 the exit rate was 6 per cent of those in wage employment. The coverage of NSSF includes some regular agricultural workers who probably have a higher exit rate. No allowance can currently be made for this. We will adopt the 6 per cent estimate of the NSSF since this lies in the centre of the range estimated from the ILO Survey data.

The next stage in our analysis of turnover-based demand is to investigate the possibility of education-bias. Various evidence suggests that turnover demand had an education-saving bias. The ILO Survey found that the total quit rates (the sum of (1) through (6)) was 11.5 per cent for skilled workers and 16.7 per cent for the unskilled, in all sectors excluding agriculture. The 1972 Manpower Survey, with a higher skill definition, found a total recruitment rate during 1971 of only 11 per cent, which must have exceeded the total quit rate by the extent of employment expansion which was 6 per cent in 1971. The NSSF data base reveals higher quit rates ((1) + (2) + (3) + (4)) for lower-paid than for higher-paid workers. It also shows that throughout the 1970s the mean age of those quitting the wage labour force was below the mean age of those staying in the wage labour force. This suggests the stylized interpretation that unskilled (low wage) workers stay in the labour force a relatively short time while skilled workers (high wage) stay in it until retirement. This would produce the odd-looking result that most quitters were younger than most stayers.

Because the educated labour force is younger than the less-educated labour force we should expect lower turnover from death and retirement among the educated. Because incomes of the educated are so much higher we would also expect smallholding to be a less attractive proposition for them than for the less educated.

Even within an occupation quit rates might vary systematically by education. A survey of young skilled manual workers in Kenya[14] found this to be the case with respect to inter-firm quitting. The rate of voluntary quits rose with education and the rate of involuntary quits fell (see Table 6.20).

Table 6.20

Quit rates by Reason for Quitting and Education among Skilled Manual Workers

	Quit rate (percentage)	
Education	Voluntary	Involuntary
Little or none	13	16
Completed primary	20	15
Secondary I–II	25	21
Secondary III–IV	22	7

Source: Collier and Rosewell (1983).

These observations lead us to expect that turnover-based demand for skilled labour would be low. For example, the ILO Survey found turnover through death and retirement to be 1.2 per cent per annum in commerce and 0.8 per cent per annum in services, both being industries with a relatively highly-educated labour force. If quitting to rural areas is negligible for the educated then an estimate of one per cent per annum for tunover-based demand might not be implausible. Our final estimates of turnover-based demand are one per cent per annum for skilled workers and 6 per cent per annum for unskilled workers. These estimates are obviously only approximate.

(4) Supply–Demand Imbalance

We now bring together the education-specific changes in demand and supply. There are several possible reactions to imbalances. Firms could choose some combination of wage adjustment and labour-quality adjustment reflected in selection criteria. Individual workers could choose to resist or accept either of these changes and, should they choose to resist, they could prove to be successful or unsuccessful. Thus, for example, in the face of excess supply wage rigidity might be compatible with no unemployment (if selection criteria are sufficiently flexible), or wage flexibility be compatible with severe unemployment (if some workers maintain their initial reservation prices).

We first infer the pattern of demand–supply imbalances, then investigate actual (as distinct from desired) behavioural responses in terms of wages and selection criteria. Finally, we examine the consequences of this behaviour for the labour market as indicated by unemployment and urban migration.

We have distinguished two separate components of demand for African wage labour, net employment growth (including the replacement of non-citizens) and the replacement of those citizens who leave the wage labour market. The former of these, summarized in Table 6.17, was biased in an education-using direction; the latter was biased in an education-saving direction. The net effect, reported in Table 6.21, is education-using. The fragility of the underlying turnover data should, however, be recalled.

We now compare these incremental employment estimates with the flows of labour by education coming on to the market in the relevant periods. It should be recalled that the stock accumulation figures do not allow for mortality. For example, some 6 per cent of the labour coming on to the market in 1964 would have been dead by 1977. The required adjustments are, however, marginal. Table 6.22 brings together the supply and demand figures.

Three criteria are jointly useful as indicating pressure of imbalance. The absolute difference between employment growth and supply growth is useful partly because it is a more reliable estimate than the percentage changes since it is invariant with respect to errors in estimates of initial stocks. Thus, we can conclude that an excess supply of 8,400 Form VI leavers in reality represented broad balance in that market. Our supply figures made no allowance for the increase in university intake over the period, nor for mortality. Further, not all Form VI leavers who did enter the labour market would have entered wage employment. A second indicator of imbalance is the absolute imbalance as a percentage of total incremental employment. For Form VI leavers this was rather low at 39 per cent. A third measure is the

Table 6.21

The Total Incremental Demand for African Labour by Education

	Education ('000s)				
	None	P 1–4	P 5–8	S I–IV	S V+
Employment in 1964	94.1	99.3	86.6	26.2	8.5
quits[a]	5.6	6.0	5.2	0.3	0.1
Employment in 1977	159.8	172.6	177.3	77.7	27.1
quits[a]	9.6	10.4	10.6	0.8	0.3
Total quits 1964–77[b]	106.4	114.8	110.6	7.7	2.8
Net employment growth 1964–77	65.7	73.3	90.7	51.5	18.6
Total Incremental Employment	172.1	188.1	201.3	59.2	21.4
Percentage Increment	183	189	232	226	252

Sources: Tables 6.16 and 6.17.
Notes:
[a] Six per cent p.a. for primary and less, one per cent p.a. for secondary.
[b] Average of 1964 and 1977 quits times 14 (years).

Table 6.22

Demand–Supply Imbalance by Education

	Education				
	None	P 1–4	P 5–8	S I–IV	S V+
(1) 1964–77 total incremental employment ('000s)	172.1	188.1	201.3	59.2	21.4
(2) 1964–77 total incremental stock ('000s).	859	564	910	411.5	29.8
(3) Imbalance ('000s)	686.9	375.9	708.7	352.3	8.4
(4) Imbalance as percentage of employment	399	200	352	595	39
(5) Percentage employment increase	183	189	232	226	252
(6) Percentage stock increase	30	92	435	921	458
(7) Difference ((6) − (5))	−153	−97	203	695	206

Sources: Tables 6.15 and 6.21.

absolute difference in the percentage growth rates of employment and the labour stock. If there is no difference then a constant proportion of the labour force can be recruited into wage employment. Depending upon what we assume about the rest of the economy, either of the latter measures could be more appropriate as an indicator of imbalance. We will therefore use all three criteria.

On all three criteria there was massive excess supply of secondary school leavers below Form V, and to a lesser extent of those with completed primary education. The increment to the stock of such secondary school leavers was 600 per cent greater than the incremental employment opportunities, the percentage growth of supply being 700 per cent greater than that of demand. In contrast, on the third indicator of imbalance, in those categories below completed primary education, there would have been substantial excess demand in the absence of any changes in selection criteria.

On constant selection criteria, flexible wages, and initial equilibrium this should have produced a widening of differentials between Form VI and lower secondary-school leavers, and wage compression with rising wages for those with less education and falling wages for those with completed primary and lower secondary education.

(5) Wage Adjustment

The attempt to test whether wage changes coincide with these predictions encounters two problems. One is the problem of data: earnings data by occupation (as opposed to industry) is scarce. The second problem is that in the early 1960s the wage labour market was not in equilibrium. The combination of economic appeasement by the colonial authorities as a prelude to Independence and the economic rewards which were its postscript, had pushed real wages of unskilled workers well above the market clearing wage. Because the minimum wage was the main instrument of these policies, the period around Independence was one of wage compression between skilled and unskilled workers. Offsetting this was a temporary severe shortage of highly-educated African labour caused by the sudden introduction of Africanization. In Table 6.23 these changes can be seen by comparing earnings in 1953, the pre-crisis equilibrium, with earnings in 1968. The data for 1953 relate to Africans and those for 1968 and subsequent years include non-citizens, but African earnings must have been close to these figures except in the two highest occupation categories. Over the period 1953–68 unskilled earnings jumped 174 per cent, skilled manual earnings by 102 per cent, and clerical earnings by 189 per cent.

Because the post-Independence period started in disequilibrium, to the extent that market forces influenced wages there were two distinct pressures on the labour market. In addition to the wage changes exerted by educational imbalance outlined above there was pressure for a widening of skill differentials as the unskilled labour market returned to equilibrium.

A final complication is that the supply price of labour from smallholdings was changing over time. This was the result of four distinct changes in the smallholder economy. First, mean incomes rose over the period. Second,

Table 6.23

Earnings by Occupation[a] 1953–1977 (spm at current prices)

	Directors administration and professional	Middle level executive and managerial	Clerical/ secretarial	Teachers	Other white-collar	Technicians foremen	Manual skilled and semi-skilled	Manual unskilled regular (non-agricultural)
1953[c]	–	194	–	–	–	130	74	
1968	2168	2304	692	541	734	1252	327	253
1972	2621	2092	783	564	796	1565	363	271
1977	6083	3212	1190	862	1397	1851	1001	447
(A) Normalized (manual unskilled earnings = 1)								
1953	–	–	2.62	–	–	–	1.76	1.00
1968	8.57	9.11	2.74	2.14	2.90	4.95	1.29	1.00
1972	9.67	7.72	2.89	2.01	2.94	5.77	1.34	1.00
1977	13.61	7.19	2.62	1.93	3.13	4.14	2.24	1.00
(B) Normalized (1972 real earnings; GDP deflator used[b])								
1953	–	–	0.35	–	–	–	0.51	0.39
1968	0.95	1.26	1.01	1.13	1.06	0.92	1.03	1.07
1972	1.00	1.00	1.00	1.00	1.00	1.00	1.00	1.00
1977	1.18	0.78	0.78	0.81	0.90	0.60	1.41	0.84

[a] *Employment and Earnings* (Central Bureau of Statistics, 1963–77) for 1972 and 1977 and House and Rempel (1978), T.2.4 for 1968.
[b] For 1972–7 the GDP deflator is 1.96. The Nairobi higher-, middle- and lower-income indexes of consumer prices rose by 1.87, 1.84 and 2.00 respectively. For 1968–72 the GDP deflator is 1.145.
[c] *Report of the Committee on African Wages* (Colony of Kenya, 1954), Table D.3 for 1953 data.

population rose so that the relationship between the marginal and the mean product of agricultural labour changed. Third, smallholder income distribution may have become less equal. Fourth, the expansion of rural education meant that education trickled down to lower income groups because of the correlation between parental income and children's education. This had the effect of lowering the supply price of labour with a given level of education over and above that change brought about directly by education expansion.[15] The combined effect of these changes probably raised the supply price of unskilled wage labour, but the data are not available to quantify this change.

Table 6.23 shows that in the period 1968–77 real wages changed very rapidly. The unskilled wage fell by 22 per cent, a trend which continued until 1980, by which time there was little difference between the earnings of smallholders and unskilled wage earners (once cost of living differences have been allowed for). That is, the unskilled labour market returned to equilibrium. The quantification of this process whereby market forces restored the wage structure to equilibrium after a series of institutional shocks requires long time-series on real earnings, covering the period from the late 1940s to the late 1970s. No such data are available for the smallholder sector. However, in the late 1940s there was no institutional intervention in the private agricultural estates labour market so that it may be reasonable to consider average smallholder living standards as being broadly equated to that of estates workers. This is the assumption made for 1949 in Table 6.24. The increase in the real income of the mean smallholder household between 1949 and 1978 cannot be estimated with any degree of precision. The CBS estimates of smallholder gross marketed output for the period 1954–77[16] indicate a real growth rate of 6 per cent p.a. The national accounts estimate a

Table 6.24
Long-Run Real Wage Adjustments
(African real wage in estates agriculture in 1949 = 100)

Year	Real earnings by sector				
	Smallholders	Estates	Nairobi minimum wage[a]	Public sector	Private non-agriculture sector
1949	100[b]	100	88	106	109
1967	143–170[c]	167	240	420	359
1978	178–236[c]	230	168	298	280

[a] The range produced by growth rate assumptions of 2 per cent and 3 per cent respectively.
[b] Allowing for an urban cost of living differential of 60 per cent; see text.
[c] Assumption, see text.

real growth of subsistence production of 4.8 per cent p.a. over the same
period. The growth rate of total smallholder output over the period was
therefore around 5.6 per cent p.a.[17] The African rural adult[18] population
grew at 3.1 per cent p.a. between 1948 and 1979, so that real smallholder
output per rural African adult grew at around 2.5 per cent p.a. This is
probably the best estimate of the growth rate of smallholder income between
1949 and 1978. However, since it is uncertain we present estimates in the
range bounded by 2 per cent and 3 per cent p.a. growth rates.[19]

The other calculation which is required to get a comparable series on
incomes of different groups is the cost of living differential between urban
and rural areas. Detailed estimates for a typical low-income family of four
were made in 1977 by COTU, the Kenyan confederation of trade unions,
which suggested a differential between estates and urban living of 60 per
cent. Scott had arrived at the same estimate of 60 per cent based on data
for 1969.[20] In 1949, prior to most institutional interventions, the mean
non-agricultural African wage was 72 per cent above that on the estates. A
small part of this probably reflected a skill premium and the need to offer a
positive inducement to migration. However, since urban employers were not
charities, most of this differential presumably reflected cost of living differences. Table 6.24 assumes a 60 per cent cost of living differential throughout
the period.

On these tentative assumptions, both in 1949 and 1978 the urban minimum-wage earner had a slightly lower real income than the mean smallholder.
Real wages on estates appear to have risen approximately in line with
smallholder incomes throughout the period. However, the enormous magnitude of the minimum-wage intervention around its peak in 1967 is clearly
shown. Between 1949 and 1967 real earnings on estates rose by 67 per cent
against 173 per cent for the urban minimum wage. Considering the scale of
this disturbance the speed at which wage adjustment restored equilibrium in
the unskilled labour market was noteworthy. We will suggest in sub-section
(7) that, in the Kenyan context, equilibrium wages may well now coexist
with quite high youth unemployment.

In the skilled labour market, the top educational category experienced
strong increases in real wages. This probably reflected the shortages created
as Africanization gradually moved up to higher-level occupations. In senior
positions age and experience may be necessary qualifications so the process
of Africanization was chasing a constant limited stock of Africans largely
educated before Independence who were gradually gaining the age and
experience needed to equip them for higher positions. This conclusion is
supported by the comparison of the 1968 IBRD Labour Force Survey, (Thias
and Carnoy, 1972) and the 1978 High and Middle Level Manpower Survey
made by Collier and Bigsten (1981). This study found that the combination
of age and education secured the largest increases in real wages. In the four
other white-collar occupations there is a uniform tendency to sharp falls in

real wages between 1968 and 1977, ranging between 38 and 15 per cent. Classification changes make the apparent trends in the two skilled manual categories unreliable.

We may conclude that the Kenyan labour market displayed considerable wage flexibility in the post-Independence era. Wages responded to both the expansion of education, which sharply depressed earnings in the white-collar occupations, and to the initial disequilibrium in the unskilled labour market.

The above evidence on occupation-specific wage change can be supplemented by evidence on education-specific wages. Data is limited, however, to four surveys which have been used to construct earnings functions, these being the IBRD Survey of 1968 (Thias and Carnoy), a sample of 3,464 African males in urban wage employment, the ID Urban Survey of 1971, Johnson (1971), a sample of 1,254 Africans in wage employment in Nairobi, the Trade Test Survey of February 1973, Godfrey (1977), a sample of 190 Africans in skilled manual wage employment, and the Nairobi High and Middle Level Manpower Survey of January 1978 (NHMLMS), conducted by the CBS, a sample of 525 non-manual Nairobi workers almost all of whom were African.

The estimated contribution of education to earnings differs quite substantially between the four surveys. The percentage increase in earnings generated by a year of schooling is 8 per cent in the Thias and Carnoy survey, while in the Johnson survey it ranges between 8.5 per cent and 34 per cent depending on the level of education, with a mean of 12.1 per cent using the Thias and Carnoy weights for the education distribution. In the Godfrey survey a year of education increases earnings by 0.7 per cent whilst in the CBS survey the increase is 18.5 per cent.

These results suggest that the importance of education differs radically by level of education and type of labour market. In white-collar occupations the quantity of education is an important factor in determining earnings while in manual activities education is fairly unimportant. Since non-manual activities tend to require post-primary education this manifests itself as a high private rate of return on secondary education compensating for a low rate of return on primary education. There is considerable evidence for this hypothesis. The return on education by level of education can be obtained from the comparable random samples of Thias and Carnoy and Johnson (Table 6.25). Both surveys show very low private returns to primary education. For example, the private return to completed primary education in 1968 was only around 3.5 per cent per annum for the seven-year investment.[21] Further, this is before taking into account a number of personal characteristics correlated both with education and earnings, such as parental socio-economic status, the inclusion of which would reduce even this modest return. Finally, whilst the Godfrey survey found each year of education added less than one per cent to the earnings of its sample of skilled manual workers, the CBS survey,

Table 6.25
Increment in Earnings by Education Level
(controlling for age)

Increment in education	Increment in earnings (%)	
	1968[a]	1971[b]
0–2 years to 2–5 years	8	18
2–5 years to 5–7 years	18	27
5–7 years to 7–9 years	54	59
7–9 years to 9–11 years	60	68

[a] From Thias and Carnoy (1973) Table 3.4 taking the average of age groups 25–29 and 35–44 (both significant throughout).
[b] Johnson (1971), Table 2.

confined to white-collar employees, found that each year of education increased earnings by 18.5 per cent.

The surveys can be used to discover how this relationship between earnings and education has changed over time. The period 1964–7 was a period of shortage of secondary school educated labour. This was because public sector expansion and Africanization raised demand at a time when the stock of African labour with secondary education was very low, even though it was increasing very rapidly (see Table 6.15). Several indicators confirm the tightness of the market for educated labour during this period. First, we noted in Chapter 2 IV(2) the sharp widening of wage differentials between manual and non-manual workers in the years 1964–8. Second, prior to 1968 very low rates of unemployment were found by the Kinyanjui Tracer Survey, (Kinyanjui, 1974), which followed a large sample of Form IV leavers for each of the years 1965–8. The unemployment rates in the first year after leaving school are shown in Table 6.26. Third, the Thias and Carnoy survey collected data on the mean delay of school leavers at different levels between leaving school and entering wage employment (note that this is not synonymous with unemployment). The data is reproduced in Table 6.27. Two features are noticeable, first the systematic tendency for secondary school leavers in general and Form IV leavers in particular to have shorter delays in entering employment. Second, the mean delay shortened for all groups but proportionately shortened most for Form IV leavers in the 1963–6 period compared to the period 1955–62.

The sudden leap to a 14 per cent unemployment rate among Form IV leavers in 1968 (see Table 6.26) was an indicator that supply was overtaking demand. Form IV output continued to expand massively between 1968 and 1972 well beyond any feasible increase in demand for white-collar labour. The emergence of a large excess supply of Form IV leavers over white-collar

Analysis

Table 6.26
Unemployment of Form IV Leavers

Year	Unemployment rate (%)
1965	2
1966	1
1967	1
1968	14

Source: Kinyanjui (1974).

Table 6.27
Average Delay (in years) between Leaving School and Starting Work
(by year of leaving school and education)
(African Males)

Year of leaving school	Education		
	completed primary	partial secondary	secondary Forms III and IV
1955–9	2.6	2.3	1.8
1960	2.4	1.8	1.5
1961	2.7	1.7	1.4
1962	1.9	1.3	1.4
1963	2.2	2.1	1.2
1964	1.9	1.4	1.3
1965	1.7	1.1	1.0
1966	1.4	1.1	0.9

Source: Thias and Carnoy (1972), Table 4.1.

employment opportunities does not appear to have led in the short run to a marked reduction in the earnings of those school leavers who succeeded in gaining wage employment.

From Table 6.25 we see that for each educational level the private return to incremental education rose slightly between January 1968 and February 1971. The Thias and Carnoy and Johnson surveys are comparable in that they are both random samples of Africans in wage employment, and such characteristics as are reported, for example the degree of unionization, suggest that the samples were similar. Note that in each case in constructing the return to incremental education no allowance is made for the probability of attaining wage employment. We are monitoring the link between the wage structure and education rather than that between the income of the labour force and education.

To summarize, the evidence of the earnings surveys suggests the following. First, primary education has little impact upon earnings. Second, earnings in manual occupations are little affected by education. Third, secondary education has a large impact upon earnings. Fourth, earnings in white-collar occupations are strongly affected by education. Fifth, while in the longer period 1964–77 occupational earnings were flexible, in the short period around 1967–72 wage changes, to the extent that they occurred, were small in relation to the imbalance between supply and demand. This is not surprising when the magnitude of supply changes is recalled from Table 6.15. Having been a tight market for educated labour in the mid-1960s (due chiefly to Africanization), the period 1967–72 saw the stocks of both those with completed primary schooling and those with secondary schooling expand at between 20 per cent and 30 per cent per annum. In the short-run wage adjustment could not be sufficient to equilibrate so large a change in the balance of supply and demand.

(6) Non-Wage Adjustment

Human capital theory does not appear to fit compatibly with either the failure of the returns to education to fall or with the very much lower returns to primary than secondary education. Superficially, it appears that the segmented labour market theories offer a better account of Kenyan experience. A composite of the Spence, Thurow and Harris-Todaro models would contain all the following postulates. First, wages are institutionally rigid. Second, years of education are used as a screening criterion by employers since this is a proxy for ability or trainability. Third, this implies that the return on education is very low below the critical number of years of education which employers require as a minimum for recruitment, but is then very high around the critical number of years. Fourth, this in turn implies that there is a private incentive to invest in more years of education so as to be over the critical minimum. Fifth, in response to this 'signalling' by job seekers, employers, wishing to preserve the same minimum ability given by a particular position in the ability hierarchy, raise the critical minimum number of years required to attain employment. Sixth, the result of this is that the expansion in the numbers with education above the critical minimum crowds or 'bumps' out of employment opportunities those whose years of education no longer afford them access to wage employment. Seventh, such expansion does not reduce the private rate of return on a particular level of education while it remains above the critical level for a given job, that is while there are job seekers with fewer years of education to be crowded out. Eighth, the social rate of return to this expansion of education is zero. Ninth, unemployment is the result of mismatching between private investment in years of education and employers' demand, combined with rigid wage differentials. Whilst educational expansion need not always increase unemployment, there are no equilibrating processes reducing unemployment.

This account of the labour market does coincide with a number of observed features. The first postulate fits with the observation that real earnings of employed school leavers did not fall sharply between 1967 and 1972. The third postulate fits if the critical level is taken to be secondary education. The fourth postulate fits the massive expansion of harambee secondary schools which occurred during the 1970s.

This is perhaps the orthodox account of the Kenyan labour market. However, it deserves close scrutiny because the basic postulate of wage rigidity is, we have seen, implausible given the massive wage increases and decreases which occurred in the years 1964–77. It is therefore worth investigating the properties of a less naïve version of the human capital model, deriving propositions which enable it to be tested against the segmented labour market model.

The standard extension which we introduce into the naïve human capital model is to allow for heterogeneity of an array of personal characteristics, some but not all of which are correlated with academic performance (A), and some but not all of which are correlated with job performance (Q). This yields four types of characteristics: those which improve both academic and job performance (C_1), those which improve academic but not job performance (C_2), those which improve job but not academic performance (C_3), and those which improve neither (C_4). Denoting years of education by E, we can stylize the naïve human capital theory as:

$$Q = Q\,(A(E)) \tag{1}$$

and the segmented model as:

$$Q = Q(C_1) \tag{2}$$

and

$$E = E(C_1). \tag{3}$$

A fully realistic account would acknowledge some validity in all these relationships and assert:

$$Q = Q\{A(E,C_1C_2)\,,C_1,C_3\} \tag{4}$$
$$E = E(C_1,C_2). \tag{5}$$

Whether (4) and (5) simplify into (1) or (2) and (3) or into anything else depends upon the coefficient values in particular cases. The extended human capital model must dismiss the importance of education as a recruitment screen used to identify C_1. That is, either it simplifies (4) to

$$Q = Q\{A(E,C_1,C_2)\,,C_3\} \tag{6}$$

or it allows C_1 to be directly observable by employers, (5) in either case ceasing to have significance for the labour market.

In contrast to the bumping model the extended human capital model postulates that employers have preference orderings over a wide array of employee characteristics. As with all preference orderings we must distinguish between lexicographic and non-lexicographic ordering. A human capital model with orderings lexicographic in years of education will give the same predictions as the bumping model concerning bumping but different predictions about search-induced unemployment. A model with non-lexicographic orderings will give different predictions for both bumping and unemployment. The unemployment predictions differ because potential job seekers who are identical with respect to years of education will be differentiated by other selection characteristics. Hence employment prospects are generally determinate rather than probabilistic.[22] The bumping predictions differ because faced with an increase in supply by years of education it may be optimal for an employer to upgrade some selection criteria other than years of education. In the extreme case in which orderings are lexicographic in some characteristic other than years of education then educational expansion would generate no filtering or displacement at all. Excluding lexicographic orderings, educational expansion could theoretically cause either filtering down *or filtering up*[23] but is most likely to generate filtering down at a much slower pace than predicted by the bumping model.

This brief statement of the theory suggests that it is important to investigate the full characteristics of recruits to discover whether, in addition to years of education, other selection criteria were also changing.

The number of years of education required for recruitment to a particular occupation did indeed rise during the period. However, the extent of this increase varied between manual and non-manual occupations. The 1972 Manpower Survey provides particularly good data for 1971, by which time the market for secondary school educated labour was in massive excess supply. In Table 6.28 we compare the educational attainment of workers hired or promoted into particular occupations during 1971 against that of the stock of workers in those occupations for the same year. In non-manual occupations a majority of the stock of workers had secondary education and here, looking at the flow of recruitment, there is a tendency for primary school leavers to be bumped out of the residual positions. In contrast, in the skilled manual occupations primary school leavers have a majority of the stock of jobs and retain this position in the flow of recruitment.

Further evidence that bumping was rather limited in the Nairobi labour market will be presented in Chapter 7, Table 3. In the period 1969–77 the proportion of net male migration to Nairobi made up of migrants with Form IV education or above was only 27 per cent. That is most male net migration to Nairobi had educational credentials which would have excluded migrants from the labour market had the bumping process been operating.

Consider now characteristics of education other than the number of years of it possessed by the applicant. It is not unlikely that firms will also be interested in what the student has studied and how well he has acquitted himself. On this we have extremely good data covering a wide range of occupations.

Table 6.28

Education of Workers Hired/Promoted in 1971 and of all Workers, by Selected Occupations

Occupation	Status	Education (percentage)				
		Primary	Form I and II	Form III and IV	Form V and VI	Unspecified
Science technicians	Stock	26	9	46	19	0
	Hired	3	0	74	23	0
Semi-professionals (health)	Stock	20	9	60	11	0
	Hired	1	0	77	21	0
Skilled clerical	Stock	27	15	46	9	3
	Hired	9	9	70	12	0
Semi-professionals (agriculture)	Stock	48	9	32	11	0
	Hired	49	5	40	5	0
Skilled health workers	Stock	74	11	11	1	2
	Hired	61	12	22	5	0
Mechanics	Stock	77	4	9	2	2
	Hired	57	24	16	3	0
Electrical workers	Stock	69	15	12	4	0
	Hired	73	22	4	0	0
Welders	Stock	n.a.		n.a.	n.a.	n.a.
	Hired	78	22	0	0	0
Printers	Stock	n.a.		n.a.	n.a.	n.a.
	Hired	99	1	0	0	0

Source: Manpower Survey 1972 (unpublished), Appendix A, Tables 19, 24, 25.

The best single data source is a guide issued to all secondary school leavers in Kenya for the period 1968–70.[24] This guide is a compendium of standardized advertisements for a range of jobs covering the vast majority of the vacancies for secondary school leavers available at that time. Educational requirements are specified. It should be stressed that these are not just the selection criteria employers used, *they are the selection criteria which all secondary school leavers knew to be in operation.* We have grouped the 141 job types open to Form IV leavers into four categories according to educational selection criteria. Educational performance is assessed at Form IV level by a graded examinatton. Some employers may be concerned with educational performance but not educational content, in which case they will specify a required grade but not a required or desired subject. Alternatively, some employers may be concerned with educational content but not performance. They will specify required subjects but not required grades. A third possibility is that employers are concerned with both educational content and performance, in which case they will specify both grade and subject. Finally, employers could require only a number of years of education, in which case they will not have specified grades or subjects.

The period 1968–70 was one of rapidly emerging imbalance. Our data thus focus on precisely the critical period by which we can judge the pace of adjustment. In Table 6.29 the 141 types of job open to Form IV leavers are assigned to the four above categories, distinguishing between private and public sector employers. The results demonstrate that only in a small minority of jobs (16 per cent) did employers fail to specify either grades or subjects. In a third of the jobs both grade and subject were specified. The table also suggests that private sector employers were more discriminating than the public sector: only 9 per cent of private sector jobs failed to specify grade or subject against 19 per cent in the public sector. This may offer some insight into why the private sector paid higher wages than the public sector for given jobs.[25]

Whilst Table 6.29 fully substantiates the human capital model by demonstrating that firms were concerned to select by a variety of criteria, the individual advertisements give added insight into the revealed preferences of firms. In response to the increased supply one employer announced that he was adding an additional required subject: Division III (or better) and Biology and Chemistry were amended to Division III (or better) and Biology, Chemistry, and English.[26] Other employers revealed a wide range of different preferences between Form IV leavers and Form VI leavers. Several were indifferent between Form VI leavers and Division II Form IV leavers.[27] Others who specify subject indicate that a Form IV leaver, Division III, with the right subjects,is preferred to a Form VI leaver with other subjects.[28] Others are indifferent between any Form VI leaver and Division III Form IV leavers with English and Mathematics.[29] Yet others actively discourage Form VI leavers.[30] All this suggests that in general

Analysis

Table 6.29

Educational Selection Criteria used in 141 Jobs for Form IV Leavers, 1968–1970

Sector	Selection Criteria				
	Grade only	Subject only	Grade and subject	Neither grade nor subject	Total
Public	15	40	32	20	107
(percentage)	(14)	(37)	(30)	(19)	
Private	4	15	12	3	34
(percentage)	(12)	(44)	(35)	(9)	
Total	19	55	44	23	141
(percentage)	(13)	(39)	(31)	(16)	

Source: Helping You to Choose a Career, Kenyanization of Personnel Bureau (1968).

preference orderings are not lexicographic by years of education between Forms IV and VI, but that the specific trade-off against other characteristics varies with the nature of the job.

The advertisements also reveal some non-academic selection criteria such as health, the wearing of glasses, proven leadership ability, personality, and various skills. Clearly with some of these characteristics the applicant is better able to make a self-evaluation than with others.

Since the data source is aimed at secondary school leavers we are not able to assess from it wider trade-offs between years of education and other characteristics. However, the data have demonstrated the importance of, and variety of, other selection criteria.

The use of examination grade as a selection criterion was also noted by the Kenyan Ministry of Labour. The 1972 *Annual Report* noted 'nearly all employers are asking for good passes in EACE . . . and it is easy to place these good passes'. Again in 1974 the *Annual Report* noted 'problem areas continue to be Form IV low grades—those below Division 2. Form IV Divisions 3, 4, and Fail may have to compete with other job seekers for unskilled jobs'.

Having investigated the use of performance in, and content of, education as selection criteria we now turn to job experience as a criterion. Smock's[31] analysis of changes in public sector recruitment criteria reveals tendencies towards internal labour markets with entry at the bottom rung followed by promotion subject to performance, experience, and training. However, these selection criteria do not indicate the full characteristics of those who get promoted. This information is needed to discover whether experience can be a substitute for educational characteristics or whether employers' preference orderings are lexicographic in education. In Table 6.30 we present the required data for the sample of 11,000 skilled workers hired or promoted in 1971. In ten occupations the sample is disaggregated according to whether

Table 6.30

Education and Experience of Persons Hired/Promoted during 1971 in Selected Occupations

Occupation	Education completed	Experience when hired or promoted		
		Total %	Up to 5 years %	More than 5 years %
Engineering technicians	Up to Form IV	100	40	60
	Above Form IV	100	73	27
Dental and pharmaceutical technicians	Up to Form IV	100	76	24
	Above Form IV	100	100	0
Professional nurses and mid-wives	Up to Form IV	100	74	26
	Above Form IV	100	92	8
Semi-professional accountants	Up to Form IV	100	46	54
	Above Form IV	100	89	11
Managers n.e.c.	Up to Form IV	100	18	82
	Above Form IV	100	37	63
Clerical and other administrative supervisors	Up to Form IV	100	60	40
	Above Form IV	100	86	14
Government executive officials	Up to Form IV	100	25	75
	Above Form IV	100	75	25
Lower-level accountants, book-keepers, and cashiers	Up to Form IV	100	70	30
	Above Form IV	100	67	33
Other clerical and related workers	Up to Form IV	100	78	22
	Above Form IV	100	85	15
Specialized sales and service workers	Up to Form IV	100	67	33
	Above Form IV	100	25	75

Source: 1972 *Manpower Survey*, Table A.20.

educational attainment was above Form IV or not, and according to whether experience in similar work was greater than or less than five years. In eight out of the ten occupations those with less education tended to have more experience. An interpretation consistent with this observation is that experience was regarded by selectors as a substitute for education.

Next consider age as a possible selection characteristic. It is not implausible that firms would prefer not to employ teenagers, or more generally, youth might be correlated with indiscipline and immaturity. The NSSF data base reveals just such a trend in the Kenyan wage labour market for the period 1971–6 (the period currently available for analysis). The modal age of entry rose steadily from nineteen in 1971 to twenty-four in 1976.[32] This is suggestive of age being a desired characteristic in this range. More powerful tests require a more detailed data base than is available from published data.

Finally, it should be emphasized that the human capital model is not just the postulate that a given list of characteristics is desired in addition to years of education. The economist can never get an exhaustive description of employee attributes. Why, for example, do employers invariably wish to *see* applicants before selecting from among them?

It thus appears that employers used the rapidly emerging excess supply of the period 1967–72 in order to raise a variety of selection criteria, of which the number of years of education formed only a small part.

This account sounds as if it is merely a 'bumping' model in which other characteristics are introduced. However, it has radically different implications from the bumping model set out above. First, let us return to the issue of wage rigidity.

Consider the recruitment problem facing the typical firm. In Figure 6.12 the horizontal axis denotes a ranking of examination performance.

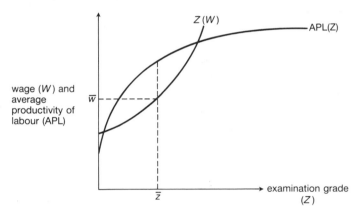

Fig. 6.12

The schedule $Z(W)$ denotes the maximum mean examination grade which can be achieved by selection of recruits for a given quantity of recruitment of labour in efficiency units. The higher the wage the more applicants come forward and the higher the selection standards which may be imposed. The schedule APL (Z) denotes, for a given quantity of recruitment and employment in efficiency units of labour, the increase in the average productivity of recruits as a function of their grade. The negative second-order derivative of this function denotes diminishing returns to this characteristic. The profit maximization problem facing the firm for any given recruitment requirement (in efficiency units) is to maximize $\phi = \text{APL}(Z) - Z(W)$ with respect to Z. Clearly, this occurs at $\bar{Z}$ where the first order derivatives are equal, the firm paying the wage $\bar{w}$ in order to secure this level of Z.

In some occupations, the cost of monitoring productivity is so high as to prevent the introduction of piece rates. In this case, regardless of variations in willingness to work among recruits, all recruits will receive the wage $\bar{w}$. Where the firm is free to vary the wage in line with variations in productivity then there will be a dispersion of wages associated with the dispersion in marginal products, but the cost of the minimizing mean wage will remain at $\bar{w}$.

Consider a supply change in the labour market for Form IV leavers. An expansion in the educational system relative to employment opportunities will shift the $Z(W)$ curve to the right (see Figure 6.13). However, the reservation price at which educated labour will transfer its search to other occupations is underpinned by the income level in these occupations. Hence, the $Z(W)$ curve flattens rather than shifts. The flatter the $Z(W)$ curve the more rewarding for the firm is an increase in mean wages in terms of the increased willingness to work of recruits. Hence, an increased supply of educated labour may be associated with an increase in or stability of the wage at which such labour is recruited. This situation, in which firms are displaying rational cost-minimization, is characterized by an apparent downwards wage rigidity in the face of an increased supply of job seekers and is therefore easy to confuse with a market imperfection.

Clearly, by the 1970s examination performance was a powerful recruitment criterion so we would expect earnings and grade to be significantly correlated. Our theory predicts that in the tighter labour market conditions of the period prior to 1968 firms did not find it worthwhile to bid up wages so as to attract workers with better grades. Supporting evidence for this prediction is provided by the Thias and Carnoy survey (February 1968) which found in estimating a wages function for Form IV leavers that EACE grades, entered as dummy variables, were all statistically insignificant. Kinyanjui, assessing his own survey results, reached the same conclusion: 'These facts

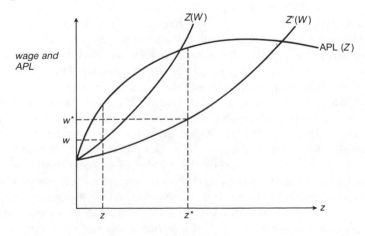

Fig. 6.13

support the hypothesis that in a period of low educational output the labour market is less selective, but it becomes progressively more selective in terms of performance as educational output expands and the labour market remains relatively static.' (Kinyanjui, 1974, p. 63.)

Hence, wage stability in the face of educational expansion need not be interpreted as institutional wage rigidity. It does not conflict with our previous evidence which suggests that wages are flexible. While this undermines the first postulate of the segmented labour market model and threatens several of the other postulates, we will delay further investigation of its implications until we have considered first a possible retort by the segmented labour market proponents, and secondly the case of the manual labour market.

A possible retort to the introduction of academic performance, (A), is of course to argue that in the place of (2) and (3) the labour market is described by:

$$Q = Q(C_1, C_3) \tag{7}$$

and

$$A = A(C_1 \ldots) \tag{8}$$

so that academic performance is not wanted *per se* by employers but is used as a screen to identify attributes of the C_1 type. Even were we to accept this it would in no way qualify our critique of the wage rigidity postulate. However, it is pertinent to a consideration of whether education is directly productive or whether it functions as a (by implication, socially very expensive) sorting device. We now introduce further evidence from the 1972 *Annual Labour Report*. We have previously cited this report as evidence that employers were concerned about grade. However, the report goes on to note: 'Nearly all employers were asking for candidates with good passes in Physics, Chemistry, General Science, Biology, Maths and English . . . Candidates with very good passes in arts were very hard to place.' Thus, employers were certainly not looking for something correlated with generalized academic performance. It is possible that employers were not interested in the fact that candidates were numerate and literate in English but only that they had discovered that such academic achievements were imperfectly correlated with characteristics which they did require. But such characteristics could not be general ones such as effort, determination, or IQ for this would also be correlated with arts performance. Yet the more narrowly the characteristics are defined the closer they approach to being perfectly correlated with, and hence indistinguishable from, the knowledge of subjects imparted by education. Certainly Kenyan personnel officers themselves perceive education as being directly useful. For example, the Nzomo survey of personnel officers in the Kenyan banking industry found that nearly all interviewees considered an academic education essential. 'In getting a job and executing functional responsibilities nearly all interviewees considered formal education to be either simply "useful" or "very useful"' (Nzomo, p. 20). Obviously, it is logically impossible to disprove the screening theory. The illiterate and innumerate job seeker might possess C_1 characteristics which make him just as good a banker as his counterpart with Grade 1 EACE, but because employers do not take the trouble to observe C_1 directly he fails to get recruited. Perhaps, though, as a plausible theory it lacks a certain robustness.

Now let us consider the Kenyan manual labour market. Recall that equation (3) loses significance either if C_1 is observable without relying upon years of education, or if C_1 in (4) has a low coefficient. In the case of the white-collar labour market we have suggested that the evidence can be interpreted either as indicating that in (4) A has a mugh higher coefficient than C_1 or, that C_1 is predicted by A rather than by E. In the case of the manual labour market we suggest that almost precisely inverse characteristics apply. Academic performance is of little significance in most manual jobs so that the coefficient upon A will be very low relative to those on C_1 and C_3. However, neither A nor E is used as a predictor of C_1 because firms have devised means of observing C_1 and C_3 directly prior to recruitment.

The way that firms typically observe the characteristics of manual workers is by hiring applicants initially only as casual workers. Casual workers, although technically paid by the day will commonly be retained by firms for anything between three months and two years. They are not, however, protected by any such job security legislation as regular workers. Only after satisfactory performance as casual workers will workers be taken onto the regular labour force. While several personnel officers have described such a process to the authors there is as yet no direct statistical confirmation. However, several pieces of evidence support both the hypotheses concerning the role of casual labour, the ability of firms to identify able workers and the absence of screening by education. First, consider the aggregate characteristics of the casual labour force. Casual workers earn considerably lower wages than regular manual workers. Over the period 1968–77 casual workers increased substantially as a proportion of all manual workers despite the absence of any significant change in relative wages. Indeed, the fastest expansion of the casual work-force between 1972 and 1977 coincided with an increase in the casual wage relative to the regular wage.[33] If the casual–regular wage differential were an institutional distortion then firms should react by having a mainly casual work-force, yet even in 1977 only 25 per cent of the manual labour force was employed on a casual basis. Yet if the differential represents only a premium for skills acquired on the job, then the movement of relative wages and relative employment in the same direction cannot be reconciled.

Our explanation is that the wage differential is determined at least in part by the difference in characteristics between probationary and permanent workers, low-effort workers (for example) having been screened out of the latter group. Further, the relative size of the casual labour force is determined primarily by the recruitment needs of employers. Recruitment is a function of turnover and net expansion of the labour force. That the 1960s were a period of falling employment would imply a low proportion of casual workers relative to the late 1970s when employment was expanding.[34]

Because of this ability to gather information on potential regular employees firms do not generally need to impose a crude proxy for unobserved characteristics by using education as a screening device for unskilled labour.

Evidence that employers in the manual labour market are able to observe relevant characteristics directly rather than rely upon education can be derived from the panel data contained in Godfrey's survey. Our approach is to suppose that a worker's wage upon leaving employment reflected his employer's fully informed assessment of his worth, while the wage of the worker at recruitment represented the employer's estimate of his worth based on information about observable characteristics.

A worker can be described by vectors of fixed and variable characteristics: $\mathbf{C}_i$, and $\mathbf{V}_i$. Together these determine the worker's productivity y_i in any particular job

$$Y_i = Y_i(\mathbf{C}_i, \mathbf{V}_i). \tag{9}$$

We may treat this function as being linear in the log of productivity:

$$\ln y_i = \alpha \mathbf{C}_i + \beta \mathbf{V}_i. \tag{10}$$

If, post-recruitment, the firm can directly observe y_i, then if we assume that the log of earnings is proportional to the log of productivity plus a random disturbance term, we have

$$\ln w_i = \gamma\alpha \mathbf{C}_i + \gamma\beta \mathbf{V}_i + \mu_i. \tag{11}$$

The assumption of log-linearity gives us a relationship which bears a strong resemblance to a standard earnings function, and the disturbance term μ_i is generated by the assumption that there will be random differences between firms which affect earnings but not productivity. If at recruitment the firm is unable to observe y_i directly, it must form an estimate based on observation of a subset of $\mathbf{C}_i$ and $\mathbf{V}_i$. It then forms an expectation of y_i conditional upon its information set:

$$E(\ln y_i \mid \mathbf{C}_i^r, \mathbf{V}_i^r) = \phi \mathbf{C}_i^r + \theta \mathbf{V}_i^r = \alpha \mathbf{C}_i + \beta \mathbf{V}_i + \lambda_i \tag{12}$$

where $\mathbf{C}_i^r$, $\mathbf{V}_i^r$ are the characteristics observed by the firm and λ_i is randomly distributed.

This function can be transformed into an earnings function in the same way as (11) above:

$$\ln w_i^r = \delta\phi \mathbf{C}_i^r + \delta\theta \mathbf{V}_i^r + \eta_i \tag{13}$$

where η_i is a firm-specific random disturbance term, and w^r is the wage at recruitment.

Now consider how well this function is approximated by the information set conventionally attributed to the firm in an earnings function which includes only research-observed characteristics such as years of education. Denoting the researcher information set as $\mathbf{C}_i^s, \mathbf{V}_i^s$, some subset of $\mathbf{C}_i, \mathbf{V}_i$, we assume that the researcher can measure the characteristics he knows about correctly, but is unable to measure at all some relevant characteristics. Thus, the conventional earnings function estimates the following relationship:

$$\ln w_i = \mathbf{a}\mathbf{C}_i^s + \mathbf{b}\mathbf{V}_i^s + u_i \tag{14}$$

$$\ln w_i^r = \mathbf{c}\mathbf{C}_i^s + \mathbf{d}\mathbf{V}_i^s + v_i . \tag{15}$$

We will assume that both pre- and post-recruitment firms and researchers correctly observe $\mathbf{V}_i$, but that $\mathbf{C}_i$ is never directly observed. What is at issue is how good firms are at recruitment at assessing these characteristics. This involves comparing $\gamma\alpha\mathbf{C}_i$ with $\delta\phi\mathbf{C}_i^r$ from our earlier equations.

Godfrey's data set permits this for it combines measures of variable characteristics with panel data which allows the estimation of the complete set of fixed characteristics. The two variable characteristics included were years of seniority (SEN) and years of experience in other firms (WEXP). Fixed educational characteristics were desribed by dummy variables for completed primary (PRIM), partial secondary (SEC 1), and Form IV secondary (SEC 2) schooling. Finally, performance on the Trade Tests (TT) was included as a measure of both skill and trainability observed by the researcher but not observable to the firm at recruitment (since the test was taken at the time of data collection). The survey data set was arranged so that each job was treated as an observation, dummy variables being assigned to $n - 1$ of the n individuals with at least two jobs. Observations in which jobs were held by workers who had held no other job were dropped.

Equation (11) was estimated with SEN and WEXP entered as variable characteristics and personal dummy variables (D_i) as the aggregates of all fixed characteristics:

$$\ln w = a_0 + \mathbf{e}\mathbf{D} + f_0 \text{ SEN} + f_1 \text{ WEXP} + \varepsilon^1. \tag{16}$$

The results are reported in Table 6.31, column 4. The dummy variables are collectively significant, e_i being our estimate of $\gamma\alpha\mathbf{C}_i$. Equation (15) is similarly estimated:

$$\ln w^r = a_1 + \mathbf{g}\mathbf{D} + f_2 \text{ WEXP} + \varepsilon^2 \tag{17}$$

the results being reported in Table 6.31, column 2. The dummy variables are again collectively significant, g_i being our estimate of $\delta\phi\mathbf{C}_i^r$. That is to say e_i is the estimate of the effect on an individual's earnings of all fixed characteristics while g_i is the effect of his characteristics on earnings at recruitment.

The proportion of full information on $\mathbf{C}_i$ known to the firm at the time of recruitment can now be estimated by regressing $\mathbf{e}$ on $\mathbf{g}$, the results being reported in Table 6.32, column 1. Some 69 per cent of full information on $\mathbf{C}_i$ was known by firms at the time of recruitment.

Table 6.31
Earnings Functions for Skilled Manual Workers

	1 w^r	2	3 w	4
PRIM	0.18 (0.16)		0.23 (0.14)	
SEC$_1$	0.25^{xx} (0.10)		0.31^{xx} (0.08)	
SEC$_2$	0.35^{xx} (0.13)		0.25^x (0.11)	
TT			0.08^{xx} (0.02)	
SEN			0.08^{xx} (0.02)	0.11^{xx} (0.02)
WEXP	0.06^{xx} (0.02)	0.10^{xx} (0.02)	0.09^{xx} (0.01)	0.10^{xx} (0.02)
F Dummy Vars		1.91^{xx}		4.29^{xx}
$\bar{R}^2$	0.36	0.53	0.39	0.60
F	16.20	3.68	15.83	4.52
SEE	0.53	0.45	0.45	0.36

^{x} Significant at the 10 per cent level.
^{xx} Significant at the 5 per cent level.
^{xxx} Significant at the 1 per cent level.

Table 6.32
Information Identified by Firms and by Conventional Earnings Functions

	1	2 Y_e	3 Y_b
R	0.83	0.58	0.48
R^2	0.69	0.34	0.23
SEE	0.28	0.24	0.20

Now consider the information set of the researcher, first in relation to full information. **e**, representing full information, is again taken as the dependent variable, the independent variables now being that vector of observed fixed characteristics found to be significant in an earnings function of the form of (14), reported in Table 6.31, column 3.

This comparison involves regressing **e** on the series

$$\hat{w}_F = 0.23 \text{ PRIM} + 0.31 \text{ SEC}_1 + 0.25 \text{ SEC}_2 + 0.08 \text{ TT} \qquad (18)$$

where $\hat{w}_F$ is the estimated effect on earnings of the measured fixed characteristics, using the coefficients from (14). The results, reported in column 2, indicate that only 34 per cent of full information on $\mathbf{C}_i$ was captured by the vector of observed characteristics.

To estimate the researcher information set in relation to that available to the firm at recruitment the procedure is repeated, the appropriate dependent variable now being **g**, and the independent variable being $\hat{w}_F^r$, derived from the estimate of (15) reported in Table 6.31, column 1:

$$\hat{w}_F^r = 0.18 \text{ PRIM} + 0.25 \text{ SEC}_1 + 0.35 \text{ EC}_2 . \qquad (19)$$

The results, reported in Table 6.32, column 3, show that only 23 per cent of the firm's information set is explained by the information set of the researcher.

We are now in a position to establish the size of the information problem faced by the firm and the researcher. This can be illustrated in a Venn diagram, Figure 6.14.

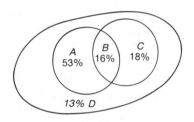

Fig. 6.14.

$A + B + C + D$ represents the total information about the individual known by the firm after recruitment. $A + B$ is the proportion of this information known by the firm at recruitment, that is 69 per cent. The researcher only knows 23 per cent of the firm's information at recruitment, and so B, that information common to the researcher and the firm at recruitment, is 16 per cent of total information, (0.23×0.69). Since $B + C$, all information known to the researcher, is 34 per cent of the total, C, information known at recruitment only to the researcher, this being the performance on the Trade Tests, is 18 per cent of the total $(0.34 - 0.16)$.

These results suggest that firms at recruitment have good information on the subsequent performance of manual workers, but that the number of years of education possessed by a recruit is only a minor component of this information set. In turn this suggests that the bumping process did not operate in the manual labour market. That is, those Form IV leavers whose grades were too low to achieve white-collar employment did not gain priority employment over those with less education.

(7) Unemployment

Unemployment is a symptom of a failure in the adjustment process. Necessary conditions for its existence on a significant scale are that wages should not fully respond to excess supplies and, in addition, that selection criteria should either not be introduced in sufficient quantity to make employment prospects determinate or, if introduced, should not be known accurately by job seekers. First, then, let us see what happened to urban unemployment.

In 1969 the male unemployment rate is estimated at around 10.3 per cent in Nairobi, but fell to below 6 per cent by 1977/8 (see Table 7.5). The decline in the Kenyan unemployment rate is perhaps explained by two different adjustment processes. In the skilled labour market the initial impact of Form IV expansion in the surge of 1968–72 was for the unemployment rate of Form IV leavers to rise very sharply. Tracer surveys found unemployment rates of 2 per cent in 1963, 1 per cent in 1966 and 1967, and then 14 per cent in 1968 (see Table 6.26). But in response to this increase in supply, employers introduced additional selection criteria and raised initial criteria. A consequence was that job search quickly reverted to being determinate rather than probabilistic for most Form IV leavers. An example of this process over the critical period 1968–74 is given in Table 6.33 which shows the relative unemployment rate of different grades of Form IV leaver. In 1968 the highest unemployment rate, that is the group for whom job search was least determinate, was among Form IV failures. By 1970 failures had an unemployment rate below average whilst the highest rate was for those with Division IV. By 1974 skilled employment prospects for Form IV failures

Table 6.33
Unemployment Prospects by Examination Performance, 1968–1974

Score	Grade	Relative unemployment prospect (percentage in unemployment/percentage in labour force)		
		1968	1970	1974
1–19	1	0	0.08	0.22
20–29	2	0	0.54	0.90
30–39	3	0.49	1.78	1.95
40–49	4	1.13	1.78	1.13
50–54	Fail	2.16	0.62	0.19
All		1.0	1.0	1.0

Sources: Kinyanjui (1974); and Ministry of Labour *Annual Reports*, 1970 and 1974.

were so (sadly) determinate that they had the *lowest* unemployment rate of all
Form IV leavers, the highest rate having moved up again to Division III.

Table 6.33 only slices unemployment by one selection criterion which we
know, was well-known to Form IV leavers. The Ministry of Labour *Annual
Reports* are filled with comments which suggest that slicing by subject, for
example, would reveal a similar process were such data available. To conclude, there is reason to suppose that in the skilled labour market unemployment was contained primarily through a process of multiple selection criteria
adjustment. Doubtless, years of education would be one of these criteria.

In the unskilled labour market the full rigours of the bumping model did
not appear to operate for the uneducated and scarcely-educated continued to
be recruited. Evidence for this in 1971 has already been cited. For the
Nairobi labour market the analysis can be extended for the periods 1969–77
and 1977–9 by comparing the education by age matrices of the male population shown in the Censuses (1969, 1979) and the National Demographic
Survey (1977). The results suggest that some 73 per cent of net migration to
Nairobi during this period was by those with less than Form IV education
(see Chapter 7). Yet had Form IV leavers always had priority in a rationed
formal labour market over those with less education, as postulated by the
bumping model, then nationally over the period 1969–77 those with below
Form IV education would have gained only around 43 per cent of all non-
agricultural wage jobs. Because Nairobi has a substantially higher skill
profile than the rest of the wage labour market, the prediction for Nairobi
would be well below 43 per cent. Our estimate of 43 per cent is derived by
interpolating the previous stock snapshots for 1964 and 1977 to generate
approximate annual flows of educated labour into employment on the bumping assumption of the priority of the educated, the flows being shown in
Table 6.34. The prediction concerning primary school leavers is more dramatically erroneous: namely that by 1979 they would have been entirely
excluded from recruitment to formal non-agricultural employment.

If the number of years of education is a less important selection criterion in
the unskilled labour market, as it seems to be, then probably so too are the
other dimensions of selection based on education. Possibly employers are
indifferent over wide ranges of characteristics. More probably, their critical
selection criteria are less well-known to applicants, being those in which self-
assessment is more difficult. But in this case the dominant explanation for the
reduction in the rate of unemployment of Kenyan unskilled labour must be
not selection criteria adjustment but wage adjustment. This is certainly
consistent with our findings on the fall in the unskilled wage rate relative to
smallholder incomes.

Let us now return to the postulates of the segmentation model. The first
postulate, wage rigidity, we have already criticized as being an unnecessary
and unlikely account of wage behaviour. The second postulate, that years of
education are used as a screen, we have suggested is accurate neither as a

Analysis

Table 6.34
Flows on to the Labour Market by Education and Job Type had Bumping Operated,
1964–1979
('000s)

		No job	None	P 1–4	P 5–8	S I–IV	S V+
					Education–type of job		
1964	Vacancies		7.2	7.7	7.8	2.3	0.8
	S V+						0.6
	S IV				2.1	2.3	0.2
	S I–II				2.3		
	P 7/8			7.5	3.5		
	P 1–4	64.6	7.2	0.2			
1965	Vacancies		7.8	8.3	8.5	2.5	0.8
	S V+						0.7
	S IV				3.1	2.5	0.1
	S I–II				3.1		
	P 7/8		2.4	8.3	2.3		
	P 1–4	62.6	5.4				
1966	Vacancies		8.4	9.0	9.3	2.7	1.0
	S V+						0.9
	S IV				2.9	2.7	0.1
	S I–II				1.9		
	P 7/8		0.5	9.0	5.5		
	P 1–4	107.1	7.9				
1967	Vacancies		9.1	9.7	10.1	2.9	1.1
	S V+						1.0
	S IV				6.3	2.9	*
	S I–II			0.6*	3.8		
	P 7/8	59.8*	9.1	9.1	*		
	P 1–4		*				
1968	Vacancies		9.8	10.5	11.0	3.2	1.2
	S V+					0.2*	1.2
	S IV				9.6	3.0	
	S I–II			5.4	1.4		
	P 7/8	63.1	9.8	5.1			
1969	Vacancies		10.6	11.3	12.0	3.5	1.3
	S V+					0.3	1.3
	S IV				11.5	3.2	
	S I–II		0.7*	11.3	0.5		
	P 7/8	83.1	9.9				

		No job	None	P 1–4	P 5–8	S I–IV	S V+
			Education–type of job				
1970	Vacancies		11.4	12.2	13.1	3.8	1.4
	S V+					0.6	1.4
	S IV				13.1	3.2	
	S I–II		0.3	12.2	*		
	P 7/8	75.9	11.1				
1971	Vacancies		12.3	13.2	14.3	4.1	1.5
	S V+					1.1	1.5
	S IV			2.2*	14.3	3.0	
	S I–II		11.9	11.0			
	P 7/8	81.6	0.4				
1972	Vacancies		13.2	14.2	15.6	4.5	1.6
	S V+					1.4	1.6
	S IV			4.8	15.6	3.1	
	S I–II		3.5	9.4			
	P 7/8	71.3	9.7				
1973	Vacancies		14.2	15.3	17.0	4.9	1.8
	S V+					1.8	1.8
	S IV			3.9	17.0	3.1	
	S I–II		3.1	11.4			
	P 7/8	78.9	11.1				
1974	Vacancies		15.3	16.4	18.6	5.3	2.0
	S V+					1.5	2.0
	S IV			4.7	18.6	3.8	
	S I–II		5.7	11.7			
	P 7/8	82.4	9.6				
1975	Vacancies		16.5	17.7	20.3	5.8	2.2
	S V+					2.0	2.2
	S IV			6.7	20.3	3.8	
	S I–II		2.1	11.0			
	P 7	78.6	14.4				
1976	Vacancies		17.8	19.1	22.1	6.3	2.4
	S V+					2.2	.2.4
	S IV			14.2	22.1	4.1	
	S I–II		7.2	4.9			
	P 7	86.4	10.6				

Table 6.34 (*cont.*)

		No job	None	P 1–4	P 5–8	S I–IV	S V+
			Education–type of job				
1977	Vacancies		19.2	20.6	24.1	6.9	2.6
	S V+					2.6	2.6
	S IV		18.2	24.1	4.3		
	S I–II	98.3	7.7				
1978	Vacancies		20.7	22.2	26.3	7.5	2.8
	S V+					2.4	2.8
	S IV			21.4	26.3	5.1	
	S I–II		17.0	0.8			
	P 7	104.3	3.7				
1979	Vacancies		22.3	23.9	28.7	8.2	3.1
	S V+					2.9	3.1
	S IV		11.0*	23.9	28.7	5.3	
	S I–II	8.8*	11.3	*			
	P 7	100	*				

* denotes the entry or exit of an education category of labour into or out of a job type.
Note: The vacancies for each year by education-type of job are derived from Table 6.21 by interpolation. For example, from Table 6.21 around 26,200 vacancies for jobs of a type appropriate for secondary school leavers from forms I–IV occurred during the period 1964–77. The Table also yields an average annual growth rate for this employment. This information is combined to infer an approximate annual profile of vacancies abstracting from actual cyclical fluctuations around the long-term trend. The flow of job seekers is taken from Table 6.14. It is assumed that the more educated have priority, and that the acceptance of one education-type precludes subsequent employment in a higher type job.

description of the white-collar labour market, where examination performance supplements years of education as a recruitment criterion, nor of the manual labour market, where years of education are largely unimportant. The third postulate, that the returns to education should be low below the critical level and high above is common to both the segmentation and human capital models. The fourth postulate, exploding private demand for education, and the seventh, that the private return to education above the critical minimum stays constant in the face of educational expansion, are best considered together. The human capital model instead predicts that the return on acquiring Form IV education would fall steadily as a smaller proportion of all Form IV leavers achieve white-collar jobs, but that this does not create an incentive to invest in more years of education because evaluation for such jobs is by performance in a non-repeatable examination rather than by years of education. This does not imply that in competitive equilibrium the demand for secondary education will only equal the number of white-collar jobs. Since examination performance at EACE is not predictable from performance at KPE[35] the competitive equilibrium is that many families will invest in their children's education fruitlessly.[36] However, in the human capital model, because firms raise the performance rather than the years of education criterion (contradicting the fifth postulate of the segmentation model), there is no 'explosive' tendency in the education market. Empirically, there is no doubt that private investment in secondary education has expanded very rapidly in the 1970s. It is too early to judge whether this is an adjustment path to a stable equilibrium or whether the expansion is a manifestation of an explosive disequilibrium.

The sixth postulate, that those with more years of education 'bump' those with less out of the wage labour market, we have suggested is contradicted by both theory and evidence. The eighth postulate, that the social return on education is zero, we have suggested lacks plausibility and is not entailed by any of the evidence on the white-collar labour market. The final postulate, on unemployment, we have suggested is radically mistaken. Empirically, as we will show in Chapter 7, the rate of urban unemployment has fallen during the 1970s. We have identified three equilibrating processes. First, wages have responded to the excess supply of unskilled labour to the extent that the smallholder–unskilled wage earner differential has been largely eliminated. Second, in the white-collar labour market we have argued that the supply of educated labour is likely to respond in an equilibrating rather than a disequilibrating manner to unemployment. Third, and most crucially, labour of a given number of years education is not perceived as being homogeneous by either employers or job seekers. Because examination performance is used as a criterion there is a known and fairly continuous ranking of job applicants rather than a discrete queue of homogeneous groups of applicants. In this case the group of applicants for whom white-collar employment is probabilistic is very much smaller than the segmentation model would suggest; for example, it might be those with a score of 6 in mathematics and English rather than all those with Form IV education.

This is not to suggest that unemployment is not a problem in Kenya, for clearly an urban unemployment rate of around 6 per cent is both inefficient and is potentially a poverty problem (though we will argue that in Kenya urban unemployment and poverty are largely unconnected). However, it does perhaps suggest that the problem is not now closely connected with either the wage level or the education system. Rather, we would return to the theme of the impact of minimum wage legislation upon the wage structure. Even though the urban unskilled wage is not now substantially higher than the supply price of the mean smallholder, starting wages for young workers are probably much higher than their supply price. This is exacerbated by two sociological features of migration and job search. First, the decision whether to migrate is not just a decision about job search and employment—

rather it is a choice between alternative household structures for the potential migrant. On the smallholding the young worker will invariably be excluded from the major farming decisions which will be taken by the household head. Further, he lacks contractual rights to the output generated by his own labour, partly because he lacks contractual rights *per se* and partly because often his output cannot be identified. As an urban wage earner, while he might choose to remit part of his income, the worker does at least get his income. The effect of this is to lower the supply price of young labour to wage employment below the supply price to smallholders. Second, the unemployed migrant seeking a job typically can expect temporary subsidy from urban relatives or friends for the duration of his search. The effect of this is to lower the supply price of labour to job search below the supply price of labour to employment and therefore ensure that a competitively determined wage will co-exist with unemployment. In Table 6.35 we demonstrate the tendency for the urban unemployed to be disproportionately drawn from young dependents of urban households. We should note that unemployment is an urban phenomenon. The Labour Force Survey of 1977[37] found less than one per cent of the rural population to be unemployed but seeking work.

During the 1960s, when the urban unskilled wage had been pushed up by minimum wage legislation to a level well above smallholder incomes, although the young had the highest unemployment rates, unemployment

Table 6.35
Characteristics of the Nairobi Male Unemployed
(percentages)

	Unemployment rate		Proportion of total unemployed	
	1970	1974	1970	1974
By household status				
heads of household	5	4	n.a.	19
sons of head	n.a.	49	n.a.	40
other relatives of head	n.a.	39	n.a.	40
no relation of head	n.a.	3	n.a.	1
By age group				
16–19	30	11	10[a]	11
20–29	20	19	53[a]	62
30–44	12	3	28[a]	13
45–59	10	8	9[a]	14

[a] Using the 1969 Census distribution of the male population of Nairobi by age and assuming that 50 per cent of those in the age group 16–19 were not in the labour market.
Sources: for 1970 Whitelaw (1971); for 1974 Nairobi Household Budget Survey conducted by CBS (unpublished data analysed in collaboration with J. W. Gunning).

was widespread in all age and household status groups. As smallholder unskilled wage-earner differentials narrowed rapidly due to rising small-holder incomes and falling real wages, the incentive for adult household heads to queue for unskilled urban employment was greatly reduced. For example, amongst males in 1968 the unemployment rate of relatives of the household head was 3.6 times that of household heads. By 1974 this differential had widened to 11.5. Between 1970 and 1974, while the unemployment rate of those aged below thirty fell from 21 per cent to 17 per cent, the unemployment rate for those aged thirty and over fell from 11 per cent to 5 per cent, so that while the young had an unemployment rate 90 per cent above the old in 1970 they had a rate 270 per cent above the old in 1974.

The effect of minimum wage laws on youth unemployment was exacerbated in 1967 by the reduction in the minimum age at which the adult wage rates applied, from twenty to eighteen. Combining our argument that the young have a much lower supply price than other workers with the argument of section III, that given the opportunity firms will adopt seniority scales in which young workers receive low pay, it would seem that a simple institutional reform which raised the minimum age at which the minimum wage legislation applies from eighteen to perhaps twenty-five would both reduce youth unemployment and accelerate the process of skill acquisition. This has become of greater importance since the increase in the minimum wage in 1980.

Notes

1. House and Rempel (1978), Table 5.6 regression 5.13.
2. Reported in House and Rempel (1978), Table 2.6.
3. Thias and Carnoy (1972), Table 3.8.
4. House and Rempel (1978), Table 5.7.
5. The argument is stated formally in an excursus to this section. A fuller treatment is provided in Collier and Knight.
6. It should be noted that in both cases the 3–5 years category might be effected by government intervention, in 1957 by Operation Anvil and in 1968 by the first Tripartite Agreement, though these do not materially effect our conclusion.
7. In 1959 employment of Africans in the town and extra-provincial district of Nairobi was 81,500. In 1968 African employment in the province of Nairobi was 122,700. However, between 1963 and 1964 coverage of urban private services was extended, the national extension of coverage being 18,100. We have assumed that the increase of 7,000 in Nairobi employment in that year was due to the change in coverage.
8. This excursus is based on Collier and Knight.
9. Note that this does not contradict our assumption about diminishing marginal utility since the compensation required for a wage transfer of $\frac{x}{2}$ can be made very much smaller than $\frac{x}{2}$ by appropriate choice of time periods. From (5), C is less than x provided that $x < - 4U'(\bar{w})/U''(\bar{w})$. Since x can be made as small as we

like for any wage structure, this condition can always be satisfied without damage to the generalization to many time periods.

10. From (7) the relation between the recruitment rate and a particular cohort-specific quit rate (q_i) is:

$$R = 1/(a + (b + bc + bcd + \ldots))(1 - q_i)$$
$$= 1/(a + g(1 - q_i))$$

where $a > 1$, $g > 0$, and $0 \leqslant q_i \leqslant 1$, with all cohort-specific quit rates (other than q_0 and q_7) between zero and unity. Then:

$$R' = \frac{\partial R}{\partial q_i} = g/(a + g(1 - q_i))^2 > 0$$
$$\text{and } R'' = \frac{\partial^2 R}{\partial q_i} = 2g^2/(a + g(1 - q_i))^2 > 0.$$

11. The timing of the payment of compensation for the postponement of consumption poses a problem to the firm which is precisely symmetrical to the larger problem of the timing of the wage payment. Although the firm would be able to pay all the compensation at the end of the first period, it can reduce quitting by phasing the compensation over the working life of the employee. This gives rise to a further compensation requirement, i.e. that required to compensate the employee for the postponement of his compensation payment. Indeed, there is an infinite regress of compensating payments of rapidly diminishing order of magnitude. However, the consequences of the phasing of compensation payments are second-order effects which we will set to zero in our subsequent analysis.

12. This section is based on Collier and Bigsten (1982).

13. Bigsten and Collier (1980), mimeo Table 16.

14. Collier and Rosewell (1983), Table 7.

15. For the period 1969–75 in Tanzania this effect has been estimated as reducing the supply price by 25 per cent. See Collier (1979).

16. Correcting for a break in the series in 1963.

17. Using the subsistence/marketed weights observed in *IRS* I.

18. Aged fifteen and over.

19. The national figure is corroborated by the comparison of the two Central Province Surveys reported in Chapter 3 II(2).

20. Scott *et al.*, p. 174.

21. 1.08 × 1.18 discounted over seven years.

22. Unemployment then becomes a function of whether job seekers are aware of selection characteristics.

23. If years of education is an 'inferior' characteristic.

24. *Helping You to Choose a Career*, Kenyanization of Personnel Bureau (1968).

25. See Table 6.6.

26. Kenyanization of Personnel Bureau (1968).

27. Ibid. p. 20, 22, 84.

28. Ibid. p. 53.

29. Ibid. p. 57.

30. Ibid. p. 25.

31. Smock (1978).

32. Bigsten and Collier (1980), Table 23.

33. The casual wage is commonly very close to the minimum wage.
34. The low proportion of casual workers in 1972 is a consequence of the 'Tripartite Agreement' of the previous year under which firms undertook to increase their regular work force by 10 per cent. This was commonly achieved by regularizing casual workers.
35. See Somerset (1974a) for an excellent account of this relationship.
36. There might of course be a return to education in either smallholder agriculture or urban self-employment. Evidence that the former does not hold beyond partial primary education is given in Chapter 8, and that the latter does not hold by Johnson (1971).
37. Reported in *IRS* II–IV, Central Bureau of Statistics (1983).

7

CONSEQUENCES FOR MIGRATION, UNEMPLOYMENT, AND URBAN POVERTY

The non-agricultural labour market is by no means synonymous with the urban labour market, though the latter has received much attention because spatial movements of labour, unemployment, and household poverty are all more visible to observers when they occur in urban areas. The spectre raised by the ILO Report (1972) was of rapid rural-to-urban migration fuelled by educational expansion. Yet employment in the formal sector was expected to grow only slowly, this being projected from the experience of the preceding decade. As a consequence of these two phenomena urban unemployment was predicted to continue to grow rapidly. Finally, unemployment was seen as being a serious problem for poverty not merely (or even primarily) because of the resource misallocation which it represented, but because of the social consequences for urban household poverty. This gloomy scenario might however be avoided, suggested the Report, by the benign rapid growth of the informal sector, which, unlike the distorted and non-maximizing formal sector, was suitably endowed with appropriate technology and evaded employment regulation.

In fact, none of these beliefs were well founded. Despite very rapid educational expansion urban migration decelerated sharply. The growth of formal sector employment by contrast accelerated so that the rate of urban unemployment declined. The urban informal sector grew quite rapidly but, given its very small base, failed to live up to the expectations of those who had regarded it as the dynamic sector of the economy. This chapter documents why the experience of the 1970s was so contrary to the expectations held at the beginning of the decade.

I. Education and Migration

In Chapter 6 section IV we analysed the links between educational characteristics and employment opportunities. It was demonstrated that employers used the opportunity presented by the expansion in the supply of educated labour to intensify selection criteria, in particular by requiring good educational performance and an appropriate academic specialization. Since this change in the critical characteristics required for employment was, with a short lag, perceived by job seekers, hopeless job search did not rise with the supply of educated labour. This thesis has corollaries for both the volume and composition of migration to urban areas. It suggests that the volume of migration would be neither an extrapolation of the past migration, nor (through fixed education-specific migration propensities) follow the path of educational growth. Rather, migration would be matched to employment opportunities except to the extent that a return to market equilibrium required a temporary reduction in migration below this level. Regarding the composition of migration, the thesis suggests that rather than those with more years of education bumping out those with less, those with good educational performance at the secondary level would displace those with poor performance who would not themselves be at a significant advantage over those with less education. Hence, a rapid fall in the propensity of Form IV leavers to migrate in search of urban employment would co-exist with continued migration of those with primary education.

The experience of urban migration in the 1970s can be calculated with reasonable accuracy through the Census of 1969, the Demographic Baseline Survey of 1973, the National Demographic Survey of 1977, and the Census of 1979. Since rather more data is available for Nairobi than for urban areas as a whole, we focus primarily upon Nairobi, which during the 1970s comprised around half of the national urban population.

In the period 1962–9 Nairobi had grown at an annual rate of 10.3 per cent, of which around 8 per cent was due to migration. Between 1969 and 1979 the growth rate fell to 5.0 per cent of which only some 2.2 per cent was due to migration. The intra-period growth rates are set out in Table 7.1. This rapid

Table 7.1
Nairobi Population Annual Growth Rates 1969–1979
(percentages)

	1969–73	1973–7	1977–9
Male			
natural increase	2.0	2.4	2.4
net migration	3.9	1.4	1.6
total	5.9	3.8	4.0
Female			
natural increase	3.5	3.8	3.8
net migration	4.7	−1.0	1.0
total	8.4	2.7	4.8
Total			
natural increase	2.6	3.0	3.0
net migration	4.2	0.3	1.3
total	6.9	3.3	4.3

Sources: 1969 Census; 1973 Demographic Baseline Survey; 1977 National Demographic Survey (unpublished data analysed in collaboration with J. W. Gunning); 1979 Census.

deceleration in net migration conceals substantial rural-to-urban migration by some age groups offset by substantial urban-to-rural migration by others, as is shown in Table 7.2. Male in-migration is heavily concentrated in the age group 20–24, female in-migration being concentrated in the wider age band 15–24. Most female migration is for the purpose of marriage rather than employment. Once married, wives and their children often return to the shamba. For example, the period 1969–73 was a marriage boom, the proportion of adult women who were married rising from 35 per cent to 53 per cent. Proximately, this yielded a baby boom[1] and by 1973–7 both children and women aged 25–9 (presumably their mothers) had high rates of out-migration. In this sense, female migration is derivative of male migration, and so we focus upon the latter.

Table 7.2
Age- and Sex-Specific Net Migration to Nairobi
('000s)

		1969–73	1973–7	1977–9
Males				
Age	0–14	16.9	−4.2	−2.8
	15–19	6.4	8.0	6.5
	20–24	20.4	19.9	36.2
	25–29	12.6	5.1	15.4
	30–39	5.0	−4.4	−7.0
	40–49	−0.7	−1.9	−7.1
	50+	−9.6	−1.9	−12.6
Females				
Age	0–14	18.8	−4.7	−0.7
	15–19	13.5	11.5	6.8
	20–24	24.6	3.6	10.6
	25–29	0.8	−11.2	1.6
	30–39	−3.3	−6.4	−3.3
	40–49	−5.8	−3.0	−0.5
	50+	−2.3	−1.5	−0.7

Sources: As for Table 7.1. These figures are only approximate, being derived by predicting the population in the absence of migration from prior fertility and mortality rates.

Table 7.2, which shows net migration by age group, demonstrates that migration is highly age-specific, male migration to Nairobi being concentrated in the age group 20–4. Indeed, all age groups over thirty display net out-migration, a theme to which we return in section (4).

Rural-to-urban migration is not only age selective but is also biased by education. Since the Censuses and the National Demographic Survey recorded educational attainments it is possible to estimate the educational profiles of migrants for the two periods 1969–77 and 1977–9. These can be compared with the survey data for the period 1964–8, collected by Rempel, Harris, and Todaro. The results (shown in Table 7.3) reveal a modest rise in the share of migrants with secondary education. However, migrants with only primary education remained a major component of the total. Indeed, the increase in the share of migrants with secondary education (from 34 per cent to 51 per cent) was less than the increase in the share of new entrants to the national labour force with secondary education (from 7 per cent to 27 per cent, from Table 6.15). Hence, the propensity of secondary school leavers to migrate probably declined relative to that of those with less education, this being precisely the converse of the 'bumping' hypothesis. The migration propensity of those leaving Form IV of secondary schooling is further investigated because in the 1960s the migration propensity of this group was known to be very high, and because the rate of stock accumulation has been between 20 and 30 per cent per annum since the late 1960s. Table 7.4 estimates the propensity of non-Nairobi male Form IV leavers to migrate to Nairobi in four sub-periods spanning 1964–79. It suggests that there has been a rapid and very substantial adjustment in Form IV leavers' expectations so that, while around 80 per cent migrated at the start of the period, little more than 10 per cent were migrating by the end.

Table 7.3
Educational Qualifications of Male Migrants to Nairobi
(percentages)

Education	1964–68[a]	1969–77[b]	1977–9[c]
None	10.8	}52.1	7.6
Primary	55.2		41.1
Secondary I–III	11.1	20.5	}51.2
Secondary IV and above	22.9	27.4	

[a] From Rempel, Harris, and Todaro; male migrants aged 15–60 in 1968.
[b] Derived from 1969 Census and 1977 NDS; male age-specific net migration over age twenty.
[c] Derived from 1979 Census and 1977 NDS; male age-specific net migration over age twenty.

To summarize the evidence on migration between urban and rural areas, the pace of urbanization slowed sharply in the 1970s. The rapid rates of urban growth experienced in the 1960s should therefore be interpreted as a temporary response to the particular circumstances of the Independence era. This deceleration in urban growth coincided with an acceleration in edu-

Table 7.4

The Propensity of Male Non-Nairobi Form IV Leavers to Migrate to Nairobi
('000s)

	1964–8	1969–72	1973–6	1977–9
National output of leavers[a]	19.6	54.5	79.9	118.4
Nairobi output of leavers[b]	3.9	6.8	10.0	14.8
Non-Nairobi leavers	15.7	47.7	69.9	103.6
Migrants with Form IV education	12.4[c]	8.7[d]	8.5[d]	13.3[e]
Propensity to migrate	0.79	0.18	0.12	0.13

[a] From Statistical Abstracts.
[b] Derived from Bigsten (1980), Table XII:2.
[c] Derived from Rempel *et al.* (gross in-migration).
[d] The 1969 Census and the 1977 NDS enable an estimate of net age-specific migration of those over twenty to be made by education for the period 1969–77. In allocating this between the sub-periods 1969–72 and 1973–6 we have assumed that the share of Form IV leavers in total migration was the same in 1969–72 as it had been in 1964–8, i.e. 23 per cent against 27 per cent for the 1969–77 period as a whole.
[e] The 1977 NDS distinguishes secondary education in to those with Forms I–III and those with Forms IV to VI. The 1979 Census distinguishes Forms I–IV from V to VI. We have assumed that those two proportions were the same in 1979 as in 1977 within an age group, so that the difference between them (around 50 per cent) is the proportion of secondary school leavers in Nairobi with Form IV education.

cational output. Despite this conjunction, those with little education were not bumped out of the urban labour market. Instead, the adjustment was borne by those with secondary education revising their expectations and accordingly reducing their propensity to migrate.

II Unemployment and the Structure of Employment

The pessimism concerning the scope for expansion of formal wage employment which prevailed by the end of the era of 'compassion' was correctly based upon experience during that era. Between 1955 and 1968 African non-agricultural formal wage employment had increased at only 1.6 per cent per annum, considerably less than the growth of the labour force. Again, the error in this pessimism was the failure to perceive the abnormality of the period. In the decade which followed, (1968–78), citizen[2] non-agricultural formal wage employment increased by 6.3 per cent per annum, well in excess of labour force growth.

Turning to the Nairobi labour market our data sources again dictate that the period of focus is 1969–79, providing four snapshots of the employment structure, the data being presented in Table 7.5. Defining the male labour

Table 7.5

The Nairobi Male Labour Force by Economic Activity, 1969–79

	1969	1973	1977	1979	Annual growth rate 1969–79
			('000s)		(per cent)
Population aged 20–54[a]	179.0	219.4	243.3	286.3	4.8
Population aged 55+[a]	11.7	11.7	17.3	15.7	3.0
Not in labour force[b]	16.3	19.6	21.9	25.4	4.5
Formal wage employment[c]	142.8	175.5	202.1	217.3	4.3
Informal sector and self-employed	13.2[d]	12.5[d]	29.3[h]	35.4[h]	10.4
Unemployment	18.4[e]	23.5[f]	14.1[g]	16.3[g]	−1.2
Discrepancies (identifiable error)	–	–	−6.8	7.6	–

[a] Sources as for Table 7.1
[b] The 1977/8 Labour Force Survey reported in *Integrated Rural Surveys 1976–79*, Table 7.9, gives age-specific labour force participation rates for urban males. These were applied to the age distributions of the Nairobi male population prevailing in each year. Hence, we do not allow changes in participation rates within age groups.
[c] *Employment Earnings*, various years.
[d] Derived as a residual, little reliance can be placed in these figures. The magnitude of identified errors in 1977 and 1979 was 2½ per cent of the population, this being ± 5,000 in 1969 or a range of 8,000 to 18,000.
[e] ILO Survey estimated male unemployment rate at 10.3 per cent in 1969.
[f] 1974 HBS (unpublished data) estimated male unemployment rate at 10.7 per cent in 1974.
[g] 1977/8 Labour Force Survey estimated unemployment rate for urban males aged twenty or more at 5.9 per cent of the labour force. Sources as for note b and the 1979 Census.
[h] CBS Informal Sector Survey combined with Employment and Earnings Survey.

force by age is problematic. As noted in Chapter 6 employers recruit very few workers into formal wage employment below the age of nineteen, the modal age of recruitment in the 1970s being twenty-four.[3] The 1977/8 Labour Force Survey found that 76 per cent of urban males aged 15–19 were outside the labour force (and only 15 per cent were in employment). Similarly, there is no discrete age of retirement from formal wage employment, though very few workers are aged over 54. The male labour force eligible for formal sector wage employment is therefore approximately that part of the population which is aged 20–54. This is clearly more restricted than that eligible for the informal sector. Probably a substantial proportion of the males aged 55 and above who are resident in Nairobi are working in the informal sector (or self-employed in the formal sector). Many youths under twenty are either unemployed or generate very low incomes in the informal sector and are certainly waiting for formal sector employment. However, they are only ambiguously part of the labour force since their youth appears to make them virtually ineligible for productive employment. (In the formal sector their marginal product would apparently be below the minimum wage; in the informal sector their marginal product is often negligible.) The labour force eligible for formal sector wage employment (aged 20–54) grew broadly in line with formal wage employment (4.8 per cent against 4.3 per cent, see Table 7.5). The labour force available for the informal sector (those aged 20+ less those in formal wage employment) grew slightly more rapidly (5.7 per cent). Snapshots of the unemployment rate are available for 1969, 1974, and 1977/8. They indicate that, far from exploding, the unemployment rate fell so rapidly to below 6 per cent by the end of the decade. So substantial was this fall that the absolute numbers in unemployment actually fell by over 10 per cent despite the increase in formal sector wage employment of over 50 per cent. The trend in the informal sector (including formal sector self-employment) cannot be identified with any accuracy because survey snapshots are only available for 1977 and 1979. The informal sector in previous years can only be estimated as a residual of the male population less all other (identified) groups. Net errors in data will therefore be wrongly included in the residual estimate. For 1977 and 1979 the reliability of the data can be subjected to consistency checks in the form of the discrepancy between the total adult male population and the sum of the separately identified components of that population. For each year the discrepancy was only 2½ per cent of the adult male population. This suggests that the underlying numbers are fairly reliable. However, even the small error of ± 2½ per cent is sufficient to make our residual estimate of the informal sector in 1969 and 1973 highly unreliable. For example, for 1969 it translates into an estimated range of 8,000 and 18,000. Our estimate of the trend growth rate of the informal sector as being 10 per cent per annum is therefore much less reliable than are the other figures (though it does coincide with the *observed* growth rate for the sub-period 1977–9).

To summarize, the acceleration in the growth of formal sector wage employment coincided with a deceleration in net migration. The proportion of the labour force in unemployment or the informal sector, which had been rising rapidly in the years 1955–68, fell substantially between 1969 and 1979. This is consistent with out hypothesis that both wage and non-wage adjustments were tending to equilibrate the labour market in this period and that these overcame the enormous supply shocks represented by increased educational output.

III Unemployment and Household Poverty

The links between unemployment and household poverty should not be expected to be powerful. Recall from Table 6.33 that 80 per cent of un-employed males were dependents rather than household heads. Of course, as non-earning members of the household labour force they will tend to depress per capita household income, but in 80 per cent of cases the un-employed would probably not be the principal earner even if in employment. In attempting to corroborate this hypothesis we are handicapped by a shortage of urban household budget survey data, the only source being that for Nairobi in 1974. Using this survey we imposed an arbitrary poverty line which attempted to take into account household economies of scale.[4]. Around 20 per cent of Nairobi households had incomes below this poverty line. The poor thus defined do indeed have an unemployment rate nearly double that of non-poor households (74 per cent greater). However, most unemployed persons (67 per cent) are not members of poor households, and most poor households have no member who is unemployed. Poverty is primarily related to low earnings rather than to unemployment. The lowest earning group of the urban labour force is that at the bottom of the informal sector distribution of earnings since there is no minimum wage guarantee. Thus, there is a more powerful link between the low-income self-employed[5] and poverty. The proportion of the labour force of poor households in low income self-employment was nearly nine times that of the non-poor, and most (71 per cent) of such workers were in households that were poor.

IV Urban-to-Rural Migration and Remittances

The phenomenon of urbanization has a counterpart in substantial migration back to rural areas. Table 7.2 reveals the important but neglected feature of net male urban-to-rural migration for all groups over thirty. Many migrants appear to work in urban wage employment for only five to ten years before returning to the shamba. This is supported by evidence of the age structure of those leaving the National Social Security Fund. This fund is entered by all formal sector wage employees who remain in the fund even if they change wage jobs. Those who leave therefore either retire or enter self-employment of which the bulk is agricultural. In fact, leaving for retirement accounts for only a small proportion of total quits, for only around 10 per cent of leavers were aged over fifty.[6] Over half of those leaving the formal wage sector were aged 26–40, the modal age group being 26–30. Indeed, the mean age of those who leave the wage sector is below that of those who stay in it. This paradoxical finding can be explained as the result of two distinct groups of urban wage earners; those who return to the shamba after only five to ten years in urban employment, and those who retire to holdings much later in life. The propensity to quit in any particular year is a U-shaped function of age which is at its minimum in the age range 35–45. This bimodal quitting propensity supports the dichotomy into young and old leavers. Again using NSSF data, young leavers have earnings below the average for their age group. This would suggest that they are manual workers, probably the less skilled. Young urban-to-rural migrants are therefore probably drawn from the less successful urban wage earners. Precisely the opposite appears to be true of older urban-to-rural migrants. Over the period 1969–77, of the 14,000 males aged over forty who left Nairobi, 50 per cent had secondary education while only 13 per cent of those remaining in Nairobi were so qualified. Alternatively stated, of those over forty years old, 40 per cent of those with secondary education left Nairobi during the period against only 10 per cent of those with less education. We will argue that in different ways each of these streams of return migration have important consequences for the smallholder economy.

The figures presented in Table 7.2 are estimates of *net* migration for each age group. Gross migration flows will be greater than this but cannot be estimated except for the brief sub-period July 1973 to January 1974 using the Retrospective Survey 1. Even this survey, which traced respondents over a substantial area of Kenya, understates out-migration since it missed cases in which entire households migrated from Nairobi to a location outside the surveyed area. With the above caveat, net migration to Nairobi was found to be almost precisely half of gross in-migration. As an order of magnitude, over the entire period 1973–7 this would suggest that the age-specific net figures in Table 7.2 understate both gross in-migration and gross out-migration by about 8,000.

To summarize, out-migration from urban areas appears to take three forms: the return of women to the shamba once married; the return of low-income wage earners once aged over thirty; and the retirement to rural areas of older, more successful urban workers.

These labour flows to rural areas have a counterpart in financial flows, for there are substantial urban-to-rural remittances. Our hypothesis that lower-income, less-educated wage earners have a higher propensity to migrate back to rural areas while still young, is corroborated by the remittance behaviour of urban wage earners. Johnson and Whitelaw, in a survey of remittance behaviour in Nairobi in 1970, found that remittances were strongly income inelastic. The greater propensity of low-wage workers to remit income is consistent with their closer psychological integration into the rural community, their propensity to return earlier to that community perhaps being a further manifestation of the same attitude. The overall volume of remittances from urban wage earners to smallholder households is large. Remittances from relatives formed 9 per cent of smallholder income.[7] As a proportion of urban wage earners income estimates differ. The Johnson and Whitelaw Survey claimed to find 21 per cent of wages were remitted, though this is regarded by some researchers as methodologically biased towards a high figure. The 1974 Nairobi HBS found 9 per cent of income remitted, but this was biased downwards since some respondents regarded the payment of school fees for rural relatives as being distinct from remittances. Were all the smallholder receipts of remittances from relatives provided by urban wage earners (probably a reasonable approximation) then remittances would be 13 per cent of the urban wage bill.[8]

Each of the three labour flows and the flow of remittances have distinct and powerful consequences for the distribution and growth of income in the smallholder economy. Indeed, developments in the smallholder sector can only be understood in terms of these urban–rural interactions. It is to this central issue that we finally turn.

Notes

1. Since Table 7.2 is based on extrapolating from previous fertility this shows up as an excess of births which are ascribed in the table to migration.
2. Data from 1968 were collected by citizenship rather than by race. This change is very slight.
3. Unpublished NSSF data.
4. The poverty line in shillings per month was related to household size and composition as follows. A child was counted as ½ an adult, the poverty line being specific to household size in the resulting adult equivalent units. That for single person households was 350 sh., for two person households 400 sh., rising in units of 100 sh. with each extra adult equivalent up to a maximum of 800 sh. for households of six or more adult equivalents.
5. Defined as earning less than 350 s.p.m.
6. Thirteen per cent in 1971, 9 per cent in 1976. Tabulations were prepared for the researchers by the NSSF.
7. *IRS* I (1974), Table 8.4.
8. From *IRS* I remittances are K£24m. and from the 1974 Employment and Earnings Survey, Table 31, urban wages total K£186m.

8

POVERTY AND GROWTH

I Introduction

Economic growth in Kenya is primarily generated through two proceses: in agriculture by the pace of smallholder innovation and investment, and in non-agriculture by the pace of skill formation. We have argued that the latter was temporarily impaired between the mid-1950s and the mid-1970s by an increase in wage levels which distorted wage structures, in particular by reducing seniority premiums. In this chapter we will suggest that smallholder innovation and investment are also intimately dependent upon the non-agricultural labour market. Since poverty in Kenya is overwhelmingly a rural phenomenon,[1] its eradication is dependent upon equitable growth within the smallholder sector. Hence, we must investigate not only how the non-agricultural labour market influences the rate of growth in smallholder agriculture but how that growth is distributed.

Whether the smallholder economy has been characterized by equitable growth is difficult to determine from existing data. The evidence on changes in income distribution and income levels in the smallholder economy was presented in Chapter 3. Recall that comparison between time periods was possible for only one region (Central Province) and for one date pair (1963–74). As Anand has recently demonstrated, comparison between budget surveys is liable to be subject to severe biases. However, to the extent that valid comparison can be made and that this generalizes to other regions and date pairs, the tentative conclusions were that all income groups gained from growth, though the benefits were perhaps disproportionately skewed towards the middle-income group of households. Recall that the skew of income distribution against the poorest 40 per cent was contentious. First, it was in conflict with the consumption data which pointed to precisely the opposite process of egalitarian growth (see Table 3.6). Second, it was in conflict with the change in wage rates in the smallholder hired labour market (see Chapter 5 IV(2)). Since the change in real wages coincided with the change in mean smallholder incomes, this suggested that growth was distributionally neutral. This evidence does not appear to sustain Kitching's view that 'up to 1970 a considerable majority of smallholders in Kenya were untouched by Kenya's agrarian revolution' (Kitching, 1980, p. 329), and directly contradicts his assertion that middle-level smallholders were a 'rapidly eroding group' (*ibid.*, p. 406). Kitching attempts to sustain these views by citing the household income distribution estimated by the ILO

Report (ILO, 1972, p. 74); and Kitching, (1980, p. 407). However, that estimate was spectacularly refuted by *IRS* I 1974/5 (Kenya, Republic of, 1977). The group of households with income in the range K£120–K£200 per annum in 1970 was identified by Kitching as containing 'the remains of the rapidly eroding group of middle-level smallholders'. This group was estimated in the ILO Report as totalling only 240,000 households of whom many were not smallholders. Yet *IRS* I found that among smallholders alone over half a million households had incomes in excess of K£120 p.a. (at 1970 prices). Similarly, the 'considerable majority' untouched by growth, earning less than K£60 p.a., formed not 63 per cent of all Kenyan households as suggested by the ILO Report, but around 29 per cent.[2] By choosing 1970 as an end-point for his analysis, Kitching denied himself by far the richest data source then available on smallholder agriculture.

However, even with the benefit of *IRS* I data the evidence on the change in smallholder income distribution is sufficiently uncertain for us to say that a more reliable basis for judgement is to study the processes which determine the pace and distribution of growth of the smallholder economy. Abstracting from changes in government policy and shocks originating in the world economy two sets of characteristics jointly determine the form of the growth process; namely, the malfunctioning of smallholder factor markets (discussed in Chapter 5) and the interactions with the urban labour market (discussed in Chapter 7). The sources of growth may be distinguished as improved resource allocation, capital formation, and innovation, so that the transmission mechanisms from factor market malfunctioning and urban employment on to growth and distribution must be via these three components. In section II our thesis starts by abstracting from rural–urban interactions. It is argued that the malfunctioning of rural factor markets has negative implications for both growth and poverty. In section III one aspect of rural–urban labour market interactions is introduced. We argue that this interaction can offset some of the damaging consequences of rural factor market malfunctioning both for growth and for poverty. Hence, given rural factor market malfunctioning, some rural–urban interactions are benign. In section IV two further aspects of rural–urban interactions are considered. We suggest, first, that land concentration is not primarily a consequence of the internal dynamics of the smallholder economy, but rather of the juxtaposition of rural–urban interactions and rural factor market malfunctioning. Second, we argue that the very extent of rural factor market malfunctioning should be regarded as a variable which is accentuated by rural–urban labour-market interactions. Section V provides a summary statement of the framework developed in the chapter. Our conclusion is that in Kenya neither the extent of poverty nor the process of its eradication can be understood in terms of the distribution of endowments of assets. Rather, they are determined by the complex influences of factor market processes, both those operating within the smallholder sector and the urban economy.

II Malfunctioning of Rural Factor Markets: Consequences for Poverty and Growth

Recall from Chapter 5 that we established that labour allocation within the smallholder sector is severely constrained by the virtual absence of a market in land rental, the curtailment of land sales, the inefficiency of the hired labour contract, and the limited extent of the market for rural credit. The cumulative consequence of these market malfunctions is the failure of the market process to secure an efficient allocation of labour. This has clear, direct effects upon both the level and the distribution of smallholder income. Consider the consequences for allocative inefficiency. First, the radically different man/land ratios on different holdings, identified in Table 5.2, imply that output is below its maximum level. Ideally, this loss of agricultural output could be quantified by means of a fitted production function; however, this would require access to individual farm observations. In the absence of such data an estimate of the output loss is made in Table 8.1 by comparing the productivity of farms in the size class 2.0–2.9 hectares with that of all farms. We would expect that farms in this middle-size category would tend to have factor proportions similar to the mean factor proportions for all farms. Hence, they would cultivate their holdings using factor proportions which would be used by all farms if factor markets succeeded in equalizing factor proportions. The failure of markets to equalize factor proportions should imply that farms which happen to employ factors in the proportions which would be used by all farms if markets worked, will have above average factor productivity. In fact, the mean labour use per hectare on farms in the size group 2.0–2.9 ha is very close to the mean for all farms (see the second row of Table 8.1), while non-labour inputs are rather below the mean for all farms. Yet net output per hectare is 11.2 per cent greater than the average for all farms. All farms could use land, labour, and inputs in the proportions employed on farms in this middle-size category if factors were reallocated. Unless there are explanations for the difference in productivity unrelated to factor inputs, we may conclude that without factor mis-

Table 8.1
An Estimate of the Loss of Output due to Allocative Inefficiency

	(1) Farm size 2.0–2.9 ha	(2) All farms	(3) (1)/(2)
Mean farm size (ha)	2.38	2.37	1.004
Total labour use per hectare (sh.)	151	147	1.027
Non-labour inputs per hectare (sh.)	155	169	0.917
Output net of non-labour inputs per hectare (sh.)	1,060	954	1.112

Source: IRS I.

allocation output would be at least 11.2 per cent higher. This is clearly an underestimate of the true output loss because most farms in the middle-size group will not actually use factors in the same proportion as the group mean.

The second consequence of allocative inefficiency in rural factor markets is that the distribution of income is different from that which would emerge were efficient transactions feasible. The loss in agricultural output is not shraed equally by all households. The groups most affected by the constraints on the market mechanism are those groups with the most atypical land/labour ratios. The effect on income distribution is thus ambiguous, because both the near landless and those with the largest holdings lose. The commonly used measure of inequality, the Gini coefficient, is more influenced by income distribution within the higher-income half of the population than by the distribution among the poorer half of the population. Therefore, the Gini coefficient of income distribution of Kenyan smallholders may tend to give an impression of egalitarianism relative to a similar economy in which market exchanges are less curtailed.

While the consequence for income distribution is ambiguous the effect on poverty is unambiguous. The near-landless, poor through their limited land endowments, have their poverty compounded by atypically low returns to labour. Poverty becomes a matter both of inadequate endowments and an atypically low return on endowments. The landless and near landless are caught between the contractual inefficiencies of factor markets and the low returns at the margin to cultivation of their own holdings. The array of choices open to poor households with little land is not attractive. The alternatives to cultivating mainly food crops with a very high input of labour per hectare are low wages due to contract-dependent inefficiency labouring for other smallholders, low wages due to monopsony power labouring on the estates, low wages in the informal sector due to competition from the young dependents of employees in the formal sector, or migration to dry land areas. It is, of course, because none of the alternatives are attractive that such smallholders decide to use their labour on their own holdings and, hence, why such widely differing factor proportions are observed.

In addition to allocative inefficiency due to malfunctioning of the land and labour markets, growth is restricted due to the malfunctioning of the rural credit market. Recall from Chapter 5 that credit is a rationed commodity largely confined to higher-income smallholders. This is borne out in Table 8.3 below, where loans outstanding are found to be broadly proportionate to current income. Since current and transient income are positively correlated,[3] credit would appear to be elastic with respect to permanent income. The lack of access to credit for most smallholders has consequences for allocative inefficiency, capital formation, and innovation. Allocative inefficiency is generated in two ways. First, the inability of most smallholders to borrow, combined with limited liquid assets, constrains consumption closely to current income. In turn this makes a given degree of income risk translate into a greater consumption risk and hence, for a given utility function, increases risk-averting behaviour. The failure of the credit market thus raises the equilibrium risk premium. One consequence of a high-risk premium is to generate substantial differences in mean rates of return between risky and less risky activities. Second, the limitations on access to credit create barriers to entry into activities which require substantial investment. The two major non-food agricultural activities both combine high rates of return with large initial investment requirements; namely, tree crops and improved livestock (the former because of the high opportunity cost of lost annual crops entailed by long gestation periods). The quantification of activity-specific risks and credit barriers requires more data than are currently available and so no attempt is made to estimate the resulting global output loss.

Direct evidence on the existence of credit constraints in smallholder agriculture has already been presented in Chapter 5. Evidence on risk as a constraint is scanty, for time-series data on individual holdings are not available. From the *IRS* I, one group of smallholders can, however, be identified as probably having taken atypically high risks, namely that group with negative income for the year observed (1974/5). Some 7 per cent of all smallholder households had negative income, mean cash income being − 3,799 sh. against 2,355 sh. for all households. Clearly, this group must have had positive permanent income, so that mean transient income was almost certainly more negative for this group than for any other. Not all those with heavily negative transient income have taken a risky stance. Some households who have adopted low-risk strategies will still have been very unlucky. However, definitionally, the proportion of households with low-risk strategies who are very unlucky is very small, while the proportion of households with high-risk strategies who make substantial losses will be large. Hence, it is reasonable to expect that many of the negative income groups of households are among those which took atypically high risks. If high risk is not a barrier which can only be overcome by the rich, then the taking of such risks will be uncorrelated with permanent income. Further, if risk were not an important barrier to activities the premium on the rate of return to risky activities would probably be small. Conversely, the more severe is the financial barrier to risk taking, the higher will be the premium on risky activities. Thus, the hypothesis that the financial ability to bear risk constitutes an important entry barrier implies the testable proposition that the permanent cash income of high-risk takers will be substantially above the average, and has the corollary that thereby the risk premium will be high so that differential risk-bearing ability will accentuate differences in permanent income.

The best guide to the permanent cash income of smallholder households is their annual cash consumption expenditure. In considering high risks, and their corollary of large losses, we must however distinguish between *ex ante* and *ex post* permanent income. The household chooses its risk strategy on the basis of *ex ante* expected permanent income. *Ex post*, unlucky households suffer large losses. Consumption can only be sustained by reducing wealth which in turn reduces permanent income. Thus, *ex post* consumption and permanent income are lower than their *ex ante* values on the basis of which risk decisions are taken. The extent to which a loss of wealth reduces permanent income depends upon the rate of return on the assets lost. We will assume that the rate of return on assets is 15 per cent which will be seen is probably on the low side. The mean wealth loss suffered by negative-income households was mean cash consumption (2,732 sh.) less mean cash income (− 3,799 sh.), that is a loss of 6,531 sh. At 15 per cent this would have lowered permanent cash income by 980 sh. p.a. so that *ex ante* permanent cash income would have been *ex post* cash consumption plus 980 sh., namely 3,712 sh. Recall that if risk were not a barrier, the *ex ante* permanent cash income of high-risk takers should not differ significantly from that of the entire population. In fact it is higher than any other current income group identified in *IRS* I, being some 75 per cent above the mean. That is, stratifying households by current income, that group with the highest *ex ante* permanent income is the group with negative current income. This suggests that the adoption of high-risk strategies is largely confined to the richest smallholders. In turn, this would imply that because entry into risky activities was restricted, the rate of return on risk-taking would be high.

The above argument has been presented in terms of allocative inefficiency: risk and financing of investment constraints constitute barriers to entry in some activities thereby preserving differential returns to factors in those activities. However, implicit in the argument have been consequences for capital formation and innovation, the other components of growth. The argument that entry to some activities requires capital investment so that limited credit restricts access, clearly contains the argument that capital formation is constrained by credit. Similarly, innovation which is both innately risky and commonly embodied in capital investments is liable to be constrained by high-risk premia and by access to credit.

The combined effect of cash flow and risk constraints as entry barriers preserving high returns to restricted agricultural activities is to make income from agricultural activities a function of the means of overcoming these barriers. This, of course, has implications for the distribution of the gains from income growth as well as for the rate of income growth. The benefits of growth will accrue to those smallholders with characteristics which enable them to overcome cash-flow and risk constraints. It is the thesis of section III that a prime component of this group are those who participate in the urban economy.

III Rural–Urban Interactions I: Urban Employment as a Substitute for Credit

While the internal operation of the smallholder economy is subject to the output-reducing factors discussed in the previous section, their effects are potentially mitigated by urban–rural labour market interactions. Those smallholder households with members in urban wage employment are both diversified against agricultural risks and receive a substantial cash inflow. Our major thesis is both that risk and credit are important constraints upon agricultural income, and that urban wage employment is an important means of breaking these constraints. We attempt to substantiate this thesis through two approaches. First, using econometric evidence from *IRS* I, we estimate a reduced-form equation in which agricultural income is explained by non-farm income as well as by direct inputs. Our second approach is to investigate the differences in the characteristics of poor and non-poor small-holder households in three major regions, so as to identify the characteristics which permit constraints on income to be overcome. Income from urban wage employment is only one means of overcoming risk and cash flow constraints in the absence of credit. The generalization of the hypothesis is that liquid wealth and all cash income from non-agricultural activities *ceteris paribus* raise agricultural income. However, urban wage employment is directly or indirectly the dominant source of non-agricultural cash income to smallholder households. Income from regular wage employment (which is predominantly urban) and remittances from relatives (which is almost entirely urban) constitute over three quarters of all non-agricultural cash income, according to *IRS* I.

In testing the hypothesis that agricultural income is a function of liquid wealth and other cash income sources we encounter the problem that the major liquid asset, livestock, also enters directly into the livestock production function. For this reason the hypothesis was reformulated on crop income rather than total agricultural income, the independent variables being liquid assets and non-crop cash income, together with a reduced-form crop production function on land, family labour, education, and purchased inputs. The OLS regression results are presented in Table 8.2. Both non-crop income and liquid wealth significantly and powerfully contribute to crop income controlling for the direct inputs into production. That is, more productive use is made of given direct inputs either by deploying them in a riskier stance, or by deploying them in higher-yield activities which cannot be entered without substantial cash. Doubting the mean level of liquid wealth raises crop output from given inputs by 16 per cent. This represents a rate of return on liquid assets of 11 per cent before allowance is made for their direct yield, hence our earlier assumption of a 15 per cent total return on assets may be an under-estimate (in which case the true permanent income of high-risk takers was even higher than our estimate). Doubling the mean level of non-crop income raises crop output by 5 per cent given direct inputs. In fact, non-crop income also enables the expenditure upon purchased inputs to be increased, as we will demonstrate below, so that this understates the positive

Table 8.2

Regression of Crop Output on Liquid Assets[a]

Dependent Variable: log of crop output

Independent Variables: $\ln L_c$ log of family labour used on crops

$\ln M_c$ log of land area devoted to crops

$\ln N_c$ log of purchased inputs for crops (including hired labour)

E_1 unity if head of household has at least 1–4 years primary education

E_2 unity if head of household has at least 5–8 years primary education

E_3 unity if head of household has at least some secondary education

Y_{nc} non-crop income

Q value of liquid assets

A constant

		s.e.	F
$\ln L_c$	0.29[xxx]	(0.03)	86.1
$\ln M_c$	0.05[xx]	(0.02)	4.9
$\ln N_c$	0.20[xxx]	(0.01)	320.7
E_1	0.18[xxx]	(0.07)	6.9
E_2	0.02	(0.10)	0.0
E_3	0.02	(0.17)	0.0
Y_{nc}	0.000018[xxx]	(0.00001)	11.9
Q	0.000052[xxx]	(0.00001)	104.8
A	3.97		
$R^2 = 0.37$			
$F = 115.5$			
$N = 1613$			

[a] From Bigsten and Collier (1983). The Cobb-Douglas form was used since experiment with CES established that the elasticity of factor substitution was not significantly different from unity.

[xxx] Variable significantly different from zero at the one per cent level (two-tail *t*-test applied throughout).

[xx] Significant at the 5 per cent level.

contribution of non-crop income, of which the urban wage income and associated remittances is the largest single component.

The principal agricultural decisions which are potentially constrained by risk and cash flow are the use of purchased inputs and the mix of activities. Of these the latter is the more important since it determines many of the input requirements. Kenyan agriculture has been characterized by two crop and livestock innovations in the activity mix which involved high risk and large cash outlays; namely the introduction of tree crops with long gestation periods and large yield and price fluctuations, and hybrid livestock with high mortality rates. The extent to which smallholders adopt these innovations we have measured by a composite index of innovation with weights based upon the values of different innovating investments.[4] We now investigate how important differences in innovation are as a factor contributing to differences in smallholder income, and to what extent such differences in innovation can be explained by differences in non-farm income.

Table 8.3 shows that poor smallholders have less land, lower inputs (purchased and own-produced) per acre, lower non-farm incomes, lower education levels, lower subsistence consumption, as well as lower levels of on-farm innovation (as measured by our innovation index) than the smallholder average.[5] Smallholder poverty is not strongly region-specific. In no region on our estimates are less than 20 per cent or more than 50 per cent of smallholders poor. Using a Thiel index only 4 per cent of the variance in household incomes is explained by inter-regional differences.[6] The major explanations for smallholder poverty, are unlikely, therefore, to be found in regional or ecological differences. Nevertheless, not surprisingly, there are differences in the reasons for smallholder poverty in the different regions. To focus on these we examine the causes of smallholder poverty in greater detail for three regions; namely, Central, Nyanza, and Western Provinces, which together accounted for 60 per cent of smallholder poverty in 1974.

These three provinces represent different stages of rural development. Thus, Central Province has had a high degree of agricultural innovation (in the form of a switch to cash crops, improved livestock, hybrid maize, and a high level of purchased inputs). By contrast, Western Province has had little agricultural innovation, whilst Nyanza is at an intermediate stage.

Table 8.3 provides some explanations for the higher incidence of poverty amongst smallholders in Western and Nyanza Provinces than in Central Province. Prima facie one would expect that differences in the average incomes of all smallholders in the three regions would be correlated with the differences in the incidence of poverty amongst their smallholders. It can be seen that the mean household income in Nyanza is about 20 per cent less than in Central Province, while that in Western Province is barely half that in Central Province. But whereas in Western Province *both* the farm and non-farm components of household incomes are lower than their respective values for Central Province, in Nyanza mean farm income levels of the average smallholder are *higher* than in Central Province, and the difference in the mean household incomes in the two provinces is explicable entirely in terms of differences in *non-farm* income. Thus, we would expect that differences in the relative incidence of poverty in the three provinces would be related to the determinants of lower *non-farm* incomes in Nyanza relative to Central Province, and to both lower farm and non-farm incomes in Western Province. For the latter, from the evidence on the mean inputs of innovation, purchased

Table 8.3

Smallholder Characteristics by Selected Income Groups and Province

Income range (s.p.a.)	0–999	1,000–1,999	4,000–5,999	6,000–7,999	Mean for all groups
Central Province					
Mean income (s.p.a.	489	1,514	4,823	6,778	5,082
Farm income (s.p.a.)	79	269	2,602	4,144	2,961
Land (hectares)	2.11	2.35	2.116	2.885	2.67
Purchased farm inputs (s.p.a.)	395	204	370	747	427
Innovation (index)	750.7	761.9	1762.0	3528.6	2,235
Education (percentage of households with)	16	16	31	35	
Non-farm income (s.p.a.)	410	1,245	2,221	2,634	2,121
Regular wage income and remittances (s.p.a.)	209	548	1,250	1,420	
Loans outstanding (shillings)	207	195	1,052	1,183	991
Estimated number of households	26,832	36,713	61,109	32,833	
Nyanza Province					
Mean income (s.p.a.)	673	1,511	4,683	7,082	4,327
Farm income (s.p.a.)	181	904	3,109	4,789	3,205
Land (hectares)	1.608	1.637	3.42	5.097	2.67
Purchased farm inputs (s.p.a.)	55	27	292	40	140
Innovation (index)	170	396	473	720.8	368
Education (percentage of households with)	5	2	20	35	
Non-farm income (s.p.a.)	492	607	1,574	2,293	1,122
Regular wage income and remittances (s.p.a.)	150	150	385	1,144	
Loans outstanding (shillings)	77	46	590	109	247
Estimated number of households	54,068	98,127	48,792	13,845	
Western Province					
Mean income (s.p.a.)	629	1,487	5,094	6,893	2,784
Farm income (s.p.a.)	222	623	3,096	1,464	1,476
Land (hectares)	1.708	3.41	4.507	3.583	3.27
Purchased farm inputs (s.p.a.)	22	43	214	157	112
Innovation (index)	1.3	20	181.5	70.1	111
Education (percentage with)	37	33	55	47	
Non-farm income (s.p.a.)	407	864	1,998	5,429	1,308
Regular wage income and remittances (s.p.a.)	168	545	1,041	3,655	
Loans outstanding (shillings)	36	100	618	0	144
Estimated number of households	52,273	99,432	24,194	5,495	

Source IRS I.

farm inputs, and labour on the average smallholder farm, it appears that all these are lower than those on a smaller average farm size in the other two provinces.

Within each province, Table 8.3 reveals that the low-income households have both low farm and low non-farm incomes. However, comparing lower- with higher-income households it appears that the relative contributions of land, innovation, and inputs to differences in farm incomes is not uniform across regions. In Central Province, which has had substantial exposure to urban employment opportunities in Nairobi, there are large absolute differences between rich and poor households in their level of innovation and in their use of purchased inputs, but only small differences in their use of land. Innovation, and hence smallholder poverty, appear not to be closely related to land size class. As indicated in Chapter 3, in Central Province the middle-income group of smallholders have matched the real per capita income growth of the richest 30 per cent. That this diffusion of innovation is relatively land-size neutral is also borne out by evidence from a survey of households making sales of milk and tea in two locations in the Central Province in 1965 and 1970 (Cowen 'Notes on Capital, Class and Household Production'). By contrast, in Nyanza and Western Province, which have lacked access to proximate urban employment opportunities, land differences between rich and poor are substantial while absolute differences in innovation and use of purchased inputs are far smaller than in Central Province.

The characteristics of smallholder poverty identified above are in terms of the determinants of farm income, and the relative contribution of farm income to total household income. Of the determinants of farm income the differences in the size of land-ownership are in a sense structural variables, for which we provide no further explanation and take them as given in what follows. For the two other inputs, innovation and the purchase of farm inputs, we need to explain differences in their values across different small-holder farms.

The importance of non-farm income and/or loans in financing innovation and the purchase of farm inputs is apparent if it is noted that, if the average poor smallholder were to increase his purchased farm inputs to the level of the mean for *all* smallholders, the financial burden would require a reduction in household consumption of 25 per cent if met out of current income. Table 8.3 shows that the levels of loans cum non-farm income are correlated with the levels of innovation and purchased farm inputs for smallholders in both Central and Western provinces. Furthermore, we would expect that the loans component of the availability of finance for smallholders would be closely correlated with non-farm income, with the level of non-farm income *determining* both the ability as well as the willingness of smallholders to borrow. The risk of borrowing without an adequate non-farm income is that land offered as collateral might have to be sold. That this is not an idle fear for smallholders in Kenya is borne out by the experience of smallholders on the Lugari settlement scheme. On this scheme, smallholders were forced to take out loans to finance both purchases of current inputs as well as the purchases of the freehold of the land. By 1977 80 per cent of the smallholders had forfeited their land because of loan defaults.

Similarly, lenders in Kenya look to the non-farm income of smallholders as a source of servicing any loans, when extending credit. For example, in a recent survey of smallholders with loans for farming purposes taken out from the Kenya Commercial Bank, David and Wyeth found that 70 per cent received income from wage employment. The survey covered Nyanza, Western, Rift, Eastern, and Central Provinces. Applying the same coverage and weights to *IRS* I data[7] yields the result that only 9.7 per cent of smallholder household heads received income from wage employment, only 20.5 per cent undertaking any activity other than operating their own holding. Hence, smallholders taking out loans for farming purposes are heavily biased towards those with above-average non-farm incomes. Further support for this is provided in David and Wyeth, which shows that most farmers taking out loans regarded their salary as more important than their farm incomes. Thus non-farm income is likely to be the most important element in the ability of smallholders to break the financial constraint which inhibits both innovation and purchases of farm inputs (to the requisite level).

This raises the obvious question as to what determines variations in non-farm incomes amongst smallholders. Table 8.4 shows variations in non-farm income between regions. The share of rural-based non-farm income in total household income is roughly the same in all three regions, and it would be plausible, therefore, to assume that this component of non-farm income was a function of farm income. The variations in non-farm incomes between the regions seem to depend entirely upon variations in the urban-based component of non-farm income.

Access to urban income is by means of the urban migration and subsequent

Table 8.4
Sources of Non-Farm Income

	Central	Nyanza	Western
Mean income (s.p.a.)	1,121	1,122	1,308
Mean urban-based income (s.p.a.)	1,431	650	1,016
Mean rural-based non-farm income (s.p.a.)	690	472	292
Rural-based non-farm income as percentage of total household income	13.6	10.9	10.5
Percentage of smallholder male labour force in urban employment	8.8	5.3	9.7

Source: IRS I.

wage employment of male household members. Urban survey data confirms that wage earners make substantial remittances to rural households. In a survey of Nairobi wage earners conducted in 1971, Johnson and Whitelaw (1974) found that 21 per cent of the urban wage bill was remitted to the rural areas. This establishes one important link, between rural–urban migration and the reverse flow of remittances, which forms an important part of non-farm rural incomes; namely, the urban-based component, which we have seen is an important determinant of differential levels of innovation amongst rural smallholder households.[8]

While remittances from urban wage income may indeed be an important stimulus to smallholder innovation, this process may generate new inequalities. Indeed, Kitching argues that remittances are predominantly sent by the richer urban households to the richer rural households, thereby constituting the most powerful mechanism for social stratification. On this hypothesis the evidence seems unambiguous. The Johnson and Whitelaw survey found the sending of remittances to be strongly income-inelastic: poor urban households remitted a considerably higher proportion of income than richer households (see Table 5 in Johnson and Whitelaw). While remittances are sent disproportionately by the urban poor, they might still be disequalizing if their receipt was disproportionately by the rural rich. On this the Johnson and Whitelaw data cannot contribute, but the receipt of remittances was recorded in both of the previously cited rural surveys. The results, reported in Table 8.5, demonstrate that both in 1963 and in 1974 the receipt of remittances was a highly equalizing component of rural income.

Table 8.5
The Distribution of Remittances
(percentage of income)

Households by income[a]	The sending of remittances by urban households	The receipt of remittances by rural households	
		Central Province 1963	Central Province 1974
Low-income households	28	16	24
Middle-income households	21	14	15
Upper-income households	15	5	9
All households	21	10	13

[a] Rural households grouped as in Table 3.6. For urban households, low income is defined as below 350 shillings per month and high income as above 900 shillings per month.
Sources: Johnson and Whitelaw (1973), and as for Table 3.6.

Thus remittances, while contributing powerfully to rural social mobility, do not appear to be a source of stratification.

This evidence on the distribution of remittance receipts is indeed consistent with the process which determines access to urban manual wage employment (the relevant job market for most smallholder households). It has long been known that such migration is educationally selective (see, for example, Rempel, Harris, and Todaro, 1968). An excellent case study of this link from education through wage employment to innovation is provided in Momanyi's comparison of two rival sub-clans in South Nyanza (Momanyi, 1976). One had invested in education, and the other had not. The reason for this was that schools take up land and the more powerful sub-clan had used its power to locate the schools on the land of the rival sub-clan. The sub-clan which acquired education was then able to get jobs in the local town (Kisii) and this money was used to purchase improved livestock and to switch into cash crops—especially coffee. All political power still lies with the uneducated sub-clan, but their economic fortunes have diverged dramatically from those of the educated sub-clan.

The above evidence on remittances would also suggest that the urban wage-earners (who are predominantly rural–urban migrants) are keen to maintain their rural links. Why?

Chapter 7 provided evidence for the following three hypotheses: (*a*) women tend to migrate to towns to get married, then return to the rural areas; (*b*) the rate of labour turnover amongst urban unskilled workers is high (see Chapter 6 IV(3)); (*c*) the rate of out-migration of males from cities to rural areas is also high (see CBS *Demographic Paper 1*). From this it would appear that the typical unskilled rural–urban migrant has primary education, obtains a formal sector job, and marries a rural bride who is then sent back to the countryside to look after the family homestead to which the urban worker later 'retires'.

Summarizing the argument, it appears that educated rural–urban migrants with formal sector jobs are the major source of urban-based off-farm income, which is in turn a major determinant of the levels of smallholder innovation. This suggests that the extent of social mobility within the rural economy is strongly influenced by changes in access to urban employment. This thesis was suggested independently by Kitching (1980) and by Collier and Lal (1980). However, while Kitching, basing his evidence primarily upon the inter-war period, saw the process as severely accentuating differentiation, Collier and Lal, studying the post-Independence period, suggested that it increased social mobility. That the pre- and post-Independence periods differed was explicitly denied by Kitching, who maintained that Independence was a non-event.

Kitching's argument was that throughout the colonial period male smallholders had migrated and entered the formal wage labour force. However, only those with either education or skills earned enough to enable them to accumulate. In the early part of the period this accumulation often took the form of bride wealth, but subsequently became directed towards agricultural investments in innovation and land purchase. Hence, 'the prime determinant of differentiation among cultivating households was the rate of savings out of off-farm income, of which wages were in turn the major form' (Kitching, 1980, p. 273), while 'a minority with literacy or simple artisan skills acquired in mission schools and elsewhere obtained better paid employment' (p. 271). Kitching complains of a dearth of data on remittances of wage income but speculates that remittances were income elastic: only the élite of wage earners are able to make remittances large enough to finance the development of the holding. But recall that this is precisely the opposite finding to the survey of Nairobi workers in early 1971 conducted by Johnson and Whitelaw.

The rapid expansion of education in rural Kenya will have had the effect of more widely diffusing the opportunities of access to wage employment, unless employers have offset educational expansion by raising educational selection criteria (the 'bumping' process). In fact, in the manual wage labour market the bumping process seems not to operate. Recall from Chapter 6 that recruitment to manual wage employment was not generally rationed by secondary education. Jobs were at least potentially accessible to a wide group of poorer smallholder households. Hence, the major cash crops—coffee, tea, and pyrethrum—were adopted by smallholders very rapidly over the period 1961–75. While in 1961 the Agricultural Census had found that the sum of the percentages of smallholders growing each of these three crops was less than 5 per cent, by 1975 *IRS* I found the sum to be 48 per cent of all smallholders. Not only had very many smallholders innovated but, as Table 5.4 demonstrated, such innovation was by no means confined to the larger holdings. There seems little basis for Kitching's claim that 'in order to be a comparatively successful smallholder farmer in Kenya in 1973 . . . an above average-size holding . . . was nearly always a necessary condition', other than his own visits to thirty large holdings (*ibid.* p. 372).

The unskilled wage bonanza of the 1960s, inimical to skill formation in the urban labour market, by enhancing remittances probably assisted this process of equitable diffusion of income-enhancing innovations in agriculture given the absence of an adequate rural credit market. The decline in un-skilled wages during the 1970s eased the process of skill formation but threatened temporarily to reduce the finance available for innovation. This threat is only a temporary one since gradually increased skill formation in the manual work-force will lead to higher productivity and hence higher real earnings. However, during the phase in which low manual wages retard the financing of innovation, smallholder income distribution may become more concentrated. Through the relative increase in fee-paying schools, and the link between children's educational performance (and hence their access to government schools) and the educational attainment of their parents, edu-cation has become correlated with rural household income levels. Thus, whereas in earlier years remittances would be a function of education, and rural household incomes primarily of farm size, in later years we would expect education, remittances, and rural household income levels to be more closely related. Thus the benign mechanism for social mobility in the 1970s whereby the random distribution (at least intra-regionally) of new assets— education and high-wage manual jobs—rather than the distribution of land was the prime determinant of household incomes, may now be curtailed.

Further, inter-regional differences in access to urban formal sector wage employment in Nairobi, the fastest growing urban centre, would also have led to regional differences in off-farm income increases and thence in rural innovation. Between 1969–77 there were 70,000 extra jobs created in Nairobi, but less than 2,000 in Kisumu—the local urban centre for Nyanza and Western province. The educated smallholders of Nyanza and Western provinces would have had to migrate longer distances (compared with their fellows in Central Province), which would have limited both their participation in the Nairobi labour market as well as the effective use of their off-farm urban incomes (if they had any) because of the greater difficulties in visiting and supervising their farms.

Nationally, at the present rates of labour turnover and wage employment growth which prevailed in the years 1964–77, some 50,000 vacancies occur each year.[9] Assuming that those urban labour market entrants who are male children of urban households gain priority access, this leaves around 40,000 opportunities for urban employment open to smallholders each year.[10] Thus, the average smallholder household has an annual probability of access of 0.027.[11] We have, of course, stressed that while this is an average probability, in fact probabilities differ systematically between households by location and education.

On the basis of the available evidence assembled and discussed above, many of the implicit assumptions underlying orthodox views should be questioned. The notion that, while allocatively efficient the Kenyan peasantry suffer from polarizing urban-bias, should be replaced by the proposition that rural–urban interactions have alleviated chronic allocative inefficiency to the particular benefit of the middle-peasantry. Growth has in no sense 'trickled down' within Kenyan agriculture. Indeed, the absence of integrated rural factor markets severely inhibits the transmission of income gains within the peasantry. But urban employment opportunities have enabled those with little land to overcome failures in the credit market and thereby achieve substantial increases in income.

IV Rural-Urban Interactions II: Land Concentration and Absenteeism

In Section III we have suggested that, given the malfunctioning of the smallholder credit market, urban wage employment provides an important means of overcoming cash and risk constraints upon agricultural innovation. We now argue that failures in the smallholder land and labour markets generate qualitatively, offsetting malign effects of urban growth on the smallholder sector. We begin with the land market.

Recall that because of the virtual absence of tenancy, changes in land ownership entail changes in land operation. Where changes in land concentration can be measured we find that concentration increased substantially (seé Table 3.7). Because larger holdings are farmed less labour-intensively than smaller holdings this concentration tended to reduce the demand for labour. Controlling for other variables, the land concentration which occurred in Central Province between 1963 and 1974 reduced the demand for labour at an average annual rate of 1.6 per cent. If it could be shown that the increase in land concentration was due to innovating smallholders purchasing land, then some at least of the beneficial effects of innovation on smallholder and landless labour poverty would be offset. To what extent is this concentration a consequence of the selective diffusion of innovation?

Though it is natural to expect that most of the land purchases are by innovating smallholders, the available evidence does not support this hypothesis. First, in the provinces where innovation had *not* occurred there is some evidence of correlation between farm incomes and farm size (the correlation being significant at the one per cent level for Nyanza and at the 5 per cent level for Western). In Central Province, which has the most innovation, our expectation would be that if the innovating farmers had increased the size of their land holdings, the correlation between farm income and farm size would be at least as strong as in Nyanza and Western Province. However, there seems to be little correlation between farm incomes and farm size for Central Province (the correlation not being significant at the 10 per cent level). This would suggest that the larger farms are being farmed relatively inefficiently compared with the small smallholder farms in Central Province. Moreover, as virtually all the land in Central Province is of high quality, this absence of a correlation between farm income and farm size cannot be explained in terms of differences in land quality. Thirdly, from the evidence in Section III, it appears that smallholder innovators in Central Province do not have more land than non-innovators. Thus it would seem unlikely that innovating smallholders (who could be expected to apply their superior agricultural skills on all parts of their land holdings) are the major net purchasers of land.

Who then are the net purchasers of land in Kenya? Our hypothesis is that they are high-income urban households, buying land both with a view to its speculative return as well as for somewhere to retire. We have six pieces of (admittedly speculative) evidence in support of this view. First, a survey by Cowen (1974) in Central Province in 1971 showed that 90 per cent of farms over three hectares had absentee landowners.

Secondly, many Nairobi residents retire outside Nairobi (see Chapter 7

IV). Further, the migration of people over the age of forty from the cities to the countryside is heavily biased towards those with at least secondary education. Moreover, we know that urban income levels are highly correlated with education levels (see Thias and Carnoy, 1972). Amongst the urban male labour force aged over forty, only 14 per cent have attained educational levels of secondary school and above, whereas amongst urban–rural migrants aged over forty 50 per cent are educated to secondary school level and above. This suggests that the stream of older urban–rural migrants contains a heavily biased proportion of the most successful urban residents.

Thirdly, recall from Chapter 6 that from NSSF data the mean age of wage earners not quitting the wage labour force has been higher than that of those who did quit (see page 000). This lends support to our thesis that the majority of wage earners quit after only a few years in the wage labour market, while fairly young, leaving a minority of stayers to remain until retirement. Moreover, from the same NSSF data it appears that turnover rates are much higher for the low than for the high earnings group, which suggests that the stayers are typically in more skilled high-wage occupations.

Fourth, from Johnson and Whitelaw we know that the high-income urban groups have a low propensity to remit funds to the countryside. This suggests that they are probably not as directly involved with the rural sector as the relatively poorer unskilled urban workers.

Fifth, from Migot-Adholla's study of the Lugari settlement scheme it appears that the settlement officers actively promoted purchases of land from the large number of defaulting smallholders by absentee urban dwellers, who had sufficient off-farm income to meet debt repayments.

Sixth, the survey by David and Wyeth supports the link between higher-income wage earners and land purchases. Of those taking out bank loans for farm purpose, 53 per cent had secondary education and 70 per cent had wage income. For this 70 per cent the mean wage was 1,480 s.p.m.—well above the average formal sector wage in 1975, the year of the survey. Only 50 per cent of borrowers were resident in rural areas and 22 per cent of all farm loans had been used to purchase land, the mean loan being 22,700 sh. Borrowers were asked to estimate the contribution of the loan to operating profits. Out of six different uses of loans land purchase had the lowest rate of profitability.

But, if land purchase is a poor way of raising operating profits it can still prove a very good investment. We estimate that the price of land has risen threefold in Central Province between 1974 and 1978, and from all accounts this rise was part of a much older trend. Given these substantial rises in the price of land it would be rational for urban residents contemplating retirement in the countryside to purchase land well ahead of their actual retirement.

Thus, we would argue that smallholder innovation cannot be held responsible for the increased concentration of land in Kenya, and hence for the effects of such concentration on the incidence of poverty. If this hypothesis is correct then changes in the concentration of land are influenced by changes in the concentration of urban incomes. Recall from Table 3.8 that such evidence as there is on this trend pointed to an increase in concentration between 1969 and 1974. This may be partly accounted for by the widening of skill differentials during that period. Perhaps of equal importance was the trend to monopoly industrial protectionism discussed in Chapter 3 I(3).

Finally, consider those influences of urban–rural interactions which arise out of the malfunctioning of the smallholder labour market. Recall that very little labour is hired. The limited extent of labour hiring of course worsens the consequences of the land concentration discussed above: large holdings simply farm less labour-intensively. However, Chapter 5 also suggested that absenteeism reduces the efficiency of labour hiring. Absenteeism is likely to result primarily from urban employment. Recall from Chapter 5 that absenteeism of the household head was indeed far above the national average level in Central Province which, as the previous section showed, has the highest level of smallholder urban-based income.

Typically, absenteeism takes the form of the husband working and hence residing in an urban area, leaving a wife in day-to-day charge of the holding. In Chapter 5 it was suggested that women might well have greater difficulty in enforcing high-productivity hired labour contracts than men.

Thus, while smallholder participation in the urban labour market helps to overcome the severe constraints upon investment and risk taking which stem from the failure of the credit market, it accentuates the allocative inefficiency generated by the failure of the smallholder hired labour market. It is, therefore, very much a second best solution to the credit problem.

V   A Framework for Analysing Growth and Poverty Redressal

A framework can now be provided to show inter-relationships between growth (especially in the urban sector) and poverty redressal, mainly in rural areas. Various policy options can be discussed within the context of the evidence and the analyses presented. To bring out the novel features of this framework, it is best contrasted with the implicit model of inter-relationships between urban growth and rural poverty redressal which seem to underlie the thinking of many observers of the Kenyan scene.

(1) The Conventional Wisdom

A caricature of conventional views on the likely consequences of Kenyan-style development might run as follows. Assets, including human capital, are unequally distributed. Various structural rigidities weaken inter-sectoral links. Therefore, the promotion of fast growth in the private formal sector and capitalist smallholder farming would increase concentration of income and wealth in both rural and urban areas. The non-formal urban labour force would become more impoverished, and the weakest groups in the rural countryside would become increasingly proletarianized. The benefits of growth would not spread evenly or fast enough among most segments of the population. Adjustment mechanisms in the form of price adjustments to correct particular sectoral imbalances in demand and supply would be weak or absent. As a result, the structural features (wage differentials for instance) would not be modified over the course of development. Maladjustments in demand and supply would become increasingly prominent in the form of quantity adjustments. Rural–urban migration would flood the low-income informal sector employment market or create vast reservoirs of unemployed urban labour.

In these implicit models, most flows of people and resources are assumed to be one way, from the rural to urban sector. Many people have therefore accepted the thesis that this type of development entails a built-in urban bias, which must therefore be corrected by deliberate acts of public policy. This intervention would be aimed at changing the structure of existing income and asset distribution, for example, and at reducing the one-way rural–urban flows. To the extent that various structural features of the economy have to be accepted, these observers see the promotion of the urban informal sector as the main panacea for urban poverty redressal. As regards the rural sector, they believe that 'for most of the rural population, the problem is not the availability of jobs, in the sense of paid work for others, but the availability of land' (Johnson, 1971a, p. 23).

(2) Some Assumptions Corrected

On the basis of the available evidence assembled and discussed above, many of the implicit assumptions underlying these views have proven false or founded on simplistic notions of interactions between rural and urban sectors in the development process. One primary assumption in particular is patently false: that the urban labour market does not function efficiently, with prices not adjusting to emerging imbalances in demand and supply. Very substantial adjustments have taken place in real wages. As a result, marked increases in urban unemployment and low-income wage employment have failed to materialize.

In the second place, the reverse links between urban and rural areas in Kenya are just as important as the one-way rural–urban links that have been emphasized in the past. When these two-way flows are taken into account, any urban bias (as exhibited, for instance, in the fast growth of urban formal sector employment) need not be at the expense of any other part of the economy. In fact, it is the close two-way linkage between rural smallholders and formal sector employees that, in our view, largely determined the pace and the extent of rural development in Kenya. Instead of siphoning off people and resources to the detriment of rural areas, these close rural–urban links imply that the growth of the urban sector has improved the rural sectors dynamic production possibilities.

The admittedly speculative evidence presented here suggests that the growth of smallholder agriculture in Kenya probably has not led to the concentration of land which has hurt the rural poor by lowering overall demand for their labour. The main culprit may well have been the proliferation of a particular type of 'rent-seeking' urban income. This remains the single most important structural source of the rural poverty problem because it fosters landlessness, out-migration to the drylands, and emerging conflict between two of Kenya's poorest groups—the out-migrants and pastoralists—who are forced to compete for meagre and dwindling supplies of marginal land.

Finally, there is some evidence that among smallholders differences in land holding have not been the major determinant of household income or poverty. Rather, it was the historically determined distribution of education which affected different smallholder households' ability to obtain the necessary urban-based off-farm income needed to finance farm innovation. As household income and education become increasingly correlated, future benefits of past accidents in the distribution of todays assets are likely to become attenuated.

In the type of two-way rural–urban interactions charted in this chapter, the notion of the 'trickling down' effects of growth is a limited and highly misleading concept. Rural innovation has in no sense trickled down in Kenya. It has been a direct function of the growth of urban formal unskilled wage employment and has led simultaneously to increases in income for most smallholder households, irrespective of farm size, as well as to increases in the outcomes of landless labourers.

Notes

1. See Chapter 3 II(1).
2. From Table 3.2 the proportion of households in poverty is 29 per cent. Our poverty line is slightly higher in real terms than the K£60 p.a. used by the ILO Report.
3. Both a priori and from Table 3.6.
4. The index of innovations is described in Appendix 2 of Collier and Lal (1980).
5. *IRS* I coverage of smallholdings is not complete since large farm areas in which illegal subdivision hs taken place are excluded. However, it clearly ranks among the best surveys of African smallholders. As discussed above, some 7 per cent of households reported negative income during the year. Since these households have high levels of both consumption and assets, negative income is not a sign of poverty. In our subsequent analysis of the poverty group we have excluded the negative-income group and also those households whose income is within the band 0–2,000 s.p.a. purely due to large (transient) livestock losses. Our poverty

group is therefore smallholders with incomes between 0 and 2,000 s.p.a. after exclusion of these groups.

6. This is not necessarily an indication that rural poverty is not location specific. Whilst regions are the appropriate units for investigating policy-induced inequalities (being the location-specific budgeting divisions) they are not the best units for the analysis of inequalities due to ecology. However, even when we grouped the *IRS* I data into eight ecological zones, only 10 per cent of the variance in incomes is explained by inter-zonal differences.

7. Table 6.4 of *IRS* I, using teaching, government, and urban employment as a proxy for wage employment.

8. Rempel and Lobdell (1978), however, have recently argued that 'the role remittances have played and are likely to play in realization of rural development is limited'. They reach this conclusion, in particular for Kenya, on the basis of survey evidence that households used remittances for the following purposes. Nearly all households (96 per cent) reported using the money to support family and friends. Twelve per cent of households reported using some to pay school fees, and 2 per cent repaid debts. From this they conclude that remittances have financed 'increased rural consumption, education and better housing' (p. 336) rather than rural development. But their argument is untenable as it fails to recognize the fungibility of the available resources of the smallholders. Even though (as is well known from the debates on the effects of foreign capital inflows) recipients of remittances claim that most of the remittances were spent on consumption, that does not mean that by increasing overall household incomes an increase in total productive investment did not also take place. To deny this, would imply that investment (future consumption) is an inferior good.

9. From Table 6.21 total incremental employment (including vacancies due to quits) was 642,000 over the period, or 49,400 per year.

10. From the 1969 Census 86,00 urban males would have entered the labour market annually during the mid-1970s.

11. Using the *IRS* I estimate of 1,483,000 smallholder households.

9

CONCLUSIONS

We have traced the evolution of Kenyan labour markets from their non-wage, pre-colonial forms through the racially segmented form in the colonial period to the current forms in which it is claimed the labour market is equally segmented. Thus, for the colonial period we have clearly identified the barriers placed in the way of African labour's access to higher income-earning opportunities, through the ban on smallholder cash-crop cultivation, the various forms of taxes and coercion used to compel Africans to work at less than their supply price as wage labourers on settler farms, and the limited provisions for Africans to acquire the educational prerequisites for high-paying urban jobs. The labour market adjusted to these barriers much as economic theory would have predicted. The notable feature of the adjustment was the practice which developed amongst African smallholders, of using their earnings from wage employment on settler farms (which was necessitated by their need to generate enough cash income to pay the colonial government's poll and hut taxes) to pay for hired labour and purchased inputs on their smallholdings. This practice has continued into the post-Independence period, and is a major reason for the beneficial two way rural–urban interactions which have characterized the more recent evolution of the Kenyan economy.

The trends in African wages and employment in the colonial period up to 1948 can be adequately explained by changing world demand for Kenyan agricultural exports, which shifted the demand curve for labour, and the varying degrees of coercion of African labour which shifted its supply curve. This coercion, as well as the initial alienation of African tribal land for white settlement which caused it, sparked African nationalism. From its inception nationalism was intimately tied to labour market issues, though at least amongst the Kikuyus it was also closely linked to the 'land question' concerning the alienation of their ancestral lands for white settlement. Its initial aim was to redress workers' grievances flowing from the coercive system designed to provide the white settlers with a cheap labour supply. In later years it sought to change the aspects of colonial educational policy which were aimed at denying Africans the means to acquire the necessary skills to rise in the urban wage hierarchy, which in turn perpetuated the racial stratification of the urban labour force.

With the growing nationalist fervour in most parts of its empire the British authorities in London became more and more concerned to divert the emerging Kenyan nationalism away from demands for independence and towards the redressal of the more narrowly defined economic aspects of workers' grievances. With the development of some local industry in the inter-war years, and the consequent growth of the urban labour force, a number of strikes had occurred in the 1930s. Under pressure from London, and its increasingly humanitarian impulses, the Kenyan authorities, by 1952, had officially recognized African trade unions and introduced minimum wage laws and a protective labour code. They then sought to divert the emerging urban labour movement in Kenya away from political agitation towards a concern for pay and working conditions. This was reflected in their new-found willingness to allow minimum wages to rise. This hit the profits of the white industrial employers whose interests now sharply diverged from those of the white settlers and the colonial authorities. The latter increasingly followed a carrot and stick policy of buying out the labour movement at the expense of industrial employers, while at the same time repressing those who sought to link economic with political demands.

The resulting rise in minimum wages and the accompanying wage policies were the major sources of the urban wage explosion, distortions in the wage structure, and the rise in urban unemployment which obsessed a whole decade of thought on Kenyan labour markets. The stylized facts of this period which various models of Kenyan labour markets sought to explain can be summarized as: a marked educational expansion, increased rural–urban migration and urban unemployment, large rural–urban wage differentials, and stagnant urban formal sector employment contrasted with growing informal urban sector employment.

Most of these structural characteristics disappeared in the 1970s, as the Kenyan government succeeded where the colonial authorities had failed in breaking the link between politics and urban labour's economic demands by the progressive emasculation of the trade unions and the reversal of its post-Independence minimum wage policies. The models of the Kenyan labour market which continue to imprison thought, however, are still implicitly based on the exceptional period of the decade from the late 1950s to the late 1960s, when policy-induced distortions led to the outcomes which various theorists attempted to rationalize in terms of institutionalist, segmented labour market type explanations. As most of the distortions underlying these theories depend upon assumed rigidities in the level and structure of urban 'formal' sector wages in the face of excess supply, we presented a detailed analytical discussion of the determinants of the urban wage structure. Our explanation, unlike those of the institutionalists, relied heavily on the so-called new 'neo-classical' theories of industrial wage structures which take account of problems concerned with imperfect information and uncertainty on both sides of the market for heterogeneous labour, many of whose relevant characteristics are unobservable. In particular, these theories stress the importance of firm-specific skills in determining the observed rigidities in the wage-structure. The concuding section of Chapter 6 provided a summary of why and in what way our conclusions about the functioning of the Kenyan urban labour market differ from those of current orthodoxy. It may be useful to reiterate these and draw their relevance for public policy on the three broad classes of issues concerning resource allocation, poverty redressal, and income distribution for which judgements of labour market behaviour are relevant.

We have shown, first, that wages are not rigid in the face of imbalances in the demand and supply of different types of labour (though they are likely to be sticky for urban labour for whom firm-specific capital is of importance). Secondly, the asserted role of completed years of education as an unproductive screening device in the labour market is not valid for either white-collar or manual labour. For jobs where educational background is important, it is examination performance (which is a test of ability and hence potential productivity) rather than years of schooling which is used as a recruitment criteria. Thus there is no inherent tendency for the educatonal system to explode, nor is there any reason to believe that social returns on education (at any level) are currently zero. Thirdly, there are no inherent structural imbalances in the labour market which would necessitate high and rising urban unemployment as an accompaniment of rising urban formal sector employment. That current urban unemployment rates at around 6 per cent are above those in rural areas is probably due to the minimum wage laws which have further exacerbated youth unemployment, as the minimum age to which adult rates apply has been reduced from twenty to eighteen.

Finally, important determinants of the formal sector wage structure are the skill requirements, and the process of their acquisition in much of modern industry. If this process of general and firm-specific skill acquisition is identified (as it rightly should be) with the most important part of the process of creating an industrial labour force, then policy-induced distortions in the wage structure (as happened during the post war period of compassionate policies in Kenya) are likely to damage this skill-acquisition process. The differential wage structure might appear to be disfunctional from the narrow, competitive-theoretical viewpoint. However, as we have argued in Chapter 6, (and as is stressed by modern neo-classical theories), this differential wage structure performs an essential role in providing adequate incentives to both sides in the labour market to acquire the requisite amount of firm-specific capital, when, given the problems of small-number bargaining, as well as the moral hazard concerning the monitoring of various unobservable (or extremely noisy) variables (relevant for productive efficiency) entailed in its acquisition and use, competitive spot markets for such firm-specific human capital do not exist.

In our view, therefore, the implicit policy implications of the segmented labour market type view are grossly misleading. On this view these wage differentials do not serve any useful efficiency function, but they do determine the distribution of income. Hence, it is implied, public policy can and should (through wages and income policies) squeeze these differentials, so that the resulting income distribution is made to conform to public preferences. As we have argued, this conclusion would be as unwarranted as its premiss. At least in Kenya, its post-war economic history provides an ample demonstration of the costs (in terms of rising urban unemployment, suboptimal levels of skill acquisition, bias against youth employment, and a general reduction in the economy's productive efficiency) which were associated with the various wage policies aimed in part at affecting the income distribution.

If one of the major aims of public policy is to redress poverty, rather than promote equality, then Kenya's post-Independence record is a success. A case can be made that the derived demand for labour in Kenya could have been higher if there were fewer product market distortions, and less concentration of land. Both these aspects, we have argued, are linked, as the major product market distortions are caused by the structure and level of protection offered by the Kenyan trade control system, while the ensuing 'rents' earned by various urban dwellers have been a major source of funds fuelling land concentration. A reform of the trade control system thus remains one of the most important policy reforms which would further improve the prospects of Kenyan labour—particularly of its poorest members.[1]

Finally, it should be noted that even though the political role that trade unions have historically played in Kenya may have been eroded, they still serve a useful economic function. For in the formal sector urban labour markets, where they predominate, it is useful for both employers and workers to have trade unions participating in collective bargaining and in industrial dispute settlement procedures. This is essentially because modern industrial labour markets cannot be converted into spot markets, due to the importance of firm-specific human capital in their production processes. To facilitate the inevitable bargaining in the bilateral monopoly position that then arises, trade unions serve an efficiency function, and to that extent would have to be invented if they did not already exist.

This, however, highlights the inevitably 'political' nature of much labour market phenomena—at least in industrial labour markets. For if these cannot be converted (for good technological and efficiency reasons) into spot markets where arms length transactions are the rule, they will involve the type of bargaining amongst human agents which is the essence of 'politics'. The government will thus invariably be under political pressure to influence the resulting outcomes, even if it does not have any distributional preferences of its own. For this reason, as the Kenyan labour market history recounted in Part One of this book shows, labour market outcomes and politics will never be completely separated. But it would be foolish to try to predict the types of political pressures that might arise in the future course of development.

However, the government will have to take a view on whether or not to accommodate these pressures, as and when they arise, as well as on the extent and form of accommodation. In forming these judgements a view on the functioning of the relevant labour markets is indispensable. The major policy implication of this book, therefore, is that there is little justification for, and much empirical and theoretical evidence against, the segmented labour market view of the Kenyan urban labour market. This market has instead functioned much closer to the manner posited by the new 'neo-classical' theories of labour markets. Certain accommodations to political pressures, which might appear economically harmless if the segmented labour market view held, will have serious efficiency costs if the alternative view we argued for is in fact valid.

In conclusion, therefore, though politics and economics will remain inextricably entwined in determining labour market outcomes, in the more recent past urban labour markets have been functioning fairly efficiently in Kenya. If the extent of poverty redressal, inequality, and allocative efficiency has been less than desirable, this has been due to distortions (either structural, or policy induced) outside the urban labour market. In particular, we have identified a structural failure of all factor markets within the smallholder sector of a magnitude seriously detrimental both to poverty, static resource allocation, and agricultural growth. The presence of the urban formal labour market has tended to mitigate these failures, notably as a substitute for a credit market. Perhaps the best that can be said of the high urban minimum wage episode was that by generating an environment which combined high wages at entry with high turnover (a disastrous configuration for skill acquisition, as we have argued), it enabled some smallholders to gain access to a means of overcoming cash constraints upon more intensive farming.

However, if there is one important lesson to be learnt from the periods of active labour market intervention, either in the coercive inter-war period or the more compassionate post-war period, it is that attempts either to offset the effects of these other distortions, or else subserve various equity objectives, through labour market interventions will most often be counterproductive. In accommodating the political pressures for such interventions which inevitably arise in the course of development, wisdom dictates that in determining the second-best forms of accommodation the direct and indirect costs of such interventions are kept in mind. In thinking about these relative costs and benefits the analytical economic framework we have utilized to exorcize the segmented labour market demon may be particularly useful.

Notes

1. Furthermore, to the extent that some of the foreign investment has been socially unproductive from Kenya's viewpoint, this too is primarily the result of a sub-optimal trade control system (see Lal, 1975).

BIBLIOGRAPHY

Alchian, A. and Demsetz, H. (1972) 'Production, Information Costs and Economic Organisation', *American Economic Review*, Dec.

Aldington, T. J. and Wilson, F. A. (1968) 'Marketing of Beef in Kenya', Staff Paper 12, IDS, Nairobi

American Technical Assistance Corporation (ATAC) (1977) SPSPC Baseline Survey, USAID, Washington

Amsden, A. (1971) *International Firms and Labour: 1945–70*, Cass, London

Anand, S. (1983) *Inequality and Poverty in Malaysia*, Oxford University Press, New York

Anderson, J. E. (1970) 'Report on the Conference of Harambee School Headmasters', Discussion Paper 95, IDS, Nairobi

Arrow, K. J. and Hahn, F. H. (1971) *General Competitive Analysis* Holden Day, San Francisco

Azariadis, C. and Stiglitz, J. E. (1983) 'Implicit Contracts and Fixed Price Equilibria', *Quarterly Journal of Economics*, Supplement Vol. 118

Bager, T. (1980) *Marketing Cooperatives and Peasants in Kenya*, Scandinavian Institute of African Studies, Uppsala

Bardhan, P. K. (1980) 'Interlocking Factor Markets and Agrarian Development: A Review of Issues', *Oxford Economic Papers*, Vol. 32, No. 1, 82–98

Bardhan, P. K. and Rudra, A. (1980) 'Terms and Conditions of Sharecropping Contracts: An Analysis of Village Data in India', *Journal of Development Studies*, 16, 287–302

Beckerman, W. (1975) *In Defence of Economic Growth*, Jonathan Cape, London

Berg-Schlosser, D. (1970) 'The Distribution of Income and Education in Kenya: Causes and Potential Political Consequences', Institut for Wirtschaftsforschung, Munich

Bigsten, A. (1980) *Regional Inequality and Development: A Case Study of Kenya*, Gower, Farnborough

Bigsten, A. (1984) *Education and Income Determination in Kenya*, Gower, Aldershot

—— and Collier, P. (1980) 'Economic Consequences of Labour Turnover in Kenya: A Pilot Application of the National Social Security Fund Data', mimeo, Oxford

—— —— (1983) 'Towards the Modelling of Smallholder Behaviour', mimeo, Oxford

Binswanger, H. P. and Rosenzweig, M. R. (1981) 'Contractual Arrangements, Employment and Wages in Rural Labour Markets', Studies in Employment and Rural Development, No. 67, World Bank, Washington DC

Blaug, M. (1978) *Economic Theory in Retrospect*, 3rd edn. Cambridge

Bliss, C. and Stern, N. (1982) *Palanpur*, Oxford University Press

Boserup, E. (1965) *The Conditions of Agricultural Growth: The Economies of Agrarian Change under Population Pressure*, Aldine, Chicago

Brett, E. A. (1973) *Colonialism and Underdevelopment in East Africa: The Politics of Economic Change 1919–1939*, NOK Publishers, New York

Brohensha, D. (n.d.) 'Mbere clans and land adjudication', Staff Paper 96, IDS, Nairobi

Brownstein, L. (1972) *Education and Development in Rural Kenya: A Study of Primary Graduates*, Prayer

British Colonial Office (1922) Devonshire White Paper *Indians in Kenya*, HMSO, London

Campbell, D. J. (1978) 'Coping with Drought in Kenya Maasailand: Pastoralists and Farmers of the Loitokitok Area', Kajiado District, Working Paper 337, IDS, Nairobi

Carlsen, J. (1980) *Economic and Social Transformation in Rural Kenya*, Scandinavian Institute of African Studies, Uppsala

Clayton, A. and Savage, D. (1974) *Government and Labour in Kenya 1895–1963*, Frank Cass, London

Cockar, S. R. (1981) *The Kenya Industrial Court: Origin Development and Practice*, Longman, Nairobi

Collier, P. (1979) 'A Dynamic General Equilibrium Analysis of Migration and Unemployment Aplied to Tanzania' *Oxford Economic Papers*, July

—— (1980) 'Concentration, Innovation and the Use of Labour in Rural Kenya', mimeo, Oxford

—— (1983) 'Malfunctioning of African Rural Factor Markets: Theory and a Kenyan Example', *Oxford Bulletin of Economics and Statistics*, 45 (2)

—— (1983a) 'Contractual Constraints upon the Processes of Labour Exchange in Rural Kenya', ILO Working Paper 59, Geneva

—— and Bigsten, A. (1981) 'A Model of Educational Expansion and Labour Market Adjustment Applied to Kenya', *Oxford Bulletin of Economics and Statistics*, Vol. 43

—— and Knight, J. B. (1986) 'Wage Structure and Labour Turnover', *Oxford Economic Papers*

—— and Lal, D. (1980) *Poverty and Growth in Kenya*, Working Paper No. 389, World Bank, Washington D.C.

—— and Rosewell, B. (1983) 'Inference and Illusion in Earnings Function Analysis', mimeo, Oxford

Court, D. and Ghai, D. (eds.), (1974) *Education, Society and Development*, Oxford University Press, Nairobi

Cowen, M. P. (n.d.) 'Notes on Capital, Class and Household Production', mimeo, Department of Economics, Nairobi University

—— (1974) 'Analysis of Nutrients in Food Consumption: Households in Magutu Location, Nyeri District 1971/72', mimeo, Department of Economics, Nairobi University

—— (n.d.) 'Real Wages in Central Kenya, 1924–1971', mimeo IDS, Nairobi

—— and Murage, F. (n.d.) 'Notes on Agricultural Wage Labour in Kenya Location', mimeo, IDS, Nairobi

Damachi, U. G., Seibel, H. D., and Tranchtman, L. (eds.), (1979) *Industrial Relations in Africa*, Macmillan, London

Darity, Jr. W. A. (1980) 'The Boserup Theory of Agricultural Growth: A Model for Anthropological Economies', *Journal of Development Economics*, June

David, M. and Wyeth, P. (1978) 'Kenya Commercial Bank Loans in Rural Areas: A Survey', IDS Working Paper 342, Nairobi

Dixit, A. (1973) 'Models of Dual Economies' in Mirrlees, J. A. and Stern, N. H. (eds.) *Models of Economic Growth*, Macmillan, London

Doeringer, P. and Piore, M. J. (1971) *Internal Labour Markets and Manpower Analysis*, Heath, Lexington

Dreze, J. (1979) 'Human Capital and Risk-Bearing', Stanford Institute for Mathematical Studiesin the Social Sciences, Reprint Series No. 288

East African High Commission (1955) *Reported Employment and Wages in Kenya, 1954*, East African Statistical Dept., Nairobi

—— (1959) *The Patterns of Income Expenditure and Consumption of Africans in Nairobi 1957/58*, East African Statistical Dept., Nairobi

—— (1959) *Reported Employment and Wages in Kenya 1958*, East African Statistical Dept., Nairobi

—— (1960) *Reported Employment and Earnings in Kenya 1959*, East African Statistical Dept., Nairobi

—— (1961) *Reported Employment and Wages in Kenya 1948–1960*, East African Statistical Dept., Nairobi

Elkan, W. (1973) 'Is a Proletariat Emerging in Nairobi?' Discussion Paper 168, IDS, Nairobi

Fei, J. C. H. and Ranis, G. (1964) *Development of the Labour Surplus Economy: Theory and Policy*, Irwin, Homewood,

Fields, G. (1974) 'The Private Demand for Education in Relation to Labour Market Conditions in less Developed Countries', *Economic Journal*, December

—— (1975) 'Rural–Urban Migration, Urban Unemployment and Under-Employment and Job-Search Activity in LDCs', *Journal of Development Economics*, June

Forrester, M. W. (1962) *Kenya Today*, Gravenhage

Garraty, J. A. (1978) *Unemployment in History*, Harper and Row, New York

Georgescu-Roegen, N. (1966) *Analytical Economics*, Harvard University Press

Ghai, D. P. (1973) 'Incomes Policy in Kenya: Needs, Criteria and Machinery' in Jolly, R. *et al.*

—— (1968) 'Strategy for Public Sector Wage Policy in Kenya', Discussion Paper 65, IDS, Nairobi

—— and Godfrey, M. (eds.), (1979), *Essays on Employment in Kenya*, Kenya Literature Bureau, Nairobi

Ghai, Y. P. and McAuslan, J. P. W. B. (1970) *Public Law and Political Change in Kenya*, Nairobi

Godfrey, E. M. (1977) 'Education, Training, Productivity and Income, a Kenyan Case Study', Discussion Paper 253, IDS, Nairobi

—— and Mutiso, G. C. M. (1979) *Politics, Economics and Technical Training: A Kenyan Case Study*, Kenya Literature Bureau, Nairobi

Griffin, K. B. (1977) 'Coffee and the Economic Development of Colombia' in *Land Concentration and Rural Poverty*, Macmillan, London

Gunning, J. W. (1979) 'Models for Income Distribution for Developing Countries: Kenya and Tanzania', D.Phil. thesis, Oxford

Gutkind, P. C. W., Cohen, R. and Copans, J. (eds.), (1978) *African Labour History*, Sage Publications, Beverly Hills, London

Gwyer, G. (1972) 'Trends in Kenya Agriculture in Relation to Employment', Discussion Paper 153, IDS, Nairobi

Harris, J. R. and Todaro, M. P. (1970) 'Migration, Unemployment and Development: A Two-Sector Analysis', *American Economic Review*

Hashimoto, M. (1981) 'Firm Specific Human Capital as a Shared Investment', *American Economic Review*, Vol. 71

Hazlewood, A. (1979) *The Economy of Kenya: The Kenyatta Era*, Oxford University Press, Oxford

Henley, J. S. (1973) 'Employment Relationships and Economic Development: The Kenyan Experience', *Journal of Modern African Studies*, Vol. 11, No. 4

Heyer, J. (1967) 'The Economics of Small-Scale Farming in Lowland Machakos', Occasional Paper 1, IDS, Nairobi

—— Maitha, J. K. and Senga, W. M. (1976), *Agricultural Development in Kenya*, Oxford University Press, Nairobi

Hickman, B. D. (1970) 'Kenya and Uganda' in Lewis, W. A. (ed.) *Tropical Development 1880–1913*, Allen and Unwin, London

Hicks, J. R. (1936) 'Review of Keynes' General Theory', *Economic Journal*

—— (1965) *Capital and Growth*, Oxford University Press, London

—— (1973) *Capital and Time: A Neo-Austrian Theory*, Oxford University Press, London

—— (1977) *Economic Perspectives*, Oxford University Press, London

—— (1979) *Causality in Economics*, Blackwell, Oxford

Hodd, M. (1976) 'Income Distribution in Kenya 1963–72', *Journal of Development Studies*, Vol. 12, No. 3

Hopcraft, P. (1974) 'Human Resources and Technical Skills in Agricultural Development: An Economic Evaluation of Educative Investments in Kenya's Small Farm Sector', Ph.D. thesis, Stanford

House, W. J. (1978) 'The 1977 Nairobi Informal Sector Survey: Some Preliminary Results', Department of Economics, Nairobi University, mimeo

—— and Rempel, H. (1976) 'The Impact of Unionization on Negotiated Wages in the Manufacturing Sector of Kenya', *Oxford Bulletin of Economics and Statistics*, Vol. 38, No. 2

—— —— (1977) 'The Impact of Unionization on Negotiated Wages in the Manufacturing Sector in Kenya: A Reply', *Oxford Bulletin of Economics and Statistics*, Vol. 39, No. 3

—— —— (1976) 'The Determinants of and Changes in the Manufacturing Sector of the Kenyan Economy, 1967–72', *Journal of Development Economies*, Vol. 3, No. 2

—— —— (1978) *Kenya Employment Problem: An Analysis of the Formal Labour Market*, Oxford University Press, Nairobi

Hunt, D. M. (1975) 'An Examination of the Distribution of Economic Status and Opportunity in Mbere, Eastern Kenya', Occasional Paper 11, IDS, Nairobi

Hunter, G. (1963) *Education for a Developing Region: A Study of East Africa*, Allen and Unwin, London

—— (1969) 'The Development of the Labour Market in Kenya', in Stewart, J. G. (ed.), (1969) *Economic Development and Structural Change*, Edinburgh University Press, Edinburgh

ILO (1972) *Employment, Incomes and Equality*, International Labour Office, Geneva

INBUCON (1973) *Survey of Salaries and Fringe Benefits in Kenya 1972/73*, Nairobi

—— (1978) *1978 Survey, Salaries and Fringe Benefits, Nairobi Area, Kenya*, Nairobi

—— (1979) *1979 Survey, Salaries and Fringe Benefits, Nairobi Area, Kenya*, Nairobi

Inukai, I. and Okello, H. (1971) 'Rural Enterprise Survey in Nyeri District Kenya. A report of the consultants to Danida', mimeo, Danida, Nairobi

Iwuji, E. C. (1979) 'Industrial Relations in Kenya', in Damachi *et al.*

Johnson, G. E. (1971) 'The Determination of Individual Hourly Earnings in Kenya', Discussion Paper 115, IDS, Nairobi

—— (1971a) 'Notes on Wages, Employment and Income Distribution in Kenya', paper read at the Conference of York University, Nairobi, 1971

—— and Whitelaw, W. E. (1974) 'Urban–Rural Income Transfers in Kenya: An Estimated Remittances Function', *Economic Development and Cultural Change*, Vol. 22

Jolly, R. *et al.* (eds.), (1973) *Third World Employment: Problems and Strategy*, Penguin, Harmondsworth

Jorgensen, D. W. (1961) 'The Development of a Dual Economy', *Economic Journal*

—— (1967) 'Surplus Agricultural Labour and the Development of a Dual Economy', *Oxford Economic Papers*, Vol. 19

—— (1967a) 'Testing Alternative Theories of the Development of a Dual Economy' in Adelman and Thorbecks (eds.), (1967) *The Theory and Design of Economic Development*, John Hopkins

Kao, C. H. C. *et al.*, (1964) 'Disguised Unemployment in Agriculture', in Eicher, C. K. and Witt, L. (eds) *Agriculture in Economic Development*, McGraw-Hill, New York

Kenya, Colony and Protectorate, *Education Department Annual Reports*, annual 1926–62, Govt. Printer, Nairobi

—— (1949) *African Education in Kenya*, The Beecher Report, Govt. Printer, Nairobi

—— *Statistical Abstract* (various years), Govt. Printer, Nairobi

—— *Economic Survey* (various years), Govt. Printer, Nairobi

—— (1954) *Report on the Committee on African Wages*, Govt. Printer, Nairobi

—— (1955) *Report of the Rural Wages Committee*, Govt. Printer, Nairobi

—— (1958) *Patterns of Income, Expenditure and Consumption of Africans in Nairobi in 1957–58*, Govt. Printer, Nairobi

—— (1959–62) *Labour Department Annual Report*, Govt. Printer, Nairobi

—— (1960) *Sessional Paper No. 10 of 1959/60: Unemployment*, Govt. Printer, Nairobi

—— (1962) *Reported Employment and Earnings in Kenya 1961–62* (Economics and Statistics Division, Office of the Minister of State for Constitutional Affairs and Economic Planning), Nairobi

Kenya, Republic of, (1976) *Report of the National Committee on Education Objectives and Policies*, Govt. Printer, Nairobi

—— (1964) *Kenya Education Commission Report*, Part I and II, Govt. Printer, Nairobi

—— (1967) *Report of the Salaries Review Commission 1967*, Govt. Printer, Nairobi

—— (1967) *Kenyanization of Personnel in the Private Sector: A Statement of Government Policy Relating to the Employment of Non-Citizens in Kenya*, Govt. Printer, Nairobi

—— (1970) *Report of the Select Committee on Unemployment*, Govt. Printer, Nairobi

—— (1971) *Report of the Commission of Inquiry (Public Service Structure and Remuneration Commission)* (The Ndegwa Report), Govt. Printer, Nairobi

—— (1972) *Report of the Training Review Committee 1971–72*, Govt. Printer, Nairobi

—— (1973) *Sessional Paper on Employment, No. 10*, Govt. Printer, Nairobi

—— *Helping You to Choose a Career*, Kenyanization of Personnel Bureau, Nairobi

—— *Mathare Valley Survey*, Department of Planning, Nairobi

—— (1963–76) *Annual·Reports of the Ministry of Labour*, Govt. Printer, Nairobi

—— (1972) 'Labour Turnover Survey', mimeo, Ministry of Labour, Nairobi

—— (1963–80) *Economic Survey*, Central Bureau of Statistics, Nairobi

—— (1963–80) *Statistical Abstract*, Central Bureau of Statistics, Nairobi

—— (1963–80) *Employment and Earnings*, Central Bureau of Statistics, Nairobi

—— (1963–71) *Agricultural Census of Large Farm Areas*, Central Bureau of Statistics, Nairobi

—— (1963) *African Agricultural Census 1960–61*, Central Bureau of Statistics, Nairobi

—— (1964) *Patterns of Income, Expenditure and Consumption of Africn Middle-class Workers in Nairobi, 1963*, Central Bureau of Statistics, Nairobi

—— (1964) *Kenya Population Census, 1962*, Central Bureau of Statistics, Nairobi

—— (1966) *A Report on Economic Studies of Farming in Nyanza Province, 1963*, Central Bureau of Statistics, Nairobi

—— (1968) *Economic Survey of Central Province, 1963/64*, Central Bureau of Statistics, Nairobi

—— (1968) *Economic Survey of Nyeri District of Central Province, 1964*, Central Bureau of Statistics, Nairobi

—— (1969) *Survey of Services 1966*, Central Bureau of Statistics, Nairobi

—— (1972) *A Comparison of the Intensity of Cultivation on Large and Small Farms in Kenya*, Statistical Digest, Central Bureau of Statistics, Nairobi

—— (1972) *Estimates of the Income Elasticity of Demand for Various Items in Nairobi, Mombasa and Kisumu*, Statistical Digest, Central Bureau of Statistics, Nairobi

—— (1972) *Population Projection by District 1970–1980*, Statistical Digest, Central Bureau of Statistics, Nairobi

—— (1977) *Consumer Price Indices, Nairobi*, Central Bureau of Statistics, Nairobi

—— (1971) *Kenya Population Census 1969*, Vols. I–IV Central Bureau of Statistics, Nairobi

—— (1973–77) *Informal Urban Sector Employment*, Annual, Central Bureau of Statistics, Nairobi

—— (1974) 'Nairobi Household Budget Survey, 1974', Central Bureau of Statistics, (unpublished)

—— (1974) *Preliminary Results of the Survey of Distribution 1971*, Central Bureau of Statistics, Statistical Digest, Nairobi

—— (1976) *Demographic Working Paper 1*, Central Bureau of Statistics, Nairobi

—— (1976) *Demographic Working Paper 3*, Central Bureau of Statistics, Nairobi

—— (1977) *Demographic Baseline Survey Report 1973*, Central Bureau of Statistics, Nairobi

—— (1977) *Basic Food Prices in 80 Rural Markets*, Central Bureau of Statistics, Nairobi

—— (1977) *Integrated Rural Survey, 1, 1974–75*, Central Bureau of Statistics, Nairobi

—— (1977) 'National Demographic Survey, 1977' (unpublished) Central Bureau of Statistics, Nairobi

—— (1983) *Integrated Rural Survey II–IV*, Central Bureau of Statistics, Nairobi

—— (forthcoming) *1978 Labour Force Survey*, Central Bureau of Statistics, Nairobi

Kenyatta, J. (1938) *Facing Mount Kenya*, Secker and Warburg, London, 1961

Keynes, J. M. (1936) *The General Theory of Employment, Interest and Money*, Macmillan, London

—— (1973) *Collected Writings Vol. XIV: The General Theory and After*, Macmillan, London

Kilby, P. (1979) *Preliminary Report on the Kenyan Informal Sector*, World Bank, Washington DC

King, A. (1978) *The African Artisan*, Heinemann, London

Kinyanjui, P. K. (1974) 'Education, Training and Employment of Secondary School Leavers in Kenya', in Court and Ghai (eds.)

—— and Shephard, D. (1972) 'Unemployment among Secondry School Leavers in Kenya', *East Africa Journal*, IX (8)

—— (1979) 'The Political Economy of Educational Inequality: A Study of the Roots of Educational Inequality and Post-Colonial Kenya', Ph.D. thesis, Harvard University

Kitching, G. (1980) *Class and Economic Change in Kenya*, Yale University Press, Newhaven

Kmietowicz, T. and Webley, P. (1975) 'Statistical Analysis of Income Distribution in the Central Province of Kenya', *East Africa Economic Review*, Vol. 7, No. 2

Kuznets, S. (1974) *Population, Capital and Growth*, Heinemann, London

Lal, D. (1974) *Methods of Project Analysis: A Review*, John Hopkins, Baltimore

—— (1975) *Appraising Foreign Investment in Developing Countries*, Heinemann Eductional Books, London

—— (1976) 'Supply Price and Surplus Labour: Some Indian Evidence', *World Development*, Nos. 10/11

—— (1977) *Unemployment and Wage Inflation in Industrial Economics*, OECD, Paris—— (1978) 'Shadow Pricing and Wage and Employment Issues in National Economic Planning', *Bangladesh Development Studies*, (reprinted as *World Bank Reprint Series*, No. 131)

—— (1979) 'Theories of Industrial Wage Structures: A Review', *Indian Journal of Industrial Relations*, Nov. (reprinted as *World Bank Reprint Series*, No. 142)

—— (1980) *Prices for Planning: Toward the Reform of Indian Planning*, Heinemann, London

—— (1982a) 'Do Keynesian Diagnoses and Remedies Need Revision?', in A. Maddison & B. S. Wilpstra (eds), *Unemployment: The European Perspective*, Croom Helm, London, 1982.

Leontief, W. *et al.* (1977) *The Future of the World Economy*, Oxford University Press, London

Lewis, W. A. (1954) 'Economic Development with Unlimited Supplies of Labour', *Manchester School*

Leys, C. (1975) *Underemployment in Kenya: The Political Economy of Neo-Colonialism*, Heinemann Educational Books, London

Little, I. M. D. and Mirrlees, J. A. (1974) *Project Appraisal and Planning for Developing Countries*, Heinemann, London

Livingstone, I (1976) *Cowboys in Africa: the Socio-Economics of Ranching*, Occasional Paper 17, IDS, Nairobi

—— (1981) *Rural Development, Incomes and Employment in Kenya*, International Labour Office, Addis Ababa

Lubembe, C. K. (1968) *The Inside of Labour Movement in Kenya*, Equatorial Publishers, Nairobi

Lugard, F. D. (1922) *The Dual Mandate in British Tropical Africa*, Blackwood, Edinburgh

Lury, D. A. (1966) 'Population Data in East Africa' Discussion Paper, IDS, Nairobi

Marris, P. and Somerset, A. (1971) *African Businessmen: A Study of Entrepreneurship and Development in Kenya*, Routledge, London

Matingu, M. N. (1974) 'Rural-to-Rural Migration and Employment', MA thesis, Department of Sociology, Nairobi University

Mbithi, P. (1971) *Rural Sociology and Rural Development*, East African Literature

Bureau, Nairobi

—— (1971) 'Non-Farm Occupation and Farm Innovation', Staff Paper 144, IDS, Nairobi

—— and Barnes, C. (1975) *Spontaneous Settlement Problem in Kenya*, East African Literature Bureau, Nairobi

Mboya, T. (1963) *Freedom and After*, Deutsch, London

Migot-Adholla, S. E. (1977) 'Migration and Rural Differentiation in Kenya', Ph.D. thesis, UCLA

Mirrlees, J. A. (1979) 'The Optimal Structure of Incentives and Authority within an Organization', *Bell Journal of Economics*, Spring

Momanyi, J. O. B. (1976) 'Socio-Economic Change in Gusiiland', BA thesis, Department of Sociology, Nairobi University

Moock, J. L. (1974) 'Pragmatism and the Primary School', in Court and Ghai (eds.)

Moock, P. R. (1981) 'Education and Technical Efficiency in Small-Farm Production', *Economic Development and Cultural Change*, Vol. 29

Morrison, C. (1973) 'Income Distribution in Kenya', mimeo, World Bank, Washington

Muir, J. D. and Brown, J. L. (1974) 'Trade Union Power and the Process of Economic Development: The Kenya Example', *Relations Industrielle*, July

Muriuki, G. (1974) *A History of the Kikuyu 1500–1900*, Oxford University Press, Nairobi

Murray-Brown, J. (1974) *Kenyatta*, Fontana/Collins, London

Musyoki, R. N. (1978) 'Socio-Economic Status of Families and Social Participation: A Multi-Dimensional Analysis of Commitment and Alienation in Rural Kenya', MA thesis, Department of Sociology, Nairobi University

Nairobi City Council (1974) *Annual Report, 1974*, Nairobi

Nigam, S. B. L. and Singer, H. W. (1974) 'Labour Turnover and Employment: Some Evidence from Kenya', International Labour Review, *International Labour Office*, Geneva

Njoroge, R. W. (1977) 'Some Factors Influencing Performance in Harambee Secondary Schools', MA thesis, Department of Sociology, Nairobi University

Nurkse, R. (1953) *Problems of Capital Formation in Underdeveloped Countries*, Blackwell, Oxford

Nyangira, N. (1975) *Relative Modernisation and Public Resource Allocation in Kenya*, East African Literature Bureau, Nairobi

Nzomo, N. (1977) 'Education for Accounting and Finance Functions in Banking', Working Paper 309, IDS, Nairobi

Okoth-Ogendo, H. W. O. (1976) 'African Land Tenure Reform' in Heyer, J. *et al.* (eds.) *Agricultural Development in Kenya*

Odour-Otieno, B. E. (1979) 'The Emergence of a National Wages and Incomes Policy for Kenya: A Survey of Experience and Prospects', mimeo, paper presented to the Seminar on Price and Marketing Controls, IDS, Nairobi

—— (1979a) 'Wage and Incomes Policy in Kenya: A Brief Survey of Experience and Prospects', in Mukui, J. T. (ed.) (1979), *Price and Marketing Controls in Kenya*, Occasional Paper 32, IDS, Nairobi

Oliver, R. (1965) *The Missionary Factor in East Africa*, Longmans, London

Phelps, M. G. and Wasow, B. (n.d.) 'Measuring Protection and its Effects in Kenya', Working Paper 37, IDS, Nairobi

Posner, R. (n.d.) 'Preliminary Results of a Survey of the Labour Force on Mixed

Farms in Trans-Nzoia', Discussion Paper 57, IDS, Nairobi

Raju, B. M. (1973) *Education in Kenya*, Heinemann, Nairobi

Rees, A. (1973) *The Economics of Work and Pay*, Harper and Row, New York

Rempel, H. (1974) 'An Estimate of Kenya's Labour Force', Discussion Paper 159, IDS, Nairobi

—— (1970) 'Labour Migration into Urban Centres and Urban Unemployment in Kenya', Ph.D. thesis, Department of Economics, University of Wisconsin

—— Harris, J. and Todaro, M. (1970) 'Rural–Urban Labour Migration: A Tabulation of Responses to the Questionnaire used in the Migration Survey', Discussion Paper 92, IDS, Nairobi

—— and Lobdell, R. A. (1978) 'The Role of Urban-to-Rural Remittances in Rural Development', *Journal of Development Studies*, Vol. 14

Richardson, H. W., Khanna, A., and Sampaio, O. A. (1977) *National Urban Development Strategy*, World Bank, Washington

Robinson, R. and Gallagher, J. (1961) *Africa and the Victorians*, Macmillan, London

Samuelson, P. (1966) 'Economic Theory and Wages', *in the Collected Scientific Papers of P. A. Samuelson*, Vol. 2, MIT Press, Mass.

Sandbrook, R. (1975) *Proletarians and African Capitalism: The Kenyan Case 1960–1972*, Cambridge University Press, Cambridge

Schumpeter, J. A. (1959) *A History of Economic Analysis*, Oxford University Press, London

Scott, M. Fg. *et al.* (1976) *Project Appraisal in Practice*, Heinemann, London

Sen, A. K. (1975) *Employment, Technology and Development*, Oxford University Press, Oxford

—— (1981) *Poverty and Famines*, Oxford University Press, Oxford

Sheffield, J. R. (1973) *Education in Kenya: An Historical Study*, Teachers College Press, Columbia University, New York

—— (ed.) (1967) *Education, Employment and Rural Development*, East Africa Publishing House, Nairobi

Simon, J. (1977) *The Economics of Population Growth*, Princeton University Press, Princeton

Singh, M. (1969) *History of Kenya's Trade Union Movement to 1952*, East Africa Publishing House, Nairobi

Smock, A. C. (1978) *Education and Career Patterns in the Public Sector in Kenya*, UNESCO, Paris

—— (1977) 'Women's Education and Roles in Kenya', Working Paper No. 316, IDS, Nairobi

Somerset, H. C. A. (1974) 'Educational Aspirations of Fourth-Form Pupils in Kenya', in Court and Ghai (eds.)

—— (1974a) 'Who Goes to Secondary School?, in Court and Ghai (eds.)

Sence, A. M. (1975) 'The Economics of Internal Organisation: An Introduction', *Bell Journal of Economics*, Spring

Squire, L. and Van der Tak, H. (1975) *Economic Analysis of Projects*, John Hopkins, Boston

Stewart, F. (1979) 'The Tripartite Agreements in Kenya', in Ghai and Godfrey (eds.)

Stichter, S. (1975) 'Women and the Labour Force in Kenya', *Rural Africana*, Vol. 29

—— (1982) *Migrant Labour in Kenya*, Longmans, London

Stiglitz, J. 'Alternative Theories of Wage Determination: The Labour Turnover

Model', *Quarterly Journal of Economics*

—— (1975) 'Incentives, Risk and Information; Notes Towards a Theory of Hierarchy', *Bell Journal of Economics*, Autumn

—— (1975a) 'Information and Economic Analysis' in Parkin and Nobay (eds.), *Current Economic Problems*, Cambridge University Press, Cambridge

Stiglitz, J. E. and Weiss, A. (1981) 'Credit Rationing in Markets with Imperfect Information', *American Economic Review*, Vol. 71, pp. 393–410

Swynnerton, R. J. M. (1954) *A Plan to Intensify the Development of African Agriculture in Kenya*, Govt. Printer, Nairobi

Thias, H. H. and Carnoy, M. (1972) *Cost-Benefit Analysis in Education: A Case Study of Kenya*, World Bank, Washington DC

Thorbecke, E. and Crawford, E. (1978) 'Employment, Income Distribution, Poverty Alleviation and Basic Needs in Kenya', mimeo, International Labour Office, Geneva

Thurow, L. C. (1976) *Generating Inequality*, London

UNIDO (1972) *Guidelines for Project Evaluation*, United Nations, New York

Von Pischle, J. D. (1977) 'The Political Economy of Farm Credit in Kenya', Ph.D., University of Glasgow

Wachter, M. L. (1974) 'Primary and Secondary Labour Markets: A Critique of the Dual Approach, Brookings Papers on Economic Activity, Brookings Institute, Washington DC

Weeks, J. (1974) 'Employment Growth in Kenyan manufacturing: Another Look at Labour Absorption', Discussion Paper in Economics No. 21, Birbeck College, London

Westley, S. B., Johnston, B. F., and David, M. (1975) 'Summary Report of a Workshop on a Food and Nutrition Strategy for Kenya', Occasional Paper 14, IDS, Nairobi

Williamson, E. *et al.* (1975) 'Understanding the Employment Relation: The Analysis of Idiosyncratic Exchange', *Bell Journal of Economics*, Spring

Wilson, R. J. A. (1971) 'Land Control in Kenya's Smallholder Farm Areas', Staff Paper 89, IDS, Nairobi

—— (1971a) 'Economic Implications of Land Registration in Kenya's Smallholder Areas', Staff Paper 91, IDS, Nairobi

Whitelaw, W. E. (1971) 'Nairobi Household Survey: Description of the Methodology and Guide to the Data', Discussion Paper 116, IDS, Nairobi

Zarembka, P. (1972) *Toward a Theory of Economic Development*, Holden-Day, San Francisco

Zwanenberg, R. M. A. van and King, A. (1975) *An Economic History of Kenya and Uganda 1800–1970*, Macmillan, London

INDEX

absentee landlords, 35–6, 118, 125–6, 138, 268–9, 270
Action against unemployment (ILO), 50–1
advertisements, 221, 222
Africanization, 60–3
  of private sector, 89, 92
  of White Highlands, 75, 85
  see also Kenyanization
agreements:
  collective, 73, 167
  demarcation, 46
agricultural labour market, 115–53
  adjustment processes, 143–51
  contractual efficiency, 143–6
  demand for labour, 148, 149
  hired labour, 120, 124, 126
  plantations, 127–8, 139–43
  seasonal variation model, 125
  smallholder
    labour transactions, 118–29
    sale of labour, 121–2, 128
  wages, 92, 146–51
agriculturalists, pre-colonial, 21–4
agriculture:
  estates *see* plantations
  Kaffir farming, 29
  labour *see* agricultural labour
  market
  policy, 74–6
  pre-colonial agriculturalists, 21–4
  settlement schemes, 75
  smallholdings *see* smallholders
Akambi tribe, 25
Alchian, A. and Demset, H., 114
alienated land *see* plantations *and* settlers
Alliance High School, Kikuyu, 55
American Technical Assistance Corporation
  (ATAC), 121, 129
Amsden, A., 40, 45, 46, 47, 48, 52
Anand, S., 252
applicants *see* recruitment
Arab traders, 26
Arrow, K. J. and Hahn, F. H., 106
Arrow–Debreu framework, 101
Asians *see* Indians *and* racial discrimin-
  ation
Asquith Commission (1943), 57
Association of Commercial and Industrial
  Employers (ACIE), 42, 46
Athi, 22

Bager, T., 120, 129, 130, 131, 132, 135
balance of payments, 77
Bardhan, P. K., 117
Bardhan, P. K. and Rudra, A., 117
bargaining, collective, 42, 46, 47, 49
Baring, Sir Evelyn, 43
bartering for labour, 24
Beecher Committee (1949), 56
Bevin (of PWIF), 46
Bigsten, A., 169
Bigsten, A. and Collier, P., 197, 206, 213
Binswanger, H. P. and Rosenzweig, M. R.,
  151
Blaug, M., 114
Bliss, C. and Stern, N., 137, 152
bonds, 183
Boserup, E., 10–11, 21
Brett, E. A., 28, 29, 30
bumping model, 218, 219, 224, 233, 234–6

capital intensity:
  unionization and, 163–4
  wages and, 159–60
caravans, 25, 26
Carlsen, J., 129, 130
Carpenter Report on African Wages (1954) 43, 49,
  63
cash crops:
  colonial restrictions on, 28, 30
  see also innovation
casual workers, 94, 95, 106, 118, 168, 227, 241
Central Minimum Wage Advisory Board, 41
Central Organization of Trade Unions
  (COTU), 48, 49, 74, 95, 168, 213
Clark, J. B., 12
coercion of wage labour, 29, 32–4, 35–6
coffee, 28, 30, 75, 135
collective agreements, 73, 167
collective bargaining, 42, 46, 47, 49
Collier, P., 147, 151, 152, 153
Collier, P. and Bigsten, A., 240
Collier, P. and Knight, J. B., 239
Collier, P. and Lal, D., 79, 265, 272
Collier, P. and Rosewell, B., 207, 240
colonial economy, 26–38
  African agriculture, 35–6
  employment and labour, 30–5
  Indians, 36–8
  intervention in labour market, 39–42
  settlers, 27–30

commodity specialization, 132–5
compensation function, 193–4
competitive model, 101–5, 106
consolidation of land *see* land
consumption distribution, 82–4
contracts:
  bonds and indentures, 183
  efficiency, 143–6
  implicit, 112
  long-term, 108
  piece-rate, 124
  plough-share, 138
  sequential spot, 106
  share tenancy, 137
  sharecropping, 129, 138
  shareholder constraints on, 137–9
cooperatives, marketing, 136–7
cost of living differentials, 95, 212, 213
cost of quitting function, 194–6
Cowen, M. P., 30, 32, 36, 71, 262
Cowen, M. P. and Murage, F., 23, 24, 124,
  125, 128
craftsmen, pre-colonial, 25
credit:
  financing innovation, 262–3, 266
  for land purchase, 130, 131, 269
  smallholders, 135–7, 255–6
  urban employment as substitute, 257–67
Crown Lands Ordinance (1938), 34

Dagleish report (1960), 50–2
Dairty, Jr. W. A., 10
David, M. and Wyeth, P., 135, 263, 269
de la Ware Commission (1937), 57
decision lag, 13
demand for labour:
  agricultural, 148, 149
  by education, 200–4, 209
  non-pecuniary characteristics, 112
  uncertainties, 111–13
demarcation agreement, 46
desertion, 40, 43, 71
differentials *see* wages; differentials
diminishing returns, 9
domestic service, 30
Dreze, J., 107, 113
dual economy models, 7, 12

East Africa Protectorate, 26
East Africa Royal Commission (1955), 44
East African Indian National Congress, 41–2
East African Trade Union Congress
  (EATUC), 41
education, 86–7
  demand for labour by, 200–4, 209
  expenditure, 56
  enrolments, 57, 60
  growth of, 54–7

Harambee schools, 57, 218
hierarchy and firm size, 159, 162
independent schools, 55–6
labour force and (1948–68), 59–60
labour turnover and, 206–7
migration and, 244–6
racially segregated, 54
recruitment criteria, 99–100, 219–22,
  224–5, 227, 242
skill acquisition and, 188–91
specific charges in labour demand and
  supply, 208–10
studying abroad, 57
supply of quality labour, 197–200
unemployment and, 232–3
wage structure and, 214–17
see also experience, skill acquisition *and*
  training
Eliot, Sir Charles, 27
Emergency, the, 43
employment:
  1946–68, 66–8
  1968–80, 87–92
  by sector, 66, 69, 88
  policy, 168
  racial segmentation, 66, 69
  security of, 164, 165, 174
  see also labour, unemployment *and* wage
    labour
endogenous uncertainties, 107
engagement rates, 50, 65, 178
estates *see* plantations *and* settlers
European Convention Association, 39
exits, 205
  see also quitting *and* retirement
exogenous uncertainties, 107
experience:
  rating, 110–11
  recruitment criteria, 223, 228–32

Factories Ordinance (1950), 40
Federation of Kenya Employers, 46
Fields, G., 99
firm-specific skills, 5
  training, 107–8
  wage structure and, 171–7
fixprice, 6
fixwage model, 4, 6
flexprice, 6
flexwage model, 4, 8
foreign firms:
  private investment, 76–7
  wages paid by, 155, 158–9
Forrester, M. W., 70, 179
full employment model, 7–9
full performance model, 7–9

'gap' farms, 75, 76, 79, 81
General Wages Advisory Board, 74
Ghai, Y. P. and McAuslan, J. P. W. B., 27, 28, 29
Gini coefficient, 255
Githunguri, 55
Godfrey, E. M., 185, 186, 189, 190, 191, 214, 229
government intervention, 73–4, 166–9
    colonial, 39–42
    employment policy, 168
    public sector, 168–9
    wages policy, 167–8
growth in smallholder economy, 252–73
Gunning, J. W., 147
Gusii tribe, 25

Harambee schools, 57, 218
Harris, J. R., 8
Harris–Todaro model, 99, 114, 217
Hazlewood, A., 53–4, 75, 76
Hickman, B. D., 38
Hicks, J. R., 8, 10, 11, 13
House, W. J. and Rempel, H., 93, 100, 155, 156, 161, 163, 165, 169, 238
household poverty, 248–9
human capital, 102–4, 105, 217, 218, 219, 221, 236–7
    see also skills
Hunter, G., 72
Hut and Poll Tax, 29, 33
Hyde Clark, E. M., 33

Immigration Act (1967), 53
Imperial British East Africa Company (IBEAC), 26
implicit contracts, 112
import licensing, 77
Inbucon survey, 93, 165, 166
incentives, wage, 110
income distribution:
    1970s, 80–2
    by economic status of household, 81
    smallholders', 81, 82, 252–5, 260, 261
    squatters', 81
    urban, 81, 84–5
    see also wages
incomes policy *see* wages; policy
indenture system, 183
independent schools, 55–6
Indians, 30, 35, 53–4, 72
    colonial period, 36–8
    money lenders, 26, 36
Indians in Kenya (1923 white paper), 37
Industrial Court, 48–9, 73
Industrial Relations Charter (1962), 48
industrialization, 6, 45–9, 76–7
innovation, rural, 252, 259–60, 272

financing, 262–3, 266
    risk strategy, 256–7
institutionalist models, 99–101
    segmentation
        by firm type, 155–61
        by government intervention, 166–9
        by race, 165–6
        by union membership, 161–5
Integrated Agricultural Development Programme, 137
International Labour Organization (ILO), 77–8, 242, 252–3
    institutionalist models, 99
intervention in labour market
    colonial, 39–42
    governmental, 73–4, 166–9
investment, 10
ivory trade, 26

job search models, 8
Johnson, G. E., 162, 163, 169, 214, 215, 216, 241, 271
Johnson, G. E. and Whitelaw, W. E., 250, 264, 269
Jorgenson, D. W., 8, 9

Kabete, 55
Kaffir farming, 29
Kenya African Union (KAU), 41
Kenya African Workers' Congress (KAWC), 48
Kenya Commercial Bank, 263
Kenya Federation of Labour (KFL), 43, 46, 48
Kenya National Farmers' Union, 33
Kenyanization, 53–4
    see also Africanization
Kenyanization of Personnel Bureau, 53, 62
Kenyatta, J., 22, 24, 41, 43, 45
Keynes, J. M., 10
Keynesianism:
    investment, 10
    involuntary unemployment, 4–6
    revolution, 3
Kibisu, P., 48
Kijabe, 41
Kikonerii, 134
Kikuyu Independent School Association (KISA), 55, 56
Kikuyu tribe:
    education and, 55
    Kaffit farming, 29
    labour organization, pre-colonial, 23–4
    land tenure, pre-colonial, 22–3
    on settler estates, 35
    reduced access to land, 29
    trade, pre-colonial, 25
    see also Mau Mau

Kikuyuland, 22, 45
King, A., 186
Kinyanjui, P. K., 215, 216, 225–6
kipande, 29, 37, 40
Kipsigi tribe, 35
Kisii, 129, 132, 152
Kisumu, 41
Kitching, G., 38, 252–3, 265, 266
Kjekshus, H., 38
Kmietowicz, T. and Webley, P., 95
Kuznets, S., 9, 10, 11

labour, labour force and labour markets, 85–7
    adjustment processes in, 196–239
    agricultural *see* agricultural labour market
    bartering for, 24
    casual workers, 94, 95, 106, 118, 168, 227, 241
    coercion, 29, 32–4, 35–6
    colonial period, 30–5
        intervention, 39–42
    contracts *see* contracts
    demand *see* demand for labour
    education and *see* education
    exits from, 205
    flow on to labour force, 198
    in Nairobi, 246–8
    institutional segmentation, 155–69
    internal, 107–11
    intervention in, 39–42, 73–4, 166–9
    monopsony *see* monopsony
    neoclassical models, 105–13
    non-agricultural, 154, 241
        rural, 128
    non-wage adjustments, 217–32
    occupational profiles, 61, 62, 63
    protective labour code, 39, 40
    quality-specific market, 196
    recruitment *see* recruitment
    regular workers, 94, 118, 168, 227
    segmented labour market model, 217–8, 226, 233, 236
    sexual division of, 35
    skills *see* skill acquisition *and* skills
    plantations *see* plantations
    smallholder, *see* agricultural labour market
    stock accumulation, 199, 200
    strikes *see* strikes
    supply, 197–200
        experience rating, 110–11
        firm-specific training, 107–8
        monitoring performance, 108–10
        port of entry restrictions, 111
        wage incentives, 110
    supply-demand imbalance, 208–10
    turnover *see* turnover of labour
    urban, 39, 45–6, 246–8
        see also migration

wage adjustment, 210–17
    see also employment, unemployment *and* wage labour
lags, 13–14
Lal, D., 8, 76, 114
Lamu, 26
Lancaster House Conference (1960), 45
land:
    alienated *see* plantations *and* settlers
    consolidation, 44–5, 267–70
    distribution, 84, 147–8
    Native Land Trust Ordinance, 34
    purchase, 130–2:
        credit for, 130, 131, 269
        financed by assets, 131–2
        for retirement, 268–9
        forbidden to Indians, 37
    reform 1970s, 75–6
    rental, 129, 130
    repossession, 136, 262–3
    smallholder transactions, 129–31
    tenure, pre-colonial, 22–3
    titles, 76
    usage, not ownership, 130–1
    use, 75–6, 148, 152, 153
    values, 27–8, 131–2
lending *see* credit
Lewis turning-point, 3–4, 8
livestock as assets, 131–2, 258, 259, 260
Livingstone, David, 54
Livingstone, Ian, 130, 152
loans *see* credit
Lockwood Commission (1958), 57
Lubembe, C. K., 40
Lugari settlement scheme, 263, 269
Luhya tribe, 35
Luo tribe, 22, 25

MacArthur, J., 75
Machakos, 55
Macleod, Ian, 45
Macmillan, Harold, 45
Malindi, 26
Malthusian principle, 3, 9
manufacturing, protection and, 76–7
marginal productivity theory, 4, 12
marketing cooperatives, 136–7
Marris, P. and Somerset, A., 25
Marshall, A., 12
Marx, Karl, 3, 7
Masai tribe, 24–5
Masters and Servants Ordinance, 29
Mau Mau, 42–3, 44, 45
mbari, 22
Mboya, Tom, 47, 48, 57
Migot-Adholla, S. E., 130, 269
migration, 16, 242–6
    age selective, 244, 250

decision to, 237–8
educational selectivity, 68, 70–1, 244–6
female, 244, 250
maintenance of rural links, 250, 265
slowing of, 87
to Nairobi, 243–6
to settler estates, 34, 35–6
to smallholdings, 119
urban to rural, 244, 249–50, 268–9
Minimum Wage Ordinance (1946), 49
minimum wages *see* wages; minimum
Mirrlees, J. A., 114
missionaries, 37, 54–5
Mitchell (Governor), 50
Mombasa, 26
post-war industries, 45
strikes, 39, 41, 46
money lenders, 26, 36
see also credit
monopsony, 30, 32, 64, 65, 95, 104, 141–3, 150
Moock, J. L., 197
muhoi, 22
multinationals *see* foreign firms
Muriuki, G., 22
Murogeto, 133
Murray-Brown, J., 37
Muscat, Imam of, 26

Nairobi:
income distribution in, 81, 84–5
migration to, 242–6
post-war industries, 45
strikes, 39–40, 41
structure of labour market, 246–8
trends in absolute poverty, 80
unemployment in, 248
urban minimum wages, 41, 49
Nandi tribe, 35
National Social Security Fund, 249
contributions, 94
data, 197, 206, 207
Native Industrial Training Depot, 55
Native Lands Trust Ordinance (1938), 34
ndungata, 23–4
neoclassical theories, 105–13
ngwatio, 23
Nigam, S. B. L. and Singer, H. W., 206
nomadic pasturalists, 24–5
non-farm income *see* remittances *and* wage
labour

Odur-Otieno, B. E., 73, 74, 95, 167
Okoth-Ogendo, H. W. O., 152
Oliver, R., 54
Omani traders, 26
Operation Anvil, 239

Palmerston, Lord, 26
Pareto efficiency, 106

pasturalists:
nomadic, 24–5
poverty and, 79
performance, monitoring of, 108–10
see also supervisors
Phelps, M. G. and Wasow, B., 77
piece-work, 124, 140
Plantation Workers International Federation,
46
plantations:
labour market, 28–9, 95, 127–8, 139–43
squatting rights, 29
wages in, 64, 140, 142–3
collusion, 32–3
see also monopsony *and* settlers
plough-share contract, 138
policy environment (1968–80), 72–7
agricultural, 74–6
labour market intervention, 73–4
manufacturing, 76–7
population:
1911–62, 37
1948–69, 58
1969–80, 85–6
colonial period, 30, 31
Indian, 36–7
pre-colonial, 22
principle, 4, 9–11
poverty:
absolute, trends in, 80
household, 248–9
line, 249, 251
smallholder, 78, 79, 254–7, 262
unemployment and, 248–9
urban, 78–9, 80
pre-colonial economy, 21–6
private sector industry:
Africanization, 62, 89, 92
wages in, 65, 67
guidelines (1971), 73, 74
productivity:
lower, of hired hands, 124
mathematical function of, 228
wage increases and, 74
profit sharing, 155, 156
promotion policy, 108, 183–4
protection of manufacturing, 76–7
public sector:
Africanization, 62
employment in, 68, 89
wages in, 65, 168–9
purchase of land *see* land; purchase
purchasing power, 73

quitting, 205–6
cost of, function, 194–6
costs, 172, 174
function, 192–3

quitting (*cont.*)
  propensity towards, 181, 249
  rates, 176, 179, 191–2
  seniority and, 184, 186
  see also exits, retirement *and* turnover
    of labour

racial discrimination:
  against Asians, 72
  segmentation in labour market, 60–3
  segregated education, 54
  skill content of labour, 171
  stratification, colonial, 32, 33, 35
  wage differentials, 165–6
  see also Africanization *and* Kenyanization
railway, Uganda, 27, 36, 54
reaction lag, 13
recognition lag, 13
recruitment, 207
  age criteria, 223–4
  experience, 223, 228–32
  of supervisors, 158
  replacement, 205, 206
  screening by education, 99–100, 219–22,
    224–5, 227, 242
  unskilled, 227–32
  see also labour turnover
Rees, A., 104, 114
Registration Ordinance (1921), 29
regular workers, 94, 118, 168, 227
remittances, 250–1, 258, 264, 273
  see also rural–urban interaction
Rempel, H., Harris, J. and Todaro, M., 245
Rempel, H. and Lobdell, R. A., 273
rental of land, 129, 130
rents, 77
  intra-occupational, 104
Report of the Committee on African Wages (1955),
    43–4
Report of the Select Committee on Unemployment
    (1970), 52–3
Resident Native Ordinance (1918), 29
retirement, 247
  land purchase for, 268–9
  to rural areas, 250
  see also exits
reverse discrimination *see* Kenyanization
rigidity of wages postulation, 218, 224, 226,
    233
rinderpest, 25, 29, 38
risk strategy, 256–7
  see also innovation
Robinson, R. and Gallagher, J., 26
Royal Technical College, Nairobi, 57
rural labour market, 128
  see also agricultural labour market
rural–urban interactions, 271–2
  land concentration and absenteeism,

    267–70
  urban employment as substitute for credit,
    257–67
  see also migration *and* remittances
Rural Wages Committee, 43, 44

Salaries Review Commission (1967), 52
Sandbrook, R., 43, 48, 49, 71, 165
Schumpeter, J. A., 3
Scott, M.Fg. *et al.*, 114, 213
screening:
  by education *see* recruitment
  for ability, 109–10
  Walras law of, 114
search employment, 6
security of employment, 164, 165, 174
segmentation of labour market:
  by firm type, 155–61
  by government intervention, 166–9
  by race, 165–6
  by union membership, 161–5
segmented labour model, 12, 217–18, 226,
    233, 236
selection *see* recruitment
Sen, A. K., 116, 124
seniority, 108, 164, 172–9, 192, 229
  labour turnover and, 179–83, 184–6
sequential causation, 13
settlers, 27–30
  coercion of labour, 29, 32–4, 35–6
  collusion on wages, 32–3
  demise of, 44–5, 74
  land values, 27–8
  see also monopsony *and* plantations
share tenancy, 137–8
sharecropping, 117, 138
  contracts, 129
Sheffield, J. R., 54, 55, 57
Simon, J., 11
Singh, M., 33, 34, 39–40, 41
sisal crop, 28, 34, 71
skill acquisition, 60–3, 169–96
  costs, 172–6
    labour turnover, 179–83
  education and, 188–91
  employee's incentive to, 187
  firm-specific, 5, 107–8, 171–7
  general, 183–8
  minimum wages and, 167, 177–9
  wage structure and, 171–7, 177–9, 183–8
  see also education, skills, *and* Training
skills:
  ability screening, 109–10
  composition of labour force, 89, 90–1
  earnings and job change by, 185
  experience rating, 110–11
  wage determinants, as, 102–4
  wage differentials, 94, 102–4, 187–8, 210

see also human capital *and* skill acquisition
slave trade, 26
smallholders, 16, 34, 35–6, 64, 65
  absentee landlords, 35–6, 118, 125–6, 138,
    268–9, 270
  colonial times, 28, 30, 35–6
  commodity specialization, 132–5
  constraints on contracts, 137–9
  consumption distribution, 82–3
  credit, 135–7, 255–6
    for land purchase, 130, 131
    urban income as substitute, 257–67
  factors market malfunctions, 116–39, 253
  poverty and growth and, 254–7
  incomes, 94, 212–13
    distribution, 81, 82, 252–3, 254–5, 260,
    261
    remittances, 250–1, 258, 264, 273
  labour allocation, 116–39
    sale of labour, 121–2, 128
  land transactions, 129–31
  marketing cooperatives, 136–7
  poverty and, 78, 79, 254–7, 262
  return migration and, 250
  risk strategy, 256–7
  social stratification, 264–5
  subsistence cultivation, 134–5
  see also agricultural labour market *and*
    rural–urban interactions
Smith, A., 9, 12, 102
Smock, A. C., 240
Smuts, General, 37
Somali tribe, 24
Somerset, H. C. A., 197, 241
specialization, commodity, 132–5
Spence, A. M., 114, 217
squatters, 29, 41, 81
standard of living, 73
'state of the poor', 2–3
Stewart, F., 94, 95, 168
Stiglitz, J., 101, 114, 172
Stiglitz, J. and Weiss, A., 135
strikes, 39–40, 41, 46, 74
  essential services, 48
  sanctioned by COTU, 48, 49
subsistence theory of wages, 3, 4, 7
supervisors, 157–8
supply–demand imbalance, 208–10
supply of labour, 197–200
Swynnerton plan (1954), 44, 74, 76

Taita, 35
tea crop, 124, 135
teachers, 86, 89
Thias, H. H. and Carnoy, M., 54, 65, 72, 158,
  159, 162, 163, 169, 213, 214, 215, 216,
  225, 238, 269
Thorbeck, E. and Crawford, E., 78

Thuku, Harry, 37, 39
Thurow, L. C., 12, 114, 217
Todara, M. P., 8
  see also Harris–Todaro model
Trade Disputes Acts (1964, 1965), 49
  Amendment (1971), 73
Trade Licensing Act (1968), 53
Trade Tests, 184–5, 190–1, 229
Trade Union Ordinance (1937), 40
trade unions, 39, 40, 71
  demarcation agreement, 46
  emasculation (1960–68), 47–9
  security of employment and, 164, 165, 174
  wage levels and, 161–4, 169
  see also Central Organization of Trade
    Unions *and* Kenya Federation of Labour
traders, pre-colonial, 25, 26
training:
  costs, 176, 181, 182
  firm-specific, 107–8, 171–7
  task-specific, 111
  see also education *and* skill acquisition
Tripartite agreements, 94, 95, 168, 239, 240
Turkana tribe, 24, 25
turnover of labour, 173–6, 204–8
  cost of, 179–83
  education-bias, 206–7
  seniority and, 179–83, 184–6
  unskilled, 34–5
  see also quitting *and* recruitment

Uganda railway, 27, 36, 54
Uhuru, 44–5
uncertainties, 107
  labour demand, 111–13
  labour supply, 107–11
  see also risk strategy
unemployment, 48, 49–53, 232–9
  Dagleish report (1960), 50–2
  education and, 232–3
  Form IV leavers, 216
  household poverty and, 248–9
  reserve army of, 3
  search, 6
  structure, in Nairobi, 248
  urban, 71, 248
urban labour force *see* labour, urban
urban migration *see* migration
urban poverty *see* poverty
urban–rural interaction *see* rural–urban
  interactions
urban to rural migration, 249–50
urban employment, 71, 248

value marginal product, 101, 104, 113
Von Pischke, J. D., 136, 152

Wachter, M. L., 114
wage labour, 5
  coercion by settlers, 29, 32–4, 35–6
  colonial period, 28–35
  non-farm income, 263
  security for credit, 135–6
  substitute for credit, 257–67
  see also employment, labour, rural–urban
    interactions and unemployment
Wages:
  1948–68, 63–7
  1968–80, 92–5
  adjustment, 210–17
  agriculture, 8–9, 64
  by occupation, 170, 211
  by sector, 64, 65, 92
  by seniority, 65–6
  by skill, 63
  collective agreements, 73, 167
  collective bargaining, 42, 46, 47, 49
  collusion by settlers, 32–3
  commissions, 43
  cyclical rigidity, 112–13
  determinants of structure, 11–12
    competitive model, 101–5
    neoclassical model, 105–13
  differentials:
    casual-regular workers, 227–8
    in teaching and C. S., 68
    inter-firm, 160–1
    inter-industry, 102
    intra-occupational, 104
    racial, 165–6
    rural–urban, 16, 64–5, 101
    skill, 94, 102–4, 187–8, 210
  education and, 214–17
  engagement rates, 50, 65, 178
  fund, 4, 7
  guidelines for private sector, 73, 74
  incentives, 110
  median, for citizens 1970s, 93
  minimum, 43–4, 49–53, 65–6, 74, 211, 213
    policy, 39, 41, 167–8, 177–9, 237–9

reduced skill differentials, 187–8
piece-rate, 140
policy, 74, 167–8
  see also minimum
productivity and, 74
rigidity postulation, 218, 224, 226, 233
rural rates, 128, 146–51
segmentation by firm type, 155–61
seniority scales, 172–83, 192
skilled, 160, 213–16
smallholders, 94, 212–13, 250–1
  income distribution, 81, 82, 252–5,
    260, 261
structure
  optimal, for firms, 191–6
  skill acquisition and, 183–8
subsistence theory of, 3
unionization and, 161–5
unskilled, 212–13
  see also income distribution
Walrasian general equilibrium theory, 4
Walras's law, 102, 114
Waruhhiu, Chief, 42
Washington, Booker T., 55
Wealth of Nations, The, 12
Webb, S., 39
Weeks, J., 71
Werugha, 134
White Highlands, 27, 44–5, 75–85
white settlers see settlers
Whitelaw, W. E., 238
Williamson, E. et al., 108–9, 114
wira, 23
Workman's Compensation Ordinance (1946),
  40

Young Kikuyu Association, 39

Zanzibar, Sultan of, 26
Zanzibar (place), 26
Zwanenberg, R. M. A. von and King, A., 22,
  23, 26, 27, 28, 36